VE RI
TAS

Procession of the Bull Apis-Osiris

From the painting by F. A. Bridgman in the Corcoran Art Gallery, Washington, D. C

THE HARVARD CLASSICS
EDITED BY CHARLES W ELIOT LL D

VOYAGES AND TRAVELS

ANCIENT AND MODERN

WITH INTRODUCTIONS AND NOTES

VOLUME 33

P F COLLIER & SON COMPANY
NEW YORK

Designed, Printed, and Bound at
The Collier Press, New York

CONTENTS

INTRODUCTORY NOTE

HERODOTUS *was born at Halicarnassus, on the southwest coast of Asia Minor, in the early part of the fifth century, B. C. Of his life we know almost nothing, except that he spent much of it traveling, to collect the material for his writings, and that he finally settled down at Thurii, in southern Italy, where his great work was composed. He died in 424 B. C.*

The subject of the history of Herodotus is the struggle between the Greeks and the barbarians, which he brings down to the battle of Mycale in 479 B. C. The work, as we have it, is divided into nine books, named after the nine Muses, but this division is probably due to the Alexandrine grammarians. His information he gathered mainly from oral sources, as he traveled through Asia Minor, down into Egypt, round the Black Sea, and into various parts of Greece and the neighboring countries. The chronological narrative halts from time to time to give opportunity for descriptions of the country, the people, and their customs and previous history; and the political account is constantly varied by rare tales and wonders.

Among these descriptions of countries the most fascinating to the modern, as it was to the ancient, reader is his account of the marvels of the land of Egypt. From the priests at Memphis, Heliopolis, and the Egyptian Thebes he learned what he reports of the size of the country, the wonders of the Nile, the ceremonies of their religion, the sacredness of their animals. He tells also of the strange ways of the crocodile and of that marvelous bird, the Phenix; of dress and funerals and embalming; of the eating of lotos and papyrus; of the pyramids and the great labyrinth; of their kings and queens and courtesans.

Yet Herodotus is not a mere teller of strange tales. However credulous he may appear to a modern judgment, he takes care to keep separate what he knows by his own observation from what he has merely inferred and from what he has been told. He is candid about acknowledging ignorance, and when versions differ he gives both. Thus the modern scientific historian, with other means of corroboration, can sometimes learn from Herodotus more than Herodotus himself knew.

There is abundant evidence, too, that Herodotus had a phi-

losophy of history. The unity which marks his work is due not only to the strong Greek national feeling running through it, the feeling that rises to a height in such passages as the descriptions of the battles of Marathon, Thermopylæ, and Salamis, but also to his profound belief in Fate and in Nemesis. To his belief in Fate is due the frequent quoting of oracles and their fulfilment, the frequent references to things foreordained by Providence. The working of Nemesis he finds in the disasters that befall men and nations whose towering prosperity awakens the jealousy of the gods. The final overthrow of the Persians, which forms his main theme, is only one specially conspicuous example of the operation of this force from which human life can never free itself.

But, above all, he is the father of story-tellers. "Herodotus is such simple and delightful reading," says Jevons; "he is so unaffected and entertaining, his story flows so naturally and with such ease that we have a difficulty in bearing in mind that, over and above the hard writing which goes to make easy reading, there is a perpetual marvel in the work of Herodotus. It is the first artistic work in prose that Greek literature produced. This prose work, which for pure literary merit no subsequent work has surpassed, than which later generations, after using the pen for centuries, have produced no prose more easy or more readable, this was the first of histories and of literary prose."

AN ACCOUNT OF EGYPT

By Herodotus

BEING THE SECOND BOOK OF HIS HISTORIES CALLED EUTERPE

WHEN Cyrus had brought his life to an end, Cambyses received the royal power in succession, being the son of Cyrus and of Cassandanē the daughter of Pharnaspes, for whose death, which came about before his own, Cyrus had made great mourning himself and also had proclaimed to all those over whom he bore rule that they should make mourning for her: Cambyses, I say, being the son of this woman and of Cyrus, regarded the Ionians and Aiolians as slaves inherited from his father; and he proceeded to march an army against Egypt, taking with him as helpers not only the other nations of which he was ruler, but also those of the Hellenes over whom he had power besides.

Now the Egyptians, before the time when Psammetichos became king over them, were wont to suppose that they had come into being first of all men; but since the time when Psammetichos having become king desired to know what men had come into being first, they suppose that the Phrygians came into being before themselves, but they themselves before all other men. Now Psammetichos, when he was not able by inquiry to find out any means of knowing who had come into being first of all men, contrived a device of the following kind:—Taking two new-born children belonging to persons of the common sort he gave them to a shepherd to bring up at the place where his flocks were, with a manner of bringing up such as I shall say, charging him namely that no man should utter any word in their presence, and that they should be placed by themselves in a room where none might come, and at the proper time he should bring to them she-goats, and when he had satisfied them with milk he should do for them whatever else was needed. These things Psammetichos did and gave him this charge wishing to hear what word the children would let break forth first, after they had ceased from wailings without sense. And accordingly so it came to pass; for after a space of two years had gone by, during which the shepherd went on acting so, at length, when he opened the door and entered, both the children fell before him in entreaty and uttered the word *bekos,* stretching forth their hands. At first when he heard this the shepherd kept silence; but since this word was often repeated, as he visited them constantly and attended to them, at last he declared the matter to his master, and at his command he brought the children before his face. Then Psammetichos having himself also heard it, began to inquire what nation of men named anything *bekos,* and inquiring he found that the Phrygians had this name for bread. In this manner and guided by an indication such as this, the Egyptians were brought to allow that the Phrygians were a more ancient people than themselves. That so it came to pass I heard from the priests of that Hephaistos who dwells at Memphis; but the Hellenes relate, besides many other idle tales, that Psammetichos cut out the tongues of certain women and then caused the children to live with these women.

With regard then to the rearing of the children they related so much as I have said: and I heard also other things at Memphis when I had speech with the priests of Hephaistos. Moreover I visited both Thebes and Heliopolis for this very cause, namely because I wished to know whether the priests at these places would agree in their accounts with those at Memphis; for the men of Heliopolis are said to be the most learned in records of the Egyptians. Those of their narrations which I heard with regard to the gods I am not earnest to relate in full, but I shall name them only, because I consider that all men are equally ignorant of these matters: and whatever things of them I may record,

I shall record only because I am compelled by the course of the story. But as to those matters which concern men, the priests agreed with one another in saying that the Egyptians were the first of all men on earth to find out the course of the year, having divided the seasons into twelve parts to make up the whole; and this they said they found out from the stars: and they reckon to this extent more wisely than the Hellenes, as it seems to me, inasmuch as the Hellenes throw in an intercalated month every other year, to make the seasons right, whereas the Egyptians, reckoning the twelve months at thirty days each, bring in also every year five days beyond the number, and thus the circle of their seasons is completed and comes round to the same point whence it set out. They said moreover that the Egyptians were the first who brought into use appellations for the twelve gods and the Hellenes took up the use from them; and that they were the first who assigned altars and images and temples to the gods, and who engraved figures on stones; and with regard to the greater number of these things they showed me by actual facts that they had happened so. They said also that the first man who became king of Egypt was Min; and that in his time all Egypt except the district of Thebes was a swamp, and none of the regions were then above water which now lie below the lake of Moiris, to which lake it is a voyage of seven days up the river from the sea: and I thought that they said well about the land; for it is manifest in truth even to a person who has not heard it beforehand but has only seen, at least if he have understanding, that the Egypt to which the Hellenes come in ships is a land which has been won by the Egyptians as an addition, and that it is a gift of the river: moreover the regions which lie above this lake also for a distance of three days' sail, about which they did not go on to say anything of this kind, are nevertheless another instance of the same thing: for the nature of the land of Egypt is as follows:—First when you are still approaching it in a ship and are distant a day's run from the land, if you let down a sounding-line you will bring up mud and you will find yourself in eleven fathoms. This then so far shows that there is a silting forward of the land. Then secondly, as to Egypt itself, the extent of it along the sea is sixty *schoines,* according to our definition of Egypt as extending from the Gulf of Plinthinē to the Serbonian lake, along which stretches Mount Casion; from this lake then the sixty *schoines* are reckoned: for those of men who are poor in land have their country measured by fathoms, those who are less poor by furlongs, those who have much land by parasangs, and those who have land in very great abundance by *schoines:* now the parasang is equal to thirty furlongs, and each *schoine,* which is an Egyptian measure, is equal to sixty furlongs. So there would be an extent of three thousand six hundred furlongs for the coast-land of Egypt. From thence and as far as Heliopolis inland Egypt is broad, and the land is all flat and without springs of water and formed of mud: and the road as one goes inland from the sea to Heliopolis is about the same in length as that which leads from the altar of the twelve gods at Athens to Pisa and the temple of Olympian Zeus: reckoning up you would find the difference very small by which these roads fail of being equal in length, not more indeed than fifteen furlongs; for the road from Athens to Pisa wants fifteen furlongs of being fifteen hundred, while the road to Heliopolis from the sea reaches that number completely. From Heliopolis however, as you go up, Egypt is narrow; for on the one side a mountain-range belonging to Arabia stretches along by the side of it, going in a direction from the North towards the midday and the South Wind, tending upwards without a break to that which is called the Erythraian Sea, in which range are the stone-quarries which were used in cutting stone for the pyramids at Memphis. On this side then the mountain ends where I have said, and then takes a turn back; and where it is widest, as I was informed, it is a journey of two months across from East to West; and the borders of it which turn towards the East are said to produce frankincense. Such then is the nature of this mountain-range; and on the side of Egypt towards Libya another range extends, rocky and enveloped in sand: in this are the pyramids, and it runs in the same direction as those parts of the Arabian mountains which go towards the midday. So then, I say, from Heliopolis the land has no longer a great extent so far as it belongs to Egypt, and for about four days' sail up the river Egypt properly so called is narrow: and the space between the mountain-ranges which have been mentioned is plain-land, but where it is narrowest it did not seem to me to exceed two hundred furlongs from the Arabian mountains to those which are called the Libyan. After this again Egypt is broad. Such is the nature of this land: and from Heliopolis to Thebes is a voyage up the river of nine days, and the distance of the journey in furlongs is four thousand eight hundred and sixty, the number of *schoines* being eighty-one. If these measures of Egypt in furlongs be put together, the result is as follows:—I have already before this shown that the distance along the sea amounts to three thousand six hundred furlongs, and I will now declare what the distance is inland from the sea to Thebes, namely six thousand one hundred and twenty furlongs: and again the distance from Thebes to the city called Elephantinē is one thousand eight hundred furlongs.

Of this land then, concerning which I have spoken, it seemed to myself also, according as the priests said, that the greater part had been won as an addition by the Egyptians; for it was evident to me that the space between the aforesaid mountain-ranges, which lie above the city of Memphis, once was a gulf of the sea, like the regions about Ilion and Teuthrania and Ephesos and the plain of the Maiander, if it be permitted to compare small things with great; and small these are in comparison, for of the rivers which heaped up the soil in those regions none is worthy to be compared in volume with a single one of the mouths of the Nile, which has five mouths. Moreover there are other rivers also, not in size at all equal to the Nile, which have performed great feats; of which I can mention the names of several, and especially the Acheloös, which flowing through Acarnania and so issuing out into the sea has already made half of the Echinades from islands into mainland. Now there is in the land of Arabia, not far from Egypt, a gulf of the sea running in from that which is called the Erythraian Sea, very long and narrow, as I am about to tell. With respect to the length of the voyage along it, one who set out from the innermost point to sail out through it into the open sea, would spend forty days upon the voyage, using oars; and with respect to breadth, where the gulf is broadest it is half a day's sail across: and there is in it an ebb and flow of tide every day. Just such another gulf I suppose that Egypt was, and that the one ran in towards Ethiopia from the Northern Sea, and the other, the Arabian, of which I am about to speak, tended from the South towards Syria, the gulfs boring in so as almost to meet at their extreme points, and passing by one another with but a small space left between. If then the stream of the Nile should turn aside into this Arabian gulf, what would hinder that gulf from being filled up with silt as the river continued to flow, at all events within a period of twenty thousand years? indeed for my part I am of opinion that it would be filled up even within ten thousand years. How, then, in all the time that has elapsed before I came into being should not a gulf be filled up even of much greater size than this by a river so great and so active? As regards Egypt then, I both believe those who say that things are so, and for myself also I am strongly of opinion that they are so; because I have observed that Egypt runs out into the sea further than the adjoining land, and that shells are found upon the mountains of it, and an efflorescence of salt forms upon the surface, so that even the pyramids are being eaten away by it, and moreover that of all the mountains of Egypt, the range which lies above Memphis is the only one which has sand: besides which I notice that Egypt resembles neither the land of Arabia, which borders upon it, nor Libya, nor yet Syria (for they are Syrians who dwell in the parts of Arabia lying along the sea), but that it has soil which is black and easily breaks up, seeing that it is in truth mud and silt brought down from Ethiopia by the river: but the soil of Libya, we know, is reddish in colour and rather sandy, while that of Arabia and Syria is somewhat clayey and rocky. The priests also gave me a strong proof concerning this land as follows, namely that in the reign of king Moiris, whenever the river reached a height of at least eight cubits it watered Egypt below Memphis; and not yet nine hundred years had gone by since the death of Moiris, when I heard these things from the priests: now however, unless the river rises to sixteen cubits, or fifteen at the least, it does not go over the land. I think too that those Egyptians who dwell below the lake of Moiris and especially in that region which is called the Delta, if that land continues to grow in height according to this proportion and to increase similarly in extent, will suffer for all remaining time, from the Nile not overflowing their land, that same thing which they themselves said that the Hellenes would at some time suffer: for hearing that the whole land of the Hellenes has rain and is not watered by rivers as theirs is, they said that the Hellenes would at some time be disappointed of a great hope and would suffer the ills of famine. This saying means that if the god shall not send them rain, but shall allow drought to prevail for a long time, the Hellenes will be destroyed by hunger; for they have in fact no other supply of water to save them except from Zeus alone. This has been rightly said by the Egyptians with reference to the Hellenes: but now let me tell how matters are with the Egyptians themselves in their turn. If, in accordance with what I before said, their land below Memphis (for this is that which is increasing) shall continue to increase in height according to the same proportion as in the past time, assuredly those Egyptians who dwell here will suffer famine, if their land shall not have rain nor the river be able to go over their fields. It is certain however that now they gather in fruit from the earth with less labour than any other men and also with less than the other Egyptians; for they have no labour in breaking up furrows with a plough nor in hoeing nor in any other of those labours which other men have about a crop; but when the river has come up of itself and watered their fields and after watering has left them again, then each man sows his own field and turns into it swine, and when he has trodden the seed into the ground by means of the swine, after that he waits for the harvest, and when he has threshed the corn by means of the swine, then he gathers it in.

If we desire to follow the opinions of the Ionians as regards Egypt, who say that the Delta alone is Egypt, reckoning its sea-coast to be from the watch-tower called of Perseus to the fish-curing houses of Pelusion, a distance of forty *schoines,* and counting it to extend inland as far as the city of Kercasoros, where the Nile divides and runs to Pelusion and Canobos, while as for the rest of Egypt, they assign it partly to Libya and partly to Arabia,—if, I say, we should follow this account, we should thereby declare that in former times the Egyptians had no land to live in; for, as we have seen, their Delta at any rate is alluvial, and has appeared (so to speak) lately, as the Egyptians themselves say and as my opinion is. If then at the first there was no land for them to live in, why did they waste their labour to prove that they had come into being before all other men? They needed not to have made trial of the children to see what language they would first utter. However I am not of opinion that the Egyptians came into being at the same time as that which is called by the Ionians the Delta, but that they existed always ever since the human race came into being, and that as their land advanced forwards, many of them were left in their first abodes and many came down gradually to the lower parts. At least it is certain that in old times Thebes had the name of Egypt, and of this the circumference measures six thousand one hundred and twenty furlongs.

If then we judge aright of these matters, the opinion of the Ionians about Egypt is not sound: but if the judgment of the Ionians is right, I declare that neither the Hellenes nor the Ionians themselves know how to reckon since they say that the whole earth is made up of three divisions, Europe, Asia, and Libya: for they ought to count in addition to these the Delta of Egypt, since it belongs neither to Asia nor to Libya; for at least it cannot be the river Nile by this reckoning which divides Asia from Libya, but the Nile is cleft at the point of this Delta so as to flow round it, and the result is that this land would come between Asia and Libya.

We dismiss then the opinion of the Ionians, and express a judgment of our own on this matter also, that Egypt is all that land which is inhabited by Egyptians, just as Kilikia is that which is inhabited by Kilikians and Assyria that which is inhabited by Assyrians, and we know of no boundary properly speaking between Asia and Libya except the borders of Egypt. If however we shall adopt the opinion which is commonly held by the Hellenes, we shall suppose that the whole of Egypt, beginning from the Cataract and the city of Elephantinē, is divided into two parts and that it thus partakes of both the names, since one side will thus belong to Libya and the other to Asia; for the Nile from the Cataract onwards flows to the sea cutting Egypt through in the midst; and as far as the city of Kercasoros the Nile flows in one single stream, but from this city onwards it is parted into three ways; and one, which is called the Pelusian mouth, turns towards the East; the second of the ways goes towards the West, and this is called the Canobic mouth; but that one of the ways which is straight runs thus,—when the river in its course downwards comes to the point of the Delta, then it cuts the Delta through the midst and so issues out to the sea. In this we have a portion of the water of the river which is not the smallest nor the least famous, and it is called the Sebennytic mouth. There are also two other mouths which part off from the Sebennytic and go to the sea, and these are called, one the Saïtic, the other the Mendesian mouth. The Bolbitinitic, and Bucolic mouths, on the other hand, are not natural but made by digging. Moreover also the answer given by the Oracle of Ammon bears witness in support of my opinion that Egypt is of the extent which I declare it to be in my account; and of this answer I heard after I had formed my own opinion about Egypt. For those of the city of Marea and of Apis, dwelling in the parts of Egypt which border on Libya, being of opinion themselves that they were Libyans and not Egyptians, and also being burdened by the rules of religious service, because they desired not to be debarred from the use of cows' flesh, sent to Ammon saying that they had nought in common with the Egyptians, for they dwelt outside the Delta and agreed with them in nothing; and they said they desired that it might be lawful for them to eat everything without distinction. The god however did not permit them to do so, but said that that land was Egypt which the Nile came over and watered, and that those were Egyptians who dwelling below the city of Elephantinē drank of that river. Thus was it answered to them by the Oracle about this: and the Nile, when it is in flood, goes over not only the Delta but also of the land which is called Libyan and of that which is called Arabian sometimes as much as two days' journey on each side, and at times even more than this or at times less.

As regards the nature of the river, neither from the priests nor yet from any other man was I able to obtain any knowledge: and I was desirous especially to learn from them about these matters, namely why the Nile comes down increasing in volume from the summer solstice onwards for a hundred days, and then, when it has reached the number of these days, turns and goes back, failing in its stream, so that through the whole winter season it continues to be low, and until the summer solstice returns. Of none of these things was I able to receive any account from the Egyptians, when I inquired of them what power the Nile has whereby it is of a nature opposite to that of all other rivers. And I made inquiry, desiring to know both this which I say and also why, unlike all other rivers, it does not give rise to any breezes blowing from it. However some of the Hellenes who desired to gain distinction for cleverness have given an account of this water in three different ways: two of these I do not think it worth while even to speak of except only to indicate their nature; of which the one says that the Etesian Winds are the cause that makes the river rise, by preventing the Nile from flowing out into the sea. But often the Etesian Winds fail and yet the Nile does the same work as it is wont to do; and moreover, if these were the cause, all the other rivers also which flow in a direction opposed to the Etesian Winds ought to have been affected in the same way as the Nile, and even more, in as much as they are smaller and present to them a feebler flow of streams: but there are many of these rivers in Syria and many also in Libya, and they are affected in no such manner as the Nile. The second way shows more ignorance than that which has been mentioned, and it is more marvellous to tell; for it says that the river produces these effects because it flows from the Ocean, and that the Ocean flows round the whole earth. The third of the ways is much the most specious, but nevertheless it is the most mistaken of all: for indeed this way has no more truth in it than the rest, alleging as it does that the Nile flows from melting snow; whereas it flows out of Libya through the midst of the Ethiopians, and so comes out into Egypt. How then should it flow from snow, when it flows from the hottest parts to those which are cooler? And indeed most of the facts are such as to convince a man (one at least who is capable of reasoning about such matters), that it is not at all likely that it flows from snow. The first and greatest evidence is afforded by the winds, which blow hot from these regions; the second is that the land is rainless always and without frost, whereas after snow has fallen rain must necessarily come within five days, so that if it snowed in those parts rain would fall there; the third evidence is afforded by the people dwelling there, who are of a black colour by reason of the burning heat. Moreover kites and swallows remain there through the year and do not leave the land; and cranes flying from the cold weather which comes on in the region of Scythia come regularly to these parts for wintering: if then it snowed ever so little in that land through which the Nile flows and in which it has its rise, none of these things would take place, as necessity compels us to admit. As for him who talked about the Ocean, he carried his tale into the region of the unknown, and so he need not be refuted; since I for my part know of no river Ocean existing, but I think that Homer or one of the poets who were before him invented the name and introduced it into his verse.

If however after I have found fault with the opinions proposed, I am bound to declare an opinion of my own about the matters which are in doubt, I will tell what to my mind is the reason why the Nile increases in the summer. In the winter season the Sun, being driven away from his former path through the heaven by the stormy winds, comes to the upper parts of Libya. If one would set forth the matter in the shortest way, all has now been said; for whatever region this god approaches most and stands directly above, this it may reasonably be supposed is most in want of water, and its native streams of rivers are dried up most. However, to set it forth at greater length, thus it is:—the Sun passing in his course by the upper parts of Libya, does thus, that is to say, since at all times the air in those parts is clear and the country is warm, because there are no cold winds, in passing through it the Sun does just as he was wont to do in the summer, when going through the midst of the heaven, that is he draws to himself the water, and having drawn it he drives it away to the upper parts of the country, and the winds take it up and scattering it abroad melt it into rain; so it is natural that the winds which blow from this region, namely the South and South-west Winds, should be much the most rainy of all the winds. I think however that the Sun does not send away from himself all the water of the Nile of each year, but that he also lets some remain behind with himself. Then when the winter becomes milder, the Sun returns back again to the midst of the heaven, and from that time onwards he draws equally from all rivers; but in the meanwhile they flow in large volume, since water of rain mingles with them in great quantity, because their country receives rain then and is filled with torrent streams. In summer however they are weak, since not only the showers of rain fail then, but also they are drawn by the Sun. The Nile however, alone of all rivers, not having rain and being drawn by the Sun, naturally flows during this time of winter in much less than its proper volume, that is much less than in summer; for then it is drawn equally with all the other waters, but in winter it bears the burden alone. Thus I suppose the Sun to be the cause of these things. He also is the cause in my opinion that the air in these parts is dry, since he makes it so by scorching up his path through the heaven: thus summer prevails always in the upper parts of Libya. If however the station of the seasons had been changed, and where now in the heaven are placed the North Wind and winter, there was the station of the South Wind and of the midday, and where now is placed the South Wind, there was the North, if this had been so, the Sun being driven from the midst of the heaven by the winter and the North Wind would go to to the upper parts of Europe, just as now he comes to the upper parts of Libya, and passing in his course throughout the whole of Europe I suppose that he would do to the Ister that which he now works upon the Nile. As to the breeze, why none blows from the river, my opinion is that from very hot places it is not natural that anything should blow, and that a breeze is wont to blow from something cold.

Let these matters then be as they are and as they were at the first: but as to the sources of the Nile, not one either of the Egyptians or of the Libyans or of the Hellenes, who came to speech with me, professed to know anything, except the scribe of the sacred treasury of Athenē at the city of Saïs in Egypt. To me however this man seemed not to be speaking seriously when he said that he had certain knowledge of it; and he said as follows, namely that there were two mountains of which the tops ran up to a sharp point, situated between the city of Syenē, which is in the district of Thebes, and Elephantinē, and the names of the mountains were, of the one Crophi and of the other Mophi. From the middle between these mountains flowed (he said) the sources of the Nile, which were fathomless in depth, and half of the water flowed to Egypt and towards the North Wind, the other half to Ethiopia and the South Wind. As for the fathomless depth of the source, he said that Psammetichos king of Egypt came to a trial of this matter; for he had a rope twisted of many thousand fathoms and let it down in this place, and it found no bottom. By this the scribe (if this which he told was really as he said) gave me to understand that there were certain strong eddies there and a backward flow, and that since the water dashed against the mountains, therefore the sounding-line could not come to any bottom when it was let down. From no other person was I able to learn anything about this matter; but for the rest I learnt so much as here follows by the most diligent inquiry; for I went myself as an eye-witness as far as the city of Elephantinē and from that point onwards I gathered knowledge by report. From the city of Elephantinē as one goes up the river there is country which slopes steeply; so that here one must attach ropes to the vessel on both sides, as one fastens an ox, and so make one's way onward; and if the rope break, the vessel is gone at once, carried away by the violence of the stream. Through this country it is a voyage of about four days in length, and in this part the Nile is winding like the river Maiander, and the distance amounts to twelve *schoines,* which one must traverse in this manner. Then you will come to a level plain, in which the Nile flows round an island named Tachompso. (Now in the regions above Elephantinē there dwell Ethiopians at once succeeding, who also occupy half of the island, and Egyptians the other half.) Adjoining this island there is a great lake, round which dwell Ethiopian nomad tribes; and when you have sailed through this you will come to the stream of the Nile again, which flows into this lake. After this you will disembark and make a journey by land of forty days; for in the Nile sharp rocks stand forth out of the water, and there are many reefs, by which it is not possible for a vessel to pass. Then after having passed through this country in the forty days which I have said, you will embark again in another vessel and sail for twelve days; and after this you will come to a great city called Meroē. This city is said to be the mother-city of all the other Ethiopians: and they who dwell in it reverence of the gods Zeus and Dionysos alone, and these they greatly honour; and they have an Oracle of Zeus established, and make warlike marches whensoever this god commands them by prophesyings and to whatsoever place he commands. Sailing from this city you will come to the "Deserters" in another period of time equal to that in which you came from Elephantinē to the mother-city of the Ethiopians. Now the name of these "Deserters" is *Asmach,* and this word signifies, when translated into the tongue of the Hellenes, "those who stand on the left hand of the king." These were two hundred and forty thousand Egyptians of the warrior class, who revolted and went over to these Ethiopians for the following cause:—In the reign of Psammetichos garrisons were set, one towards the Ethiopians at the city of Elephantinē, another towards the Arabians and Assyrians at Daphnai of Pelusion, and another towards Libya at Marea: and even in my own time the garrisons of the Persians too are ordered in the same manner as these were in the reign of Psammetichos, for both at Elephantinē and at Daphnai the

Persians have outposts. The Egyptians then of whom I speak had served as outposts for three years and no one relieved them from their guard; accordingly they took counsel together, and adopting a common plan they all in a body revolted from Psammetichos and set out for Ethiopia. Hearing this Psammetichos set forth in pursuit, and when he came up with them he entreated them much and endeavoured to persuade them not to desert the gods of their country and their children and wives: upon which it is said that one of them pointed to his privy member and said that wherever this was, there would they have both children and wives. When these came to Ethiopia they gave themselves over to the king of the Ethiopians; and he rewarded them as follows:—there were certain of the Ethiopians who had come to be at variance with him; and he bade them drive these out and dwell in their land. So since these men settled in the land of the Ethiopians, the Ethiopians have come to be of milder manners, from having learnt the customs of the Egyptians.

The Nile then, besides that part of its course which is in Egypt, is known as far as a four months' journey by river and land: for that is the number of months which are found by reckoning to be spent in going from Elephantinē to these "Deserters": and the river runs from the West and the setting of the sun. But what comes after that point no one can clearly say; for this land is desert by reason of the burning heat. Thus much however I heard from men of Kyrenē, who told me that they had been to the Oracle of Ammon, and had come to speech with Etearchos king of the Ammonians: and it happened that after speaking of other matters they fell to discourse about the Nile and how no one knew the sources of it; and Etearchos said that once there came to him men of the Nasamonians (this is a Libyan race which dwells in the Syrtis, and also in the land to the East of the Syrtis reaching to no great distance), and when the Nasamonians came and were asked by him whether they were able to tell him anything more than he knew about the desert parts of Libya, they said that there had been among them certain sons of chief men, who were of unruly disposition; and these when they grew up to be men had devised various other extravagant things and also they had told off by lot five of themselves to go to see the desert parts of Libya and to try whether they could discover more than those who had previously explored furthest: for in those parts of Libya which are by the Northern Sea, beginning from Egypt and going as far as the headland of Soloeis, which is the extreme point of Libya, Libyans (and of them many races) extend along the whole coast, except so much as the Hellenes and Phenicians hold; but in the upper parts, which lie above the sea-coast and above those people whose land comes down to the sea, Libya is full of wild beasts; and in the parts above the land of wild beasts it is full of sand, terribly waterless and utterly desert. These young men then (said they), being sent out by their companions well furnished with supplies of water and provisions, went first through the inhabited country, and after they had passed through this they came to the country of wild beasts, and after this they passed through the desert, making their journey towards the West Wind; and having passed through a great tract of sand in many days, they saw at last trees growing in a level place; and having come up to them, they were beginning to pluck the fruit which was upon the trees: but as they began to pluck it, there came upon them small men, of less stature than men of the common size, and these seized them and carried them away; and neither could the Nasamonians understand anything of their speech nor could those who were carrying them off understand anything of the speech of the Nasamonians: and they led them (so it was said) through very great swamps, and after passing through these they came to a city in which all the men were in size like those who carried them off and in colour of skin black; and by the city ran a great river, which ran from the West towards the sunrising, and in it were seen crocodiles. Of the account given by Etearchos the Ammonian let so much suffice as is here said, except that, as the men of Kyrēnē told me, he alleged that the Nasamonians returned safe home, and that the people to whom they had come were all wizards. Now this river which ran by the city, Etearchos conjectured to be the Nile, and moreover reason compels us to think so; for the Nile flows from Libya and cuts Libya through in the midst, and as I conjecture, judging of what is not known by that which is evident to the view, it starts at a distance from its mouth equal to that of the Ister: for the river Ister begins from the Keltoi and the city of Pyrenē and so runs that it divides Europe in the midst (now the Keltoi are outside the Pillars of Heracles and border upon the Kynesians, who dwell furthest towards the sunset of all those who have their dwelling in Europe); and the Ister ends, having its course through the whole of Europe, by flowing into the Euxine Sea at the place where the Milesians have their settlement of Istria. Now the Ister, since it flows through land which is inhabited, is known by the reports of many; but of the sources of the Nile no one can give an account, for the part of Libya through which it flows is uninhabited and desert. About its course however so much as it was possible to learn by the most diligent inquiry has been told; and it runs out into Egypt. Now Egypt lies nearly opposite to the mountain districts of Kilikia; and from thence to Sinopē, which lies upon the Euxine Sea, is a journey in the same straight line of five days for a man without encumbrance; and Sinopē lies opposite to the place where the Ister runs out into the sea: thus I think that the Nile passes through the whole of Libya and is of equal measure with the Ister.

Of the Nile then let so much suffice as has been said. Of Egypt however I shall make my report at length, because it has wonders more in number than any other land, and works too it has to show as much as any land, which are beyond expression great: for this reason then more shall be said concerning it.

The Egyptians in agreement with their climate, which is unlike any other, and with the river, which shows a nature different from all other rivers, established for themselves manners and customs in a way opposite to other men in almost all matters: for among them the women frequent the market and carry on trade, while the men remain at home and weave; and whereas others weave pushing the woof upwards, the Egyptians push it downwards: the men carry their burdens upon their heads and the women upon their shoulders: the women make water standing up and the men crouching down: they ease themselves in their houses and they eat without in the streets, alleging as reason for this that it is right to do secretly the things that are unseemly though necessary, but those which are not unseemly, in public: no woman is a minister either of male or female divinity, but men of all, both male and female: to support their parents the sons are in no way compelled, if they do not desire to do so, but the daughters are forced to do so, be they never so unwilling. The priests of the gods in other lands wear long hair, but in Egypt they shave their heads: among other men the custom is that in mourning those whom the matter concerns most nearly have their hair cut short, but the Egyptians, when deaths occur, let their hair grow long, both that on the head and that on the chin, having before been close shaven: other men have their daily living separated from beasts, but the Egyptians have theirs together with beasts: other men live on wheat and on barley, but to any one of the Egyptians who makes his living on these it is a great reproach; they make their bread of maize, which some call spelt: they knead dough with their feet and clay with their hands, with which also they gather up dung: and whereas other men, except such as have learnt otherwise from the Egyptians, have their members as nature made them, the Egyptians practice circumcision: as to garments, the men wear two each and the women but one: and whereas others make fast the rings and ropes of the sails outside the ship, the Egyptians do this inside: finally in the writing of characters and reckoning with pebbles, while the Hellenes carry the hand from the left to the right, the Egyptians do this from the right to the left; and doing so they say that they do it themselves rightwise and the Hellenes leftwise: and they use two kinds of characters for writing, of which the one kind is called sacred and the other common.

They are religious excessively beyond all other men, and with regard to this they have customs as follows:—they drink from cups of bronze and rinse them out every day, and not some only do this but all: they wear garments of linen always newly washed, and this they make a special point of practice: they circumcise themselves for the sake of cleanliness, preferring to be clean rather than comely. The priests shave themselves all over their body every other day, so that no lice or any other foul thing may come to be upon them when they minister to the gods; and the priests wear garments of linen only and sandals of papyrus, and any other garment they may not take nor other sandals; these wash themselves in cold water twice in a day and twice again in the night; and other religious services they perform (one may almost say) of infinite number. They enjoy also good things not a few, for they do not consume or spend anything of their own substance, but there is sacred bread baked for them and they have each great quantity of flesh of oxen and geese coming in to them each day, and also wine of grapes is given to them; but it is not permitted to them to taste of fish: beans moreover the Egyptians do not at all sow in their land, and those which grow they neither eat raw nor boil for food; nay the priests do not endure even to look upon them, thinking this to be an unclean kind of pulse: and there is not one priest only for each of the gods but many, and of them one is chief-priest, and whenever a priest dies his son is appointed to his place.

The males of the ox kind they consider to belong to Epaphos, and on account of him they test them in the following manner:—If the priest sees one single black hair upon the beast he counts it not clean for sacrifice; and one of the priests who is appointed for the purpose makes investigation of these matters, both when the beast is standing upright and when it is lying on its back, drawing out its tongue moreover, to see if it is clean in respect of the appointed signs, which I shall tell of in another part of the history: he looks also at the hairs of the tail to see if it has them growing in the natural manner; and if it be clean in respect of all these things, he marks it with a piece of papyrus, rolling this round the horns, and then when he has plastered sealing-earth over it he sets upon it the seal of his signet-ring, and after that they take the animal away. But for one who sacrifices a beast not sealed the penalty appointed is death. In this way then the beast is tested; and their appointed manner of sacrifice is as follows:—they lead the sealed beast to the altar where they happen to be sacrificing, and then kindle a fire: after that, having poured libations of wine over the altar so that it runs down upon the victim and having called upon the god, they cut its throat, and having cut its throat they sever the head from the body. The body then of the beast they flay, but upon the head they make many imprecations first, and then they who have a market and Hellenes sojourning among them for trade, these carry it to the market-place and sell it, while they who have no Hellenes among them cast it away into the river: and this is the form of imprecation which they utter upon the heads, praying that if any evil be about to befall either themselves who are offering sacrifice or the land of Egypt in general, it may come rather upon this head. Now as regards the heads of the beasts which are sacrificed and the pouring over them of the wine, all the Egyptians have the same customs equally for all their sacrifices; and by reason of this custom none of the Egyptians eat of the head either of this or of any other kind of animal: but the manner of disembowelling the victims and of burning them is appointed among them differently for different sacrifices; I shall speak however of the sacrifices to that goddess whom they regard as the greatest of all, and to whom they celebrate the greatest feast.—When they have flayed the bullock and made imprecation, they take out the whole of its lower entrails but leave in the body the upper entrails and the fat; and they sever from it the legs and the end of the loin and the shoulders and the neck: and this done, they fill the rest of the body of the animal with consecrated loaves and honey and raisins and figs and frankincense and myrrh and every other kind of spices, and having filled it with these they offer it, pouring over it great abundance of oil. They make their sacrifice after fasting, and while the offerings are being burnt, they all beat themselves for mourning, and when they have finished beating themselves they set forth as a feast that which they left unburnt of the sacrifice.

The clean males then of the ox kind, both full-grown animals and calves, are sacrificed by all the Egyptians; the females however they may not sacrifice, but these are sacred to Isis; for the figure of Isis is in the form of a woman with cow's horns, just as the Hellenes present Io in pictures, and all the Egyptians without distinction reverence cows far more than any other kind of cattle; for which reason neither man nor woman of Egyptian race would kiss a man who is a Hellene on the mouth, nor will they use a knife or roasting-spits or a caldron belonging to a Hellene, nor taste of the flesh even of a clean animal if it has been cut with the knife of a Hellene. And the cattle of this kind which die they bury in the following manner:—the females they cast into the river, but the males they bury, each people in the suburb of their town, with one of the horns, or sometimes both, protruding to mark the place; and when the bodies have rotted away and the appointed time comes on, then to each city comes a boat from that which is called the island of Prosopitis (this is in the Delta, and the extent of its curcuit is nine *schoines*). In this island of Prosopitis is situated, besides many other cities, that one from which the boats come to take up the bones of the oxen, and the name of the city is Atarbechis, and in it there is set up a holy temple of Aphroditē. From this city many go abroad in various directions, some to one city and others to another, and when they have dug up the bones of the oxen they carry them off, and coming together they bury them in one single place. In the same manner as they bury the oxen they bury also their other cattle when they die; for about them also they have the same law laid down, and these also they abstain from killing.

Now all who have a temple set up to the Theban Zeus or who are of the district of Thebes, these, I say, all sacrifice goats and abstain from sheep: for not all the Egyptians equally reverence the same gods, except only Isis and Osiris (who they say is Dionysos), these they all reverence alike: but they who have a temple of Mendes or belong to the Mendesian district, these abstain from goats and sacrifice sheep. Now the men of Thebes and those who after their example abstain from sheep, say that this custom was established among them for the cause which follows:—Heracles (they say) had an earnest desire to see Zeus, and Zeus did not desire to be seen of him; and at last when Heracles was urgent in entreaty Zeus contrived this device, that is to say, he flayed a ram and held in front of him the head of the ram which he had cut off, and he put on over him the fleece and then showed himself to him. Hence the Egyptians make the image of Zeus with the face of a ram; and the Ammonians do so also after their example, being settlers both from the Egyptians and from the Ethiopians, and using a language which is a medley of both tongues: and in my opinion it is from this god that the Ammonians took the name which they have, for the Egyptians call Zeus *Amun.* The Thebans then do not sacrifice rams but hold them sacred for this reason; on one day however in the year, on the feast of Zeus, they cut up in the same manner and flay one single ram and cover with its skin the image of Zeus, and then they bring up to it another image of Heracles. This done, all who are in the temple beat themselves in lamentation for the ram, and then they bury it in a sacred tomb.

About Heracles I heard the account given that he was of the number of the twelve gods; but of the other Heracles whom the Hellenes know I was not able to hear in any part of Egypt: and moreover to prove that the Egyptians did not take the name of Heracles from the Hellenes, but rather the Hellenes from the Egyptians,—that is to say those of the Hellenes who gave the name Heracles to the son of Amphitryon,—of that, I say, besides many other evidences there is chiefly this, namely that the parents of this Heracles, Amphitryon and Alcmenē, were both of Egypt by descent, and also that the Egyptians say that they do not know the names either of Poseidon or of the Dioscuroi, nor have these been accepted by them as gods among the other gods; whereas if they had received from the Hellenes the name of any divinity, they would naturally have preserved the memory of these most of all, assuming that in those times as now some of the Hellenes were wont to make voyages and were seafaring folk, as I suppose and as my judgment compels me to think; so that the Egyptians would have learnt the names of these gods even more than that of Heracles. In fact however Heracles is a very ancient Egyptian god; and (as they say themselves) it is seventeen thousand years to the beginning of the reign of Amasis from the time when the twelve gods, of whom they count that Heracles is one, were begotten of the eight gods. I moreover, desiring to know something certain of these matters so far as might be, made a voyage also to Tyre of Phenicia, hearing that in that place there was a holy temple of Heracles; and I saw that it was richly furnished with many votive offerings besides, and especially there were in it two pillars, the one of pure gold and the other of an emerald stone of such size as to shine by night: and having come to speech with the priests of the god, I asked them how long a time it was since their temple had been set up: and these also I found to be at variance with the Hellenes, for they said that at the same time when Tyre was founded, the temple of the god also had been set up, and that it was a period of two thousand three hundred years since their people began to dwell at Tyre. I saw also at Tyre another temple of Heracles, with the surname Thasian; and I came to Thasos also and there I found a temple of Heracles set up by the Phenicians, who had sailed out to seek for Europa and had colonised Thasos; and these things happened full five generations of men before Heracles the son of Amphitryon was born in Hellas. So then my inquiries show clearly that Heracles is an ancient god, and those of the Hellenes seem to me to act most rightly who have two temples of Heracles set up, and who sacrifice to the one as an immortal god and with the title Olympian, and make offerings of the dead to the other as a hero. Moreover, besides many other stories which the Hellenes tell without due consideration, this tale is especially foolish which they tell about Heracles, namely that when he came to Egypt, the Egyptians put on him wreaths and led him forth in procession to sacrifice him to Zeus; and he for some time kept quiet, but when they were beginning the sacrifice of him at the altar, he betook himself to prowess and slew them all. I for my part am of opinion that the Hellenes when they tell this tale are altogether without knowledge of the nature and customs of the Egyptians; for how should they for whom it is not lawful to sacrifice even beasts, except swine and the males of oxen and calves (such of them as are clean) and geese, how should these sacrifice human beings? Besides this, how is it in nature possible that Heracles, being one person only and moreover a man (as they assert), should slay many myriads? Having said so much of these matters, we pray that we may have grace from both the gods and the heroes for our speech.

Now the reason why those of the Egyptians whom I have mentioned do not sacrifice goats, female or male, is this:—the Mendesians count Pan to be one of the eight gods (now these eight gods they say came into being before the twelve gods), and the painters and image-makers represent in painting and in sculpture the figure of Pan, just as the Hellenes do, with goat's face and legs, not supposing him to be really like this but to resemble the other gods; the cause however why they represent him in this form I prefer not to say. The Mendesians then reverence all goats and the males more than the females (and the goatherds too have greater honour than other herdsmen), but of the goats one especially is reverenced, and when he dies there is great mourning in all the Mendesian district: and both the goat and Pan are called in the Egyptian tongue *Mendes*. Moreover in my lifetime there happened in that district this marvel, that is to say a he-goat had intercourse with a woman publicly, and this was so done that all men might have evidence of it.

The pig is accounted by the Egyptians an abominable animal; and first, if any of them in passing by touch a pig, he goes into the river and dips himself forthwith in the water together with his garments; and then too swineherds, though they be native Egyptians, unlike all others do not enter any of the temples in Egypt, nor is anyone willing to give his daughter in marriage to one of them or to take a wife from among them; but the swineherds both give in marriage to one another and take from one another. Now to the other gods the Egyptians do not think it right to sacrifice swine; but to the Moon and to Dionysos alone at the same time and on the same full-moon they sacrifice swine, and then eat their flesh: and as to the reason why, when they abominate swine at all their other feasts, they sacrifice them at this, there is a story told by the Egyptians; and this story I know, but it is not a seemly one for me to tell. Now the sacrifice of the swine to the Moon is performed as follows:—when the priest has slain the victim, he puts together the end of the tail and the spleen and the caul, and covers them up with the whole of the fat of the animal which is about the paunch, and then he offers them with fire; and the rest of the flesh they eat on that day of full moon upon which they have held the sacrifice, but on any day after this they will not taste of it: the poor however among them by reason of the scantiness of their means shape pigs of dough and having baked them they offer these as a sacrifice. Then for Dionysos on the eve of the festival each one kills a pig by cutting its throat before his own doors, and after that he gives the pig to the swineherd who sold it to him, to carry away again; and the rest of the feast of Dionysos is celebrated by the Egyptians in the same way as by the Hellenes in almost all things except choral dances, but instead of the *phallos* they have invented another contrivance, namely figures of about a cubit in height worked by strings, which women carry about the villages, with the privy member made to move and not much less in size than the rest of the body: and a flute goes before and they follow singing the praises of Dionysos. As to the reason why the figure has this member larger than is natural and moves it, though it moves no other part of the body, about this there is a sacred story told. Now I think that Melampus the son of Amytheon was not without knowledge of these rites of sacrifice, but was acquainted with them: for Melampus is he who first set forth to the Hellenes the name of Dionysos and the manner of sacrifice and the procession of the *phallos*. Strictly speaking indeed, he when he made it known did not take in the whole, but those wise men who came after him made it known more at large. Melampus then is he who taught of the *phallos* which is carried in procession for Dionysos, and from him the Hellenes learnt to do that which they do. I say then that Melampus being a man of ability contrived for himself an art of divination, and having learnt from Egypt he taught the Hellenes many things, and among them those that concern Dionysos, making changes in some few points of them: for I shall not say that that which is done in worship of the god in Egypt came accidentally to be the same with that which is done among the Hellenes, for then these rites would have been in character with the Hellenic worship and not lately brought in; nor certainly shall I say that the Egyptians took from the Hellenes either this or any other customary observance: but I think it most probable that Melampus learnt the matters concerning Dionysos from Cadmos the Tyrian and from those who came with him from Phenicia to the land which we now call Bœotia.

Moreover the naming of almost all the gods has come to Hellas from Egypt: for that it has come from the Barbarians I find by inquiry is true, and I am of opinion that most probably it has come from Egypt, because, except in the case of Poseidon and the Dioscuroi (in accordance with that which I have said before), and also of Hera and Hestia and Themis and the Charites and Nereïds, the Egyptians have had the names of all the other gods in their country for all time. What I say here is that which the Egyptians say themselves: but as for the gods whose names they profess that they do not know, these I think received their naming from the Pelasgians, except Poseidon; but about this god the Hellenes learnt from the Libyans, for no people except the Libyans have had the name of Poseidon from the first and have paid honour to this god always. Nor, it may be added, have the Egyptians any custom of worshipping heroes. These observances then, and others besides these which I shall mention, the Hellenes have adopted from the Egyptians; but to make, as they do, the images of Hermes with the *phallos* they have learnt not from the Egyptians but from the Pelasgians, the custom having been received by the Athenians first of all the Hellenes and from these by the rest; for just at the time when the Athenians were beginning to rank among the Hellenes, the Pelasgians became dwellers with them in their land, and from this very cause it was that they began to be counted as Hellenes. Whosoever has been initiated in the mysteries of the Cabeiroi, which the Samothrakians perform having received them from the Pelasgians, that man knows the meaning of my speech; for these very Pelasgians who became dwellers with the Athenians used to dwell before that time in Samothrakē, and from them the Samothrakians received their mysteries. So then the Athenians were the first of the Hellenes who made the images of Hermes with the *phallos,* having learnt from the Pelasgians; and the Pelasgians told a sacred story about it, which is set forth in the mysteries in Samothrakē. Now the Pelasgians formerly were wont to make all their sacrifices calling upon the gods in prayer, as I know from that which I heard at Dodona, but they gave no title or name to any of them, for they had not yet heard any, but they called them gods (*θεούς*) from some such notion as this, that they had set (*θέντες*) in order all things and so had the distribution of everything. Afterwards when much time had elapsed, they learnt from Egypt the names of the gods, all except Dionysos, for his name they learnt long afterwards; and after a time the Pelasgians consulted the Oracle at Dodona about the names, for this prophetic seat is accounted to be the most ancient of the Oracles which are among the Hellenes, and at that time it was the only one. So when the Pelasgians asked the Oracle at Dodona whether they should adopt the names which had come from the Barbarians, the Oracle in reply bade them make use of the names. From this time they sacrificed using the names of the gods, and from the Pelasgians the Hellenes afterwards received them: but whence the several gods had their birth, or whether they all were from the beginning, and of what form they are, they did not learn till yesterday, as it were, or the day before: for Hesiod and Homer I suppose were four hundred years before my time and not more, and these are they who made a theogony for the Hellenes and gave the titles to the gods and distributed to them honours and arts, and set forth their forms: but the poets who are said to have been before these men were really in my opinion after them. Of these things the first are said by the priestesses of Dodona, and the latter things, those namely which have regard to Hesiod and Homer, by myself.

As regards the Oracles both that among the Hellenes and that in Libya, the Egyptians tell the following tale. The priests of the Theban Zeus told me that two women in the service of the temple had been carried away from Thebes by Phenicians, and that they had heard that one of them had been sold to go into Libya and the other to the Hellenes; and these women, they said, were they who first founded the prophetic seats among the nations which have been named: and when I inquired whence they knew so perfectly of this tale which they told, they said in reply that a great search had been made by the priests after these women, and that they had not been able to find them, but they had heard afterwards this tale about them which they were telling. This I heard from the priests at Thebes, and what follows is said by the prophetesses of Dodona. They say that two black doves flew from Thebes in Egypt, and came one of them to Libya and the other to their land. And this latter settled upon an oak-tree and spoke with human voice, saying that it was necessary that a prophetic seat of Zeus should be established in that place; and they supposed that that was of the gods which was announced to them, and made one accordingly: and the dove which went away to the Libyans, they say, bade the Libyans make an Oracle of Ammon; and this also is of Zeus. The priestesses of Dodona told me these things, of whom the eldest was named Promeneia, the next after her Timaretē, and the youngest Nicandra; and the other people of Dodona who were engaged about the temple gave accounts agreeing with theirs. I however have an opinion about the matter as follows:—If the Phenicians did in truth carry away the consecrated women and sold one of them into Libya and the other into Hellas, I suppose that in the country now called Hellas, which was formerly called Pelasgia, this woman was sold into the land of the Thesprotians; and then being a slave there she set up a sanctuary of Zeus under a real oak-tree; as indeed it was natural that being an attendant of the sanctuary of Zeus at Thebes, she should there, in the place to which she had come, have a memory of him; and after this, when she got understanding of the Hellenic tongue, she established an Oracle, and she reported, I suppose, that her sister had been sold in Libya by the same Phenicians by whom she herself had been sold. Moreover, I think that the women were called doves by the people of Dodona for the reason that they were Barbarians and because it seemed to them that they uttered voice like birds; but after a time (they say) the dove spoke with human voice, that is when the woman began to speak so that they could understand; but so long as she spoke a Barbarian tongue she seemed to them to be uttering voice like a bird: for if it had been really a dove, how could it speak with human voice? And in saying that the dove was black, they indicate that the woman was Egyptian. The ways of delivering oracles too at Thebes in Egypt and at Dodona closely resemble one another, as it happens, and also the method of divination by victims has come from Egypt.

Moreover, it is true also that the Egyptians were the first of men who made solemn assemblies and processions and approaches to the temples, and from them the Hellenes have learnt them, and my evidence for this is that the Egyptian celebrations of these have been held from a very ancient time, whereas the Hellenic were introduced but lately. The Egyptians hold their solemn assemblies not once in the year but often, especially and with the greatest zeal and devotion at the city of Bubastis for Artemis, and next at Busiris for Isis; for in this last-named city there is a very great temple of Isis, and this city stands in the middle of the Delta of Egypt; now Isis is in the tongue of the Hellenes Demeter: thirdly, they have a solemn assembly at the city of Saïs for Athenē, fourthly at Heliopolis for the Sun (Helios), fifthly at the city of Buto in honour of Leto, and sixthly at the city of Papremis for Ares. Now, when they are coming to the city of Bubastis they do as follows:—they sail men and women together, and a great multitude of each sex in every boat; and some of the women have rattles and rattle with them, while some of the men play the flute during the whole time of the voyage, and the rest, both women and men, sing and clap their hands; and when as they sail they come opposite to any city on the way they bring the boat to land,

and some of the women continue to do as I have said, others cry aloud and jeer at the women in that city, some dance, and some stand up and pull up their garments. This they do by every city along the river-bank; and when they come to Bubastis they hold festival celebrating great sacrifices, and more wine of grapes is consumed upon that festival than during the whole of the rest of the year. To this place (so say the natives) they come together year by year even to the number of seventy myriads of men and women, besides children. Thus it is done here; and how they celebrate the festival in honour of Isis at the city of Busiris has been told by me before: for, as I said, they beat themselves in mourning after the sacrifice, all of them both men and women, very many myriads of people; but for whom they beat themselves it is not permitted to me by religion to say: and so many as there are of the Carians dwelling in Egypt do this even more than the Egyptians themselves, inasmuch as they cut their foreheads also with knives; and by this it is manifested that they are strangers and not Egyptians. At the times when they gather together at the city of Saïs for their sacrifices, on a certain night they all kindle lamps many in number in the open air round about the houses; now the lamps are saucers full of salt and oil mixed, and the wick floats by itself on the surface, and this burns during the whole night; and to the festival is given the name *Lychnocaia* (the lighting of lamps). Moreover those of the Egyptians who have not come to this solemn assembly observe the night of the festival and themselves also light lamps all of them, and thus not in Saïs alone are they lighted, but over all Egypt: and as to the reason why light and honour are allotted to this night, about this there is a sacred story told. To Heliopolis and Buto they go year by year and do sacrifice only: but at Papremis they do sacrifice and worship as elsewhere, and besides that, when the sun begins to go down, while some few of the priests are occupied with the image of the god, the greater number of them stand in the entrance of the temple with wooden clubs, and other persons to the number of more than a thousand men with purpose to perform a vow, these also having all of them staves of wood, stand in a body opposite to those: and the image, which is in a small shrine of wood covered over with gold, they take out on the day before to another sacred building. The few then who have been left about the image, draw a wain with four wheels, which bears the shrine and the image that is within the shrine, and the other priests standing in the gateway try to prevent it from entering, and the men who are under a vow come to the assistance of the god and strike them, while the others defend themselves. Then there comes to be a hard fight with staves, and they break one another's heads, and I am of opinion that many even die of the wounds they receive; the Egyptians however told me that no one died. This solemn assembly the people of the place say that they established for the following reason:—the mother of Ares, they say, used to dwell in this temple, and Ares, having been brought up away from her, when he grew up came thither desiring to visit his mother, and the attendants of his mother's temple, not having seen him before, did not permit him to pass in, but kept him away; and he brought men to help him from another city and handled roughly the attendants of the temple, and entered to visit his mother. Hence, they say, this exchange of blows has become the custom in honour of Ares upon his festival.

The Egyptians were the first who made it a point of religion not to lie with women in temples, nor to enter into temples after going away from women without first bathing: for almost all other men except the Egyptians and the Hellenes lie with women in temples and enter into a temple after going away from women without bathing, since they hold that there is no difference in this respect between men and beasts: for they say that they see beasts and the various kinds of birds coupling together both in the temples and in the sacred enclosures of the gods; if then this were not pleasing to the god, the beasts would not do so.

Thus do these defend that which they do, which by me is disallowed: but the Egyptians are excessively careful in their observances, both in other matters which concern the sacred rites and also in those which follow:—Egypt, though it borders upon Libya, does not very much abound in wild animals, but such as they have are one and all accounted by them sacred, some of them living with men and others not.

But if I should say for what reasons the sacred animals have been thus dedicated, I should fall into discourse of matters pertaining to the gods, of which I most desire not to speak; and what I have actually said touching slightly upon them, I said because I was constrained by necessity. About these animals there is a custom of this kind:—persons have been appointed of the Egyptians, both men and women, to provide the food for each kind of beast separately, and their office goes down from father to son; and those who dwell in the various cities perform vows to them thus, that is, when they make a vow to the god to whom the animal belongs, they shave the head of their children either the whole or the half or the third part of it, and then set the hair in the balance against silver, and whatever it weighs, this the man gives to the person who provides for the animals, and she cuts up fish of equal value and gives it for food to the animals. Thus food for their support has been appointed: and if any one kill any of these animals, the penalty, if he do it with his own will, is death, and if against his will, such penalty as the priests may appoint: but whosoever shall kill an ibis or a hawk, whether it be with his will or against his will, must die. Of the animals that live with men there are great numbers, and would be many more but for the accidents which befall the cats. For when the females have produced young they are no longer in the habit of going to the males, and these seeking to be united with them are not able. To this end then they contrive as follows,—they either take away by force or remove secretly the young from the females and kill them (but after killing they do not eat them), and the females being deprived of their young and desiring more, therefore come to the males, for it is a creature that is fond of its young. Moreover when a fire occurs, the cats seem to be divinely possessed; for while the Egyptians stand at intervals and look after the cats, not taking any care to extinguish the fire, the cats slipping through or leaping over the men, jump into the fire; and when this happens, great mourning comes upon the Egyptians. And in whatever houses a cat has died by a natural death, all those who dwell in this house shave their eyebrows only, but those in whose houses a dog has died shave their whole body and also their head. The cats when they are dead are carried away to sacred buildings in the city of Bubastis, where after being embalmed they are buried; but the dogs they bury each people in their own city in sacred tombs; and the ichneumons are buried just in the same way as the dogs. The shrew-mice however and the hawks they carry away to the city of Buto, and the ibises to Hermopolis; the bears (which are not commonly seen) and the wolves, not much larger in size than foxes, they bury on the spot where they are found lying.

Of the crocodile the nature is as follows:—during the four most wintry months this creature eats nothing: she has four feet and is an animal belonging to the land and the water both; for she produces and hatches eggs on the land, and the most part of the day she remains upon dry land, but the whole of the night in the river, for the water in truth is warmer than the unclouded open air and the dew. Of all the mortal creatures of which we have knowledge this grows to the greatest bulk from the smallest beginning; for the eggs which she produces are not much larger than those of geese and the newly-hatched young one is in proportion to the egg, but as he grows he becomes as much as seventeen cubits long and sometimes yet larger. He has eyes like those of a pig and teeth large and tusky, in proportion to the size of his body; but unlike all other beasts he grows no tongue, neither does he move his lower jaw, but brings the upper jaw towards the lower, being in this too unlike all other beasts. He has moreover strong claws and a scaly hide upon his back which cannot be pierced; and he is blind in the water, but in the air he is of a very keen sight. Since he has his living in the water he keeps his mouth all full within of leeches; and whereas all other birds and beasts fly from him, the trochilus is a creature which is at peace with him, seeing that from her he receives benefit; for the crocodile having come out of the water to the land and then having opened his mouth (this he is wont to do generally towards the West Wind), the trochilus upon that enters into his mouth and swallows down the leeches, and he being benefited is pleased and does no harm to the trochilus. Now for some of the Egyptians the crocodiles are sacred animals, and for others not so, but they treat them on the contrary as enemies: those however who dwell about Thebes and about the lake of Moiris hold them to be most sacred, and each of these two peoples keeps one crocodile selected from the whole number, which has been trained to tameness, and they put hanging ornaments of molten stone and of gold into the ears of these and anklets round the front feet, and they give them food appointed and victims of sacrifices and treat them as well as possible while they live, and after they are dead they bury them in sacred tombs, embalming them: but those who dwell about the city of Elephantinē even eat them, not holding them to be sacred. They are called not crocodiles but *champsai,* and the Ionians gave them the name of crocodile, comparing their form to that of the crocodiles (lizards) which appear in their country in the stone walls. There are many ways in use of catching them and of various kinds: I shall describe that which to me seems the most worthy of being told. A man puts the back of a pig upon a hook as bait, and lets it go into the middle of the river, while he himself upon the bank of the river has a young live pig, which he beats; and the crocodile hearing its cries makes for the direction of the sound, and when he finds the pig's back he swallows it down: then they pull, and when he is drawn out to land, first of all the hunter forthwith plasters up his eyes with mud, and having so done he very easily gets the mastery of him, but if he does not do so he has much trouble.

The river-horse is sacred in the district of Papremis, but for the other Egyptians he is not sacred; and this is the appearance which he presents: he is four-footed, cloven-hoofed like an ox, flat-nosed, with a mane like a horse and showing teeth like tusks, with a tail and voice like a horse, and in size as large as the largest ox; and his hide is so exceedingly thick that when it has been dried shafts of javelins are made of it. There are moreover otters in the river, which they consider to be sacred; and of fish also they esteem that which is called the *lepidotos* to be sacred, and also the eel; and these they say are sacred to the Nile: and of birds the fox-goose.

There is also another sacred bird called the phœnix which I did not myself see except in painting, for in truth he comes to them very rarely, at intervals, as the people of Heliopolis say, of five hundred years; and these say that he comes regularly when his father dies; and if he be like the painting, he is of this size and nature, that is to say, some of his feathers are of gold colour and others red, and in outline and size he is as nearly as possible like an eagle. This bird they say (but I cannot believe the story) contrives as follows:—setting forth from Arabia he conveys his father, they say, to the temple of the Sun (Helios) plastered up in myrrh, and buries him in the temple of the Sun; and he conveys him thus:—he forms first an egg of myrrh as large as he is able to carry, and then he makes trial of carrying it, and when he has made trial sufficiently, then he hollows out the egg and places his father within it and plasters over with other myrrh that part of the egg where he hollowed it out to put his father in, and when his father is laid in it, it proves (they say) to be of the same weight as it was; and after he has plastered it up, he conveys the whole to Egypt to the temple of the Sun. Thus they say that this bird does.

There are also about Thebes sacred serpents, not at all harmful to men, which are small in size and have two horns growing from the top of the head: these they bury when they die in the temple of Zeus, for to this god they say that they are sacred. There is a region moreover in Arabia, situated nearly over against the city of Buto, to which place I came to inquire about the winged serpents: and when I came thither I saw bones of serpents and spines in quantity so great that it is impossible to make report of the number, and there were heaps of spines, some heaps large and others less large and others smaller still than these, and these heaps were many in number. This region in which the spines are scattered upon the ground is of the nature of an entrance from a narrow mountain pass to a great plain, which plain adjoins the plain of Egypt; and the story goes that at the beginning of spring winged serpents from Arabia fly towards Egypt, and the birds called ibises meet them at the entrance to this country and do not suffer the serpents to go by but kill them. On account of this deed it is (say the Arabians) that the ibis has come to be greatly honoured by the

Egyptians, and the Egyptians also agree that it is for this reason that they honour these birds. The outward form of the ibis is this:—it is a deep black all over, and has legs like those of a crane and a very curved beak, and in size it is about equal to a rail: this is the appearance of the black kind which fight with the serpents, but of those which most crowd round men's feet (for there are two several kinds of ibises) the head is bare and also the whole of the throat, and it is white in feathering except the head and neck and the extremities of the wings and the rump (in all these parts of which I have spoken it is a deep black), while in legs and in the form of the head it resembles the other. As for the serpent its form is like that of the watersnake; and it has wings not feathered but most nearly resembling the wings of the bat. Let so much suffice as has been said now concerning sacred animals.

Of the Egyptians themselves, those who dwell in the part of Egypt which is sown for crops practise memory more than any other men and are the most learned in history by far of all those of whom I have had experience: and their manner of life is as follows:—For three successive days in each month they purge, hunting after health with emetics and clysters, and they think that all the diseases which exist are produced in men by the food on which they live: for the Egyptians are from other causes also the most healthy of all men next after the Libyans (in my opinion on account of the seasons, because the seasons do not change, for by the changes of things generally, and especially of the seasons, diseases are most apt to be produced in men), and as to their diet, it is as follows:—they eat bread, making loaves of maize, which they call *kyllestis,* and they use habitually a wine made out of barley, for vines they have not in their land. Of their fish some they dry in the sun and then eat them without cooking, others they eat cured in brine. Of birds they eat quails and ducks and small birds without cooking, after first curing them; and everything else which they have belonging to the class of birds or fishes, except such as have been set apart by them as sacred, they eat roasted or boiled. In the entertainments of the rich among them, when they have finished eating, a man bears round a wooden figure of a dead body in a coffin, made as like the reality as may be both by painting and carving, and measuring about a cubit or two cubits each way; and this he shows to each of those who are drinking together, saying: "When thou lookest upon this, drink and be merry, for thou shalt be such as this when thou art dead." Thus they do at their carousals. The customs which they practise are derived from their fathers and they do not acquire others in addition; but besides other customary things among them which are worthy of mention, they have one song, that of Linos, the same who is sung of both in Phenicia and in Cyprus and elsewhere, having however a name different according to the various nations. This song agrees exactly with that which the Hellenes sing calling on the name of Linos, so that besides many other things about which I wonder among those matters which concern Egypt, I wonder especially about this, namely whence they got the song of Linos. It is evident however that they have sung this song from immemorial time, and in the Egyptian tongue Linos is called Manerōs. The Egyptians told me that he was the only son of him who first became king of Egypt, and that he died before his time and was honoured with these lamentations by the Egyptians, and that this was their first and only song. In another respect the Egyptians are in agreement with some of the Hellenes, namely with the Lacedemonians, but not with the rest, that is to say, the younger of them when they meet the elder give way and move out of the path, and when their elders approach, they rise out of their seat. In this which follows however they are not in agreement with any of the Hellenes,—instead of addressing one another in the roads they do reverence, lowering their hand down to their knee. They wear tunics of linen about their legs with fringes, which they call *calasiris;* above these they have garments of white wool thrown over: woolen garments however are not taken into the temples, nor are they buried with them, for this is not permitted by religion. In these points they are in agreement with the observances called Orphic and Bacchic (which are really Egyptian), and also with those of the Pythagoreans, for one who takes part in these mysteries is also forbidden by religious rule to be buried in woolen garments; and about this there is a sacred story told.

Besides these things the Egyptians have found out also to what god each month and each day belongs, and what fortunes a man will meet with who is born on any particular day, and how he will die, and what kind of a man he will be: and these inventions were taken up by those of the Hellenes who occupied themselves about poesy. Portents too have been found out by them more than by all other men besides; for when a portent has happened, they observe and write down the event which comes of it, and if ever afterwards anything resembling this happens, they believe that the event which comes of it will be similar. Their divination is ordered thus:—the art is assigned not to any man but to certain of the gods, for there are in their land Oracles of Heracles, of Apollo, of Athenē, of Artemis, of Ares, and of Zeus, and moreover that which they hold most in honour of all, namely the Oracle of Leto which is in the city of Buto. The manner of divination however is not established among them according to the same fashion everywhere, but is different in different places. The art of medicine among them is distributed thus:—each physician is a physician of one disease and of no more; and the whole country is full of physicians, for some profess themselves to be physicians of the eyes, others of the head, others of the teeth, others of the affections of the stomach, and others of the more obscure ailments.

Their fashions of mourning and of burial are these:—Whenever any household has lost a man who is of any regard amongst them, the whole number of women of that house forthwith plaster over their heads or even their faces with mud. Then leaving the corpse within the house they go themselves to and fro about the city and beat themselves, with their garments bound up by a girdle and their breasts exposed, and with them go all the women who are related to the dead man, and on the other side the men beat themselves, they too having their garments bound up by a girdle; and when they have done this, they then convey the body to the embalming. In this occupation certain persons employ themselves regularly and inherit this as a craft. These, whenever a corpse is conveyed to them, show to those who brought it wooden models of corpses made like reality by painting, and the best of the ways of embalming they say is that of him whose name I think it impiety to mention when speaking of a matter of such a kind; the second which they show is less good than this and also less expensive; and the third is the least expensive of all. Having told them about this, they inquire of them in which way they desire the corpse of their friend to be prepared. Then they after they have agreed for a certain price depart out of the way, and the others being left behind in the buildings embalm according to the best of these ways thus:—First with a crooked iron tool they draw out the brain through the nostrils, extracting it partly thus and partly by pouring in drugs; and after this with a sharp stone of Ethiopia they make a cut along the side and take out the whole contents of the belly, and when they have cleared out the cavity and cleansed it with palm-wine they cleanse it again with spices pounded up: then they fill the belly with pure myrrh pounded up and with cassia and other spices except frankincense, and sew it together again. Having so done they keep it for embalming covered up in natron for seventy days, but for a longer time than this it is not permitted to embalm it; and when the seventy days are past, they wash the corpse and roll its whole body up in fine linen cut into bands, smearing these beneath with gum, which the Egyptians use generally instead of glue. Then the kinsfolk receive it from them and have a wooden figure made in the shape of a man, and when they have had this made they enclose the corpse, and having shut it up within, they store it then in a sepulchral chamber, setting it to stand upright against the wall. Thus they deal with the corpses which are prepared in the most costly way; but for those who desire the middle way and wish to avoid great cost they prepare the corpse as follows:—having filled their syringes with the oil which is got from cedar-wood, with this they forthwith fill the belly of the corpse, and this they do without having either cut it open or taken out the bowels, but they inject the oil by the breech, and having stopped the drench from returning back they keep it then the appointed number of days for embalming, and on the last of the days they let the cedar oil come out from the belly, which they before put in; and it has such power that it brings out with it the bowels and interior organs of the body dissolved; and the natron dissolves the flesh, so that there is left of the corpse only the skin and the bones. When they have done this they give back the corpse at once in that condition without working upon it any more. The third kind of embalming, by which are prepared the bodies of those who have less means, is as follows:—they cleanse out the belly with a purge and then keep the body for embalming during the seventy days, and at once after that they give it back to the bringers to carry away. The wives of men of rank when they die are not given at once to be embalmed, nor such women as are very beautiful or of greater regard than others, but on the third or fourth day after their death (and not before) they are delivered to the embalmers. They do so about this matter in order that the embalmers may not abuse their women, for they say that one of them was taken once doing so to the corpse of a woman lately dead, and his fellow-craftsman gave information. Whenever any one, either of the Egyptians themselves or of strangers, is found to have been carried off by a crocodile or brought to his death by the river itself, the people of any city by which he may have been cast up on land must embalm him and lay him out in the fairest way they can and bury him in a sacred burial-place, nor may any of his relations or friends besides touch him, but the priests of the Nile themselves handle the corpse and bury it as that of one who was something more than man.

Hellenic usages they will by no means follow, and to speak generally they follow those of no other men whatever. This rule is observed by most of the Egyptians; but there is a large city named Chemmis in the Theban district near Neapolis, and in this city there is a temple of Perseus the son of Danaē which is of a square shape, and round it grow date-palms: the gateway of the temple is built of stone and of very great size, and at the entrance of it stand two great statues of stone. Within this enclosure is a temple-house and in it stands an image of Perseus. These people of Chemmis say that Perseus is wont often to appear in their land and often within the temple, and that a sandal which has been worn by him is found sometimes, being in length two cubits, and whenever this appears all Egypt prospers. This they say, and they do in honour of Perseus after Hellenic fashion thus,—they hold an athletic contest, which includes the whole list of games, and they offer in prizes cattle and cloaks and skins: and when I inquired why to them alone Perseus was wont to appear, and wherefore they were separated from all the other Egyptians in that they held an athletic contest, they said that Perseus had been born of their city, for Danaos and Lynkeus were men of Chemmis and had sailed to Hellas, and from them they traced a descent and came down to Perseus: and they told me that he had come to Egypt for the reason which the Hellenes also say, namely to bring from Libya the Gorgon's head, and had then visited them also and recognised all his kinsfolk, and they said that he had well learnt the name of Chemmis before he came to Egypt, since he had heard it from his mother, and that they celebrated an athletic contest for him by his own command.

All these are customs practised by the Egyptians who dwell above the fens: and those who are settled in the fen-land have the same customs for the most part as the other Egyptians, both in other matters and also in that they live each with one wife only, as do the Hellenes; but for economy in respect of food they have invented these things besides:—when the river has become full and the plains have been flooded, there grow in the water great numbers of lilies, which the Egyptians call *lotos;* these they cut with a sickle and dry in the sun, and then they pound that which grows in the middle of the lotos and which is like the head of a poppy, and they make of it loaves baked with fire. The root also of this lotos is edible and has a rather sweet taste: it is round in shape and about the size of an apple. There are other lilies too, in flower resembling roses, which also grow in the river, and from them the fruit is produced in a separate vessel springing from the root by the side of the plant itself, and very nearly resembles a wasp's comb: in this there grow edible seeds in great numbers of the size of an olive-stone, and they are eaten either fresh or dried. Besides this they pull up from the fens the papyrus which grows every year, and the upper parts of it they cut off and turn to other uses, but that which is left below for about a cubit in length they eat or sell: and those who desire to have the papyrus at its very best bake it in an oven heated red-hot, and then eat it. Some too of these people live on fish alone, which they dry in the sun after having caught them and taken out the entrails, and then when they are dry, they use them for food.

Fish which swim in shoals are not much produced in the rivers, but are bred in the lakes, and they do as follows:—When there comes upon them the desire to breed, they swim out in shoals towards the sea; and the males lead the way shedding forth their milt as they go, while the females, coming after and swallowing it up, from it become impregnated: and when they have become full of young in the sea they swim up back again, each shoal to its own haunts. The same however no longer lead the way as before, but the lead comes now to the females, and they leading the way in shoals do just as the males did, that is to say they shed forth their eggs by a few grains at a time, and the males coming after swallow them up. Now these grains are fish, and from the grains which survive and are not swallowed, the fish grow which afterwards are bred up. Now those of the fish which are caught as they swim out towards the sea are found to be rubbed on the left side of the head, but those which are caught as they swim up again are rubbed on the right side. This happens to them because as they swim down to the sea they keep close to the land on the left side of the river, and again as they swim up they keep to the same side, approaching and touching the bank as much as they can, for fear doubtless of straying from their course by reason of the stream. When the Nile begins to swell, the hollow places of the land and the depressions by the side of the river first begin to fill, as the water soaks through from the river, and so soon as they become full of water, at once they are all filled with little fishes; and whence these are in all likelihood produced, I think that I perceive. In the preceding year, when the Nile goes down, the fish first lay eggs in the mud and then retire with the last of the retreating waters; and when the time comes round again, and the water once more comes over the land, from these eggs forthwith are produced the fishes of which I speak.

Thus it is as regards the fish. And for anointing those of the Egyptians who dwell in the fens use oil from the castor-berry, which oil the Egyptians call *kiki,* and thus they do:—they sow along the banks of the rivers and pools these plants, which in a wild form grow of themselves in the land of the Hellenes; these are sown in Egypt and produce berries in great quantity but of an evil smell; and when they have gathered these, some cut them up and press the oil from them, others again roast them first and then boil them down and collect that which runs away from them. The oil is fat and not less suitable for burning than olive-oil, but it gives forth a disagreeable smell. Against the gnats, which are very abundant, they have contrived as follows:—those who dwell above the fen-land are helped by the towers, to which they ascend when they go to rest; for the gnats by reason of the winds are not able to fly up high: but those who dwell in the fen-land have contrived another way instead of the towers, and this it is:—every man of them has got a casting net, with which by day he catches fish, but in the night he uses it for this purpose, that is to say he puts the casting-net round about the bed in which he sleeps, and then creeps in under it and goes to sleep: and the gnats, if he sleeps rolled up in a garment or a linen sheet, bite through these, but through the net they do not even attempt to bite.

Their boats with which they carry cargoes are made of the thorny acacia, of which the form is very like that of the Kyrenian lotos, and that which exudes from it is gum. From this tree they cut pieces of wood about two cubits in length and arrange them like bricks, fastening the boat together by running a great number of long bolts through the two-cubit pieces; and when they have thus fastened the boat together, they lay cross-pieces over the top, using no ribs for the sides; and within they caulk the seams with papyrus. They make one steering-oar for it, which is passed through the bottom of the boat; and they have a mast of acacia and sails of papyrus. These boats cannot sail up the river unless there be a very fresh wind blowing, but are towed from the shore: down-stream however they travel as follows:—they have a door-shaped crate made of tamarisk wood and reed mats sewn together, and also a stone of about two talents weight bored with a hole; and of these the boatman lets the crate float on in front of the boat, fastened with a rope, and the stone drags behind by another rope. The crate then, as the force of the stream presses upon it, goes on swiftly and draws on the *baris* (for so these boats are called), while the stone dragging after it behind and sunk deep in the water keeps its course straight. These boats they have in great numbers and some of them carry many thousands of talents' burden.

When the Nile comes over the land, the cities alone are seen rising above the water, resembling more nearly than anything else the islands in the Egean Sea; for the rest of Egypt becomes a sea and the cities alone rise above water. Accordingly, whenever this happens, they pass by water not now by the channels of the river but over the midst of the plain: for example, as one sails up from Naucratis to Memphis the passage is then close by the pyramids, whereas the usual passage is not the same even here, but goes by the point of the Delta and the city of Kercasoros; while if you sail over the plain to Naucratis from the sea and from Canobos, you will go by Anthylla and the city called after Archander. Of these Anthylla is a city of note and is especially assigned to the wife of him who reigns over Egypt, to supply her with sandals, (this is the case since the time when Egypt came to be under the Persians): the other city seems to me to have its name from Archander the son-in-law of Danaos, who was the son of Phthios, the son of Achaios; for it is called the City of Archander. There might indeed be another Archander, but in any case the name is not Egyptian.

Hitherto my own observation and judgment and inquiry are the vouchers for that which I have said; but from this point onwards I am about to tell the history of Egypt according to that which I heard, to which will be added also something of that which I have myself seen.

Of Min, who first became king of Egypt, the priests said

that on the one hand he banked off the site of Memphis from the river: for the whole stream of the river used to flow along by the sandy mountain-range on the side of Libya, but Min formed by embankments that bend of the river which lies to the South about a hundred furlongs above Memphis, and thus he dried up the old stream and conducted the river so that it flowed in the middle between the mountains: and even now this bend of the Nile is by the Persians kept under very careful watch, that it may flow in the channel to which it is confined, and the bank is repaired every year; for if the river should break through and overflow in this direction, Memphis would be in danger of being overwhelmed by flood. When this Min, who first became king, had made into dry land the part which was dammed off, on the one hand, I say, he founded in it that city which is now called Memphis; for Memphis too is in the narrow part of Egypt; and outside the city he dug round it on the North and West a lake communicating with the river, for the side towards the East is barred by the Nile itself. Then secondly he established in the city the temple of Hephaistos a great work and most worthy of mention. After this man the priests enumerated to me from a papyrus roll the names of other kings, three hundred and thirty in number; and in all these generations of men eighteen were Ethiopians, one was a woman, a native Egyptian, and the rest were men and of Egyptian race: and the name of the woman who reigned was the same as that of the Babylonian queen, namely Nitocris. Of her they said that desiring to take vengeance for her brother, whom the Egyptians had slain when he was their king and then, after having slain him, had given his kingdom to her,—desiring, I say, to take vengeance for him, she destroyed by craft many of the Egyptians. For she caused to be constructed a very large chamber under ground, and making as though she would handsel it but in her mind devising other things, she invited those of the Egyptians whom she knew to have had most part in the murder, and gave a great banquet. Then while they were feasting, she let in the river upon them by a secret conduit of large size. Of her they told no more than this, except that, when this had been accomplished, she threw herself into a room full of embers, in order that she might escape vengeance. As for the other kings, they could tell me of no great works which had been produced by them, and they said that they had no renown except only the last of them, Moiris: he (they said) produced as a memorial of himself the gateway of the temple of Hephaistos which is turned towards the North Wind, and dug a lake, about which I shall set forth afterwards how many furlongs of circuit it has, and in it built pyramids of the size which I shall mention at the same time when I speak of the lake itself. He, they said, produced these works, but of the rest none produced any.

Therefore passing these by I shall make mention of the king who came after these, whose name was Sesostris. He (the priests said) first of all set out with ships of war from the Arabian gulf and subdued those who dwelt by the shores of the Erythraian Sea, until as he sailed he came to a sea which could no further be navigated by reason of shoals: then secondly, after he had returned to Egypt, according to the report of the priests he took a great army and marched over the continent, subduing every nation which stood in his way: and those of them whom he found valiant and fighting desperately for their freedom, in their lands he set up pillars which told by inscriptions his own name and the name of his country, and how he had subdued them by his power; but as to those of whose cities he obtained possession without fighting or with ease, on their pillars he inscribed words after the same tenor as he did for the nations which had shown themselves courageous, and in addition he drew upon them the hidden parts of a woman, desiring to signify by this that the people were cowards and effeminate. Thus doing he traversed the continent, until at last he passed over to Europe from Asia and subdued the Scythians and also the Thracians. These, I am of opinion, were the furthest people to which the Egyptian army came, for in their country the pillars are found to have been set up, but in the land beyond this they are no longer found. From this point he turned and began to go back; and when he came to the river Phasis, what happened then I cannot say for certain, whether the king Sesostris himself divided off a certain portion of his army and left the men there as settlers in the land, or whether some of his soldiers were wearied by his distant marches and remained by the river Phasis. For the people of Colchis are evidently Egyptian, and this I perceived for myself before I heard it from others. So when I had come to consider the matter I asked them both; and the Colchians had remembrance of the Egyptians more than the Egyptians of the Colchians; but the Egyptians said they believed that the Colchians were a portion of the army of Sesostris. That this was so I conjectured myself not only because they are dark-skinned and have curly hair (this of itself amounts to nothing, for there are other races which are so), but also still more because the Colchians, Egyptians, and Ethiopians alone of all the races of men have practised circumcision from the first. The Phenicians and the Syrians who dwell in Palestine confess themselves that they have learnt it from the Egyptians, and the Syrians about the river Thermodon and the river Parthenios, and the Macronians, who are their neighbours, say that they have learnt it lately from the Colchians. These are the only races of men who practise circumcision, and these evidently practise it in the same manner as the Egyptians. Of the Egyptians themselves however and the Ethiopians, I am not able to say which learnt from the other, for undoubtedly it is a most ancient custom; but that the other nations learnt it by intercourse with the Egyptians, this among others is to me a strong proof, namely that those of the Phenicians who have intercourse with Hellas cease to follow the example of the Egyptians in this matter, and do not circumcise their children. Now let me tell another thing about the Colchians to show how they resemble the Egyptians:—they alone work flax in the same fashion as the Egyptians, and the two nations are like one another in their whole manner of living and also in their language: now the linen of Colchis is called by the Hellenes Sardonic, whereas that from Egypt is called Egyptian. The pillars which Sesostris king of Egypt set up in the various countries are for the most part no longer to be seen extant; but in Syria Palestine I myself saw them existing with the inscription upon them which I have mentioned and the emblem. Moreover in Ionia there are two figures of this man carved upon rocks, one on the road by which one goes from the land of Ephesos to Phocaia, and the other on the road from Sardis to Smyrna. In each place there is a figure of a man cut in the rock, of four cubits and a span in height, holding in his right hand a spear and in his left a bow and arrows, and the other equipment which he has is similar to this, for it is both Egyptian and Ethiopian: and from the one shoulder to the other across the breast runs an inscription carved in sacred Egyptian characters, saying thus, "This land with my shoulders I won for myself." But who he is and from whence, he does not declare in these places, though in other places he has declared this. Some of those who have seen these carvings conjecture that the figure is that of Memnon, but herein they are very far from the truth.

As this Egyptian Sesostris was returning and bringing back many men of the nations whose lands he had subdued, when he came (said the priests) to Daphnai in the district of Pelusion on his journey home, his brother to whom Sesostris had entrusted the charge of Egypt invited him and with him his sons to a feast; and then he piled the house round with brushwood and set it on fire: and Sesostris when he discovered this forthwith took counsel with his wife, for he was bringing with him (they said) his wife also; and she counselled him to lay out upon the pyre two of his sons, which were six in number, and so to make a bridge over the burning mass, and that they passing over their bodies should thus escape. This, they said, Sesostris did, and two of his sons were burnt to death in this manner, but the rest got away safe with their father. Then Sesostris, having returned to Egypt and having taken vengeance on his brother, employed the multitude which he had brought in of those whose lands he had subdued, as follows:—these were they who drew the stones which in the reign of this king were brought to the temple of Hephaistos, being of very great size; and also these were compelled to dig all the channels which now are in Egypt; and thus (having no such purpose) they caused Egypt, which before was all fit for riding and driving, to be no longer fit for this from thenceforth: for from that time forward Egypt, though it is plain land, has become all unfit for riding and driving, and the cause has been these channels, which are many and run in all directions. But the reason why the king cut up the land was this, namely because those of the Egyptians who had their cities not on the river but in the middle of the country, being in want of water when the river went down from them, found their drink brackish because they had it from wells. For this reason Egypt was cut up: and they said that this king distributed the land to all the Egyptians, giving an equal square portion to each man, and from this he made his revenue, having appointed them to pay a certain rent every year: and if the river should take away anything from any man's portion, he would come to the king and declare that which had happened, and the king used to send men to examine and to find out by measurement how much less the piece of land had become, in order that for the future the man might pay less, in proportion to the rent appointed: and I think that thus the art of geometry was found out and afterwards came into Hellas also. For as touching the sun-dial and the gnomon and the twelve divisions of the day, they were learnt by the Hellenes from the Babylonians. He moreover alone of all the Egyptian kings had rule over Ethiopia; and he left as memorials of himself in front of the temple of Hephaistos two stone statues of thirty cubits each, representing himself and his wife, and others of twenty cubits each representing his four sons: and long afterwards the priest of Hephaistos refused to permit Dareios the Persian to set up a statue of himself in front of them, saying that deeds had not been done by him equal to those which were done by Sesostris the Egyptian; for Sesostris had subdued other nations besides, not fewer than he, and also the Scythians; but Dareios had not been able to conquer the Scythians: wherefore it was not just that he should set up a statue in front of those which Sesostris had dedicated, if he did not surpass him in his deeds. Which speech, they say, Dareios took in good part.

Now after Sesostris had brought his life to an end, his son Pheros, they told me, received in succession the kingdom, and he made no warlike expedition, and moreover it chanced to him to become blind by reason of the following accident:—when the river had come down in flood rising to a height of eighteen cubits, higher than ever before that time, and had gone over the fields, a wind fell upon it and the river became agitated by waves: and this king (they say) moved by presumptuous folly took a spear and cast it into the midst of the eddies of the stream; and immediately upon this he had a disease of the eyes and was by it made blind. For ten years then he was blind, and in the eleventh year there came to him an oracle from the city of Buto, saying that the time of his punishment had expired, and that he should see again if he washed his eyes with the water of a woman who had accompanied with her own husband only and had not had knowledge of other men: and first he made trial of his own wife, and then, as he continued blind, he went on to try all the women in turn; and when he had at last regained his sight he gathered together all the women of whom he had made trial, excepting her by whose means he had regained his sight, to one city which now is named Erythrabolos, and having gathered them to this he consumed them all by fire, as well as the city itself; but as for her by whose means he had regained his sight, he had her himself to wife. Then after he had escaped the malady of his eyes he dedicated offerings at each one of the temples which were of renown, and especially (to mention only that which is most worthy of mention) he dedicated at the temple of the Sun works which are worth seeing, namely two obelisks of stone, each of a single block, measuring in length a hundred cubits each one and in breadth eight cubits.

After him, they said, there succeeded to the throne a man of Memphis, whose name in the tongue of the Hellenes was Proteus; for whom there is now a sacred enclosure at Memphis, very fair and well ordered, lying on that side of the temple of Hephaistos which faces the North Wind. Round about this enclosure dwell Phenicians of Tyre, and this whole region is called the Camp of the Tyrians. Within the enclosure of Proteus there is a temple called the temple of the "foreign Aphroditē," which temple I conjecture to be one of Helen the daughter of Tyndareus, not only because I have heard the tale how Helen dwelt with Proteus, but also especially because it is called by the name of the "foreign Aphroditē," for the other temples of Aphroditē which there are have none of them the addition of the word "foreign" to the name.

And the priests told me, when I inquired, that the things concerning Helen happened thus:—Alexander having carried off Helen was sailing away from Sparta to his own land, and when he had come to the Egean Sea contrary winds drove him from his course to the Sea of Egypt; and after that, since the blasts did not cease to blow, he came to Egypt itself, and in Egypt to that which is now named the Canobic mouth of the Nile and to Taricheiai. Now there was upon the shore, as still there is now, a temple of Heracles, in which if any man's slave take refuge and have the sacred marks set upon him, giving himself over to the god, it is not lawful to lay hands upon him; and this custom has continued still unchanged from the beginning down to my own time. Accordingly the attendants of Alexandria, having heard of the custom which existed about the temple, ran away from him, and sitting down as suppliants of the god, accused Alexander, because they desired to do him hurt, telling the whole tale how things were about Helen and about the wrong done to Menelaos; and this accusation they made not only to the priests but also to the warden of this river-mouth, whose name was Thonis. Thonis then having heard their tale sent forthwith a message to Proteus at Memphis, which said as follows: "There hath come a stranger, a Teucrian by race, who hath done in Hellas an unholy deed; for he hath deceived the wife of his own host, and is come hither bringing with him this woman herself and very much wealth, having been carried out of his way by winds to thy land. Shall we then allow him to sail out unharmed, or shall we first take away from him that which he brought with him?" In reply to this Proteus sent back a messenger who said thus: "Seize this man, whosoever he may be, who has done impiety to his own host, and bring him away into my presence, that I may know what he will find to say." Hearing this, Thonis seized Alexander and detained his ships, and after that he brought the man himself up to Memphis and with him Helen and the wealth he had, and also in addition to them the suppliants. So when all had been conveyed up thither, Proteus began to ask Alexander who he was and from whence he was voyaging; and he both recounted to him his descent and told him the name of his native land, and moreover related of his voyage, from whence he was sailing. After this Proteus asked him whence he had taken Helen; and when Alexander went astray in his account and did not speak the truth, those who had become suppliants convicted him of falsehood, relating in full the whole tale of the wrong done. At length Proteus declared to them this sentence, saying, "Were it not that I count it a matter of great moment not to slay any of those strangers who being driven from their course by winds have come to my land hitherto, I should have taken vengeance on thee on behalf of the man of Hellas, seeing that thou, most base of men, having received from him hospitality, didst work against him a most impious deed. For thou didst go in to the wife of thine own host; and even this was not enough for thee, but thou didst stir her up with desire and hast gone away with her like a thief. Moreover not even this by itself was enough for thee, but thou art come hither with plunder taken from the house of thy host. Now therefore depart, seeing that I have counted it of great moment not to be a slayer of strangers. This woman indeed and the wealth which thou hast I will not allow thee to carry away, but I shall keep them safe for the Hellene who was thy host, until he come himself and desire to carry them off to his home; to thyself however and thy fellow-voyagers I proclaim that ye depart from your anchoring within three days and go from my land to some other; and if not, that ye will be dealt with as enemies."

This the priests said was the manner of Helen's coming to Proteus; and I suppose that Homer also had heard this story, but since it was not so suitable to the composition of his poem as the other which he followed, he dismissed it finally, making it clear at the same time that he was acquainted with that story also: and according to the manner in which he described the wanderings of Alexander in the Iliad (nor did he elsewhere retract that which he had said) it is clear that when he brought Helen he was carried out of his course, wandering to various lands, and that he came among other places to Sidon in Phenicia. Of this the poet has made mention in the "prowess of Diomede," and the verses run thus:

> "There she had robes many-coloured, the works of women of Sidon,
> Those whom her son himself the god-like of form Alexander
> Carried from Sidon, what time the broad sea-path he sailed over
> Bringing back Helenē home, of a noble father begotten."

And in the Odyssey also he has made mention of it in these verses:

> "Such had the daughter of Zeus, such drugs of exquisite cunning,
> Good, which to her the wife of Thon, Polydamna, had given,
> Dwelling in Egypt, the land where the bountiful meadow produces
> Drugs more than all lands else, many good being mixed, many evil."

And thus too Menelaos says to Telemachos:

> "Still the gods stayed me in Egypt, to come back hither desiring,
> Stayed me from voyaging home, since sacrifice due I performed not."

In these lines he makes it clear that he knew of the wandering of Alexander to Egypt, for Syria borders upon Egypt and the Phenicians, of whom is Sidon, dwell in Syria. By these lines and by this passage it is also most clearly shown that the "Cyprian Epic" was not written by Homer but by some other man: for in this it is said that on the third day after leaving Sparta Alexander came to Ilion bringing with him Helen, having had a "gently-blowing wind and a smooth sea," whereas in the Iliad it says that he wandered from his course when he brought her.

Let us now leave Homer and the "Cyprian Epic"; but this I will say, namely that I asked the priests whether it is but an idle tale which the Hellenes tell of that which they say happened about Ilion; and they answered me thus, saying that they had their knowledge by inquiries from Menelaos himself. After the rape of Helen there came indeed, they said, to the Teucrian land a large army of Hellenes to help Menelaos; and when the army had come out of the ships to land and had pitched its camp there, they sent messengers to Ilion, with whom went also Menelaos himself; and when these entered within the wall they demanded back Helen and the wealth which Alexander had stolen from Menelaos and had taken away; and moreover they demanded satisfaction for the wrongs done: and the Teucrians told the same tale then and afterwards, both with oath and without oath, namely that in deed and in truth they had not Helen nor the wealth for which demand was made, but that both were in Egypt; and that they could not justly be compelled to give satisfaction for that which Proteus the king of Egypt had. The Hellenes however thought that they were being mocked by them and besieged the city, until at last they took it; and when they had taken the wall and did not find Helen, but heard the same tale as before, then they believed the former tale and sent Menelaos himself to Proteus. And Menelaos having come to Egypt and having sailed up to Memphis, told the truth of these matters, and not only found great entertainment, but also received Helen unhurt, and all his own wealth besides. Then, however, after he had been thus dealt with, Menelaos showed himself ungrateful to the Egyptians; for when he set forth to sail away, contrary winds detained him, and as this condition of things lasted long, he devised an impious deed; for he took two children of natives and made sacrifice of them. After this, when it was known that he had done so, he became abhorred, and being pursued he escaped and got away in his ships to Libya; but whither he went besides after this, the Egyptians were not able to tell. Of these things they said that they found out part by inquiries, and the rest, namely that which happened in their own land, they related from sure and certain knowledge.

Thus the priests of the Egyptians told me; and I myself also agree with the story which was told of Helen, adding this consideration, namely that if Helen had been in Ilion she would have been given up to the Hellenes, whether Alexander consented or no; for Priam assuredly was not so mad, nor yet the others of his house, that they were desirous to run risk of ruin for themselves and their children and their city, in order that Alexander might have Helen as his wife: and even supposing that during the first part of the time they had been so inclined, yet when many others of the Trojans besides were losing their lives as often as they fought with the Hellenes, and of the sons of Priam himself always two or three or even more were slain when a battle took place (if one may trust at all to the Epic poets),—when, I say, things were coming thus to pass, I consider that even if Priam himself had had Helen as his wife, he would have given her back to the Achaians, if at least by so doing he might be freed from the evils which oppressed him. Nor even was the kingdom coming to Alexander next, so that when Priam was old the government was in his hands; but Hector, who was both older and more of a man than he, would certainly have received it after the death of Priam; and him it behoved not to allow his brother to go on with his wrong-doing, considering that great evils were coming to pass on his account both to himself privately and in general to the other Trojans. In truth however they lacked the power to give Helen back; and the Hellenes did not believe them, though they spoke the truth; because, as I declare my opinion, the divine power was purposing to cause them utterly to perish, and so make it evident to men that for great wrongs great also are the chastisements which come from the gods. And thus have I delivered my opinion concerning these matters.

After Proteus, they told me, Rhampsinitos received in succession the kingdom, who left as a memorial of himself that gateway to the temple of Hephaistos which is turned towards the West, and in front of the gateway he set up two statues, in height five-and-twenty cubits, of which the one which stands on the North side is called by the Egyptians Summer and the one on the South side Winter; and to that one which they call Summer they do reverence and make offerings, while to the other which is called Winter they do the opposite of these things. This king, they said, got great wealth of silver, which none of the kings born after him could surpass or even come near to; and wishing to store his wealth in safety he caused to be built a chamber of stone, one of the walls whereof was towards the outside of his palace: and the builder of this, having a design against it, contrived as follows, that is, he disposed one of the stones in such a manner that it could be taken out easily from the wall either by two men or even by one. So when the chamber was finished, the king stored his money in it, and after some time the builder, being near the end of his life, called to him his sons (for he had two) and to them he related how he had contrived in building the treasury of the king, and all in forethought for them, that they might have ample means of living. And when he had clearly set forth to them everything concerning the taking out of the stone, he gave them the measurements, saying that if they paid heed to this matter they would be stewards of the king's treasury. So he ended his life, and his sons made no long delay in setting to work, but went to the palace by night, and having found the stone in the wall of the chamber they dealt with it easily and carried forth for themselves great quantity of the wealth within. And the king happening to open the chamber, he marvelled when he saw the vessels falling short of the full amount, and he did not know on whom he should lay the blame, since the seals were unbroken and the chamber had been close shut; but when upon his opening the chamber a second and a third time the money was each time seen to be diminished, for the thieves did not slacken in their assaults upon it, he did as follows:—having ordered traps to be made he set these round about the vessels in which the money was; and when the thieves had come as at former times and one of them had entered, then so soon as he came near to one of the vessels he was straightway caught in the trap: and when he perceived in what evil case he was, straightway calling his brother he showed him what the matter was, and bade him enter as quickly as possible and cut off his head, for fear lest being seen and known he might bring about the destruction of his brother also. And to the other it seemed that he spoke well, and he was persuaded and did so; and fitting the stone into its place he departed home bearing with him the head of his brother. Now when it became day, the king entered into the chamber and was very greatly amazed, seeing the body of the thief held in the trap without his head, and the chamber unbroken, with no way to come in by or go out: and being at a loss he hung up the dead body of the thief upon the wall and set guards there, with charge if they saw any one weeping or bewailing himself to seize him and bring him before the king. And when the dead body had been hung up, the mother was greatly grieved, and speaking with the son who survived she enjoined him, in whatever way he could, to contrive means by which he might take down and bring home the body of his brother; and if he should neglect to do this, she earnestly threatened that she would go and give information to the king that he had the money. So as the mother dealt hardly with the surviving son, and he though saying many things to her did not persuade her, he contrived for his purpose a device as follows:—Providing himself with asses he filled some skins with wine and laid them upon the asses, and after that he drove them along: and when he came opposite to those who were guarding the corpse hung up, he drew towards him two or three of the necks of the skins and loosened the cords with which they were tied. Then when the wine was running out, he began to beat his head and cry out loudly, as if he did not know to which of the asses he should first turn; and when the guards saw the wine flowing out in streams, they ran together to the road with drinking vessels in their hands and collected the wine that was poured out, counting it so much gain; and he abused them all violently, making as if he were angry, but when the guards tried to appease him, after a time he feigned to be pacified and to abate his anger, and at length he drove his asses out of the road and began to set their loads right. Then more talk arose among them, and one or two of them made jests at him and brought him to laugh with them; and in the end he made them a present of one of the skins in addition to what they had. Upon that they lay down there without more ado, being minded to drink, and they took him into their company and invited him to remain with them and join them in their drinking: so he (as may be supposed) was persuaded and stayed. Then as they in their drinking bade him welcome in a friendly manner, he made a present to them also of another of the skins; and so at length having drunk liberally the guards became completely intoxicated; and being overcome by sleep they went to bed on the spot where they had been drinking. He then, as it was now far on in the night, first took down the body of his brother, and then in mockery shaved the right cheeks of all the guards; and after that he put the dead body upon the asses and drove them away home, having accomplished that which was enjoined him by his mother. Upon this the king, when it was reported to him that the dead body of the thief had been stolen away, displayed great anger; and desiring by all means that it should be found out who it might be who devised these things, did this (so at least they said, but I do not believe the account),—he caused his own daughter to sit in the stews, and enjoined her to receive all equally, and before having commerce with any one to compel him to tell her what was the most cunning and what the most unholy deed which had been done by him in all his life-time; and whosoever should relate that which had happened about the thief, him she must seize and not let him go out. Then as she was doing that which was enjoined by her father, the thief, hearing for what purpose this was done and having a desire to get the better of the king in resource, did thus:—from the body of one lately dead he cut off the arm at the shoulder and went with it under his mantle: and having gone in to the daughter of the king, and being asked that which the others also were asked, he related that he had done the most unholy deed when he cut off the head of his brother, who had been caught in a trap in the king's treasure-chamber, and the most cunning deed in that he made drunk the guards and took down the dead body of his brother hanging up; and she when she heard it tried to take hold of him, but the thief held out to her in the darkness the arm of the corpse, which she grasped and held, thinking that she was holding the arm of the man himself; but the thief left it in her hands and departed, escaping through the door. Now when this also was reported to the king, he was at first amazed at the ready invention and daring of the fellow, and then afterwards he sent round to all the cities and made proclamation granting a free pardon to the thief, and also promising a great reward if he would come into his presence. The thief accordingly trusting to the proclamation came to the king, and Rhampsinitos greatly marvelled at him, and gave him this daughter of his to wife, counting him to be the most knowing of all men; for as the Egyptians were distinguished from all other men, so was he from the other Egyptians.

After these things they said this king went down alive to that place which by the Hellenes is called Hades, and there played at dice with Demeter, and in some throws he overcame her and in others he was overcome by her; and he came back again having as a gift from her a handkerchief of gold: and they told me that because of the going down of Rhampsinitos the Egyptians after he came back celebrated a feast, which I know of my own knowledge also that they still observe even to my time; but whether it is for this cause that they keep the feast or for some other, I am not able to say. However, the priests weave a robe completely on the very day of the feast, and forthwith they bind up the eyes of one of them with a fillet, and having led him with the robe to the way by which one goes to the temple of Demeter, they depart back again themselves. This priest, they say, with his eyes bound up is led by two wolves to the temple of Demeter, which is distant from the city twenty furlongs, and then afterwards the wolves lead him back again from the temple to the same spot. Now as to the tales told by the Egyptians, any man may accept them to whom such things appear credible; as for me, it is to be understood throughout the whole of the history that I write by hearsay that which is reported by the people in each place. The Egyptians say that Demeter and Dionysos are rulers of the world below; and the Egyptians are also the first who reported the doctrine that the soul of man is immortal, and that when the body dies, the soul enters into another creature which chances then to be coming to the birth, and when it has gone the round of all the creatures of land and sea and of the air, it enters again into a human body as it comes to the birth; and that it makes this round in a period of three thousand years. This doctrine certain Hellenes adopted, some earlier and some later, as if it were of their own invention, and of these men I know the names but I abstain from recording them.

Down to the time when Rhampsinitos was king, they told me there was in Egypt nothing but orderly rule, and

Egypt prospered greatly; but after him Cheops became king over them and brought them to every kind of evil: for he shut up all the temples, and having first kept them from sacrifices there, he then bade all the Egyptians work for him. So some were appointed to draw stones from the stone-quarries in the Arabian mountains to the Nile, and others he ordered to receive the stones after they had been carried over the river in boats, and to draw them to those which are called the Libyan mountains; and they worked by a hundred thousand men at a time, for each three months continually. Of this oppression there passed ten years while the causeway was made by which they drew the stones, which causeway they built, and it is a work not much less, as it appears to me, than the pyramid; for the length of it is five furlongs and the breadth ten fathoms and the height, where it is highest, eight fathoms, and it is made of stone smoothed and with figures carved upon it. For this they said, the ten years were spent, and for the underground chambers on the hill upon which the pyramids stand, which he caused to be made as sepulchral chambers for himself in an island, having conducted thither a channel from the Nile. For the making of the pyramid itself there passed a period of twenty years; and the pryamid is square, each side measuring eight hundred feet, and the height of it is the same. It is built of stone smoothed and fitted together in the most perfect manner, not one of the stones being less than thirty feet in length. This pyramid was made after the manner of steps, which some called "rows" and others "bases": and when they had first made it thus, they raised the remaining stones with machines made of short pieces of timber, raising them first from the ground to the first stage of the steps, and when the stone got up to this it was placed upon another machine standing on the first stage, and so from this it was drawn to the second upon another machine; for as many as were the courses of the steps, so many machines there were also, or perhaps they transferred one and the same machine, made so as easily to be carried, to each stage successively, in order that they might take up the stones; for let it be told in both ways, according as it is reported. However that may be, the highest parts of it were finished first, and afterwards they proceeded to finish that which came next to them, and lastly they finished the parts of it near the ground and the lowest ranges. On the pyramid it is declared in Egyptian writing how much was spent on radishes and onions and leeks for the workmen, and if I rightly remember that which the interpreter said in reading to me this inscription, a sum of one thousand six hundred talents of silver was spent; and if this is so, how much besides is likely to have been expended upon the iron with which they worked, and upon bread and clothing for the workmen, seeing that they were building the works for the time which has been mentioned and were occupied for no small time besides, as I suppose, in the cutting and bringing of the stones and in working at the excavation under the ground? Cheops moreover came, they said, to such a pitch of wickedness, that being in want of money he caused his own daughter to sit in the stews, and ordered her to obtain from those who came a certain amount of money (how much it was they did not tell me); and she not only obtained the sum appointed by her father, but also she formed a design for herself privately to leave behind her a memorial, and she requested each man who came in to her to give her one stone upon her building: and of these stones, they told me, the pyramid was built which stands in front of the great pyramid in the middle of the three, each side being one hundred and fifty feet in length.

This Cheops, the Egyptians said, reigned fifty years; and after he was dead his brother Chephren succeeded to the kingdom. This king followed the same manner of dealing as the other, both in all the rest and also in that he made a pyramid, not indeed attaining to the measurements of that which was built by the former (this I know, having myself also measured it), and moreover there are no underground chambers beneath nor does a channel come from the Nile flowing to this one as to the other, in which the water coming through a conduit built for it flows round an island within, where they say that Cheops himself is laid: but for a basement he built the first course of Ethiopian stone of divers colours; and this pyramid he made forty feet lower than the other as regards size, building it close to the great pyramid. These stand both upon the same hill, which is about a hundred feet high. And Chephren tney said reigned fifty and six years. Here then they reckon one hundred and six years, during which they say that there was nothing but evil for the Egyptians, and the temples were kept closed and not opened during all that time. These kings the Egyptians by reason of their hatred of them are not very willing to name; nay, they even call the pyramids after the name of Philitis the shepherd, who at that time pastured flocks in those regions. After him, they said, Mykerinos became king over Egypt, who was the son of Cheops; and to him his father's deeds were displeasing, and he both opened the temples and gave liberty to the people, who were ground down to the last extremity of evil, to return to their own business and to their sacrifices: also he gave decisions of their causes juster than those of all the other kings besides. In regard to this then they commend this king more than all the other kings who had arisen in Egypt before him; for he not only gave good decisions, but also when a man complained of the decision, he gave him recompense from his own goods and thus satisfied his desire. But while Mykerinos was acting mercifully to his subjects and practising this conduct which has been said, calamities befell him, of which the first was this, namely that his daughter died, the only child whom he had in his house: and being above measure grieved by that which had befallen him, and desiring to bury his daughter in a manner more remarkable than others, he made a cow of wood, which he covered over with gold, and then within it he buried this daughter who, as I said, had died. This cow was not covered up in the ground, but it might be seen even down to my own time in the city of Saïs, placed within the royal palace in a chamber which was greatly adorned; and they offer incense of all kinds before it every day, and each night a lamp burns beside it all through the night. Near this cow in another chamber stand images of the concubines of Mykerinos, as the priests at Saïs told me; for there are in fact colossal wooden statues, in number about twenty, made with naked bodies; but who they are I am not able to say, except only that which is reported. Some however tell about this cow and the colossal statues the following tale, namely that

Mykerinos was enamoured of his own daughter and afterwards ravished her; and upon this they say that the girl strangled herself for grief, and he buried her in this cow; and her mother cut off the hands of the maids who had betrayed the daughter to her father; wherefore now the images of them have suffered that which the maids suffered in their life. In thus saying they speak idly, as it seems to me, especially in what they say about the hands of the statues; for as to this, even we ourselves saw that their hands had dropped off from lapse of time, and they were to be seen still lying at their feet even down to my time. The cow is covered up with a crimson robe, except only the head and the neck, which are seen, overlaid with gold very thickly; and between the horns there is the disc of the sun figured in gold. The cow is not standing up but kneeling, and in size it is equal to a large living cow. Every year it is carried forth from the chamber, at those times, I say, the Egyptians beat themselves for that god whom I will not name upon occasion of such a matter; at these times, I say, they also carry forth the cow to the light of day, for they say that she asked of her father Mykerinos, when she was dying, that she might look upon the sun once in the year.

After the misfortune of his daughter it happened, they said, secondly to this king as follows:—An oracle came to him from the city of Buto, saying that he was destined to live but six years more, in the seventh year to end his life: and he being indignant at it sent to the Oracle a reproach against the god, making complaint in reply that whereas his father and uncle, who had shut up the temples and had not only not remembered the gods, but also had been destroyers of men, had lived for a long time, he himself, who practised piety, was destined to end his life so soon: and from the Oracle there came a second message, which said that it was for this very cause that he was bringing his life to a swift close; for he had not done that which it was appointed for him to do, since it was destined that Egypt should suffer evils for a hundred and fifty years, and the two kings who had arisen before him had perceived this, but he had not. Mykerinos having heard this, and considering that this sentence had passed upon him beyond recall, procured many lamps, and whenever night came on he lighted these and began to drink and take his pleasure, ceasing neither by day nor by night; and he went about to the fen-country and to the woods and wherever he heard there were the most suitable places of enjoyment. This he devised (having a mind to prove that the Oracle spoke falsely) in order that he might have twelve years of life instead of six, the nights being turned into days.

This king also left behind him a pyramid, much smaller than that of his father, of a square shape and measuring on each side three hundred feet lacking twenty, built moreover of Ethiopian stone up to half the height. This pyramid some of the Hellenes say was built by the courtesan Rhodopis, not therein speaking rightly: and besides this it is evident to me that they who speak thus do not even know who Rhodopis was, for otherwise they would not have attributed to her the building of a pyramid like this, on which have been spent (so to speak) innumerable thousands of talents: moreover they do not know that Rhodopis flourished in the reign of Amasis, and not in this king's reign; for Rhodopis lived very many years later than the kings who left behind them these pyramids. By descent she was of Thrace, and she was a slave of Iadmon the son of Hephaistopolis a Samian, and a fellow-slave of Esop the maker of fables; for he too was once the slave of Iadmon, as was proved especially by this fact, namely that when the people of Delphi repeatedly made proclamation in accordance with an oracle, to find some one who would take up the blood-money for the death of Esop, no one else appeared, but at length the grandson of Iadmon, called Iadmon also, took it up; and thus it is shown that Esop too was the slave of Iadmon. As for Rhodopis, she came to Egypt brought by Xanthes the Samian, and having come thither to exercise her calling she was redeemed from slavery for a great sum by a man of Mytilenē, Charaxos son of Scamandronymos and brother of Sappho the lyric poet. Thus was Rhodopis set free, and she remained in Egypt and by her beauty won so much liking that she made great gain of money for one like Rhodopis, though not enough to suffice for the cost of such a pyramid as this. In truth there is no need to ascribe to her very great riches, considering that the tithe of her wealth may still be seen even to this time by any one who desires it: for Rhodopis wished to leave behind her a memorial of herself in Hellas, namely to cause a thing to be made such as happens not to have been thought of or dedicated in a temple by any besides, and to dedicate this at Delphi as a memorial of herself. Accordingly with the tithe of her wealth she caused to be made spits of iron of size large enough to pierce a whole ox, and many in number, going as far therein as her tithe allowed her, and she sent them to Delphi: these are even at the present time lying there, heaped all together behind the altar which the Chians dedicated, and just opposite to the cell of the temple. Now at Naucratis, as it happens, the courtesans are rather apt to win credit; for this woman first, about whom the story to which I refer is told, became so famous that all the Hellenes without exception came to know the name of Rhodopis, and then after her one whose name was Archidichē became a subject of song all over Hellas, though she was less talked of than the other. As for Charaxos, when after redeeming Rhodopis he returned back to Mytilenē, Sappho in an ode violently abused him. Of Rhodopis then I shall say no more.

After Mykerinos the priests said Asychis became king of Egypt, and he made for Hephaistos the temple gateway which is towards the sunrising, by far the most beautiful and the largest of the gateways; for while they all have figures carved upon them and innumerable ornaments of building besides, this has them very much more than the rest. In this king's reign they told me that, as the circulation of money was very slow, a law was made for the Egyptians that a man might have that money lent to him which he needed, by offering as security the dead body of his father; and there was added moreover to this law another, namely that he who lent the money should have a claim also to the whole of the sepulchral chamber belonging to him who received it, and that the man who offered that security should be subject to this penalty, if he refused to pay back the debt, namely that neither the man himself should be allowed to have burial, when he died, either in that family burial-place or in any other, nor should he be allowed to bury any of his kinsmen whom he lost by death. This king desiring to surpass the kings of Egypt who had arisen before him left as a memorial of himself a pyramid which he made of bricks, and on it there is an inscription carved in stone and saying thus: "Despise not me in comparison with the pyramids of stone, seeing that I excel them as much as Zeus excels the other gods; for with a pole they struck into the lake, and whatever of the mud attached itself to the pole, this they gathered up and made bricks, and in such manner they finished me."

Such were the deeds which this king performed: and after him reigned a blind man of the city of Anysis, whose name was Anysis. In his reign the Ethiopians and Sabacōs the king of the Ethiopians marched upon Egypt with a great host of men; so this blind man departed, flying to the fen-country, and the Ethiopian was king over Egypt for fifty years, during which he performed deeds as follows:—whenever any man of the Egyptians committed any transgression, he would never put him to death, but he gave sentence upon each man according to the greatness of the wrong-doing, appointing them to work at throwing up an embankment before that city from whence each man came of those who committed wrong. Thus the cities were made higher still than before; for they were embanked first by those who dug the channels in the reign of Sesostris, and then secondly in the reign of the Ethiopian, and thus they were made very high: and while other cities in Egypt also stood high, I think in the town at Bubastis especially the earth was piled up. In this city there is a temple very well worthy of mention, for though there are other temples which are larger and built with more cost, none more than this is a pleasure to the eyes. Now Bubastis in the Hellenic tongue is Artemis, and her temple is ordered thus:—Except the entrance it is completely surrounded by water; for channels come in from the Nile, not joining one another, but each extending as far as the entrance of the temple, one flowing round on the one side and the other on the other side, each a hundred feet broad and shaded over with trees; and the gateway has a height of ten fathoms, and it is adorned with figures six cubits high, very noteworthy. This temple is in the middle of the city and is looked down upon from all sides as one goes round, for since the city has been banked up to a height, while the temple has not been moved from the place where it was at the first built, it is possible to look down into it: and round it runs a stone wall with figures carved upon it, while within it there is a grove of very large trees planted round a large temple-house, within which is the image of the goddess: and the breadth and length of the temple is a furlong every way. Opposite the entrance there is a road paved with stone for about three furlongs, which leads through the market-place towards the East, with a breadth of about four hundred feet; and on this side and on that grow trees of height reaching to heaven: and the road leads to the temple of Hermes. This temple then is thus ordered.

The final deliverance from the Ethiopian came about (they said) as follows:—he fled away because he had seen in his sleep a vision, in which it seemed to him that a man came and stood by him and counselled him to gather together all the priests in Egypt and cut them asunder in the midst. Having seen this dream, he said that it seemed to him that the gods were foreshowing him this to furnish an occasion against him, in order that he might do an impious deed with respect to religion, and so receive some evil either from the gods or from men: he would not however do so, but in truth (he said) the time had expired, during which it had been prophesied to him that he should rule Egypt before he departed thence. For when he was in Ethiopia the Oracles which the Ethiopians consult had told him that it was fated for him to rule Egypt fifty years: since then this time was now expiring, and the vision of the dream also disturbed him, Sabacōs departed out of Egypt of his own free will.

Then when the Ethiopian had gone away out of Egypt, the blind man came back from the fen-country and began to rule again, having lived there during fifty years upon an island which he had made by heaping up ashes and earth: for whenever any of the Egyptians visited him bringing food, according as it had been appointed to them severally to do without the knowledge of the Ethiopian, he bade them bring also some ashes for their gift. This island none was able to find before Amyrtaios; that is, for more than seven hundred years the kings who arose before Amyrtaios were not able to find it. Now the name of this island is Elbo, and its size is ten furlongs each way.

After him there came to the throne the priest of Hephaistos, whose name was Sethōs. This man, they said, neglected and held in no regard the warrior class of the Egyptians, considering that he would have no need of them; and besides other slights which he put upon them, he also took from them the yokes of corn-land which had been given to them as a special gift in the reigns of the former kings, twelve yokes to each man. After this, Sanacharib king of the Arabians and of the Assyrians marched a great host against Egypt. Then the warriors of the Egyptians refused to come to the rescue, and the priest, being driven into a strait, entered into the sanctuary of the temple and bewailed to the image of the god the danger which was impending over him; and as he was thus lamenting, sleep came upon him, and it seemed to him in his vision that the god came and stood by him and encouraged him, saying that he should suffer no evil if he went forth to meet the army of the Arabians; for he would himself send him helpers. Trusting in these things seen in sleep, he took with him, they said, those of the Egyptians who were willing to follow him, and encamped in Pelusion, for by this way the invasion came: and not one of the warrior class followed him, but shop-keepers and artisans and men of the market. Then after they came, there swarmed by night upon their enemies mice of the fields, and ate up their quivers and their bows, and moreover the handles of their shields, so that on the next day they fled, and being without defence of arms great numbers fell. And at the present time this king stands in the temple of Hephaistos in stone, holding upon his hand a mouse, and by letters inscribed he says these words: "Let him who looks upon me learn to fear the gods."

So far in the story the Egyptians and the priests were they who made the report, declaring that from the first king down to this priest of Hephaistos who reigned last, there had been three hundred and forty-one generations of men, and that in them there had been the same number of chief-priests and of kings: but three hundred generations of men are equal to ten thousand years, for a hundred years is three generations of men; and in the one-and-forty generations which remain, those I mean which were added to the three hundred, there are one thousand three hundred and forty years. Thus in the period of eleven thousand three hundred and forty years they said that there had arisen no god in human form; nor even before that time or afterwards among the remaining kings who arose in Egypt, did they report that anything of that kind had come to pass. In this time they said that the sun had moved four times from his accustomed place of rising, and where he now sets he had thence twice had his rising, and in the place from whence he now rises he had twice had his setting; and in the meantime nothing in Egypt had been changed from its usual state, neither that which comes from the earth nor that which comes to them from the river nor that which concerns diseases or deaths. And formerly when Hecataios the historian was in Thebes, and had traced his descent and connected his family with a god in the sixteenth generation before, the priests of Zeus did for him much the same as they did for me (though I had not traced my descent). They led me into the sanctuary of the temple, which is of great size, and they counted up the number, showing colossal wooden statues in number the same as they said; for each chief-priest there sets up in his lifetime an image of himself: accordingly the priests, counting and showing me these, declared to me that each one of them was a son succeeding his own father, and they went up through the series of images from the image of the one who had died last, until they had declared this of the whole number. And when Hecataios had traced his descent and connected his family with a god in the sixteenth generation, they traced a descent in opposition to his, besides their numbering, not accepting it from him that a man had been born from a god; and they traced their counter-descent thus, saying that each one of the statues had been *piromis* son of *piromis,* until they had declared this of the whole three hundred and forty-five statues, each one being surnamed *piromis;* and neither with a god nor a hero did they connect their descent. Now *piromis* means in the tongue of Hellas "honourable and good man." From their declaration then it followed, that they of whom the images were had been of form like this, and far removed from being gods: but in the time before these men they said that gods were the rulers in Egypt, not mingling with men, and that of these always one had power at a time; and the last of them who was king over Egypt was Oros the son of Osiris, whom the Hellenes call Apollo: he was king over Egypt last, having deposed Typhon. Now Osiris in the tongue of Hellas is Dionysos.

Among the Hellenes Heracles and Dionysos and Pan are accounted the latest-born of the gods; but with the Egyptians Pan is a very ancient god, and he is one of those which are called the eight gods, while Heracles is of the second rank, who are called the twelve gods, and Dionysos is of the third rank, namely of those who were born of the twelve gods. Now as to Heracles I have shown already how many years old he is according to the Egyptians themselves, reckoning down to the reign of Amasis, and Pan is said to have existed for yet more years than these, and Dionysos for the smallest number of years as compared with the others; and even for this last they reckon down to the reign of Amasis fifteen thousand years. This the Egyptians say that they know for a certainty, since they always kept a reckoning and wrote down the years as they came. Now the Dionysos who is said to have been born of Semelē the daughter of Cadmos, was born about sixteen hundred years before my time, and Heracles who was the son of Alcmenē, about nine hundred years, and that Pan who was born of Penelopē, for of her and of Hermes Pan is said by the Hellenes to have been born, came into being later than the wars of Troy, about eight hundred years before my time. Of these two accounts every man may adopt that one which he shall find the more credible when he hears it. I however, for my part, have already declared my opinion about them. For if these also, like Heracles the son of Amphitryon, had appeared before all men's eyes and had lived their lives to old age in Hellas, I mean Dionysos the son of Semelē and Pan the son of Penelopē, then one would have said that these also had been born mere men, having the names of those gods who had come into being long before: but as it is, with regard to Dionysos the Hellenes say that as soon as he was born Zeus sewed him up in his thigh and carried him to Nysa, which is above Egypt in the land of Ethiopia; and as to Pan, they cannot say whither he went after he was born. Hence it has become clear to me that the Hellenes learnt the names of these gods later than those of the other gods, and trace their descent as if their birth occurred at the time when they first learnt their names.

Thus far then the history is told by the Egyptians themselves; but I will now recount that which other nations also tell, and the Egyptians in agreement with the others, of that which happened in this land: and there will be added to this also something of that which I have myself seen.

Being set free after the reign of the priest of Hephaistos, the Egyptians, since they could not live any time without a king, set up over them twelve kings, having divided all Egypt into twelve parts. These made intermarriages with one another and reigned, making agreement that they would not put down one another by force, nor seek to get an advantage over one another, but would live in perfect friendship: and the reason why they made these agreements, guarding them very strongly from violation, was this, namely that an oracle had been given to them at first when they began to exercise their rule, that he of them who should pour a libation with a bronze cup in the temple of Hephaistos, should be king of all Egypt (for they used to assemble together in all the temples). Moreover they resolved to join all together and leave a memorial of themselves; and having so resolved they caused to be made a labyrinth, situated a little above the lake of Moiris and nearly opposite to that which is called the City of Crocodiles. This I saw myself, and I found it greater than words can say. For if one should put together and reckon up all the buildings and all the great works produced by Hellenes, they would prove to be inferior in labour and expense to this labyrinth, though it is true that both the temple at Ephesos and that at Samos are works worthy of note. The pyramids also were greater than words can say, and each one of them is equal to many works of the Hellenes, great as they may be; but the labyrinth surpasses even the pyramids. It has twelve courts covered in, with gates facing one another, six upon the North side and six upon the South, joining on one to another, and the same wall surrounds them all outside; and there are in it two kinds of chambers, the one kind below the ground and the other above upon these, three thousand in number, of each kind fifteen hundred. The upper set of chambers we ourselves saw, going through them, and we tell of them having looked upon them with our own eyes; but the chambers under ground we heard about only; for the Egyptians who had charge of them were not willing on any account to show them, saying that here were the sepulchres of the kings who had first built this labyrinth and of the sacred crocodiles. Accordingly we speak of the chambers below by what we received from hearsay, while those above we saw ourselves and found them to be works of more than human greatness. For the passages through the chambers, and the goings this way and that way through the courts, which were admirably adorned, afforded endless matter for marvel, as we went through from a court to the chambers beyond it, and from the chambers to colonnades, and from the colonnades to other rooms, and then from the chambers again to other courts. Over the whole of these is a roof made of stone like the walls; and the walls are covered with figures carved upon them, each court being surrounded with pillars of white stone fitted together most perfectly; and at the end of the labyrinth, by the corner of it, there is a pyramid of forty fathoms, upon which large figures are carved, and to this there is a way made under ground.

Such is this labyrinth: but a cause for marvel even greater than this is afforded by the lake, which is called the lake of Moiris, along the side of which this labyrinth is built. The measure of its circuit is three thousand six hundred furlongs (being sixty *schoines*), and this is the same number of furlongs as the extent of Egypt itself along the sea. The lake lies extended lengthwise from North to South, and in depth where it is deepest it is fifty fathoms. That this lake is artificial and formed by digging is self-evident, for about in the middle of the lake stand two pyramids, each rising above the water to a height of fifty fathoms, the part which is built below the water being of just the same height; and upon each is placed a colossal statue of stone sitting upon a chair. Thus the pyramids are a hundred fathoms high; and these hundred fathoms are equal to a furlong of six hundred feet, the fathom being measured as six feet or four cubits, the feet being four palms each, and the cubits six. The water in the lake does not come from the place where it is, for the country there is very deficient in water, but it has been brought thither from the Nile by a canal; and for six months the water flows into the lake, and for six months out into the Nile again; and whenever it flows out, then for the six months it brings into the royal treasury a talent of silver a day from the fish which are caught, and twenty pounds when the water comes in. The natives of the place moreover said that this lake had an outlet under ground to the Syrtis which is in Libya, turning towards the interior of the continent upon the Western side and running along by the mountain which is above Memphis. Now since I did not see anywhere existing the earth dug out of this excavation (for that was a matter which drew my attention), I asked those who dwelt nearest to the lake where the earth was which had been dug out. These told me to what place it had been carried away; and I readily believed them, for I knew by report that a similar thing had been done at Nineveh, the city of the Assyrians. There certain thieves formed a design once to carry away the wealth of Sardanapallos son of Ninos, the king, which wealth was very great and was kept in treasure-houses under the earth. Accordingly they began from their own dwelling, and making estimate of their direction they dug under ground towards the king's palace; and the earth which was brought out of the excavation they used to carry away, when night came on, to the river Tigris which flows by the city of Nineveh, until at last they accomplished that which they desired. Similarly, as I heard, the digging of the lake in Egypt was effected, except that it was done not by night but during the day; for as they dug the Egyptians carried to the Nile the earth which was dug out; and the river, when it received it, would naturally bear it away and disperse it. Thus is this lake said to have been dug out.

Now the twelve kings continued to rule justly, but in course of time it happened thus:—After sacrifice in the temple of Hephaistos they were about to make libation on the last day of the feast, and the chief-priest, in bringing out for them the golden cups with which they had been wont to pour libations, missed his reckoning and brought eleven only for the twelve kings. Then that one of them who was standing last in order, namely Psammetichos, since he had no cup took off from his head his helmet, which was of bronze, and having held it out to receive the wine he proceeded to make libation: likewise all the other kings were wont to wear helmets and they happened to have them then. Now Psammetichos held out his helmet with no treacherous meaning; but they taking note of that which had been done by Psammetichos and of the oracle, namely how it had been declared to them that whosoever of them should make libation with a bronze cup should be sole king of Egypt, recollecting, I say, the saying of the Oracle, they did not indeed deem it right to slay Psammetichos, since they found by examination that he had not done it with any forethought, but they determined to strip him of almost all his power and to drive him away into the fen-country, and that from the fen-country he should not hold any dealings with the rest of Egypt. This Psammetichos had formerly been a fugitive from the Ethiopian Sabacōs who had killed his father Necōs, from him, I say, he had then been a fugitive in Syria; and when the Ethiopian had departed in consequence of the vision of the dream, the Egyptians who were of the district of Saïs brought him back to his own country. Then afterwards, when he was king, it was his fate to be a fugitive a second time on account of the helmet, being driven by the eleven kings into the fen-country. So then holding that he had been grievously wronged by them, he thought how he might take vengeance on those who had driven him out: and when he had sent to the Oracle of Leto in the city of Buto, where the Egyptians have their most truthful Oracle, there was given to him the reply that vengeance would come when men of bronze appeared from the sea. And he was strongly disposed not to believe that bronze men would come to help him; but after no long time had passed, certain

Ionians and Carians who had sailed forth for plunder were compelled to come to shore in Egypt, and they having landed and being clad in bronze armour, one of the Egyptians, not having before seen men clad in bronze armour, came to the fen-land and brought a report to Psammetichos that bronze men had come from the sea and were plundering the plain. So he, perceiving that the saying of the Oracle was coming to pass, dealt in a friendly manner with the Ionians and Carians, and with large promises he persuaded them to take his part. Then when he had persuaded them, with the help of those Egyptians who favoured his cause and of these foreign mercenaries he overthrew the kings. Having thus got power over all Egypt, Psammetichos made for Hephaistos that gateway of the temple at Memphis which is turned towards the South Wind; and he built a court for Apis, in which Apis is kept when he appears, opposite to the gateway of the temple, surrounded all with pillars and covered with figures; and instead of columns there stand to support the roof of the court colossal statues twelve cubits high. Now Apis is in the tongue of the Hellenes Epaphos. To the Ionians and to the Carians who had helped him Psammetichos granted portions of land to dwell in, opposite to one another with the river Nile between, and these were called "Encampments"; these portions of land he gave them, and he paid them besides all that he had promised: moreover he placed with them Egyptian boys to have them taught the Hellenic tongue; and from these, who learnt the language thoroughly, are descended the present class of interpreters in Egypt. Now the Ionians and Carians occupied these portions of land for a long time, and they are towards the sea a little below the city of Bubastis, on that which is called the Pelusian mouth of the Nile. These men king Amasis afterwards removed from thence and established them at Memphis, making them into a guard for himself against the Egyptians: and they being settled in Egypt, we who are Hellenes know by intercourse with them the certainty of all that which happened in Egypt beginning from king Psammetichos and afterwards; for these were the first men of foreign tongue who settled in Egypt: and in the land from which they were removed there still remained down to my time the sheds where their ships were drawn up and the ruins of their houses.

Thus then Psammetichos obtained Egypt: and of the Oracle which is in Egypt I have made mention often before this, and now I will give an account of it, seeing that it is worthy to be described. This Oracle which is in Egypt is sacred to Leto, and it is established in a great city near that mouth of the Nile which is called Sebennytic, as one sails up the river from the sea; and the name of this city where the Oracle is found is Buto, as I have said before in mentioning it. In this Buto there is a temple of Apollo and Artemis; and the temple-house of Leto, in which the Oracle is, is both great in itself and has a gateway of the height of ten fathoms: but that which caused me most to marvel of the things to be seen there, I will now tell. There is in this sacred enclosure a house of Leto made of one single stone as regards both height and length, and of which all the walls are in these two directions equal, each being forty cubits; and for the covering in of the roof there lies another stone upon the top, the cornice measuring four cubits. This house then of all the things that were to be seen by me in that temple is the most marvellous, and among those which come next in the island called Chemmis. This is situated in a deep and broad lake by the side of the temple at Buto, and it is said by the Egyptians that this island is a floating island. I myself did not see it either floating about or moved from its place, and I feel surprise at hearing of it, wondering if it be indeed a floating island. In this island of which I speak there is a great temple-house of Apollo, and three several altars are set up within, and there are planted in the island many palm-trees and other trees, both bearing fruit and not bearing fruit. And the Egyptians, when they say that it is floating, add this story, namely that in this island, which formerly was not floating, Leto, being one of the eight gods who came into existence first, and dwelling in the city of Buto where she has this Oracle, received Apollo from Isis as a charge and preserved him, concealing him in the island which is said now to be a floating island, at that time when Typhon came after him seeking everywhere and desiring to find the son of Osiris. Now they say that Apollo and Artemis are children of Dionysos and of Isis, and that Leto became their nurse and preserver; and in the Egyptian tongue Apollo is Oros, Demeter is Isis, and Artemis is Bubastis. From this story and from no other Æschylus the son of Euphorion took this which I shall say, wherein he differs from all the preceding poets; he represented namely that Artemis was the daughter of Demeter. For this reason then, they say, it became a floating island.

Such is the story which they tell; but as for Psammetichos, he was king over Egypt for four-and-fifty years, of which for thirty years save one he was sitting before Azotos, a great city of Syria, besieging it, until at last he took it: and this Azotos of all cities about which we have knowledge held out for the longest time under a siege.

The son of Psammetichos was Necos, and he became king of Egypt. This man was the first who attempted the channel leading to the Erythraian Sea, which Dareios the Persian afterwards completed: the length of this is a voyage of four days, and in breadth it was so dug that two triremes could go side by side driven by oars; and the water is brought into it from the Nile. The channel is conducted a little above the city of Bubastis by Patumos the Arabian city, and runs into the Erythraian Sea: and it is dug first along those parts of the plain of Egypt which lie towards Arabia, just above which run the mountains which extend opposite Memphis, where are the stone-quarries,—along the base of these mountains the channel is conducted from West to East for a great way; and after that it is directed towards a break in the hills and tends from these mountains towards the noon-day and the South Wind to the Arabian gulf. Now in the place where the journey is least and shortest from the Northern to the Southern Sea (which is also called Erythraian), that is from Mount Casion, which is the boundary between Egypt and Syria, the distance is exactly a thousand furlongs to the Arabian gulf; but the channel is much longer, since it is more winding; and in the reign of Necōs there perished while digging it twelve myriads of the Egyptians. Now Necōs ceased in the midst of his digging, because the utterance of an Oracle impeded him, which was to the effect that he was working for the Barbarian: and the

Egyptians call all men Barbarians who do not agree with them in speech. Thus having ceased from the work of the channel, Necōs betook himself to waging wars, and triremes were built by him, some for the Northern Sea and others in the Arabian gulf for the Erythraian Sea; and of these the sheds are still to be seen. These ships he used when he needed them; and also on land Necōs engaged battle at Magdolos with the Syrians, and conquered them; and after this he took Cadytis, which is a great city of Syria: and the dress which he wore when he made these conquests he dedicated to Apollo, sending it to Branchidai of the Milesians. After this, having reigned in all sixteen years, he brought his life to an end, and handed on the kingdom to Psammis his son.

While this Psammis was king of Egypt, there came to him men sent by the Eleians, who boasted that they ordered the contest at Olympia in the most just and honourable manner possible and thought that not even the Egyptians, the wisest of men, could find out anything besides, to be added to their rules. Now when the Eleians came to Egypt and said that for which they had come, then this king called together those of the Egyptians who were reputed the wisest, and when the Egyptians had come together they heard the Eleians tell of all that which it was their part to do in regard to the contest; and when they had related everything, they said that they had come to learn in addition anything which the Egyptians might be able to find out besides, which was juster than this. They then having consulted together asked the Eleians whether their own citizens took part in the contest; and they said that it was permitted to any one who desired it, both of their own people and of the other Hellenes equally, to take part in the contest: upon which the Egyptians said that in so ordering the games they had wholly missed the mark of justice; for it could not be but that they would take part with the man of their own State, if he was contending, and so act unfairly to the stranger: but if they really desired, as they said, to order the games justly, and if this was the cause for which they had come to Egypt, they advised them to order the contest so as to be for strangers alone to contend in, and that no Eleian should be permitted to contend. Such was the suggestion made by the Egyptians to the Eleians.

When Psammis had been king of Egypt for only six years and had made an expedition to Ethiopia and immediately afterwards had ended his life, Apries the son of Psammis received the kingdom in succession. This man came to be the most prosperous of all the kings up to that time except only his forefather Psammetichos; and he reigned five-and-twenty years, during which he led an army against Sidon and fought a sea-fight with the king of Tyre. Since however it was fated that evil should come upon him, it came by occasion of a matter which I shall relate at greater length in the Libyan history, and at present but shortly. Apries having sent a great expedition against the Kyrenians, met with correspondingly great disaster; and the Egyptians considering him to blame for this revolted from him, supposing that Apries had with forethought sent them out to evident calamity, in order (as they said) that there might be a slaughter of them, and he might the more securely rule over the other Egyptians. Being indignant at this, both these men who had returned from the expedition and also the friends of those who had perished made revolt openly. Hearing this Apries sent to them Amasis, to cause them to cease by persuasion; and when he had come and was seeking to restrain the Egyptians, as he was speaking and telling them not to do so, one of the Egyptians stood up behind him and put a helmet upon his head, saying as he did so that he put it on to crown him king. And to him this that was done was in some degree not unwelcome, as he proved by his behaviour; for as soon as the revolted Egyptians had set him up as king, he prepared to march against Apries: and Apries hearing this sent to Amasis one of the Egyptians who were about his own person, a man of reputation, whose name was Patarbemis, enjoining him to bring Amasis alive into his presence. When this Patarbemis came and summoned Amasis, the latter, who happened to be sitting on horseback, lifted up his leg and behaved in an unseemly manner, bidding him take that back to Apries. Nevertheless, they say, Patarbemis made demand of him that he should go to the king, seeing that the king had sent to summon him; and he answered him that he had for some time past been preparing to do so, and that Apries would have no occasion to find fault with him, for he would both come himself and bring others with him. Then Patarbemis both perceiving his intention from that which he said, and also seeing his preparations, departed in haste, desiring to make known as quickly as possible to the king the things which were being done: and when he came back to Apries not bringing Amasis, the king paying no regard to that which he said, but being moved by violent anger, ordered his ears and his nose to be cut off. And the rest of the Egyptians who still remained on his side, when they saw the man of most repute among them thus suffering shameful outrage, waited no longer but joined the others in revolt, and delivered themselves over to Amasis. Then Apries having heard this also, armed his foreign mercenaries and marched against the Egyptians: now he had about him Carian and Ionian mercenaries to the number of thirty thousand; and his royal palace was in the city of Saïs, of great size and worthy to be seen. So Apries and his army were going against the Egyptians, and Amasis and those with him were going against the mercenaries; and both sides came to the city of Momemphis and were about to make trial of one another in fight.

Now of the Egyptians there are seven classes, and of these one class is called that of the priests, and another that of the warriors, while the others are the cowherds, swineherds, shopkeepers, interpreters, and boatmen. This is the number of the classes of the Egyptians, and their names are given them from the occupations which they follow. Of them the warriors are called Calasirians and Hermotybians, and they are of the following districts,—for all Egypt is divided into districts. The districts of the Hermotybians are those of Busiris, Saïs, Chemmis, Papremis, the island called Prosopitis, and the half of Natho,—of these districts are the Hermotybians, who reached when most numerous the number of sixteen myriads. Of these not one has learnt anything of handicraft, but they are given up to war entirely. Again the districts of the Calasirians are those of Thebes, Bubastis, Aphthis, Tanis, Mendes, Sebennytos, Athribis,

Pharbaithos, Thmuïs, Onuphis, Anytis, Myecphoris,—this last is on an island opposite to the city of Bubastis. These are the districts of the Calasirians; and they reached, when most numerous, to the number of five-and-twenty myriads of men; nor is it lawful for these, any more than for the others, to practise any craft; but they practise that which has to do with war only, handing down the tradition from father to son. Now whether the Hellenes have learnt this also from the Egyptians, I am not able to say for certain, since I see that the Thracians also and Scythians and Persians and Lydians and almost all the Barbarians esteem those of their citizens who learn the arts, and the descendants of them, as less honourable than the rest; while those who have got free from all practice of manual arts are accounted noble, and especially those who are devoted to war: however that may be, the Hellenes have all learnt this, and especially the Lacedemonians; but the Corinthians least of all cast slight upon those who practise handicraft.

The following privilege was specially granted to this class and to none others of the Egyptians except the priests, that is to say, each man had twelve yokes of land specially granted to him free from imposts: now the yoke of land measures a hundred Egyptian cubits every way, and the Egyptian cubit is, as it happens, equal to that of Samos. This, I say, was a special privilege granted to all, and they also had certain advantages in turn and not the same men twice; that is to say, a thousand of the Calasirians and a thousand of the Hermotybians acted as body-guard to the king during each year; and these had besides their yokes of land an allowance given them for each day of five pounds weight of bread to each man, and two pounds of beef, and four half-pints of wine. This was the allowance given to those who were serving as the king's body-guard for the time being.

So when Apries leading his foreign mercenaries, and Amasis at the head of the whole body of the Egyptians, in their approach to one another had come to the city of Momemphis, they engaged battle: and although the foreign troops fought well, yet being much inferior in number they were worsted by reason of this. But Apries is said to have supposed that not even a god would be able to cause him to cease from his rule, so firmly did he think that it was established. In that battle then, I say, he was worsted, and being taken alive was brought away to the city of Saïs, to that which had formerly been his own dwelling but from thenceforth was the palace of Amasis. There for some time he was kept in the palace, and Amasis dealt well with him but at last, since the Egyptians blamed him, saying that he acted not rightly in keeping alive him who was the greatest foe both to themselves and to him, therefore he delivered Apries over to the Egyptians; and they strangled him, and after that buried him in the burial-place of his fathers: this is in the temple of Athenē, close to the sanctuary, on the left hand as you enter. Now the men of Saïs buried all those of this district who had been kings, within the temple; for the tomb of Amasis also, though it is further from the sanctuary than that of Apries and his forefathers, yet this too is within the court of the temple, and it consists of a colonnade of stone of great size, with pillars carved to imitate date-palms, and otherwise sumptuously adorned; and within the colonnade are double doors, and inside the doors a sepulchral chamber. Also at Saïs there is the burial-place of him whom I account it not pious to name in connexion with such a matter, which is in the temple of Athenē behind the house of the goddess, stretching along the whole wall of it; and in the sacred enclosure stand great obelisks of stone, and near them is a lake adorned with an edging of stone and fairly made in a circle, being in size, as it seemed to me, equal to that which is called the "Round Pool" in Delos. On this lake they perform by night the show of his sufferings, and this the Egyptians call Mysteries. Of these things I know more fully in detail how they take place, but I shall leave this unspoken; and of the mystic rites of Demeter, which the Hellenes call *thesmophoria,* of these also, although I know, I shall leave unspoken all except so much as piety permits me to tell. The daughters of Danaos were they who brought this rite out of Egypt and taught it to the women of the Pelasgians; then afterwards when all the inhabitants of Peloponnese were driven out by the Dorians, the rite was lost, and only those who were left behind of the

Peloponnesians and not driven out, that is to say the Arcadians, preserved it.

Apries having thus been overthrown, Amasis became king, being of the district of Saïs, and the name of the city whence he was is Siuph. Now at the first the Egyptians despised Amasis and held him in no great regard, because he had been a man of the people and was of no distinguished family; but afterwards Amasis won them over to himself by wisdom and not wilfulness. Among innumerable other things of price which he had, there was a foot-basin of gold in which both Amasis himself and all his guests were wont always to wash their feet. This he broke up, and of it he caused to be made the image of a god, and set it up in the city, where it was most convenient; and the Egyptians went continually to visit the image and did great reverence to it. Then Amasis, having learnt that which was done by the men of the city, called together the Egyptians and made known to them the matter, saying that the image had been produced from the foot-basin, into which formerly the Egyptians used to vomit and make water, and in which they washed their feet, whereas now they did to it great reverence; and just so, he continued, had he himself now fared, as the foot-basin; for though formerly he was a man of the people, yet now he was their king, and he bade them accordingly honour him and have regard for him. In such manner he won the Egyptians to himself, so that they consented to be his subjects; and his ordering of affairs was this:—In the early morning, and until the time of the filling of the market he did with a good will the business which was brought before him; but after this he passed the time in drinking and in jesting at his boon-companions, and was frivolous and playful. And his friends being troubled at it admonished him in some such words as these: "O king, thou dost not rightly govern thyself in thus letting thyself descend to behaviour so trifling; for thou oughtest rather to have been sitting throughout the day stately upon a stately throne and administering thy business; and so the Egyptians would have been assured that they were ruled by a great man, and thou wouldest have had a better report: but as it is, thou art acting by no means in a kingly fashion." And he answered them thus: "They who have bows stretch them at such time as they wish to use them, and when they have finished using them they loose them again; for if they were stretched tight always they would break, so that the men would not be able to use them when they needed them. So also is the state of man: if he should always be in earnest and not relax himself for sport at the due time, he would either go mad or be struck with stupor before he was aware; and knowing this well, I distribute a portion of the time to each of the two ways of living." Thus he replied to his friends. It is said however that Amasis, even when he was in a private station, was a lover of drinking and of jesting, and not at all seriously disposed; and whenever his means of livelihood failed him through his drinking and luxurious living, he would go about and steal; and they from whom he stole would charge him with having their property, and when he denied it would bring him before the judgment of an Oracle, whenever there was one in their place; and many times he was convicted by the Oracles and many times he was absolved: and then when finally he became king he did as follows:—as many of the gods as had absolved him and pronounced him not to be a thief, to their temples he paid no regard, nor gave anything for the further adornment of them, nor even visited them to offer sacrifice, considering them to be worth nothing and to possess lying Oracles; but as many as had convicted him of being a thief, to these he paid very great regard, considering them to be truly gods, and to present Oracles which did not lie. First in Saïs he built and completed for Athenē a temple-gateway which is a great marvel, and he far surpassed herein all who had done the like before, both in regard to height and greatness, so large are the stones and of such quality. Then secondly he dedicated great colossal statues and man-headed sphinxes very large, and for restoration he brought other stones of monstrous size. Some of these he caused to be brought from the stone-quarries which are opposite Memphis, others of very great size from the city of Elephantinē, distant a voyage of not less than twenty days from Saïs: and of them all I marvel most at this, namely a monolith chamber which he brought from the city of Elephantinē; and they were three years engaged in bringing this, and two thousand men were appointed to convey it, who all were of the class of boatmen. Of this house the length outside is one-and-twenty cubits, the breadth is fourteen cubits, and the height eight. These are the measures of the monolith house outside; but the length inside is eighteen cubits and five-sixths of a cubit, the breadth twelve cubits, and the height five cubits. This lies by the side of the entrance to the temple; for within the temple they did not draw it, because, as it is said, while the house was being drawn along, the chief artificer of it groaned aloud, seeing that much time had been spent and he was wearied by the work; and Amasis took it to heart as a warning and did not allow them to draw it further onwards. Some say on the other hand that a man was killed by it, of those who were heaving it with levers, and that it was not drawn in for that reason. Amasis also dedicated in all the other temples which were of repute, works which are worth seeing for their size, and among them also at Memphis the colossal statue which lies on its back in front of the temple of Hephaistos, whose length is five-and-seventy feet; and on the same base made of the same stone are set two colossal statues, each of twenty feet in length, one on this side and the other on that side of the large statue. There is also another of stone of the same size in Saïs, lying in the same manner as that at Memphis. Moreover Amasis was he who built and finished for Isis her temple at Memphis, which is of great size and very worthy to be seen.

In the reign of Amasis it is said that Egypt became more prosperous than at any other time before, both in regard to that which comes to the land from the river and in regard to that which comes from the land to its inhabitants, and that at this time the inhabited towns in it numbered in all twenty thousand. It was Amasis too who established the law that every year each one of the Egyptians should declare to the ruler of his district, from what source he got his livelihood, and if any man did not do this or did not make declaration of an honest way of living, he should be punished with death. Now Solon the Athenian received from Egypt this law and had it enacted for the Athenians, and they have continued to observe it, since it is a law with which none can find fault.

Moreover Amasis became a lover of the Hellenes; and besides other proofs of friendship which he gave to several among them, he also granted the city of Naucratis for those of them who came to Egypt to dwell in; and to those who did not desire to stay, but who made voyages thither, he granted portions of land to set up altars and make sacred enclosures for their gods. Their greatest enclosure and that one which has most name and is most frequented is called the Hellenion, and this was established by the following cities in common:—of the Ionians Chios, Teos, Phocaia, Clazomenai, of the Dorians Rhodes, Cnidos, Halicarnassos, Phaselis, and of the Aiolians Mytilenē alone. To these belongs this enclosure and these are the cities which appoint superintendents of the port; and all other cities which claim a share in it, are making a claim without any right. Besides this the Eginetans established on their own account a sacred enclosure dedicated to Zeus, the Samians one to Hera, and the Milesians one to Apollo. Now in old times Naucratis alone was an open trading-place, and no other place in Egypt: and if any one came to any other of the Nile mouths, he was compelled to swear that he came not thither of his own will, and when he had thus sworn his innocence he had to sail with his ship to the Canobic mouth, or if it were not possible to sail by reason of contrary winds, then he had to carry his cargo round the head of the Delta in boats to Naucratis: thus highly was Naucratis privileged. Moreover when the Amphictyons had let out the contract for building the temple which now exists at Delphi, agreeing to pay a sum of three hundred talents (for the temple which formerly stood there had been burnt down of itself), it fell to the share of the people of Delphi to provide the fourth part of the payment; and accordingly the Delphians went about to various cities and collected contributions. And when they did this they got from Egypt as much as from any place, for Amasis gave them a thousand talents' weight of alum, while the Hellenes who dwelt in Egypt gave them twenty pounds of silver.

Also with the people of Kyrenē Amasis made an agreement for friendship and alliance; and he resolved too to marry a wife from thence, whether because he desired to have a wife of Hellenic race, or, apart from that, on account of friendship for the people of Kyrenē: however that may be, he married, some say the daughter of Battos, others of Arkesilaos, and others of Critobulos, a man of repute among the citizens; and her name was Ladikē. Now whenever Amasis lay with her he found himself unable to have intercourse, but with his other wives he associated as he was wont; and as this happened repeatedly, Amasis said to his wife, whose name was Ladikē: "Woman, thou hast given me drugs, and thou shalt surely perish more miserably than any other." Then Ladikē, when by her denials Amasis was not at all appeased in his anger against her, made a vow in her soul to Aphroditē, that if Amasis on that night had intercourse with her (seeing that this was the remedy for her danger), she would send an image to be dedicated to her at Kyrenē; and after the vow immediately Amasis had intercourse, and from thenceforth whenever Amasis came in to her he had intercourse with her; and after this he became very greatly attached to her. And Ladikē paid the vow that she had made to the goddess; for she had an image made and sent it to Kyrenē, and it was still preserved even to my own time, standing with its face turned away from the city of the Kyrenians. This Ladikē Cambyses, having conquered Egypt and heard from her who she was, sent back unharmed to Kyrenē.

Amasis also dedicated offerings in Hellas, first at Kyrenē an image of Athenē covered over with gold and a figure of himself made like by painting; then in the temple of Athenē at Lindos two images of stone and a corslet of linen worthy to be seen; and also at Samos two wooden figures of himself dedicated to Hera, which were standing even to my own time in the great temple, behind the doors. Now at Samos he dedicated offerings because of the guest-friendship between himself and Polycrates the son of Aiakes; at Lindos for no guest-friendship but because the temple of Athenē at Lindos is said to have been founded by the daughters of Danaos, who had touched land there at the time when they were fleeing from the sons of Aigyptos. These offerings were dedicated by Amasis; and he was the first of men who conquered Cyprus and subdued it so that it paid him tribute.

TACITUS ON GERMANY

TRANSLATED BY

THOMAS GORDON

INTRODUCTORY NOTE

THE *dates of the birth and death of Tacitus are uncertain, but it is probable that he was born about 54 A. D. and died after 117. He was a contemporary and friend of the younger Pliny, who addressed to him some of his most famous epistles, to be found in another volume of the Harvard Classics. Tacitus was apparently of the equestrian class, was an advocate by training, and had a reputation as an orator, though none of his speeches has survived. He held a number of important public offices, and married the daughter of Agricola, the conqueror of Britain, whose life he wrote.*

The two chief works of Tacitus, the "Annals" and the "Histories," covered the history of Rome from the death of Augustus to A. D. 96; but the greater part of the "Histories" is lost, and the fragment that remains deals only with the year 69 and part of 70. In the "Annals" there are several gaps, but what survives describes a large part of the reigns of Tiberius, Claudius, and Nero. His minor works, besides the life of Agricola, already mentioned, are a "Dialogue on Orators" and the account of Germany, its situation, its inhabitants, their character and customs, which is here printed.

Tacitus stands in the front rank of the historians of antiquity for the accuracy of his learning, the fairness of his judgments, the richness, concentration, and precision of his style. His great successor, Gibbon, called him a "philosophical historian, whose writings will instruct the last generations of mankind"; and Montaigne knew no author "who, in a work of history, has taken so broad a view of human events or given a more just analysis of particular characters."

The "Germany" is a document of the greatest interest and importance, since it gives us by far the most detailed account of the state of culture among the tribes that are the ancestors of the modern Teutonic nations, at the time when they first came into contact with the civilization of the Mediterranean.

TACITUS ON GERMANY

THE whole of Germany is thus bounded; separated from Gaul, from Rhœtia and Pannonia, by the rivers Rhine and Danube; from Sarmatia and Dacia by mutual fear, or by high mountains: the rest is encompassed by the ocean, which forms huge bays, and comprehends a tract of islands immense in extent: for we have lately known certain nations and kingdoms there, such as the war discovered. The Rhine rising in the Rhœtian Alps from a summit altogether rocky and perpendicular, after a small winding towards the west, is lost in the Northern Ocean. The Danube issues out of the mountain Abnoba, one very high but very easy of ascent, and traversing several nations, falls by six streams into the Euxine Sea; for its seventh channel is absorbed in the Fenns.

The Germans, I am apt to believe, derive their original from no other people; and are nowise mixed with different nations arriving amongst them: since anciently those who went in search of new dwellings, travelled not by land, but were carried in fleets; and into that mighty ocean so boundless, and, as I may call it, so repugnant and forbidding, ships from our world rarely enter. Moreover, besides the dangers from a sea tempestuous, horrid and unknown, who would relinquish Asia, or Africa, or Italy, to repair to Germany, a region hideous and rude, under a rigorous climate, dismal to behold or to manure[1] unless the same were his native country? In their old ballads (which amongst them are the only sort of registers and history) they celebrate *Tuisto,* a God sprung from the earth, and *Mannus* his son, as the fathers and founders of the nation. To *Mannus* they assign three sons, after whose names so many people are called; the Ingævones, dwelling next the ocean; the Herminones,

[1] To cultivate.

in the middle country; and all the rest, Instævones. Some, borrowing a warrant from the darkness of antiquity, maintain that the God had more sons, that thence came more denominations of people, the Marsians, Gambrians, Suevians, and Vandalians, and that these are the names truly genuine and original. For the rest, they affirm Germany to be a recent word, lately bestowed: for that those who first passed the Rhine and expulsed the Gauls, and are now named Tungrians, were then called Germans: and thus by degrees the name of a tribe prevailed, not that of the nation; so that by an appellation at first occasioned by terror and conquest, they afterwards chose to be distinguished, and assuming a name lately invented were universally called *Germans*.

They have a tradition that Hercules also had been in their country, and him above all other heroes they extol in their songs when they advance to battle. Amongst them too are found that kind of verses by the recital of which (by them called *Barding*) they inspire bravery; nay, by such chanting itself they divine the success of the approaching fight. For, according to the different din of the battle, they urge furiously, or shrink timorously. Nor does what they utter, so much seem to be singing as the voice and exertion of valour. They chiefly study a tone fierce and harsh, with a broken and unequal murmur, and therefore apply their shields to their mouths, whence the voice may by rebounding swell with greater fulness and force. Besides there are some of opinion, that Ulysses, whilst he wandered about in his long and fabulous voyages, was carried into this ocean and entered Germany, and that by him Asciburgium was founded and named, a city at this day standing and inhabited upon the bank of the Rhine: nay, that in the same place was formerly found an altar dedicated to Ulysses, with the name of his father Laertes added to his own, and that upon the confines of Germany and Rhœtia are still extant certain monuments and tombs inscribed with Greek characters. Traditions these which I mean not either to confirm with arguments of my own or to refute. Let every one believe or deny the same according to his own bent.

For myself, I concur in opinion with such as suppose the people of Germany never to have mingled by inter-marriages with other nations, but to have remained a people pure, and independent, and resembling none but themselves. Hence amongst such a mighty multitude of men, the same make and form is found in all, eyes stern and blue, yellow hair, huge bodies, but vigorous only in the first onset. Of pains and labour they are not equally patient, nor can they at all endure thrift and heat. To bear hunger and cold they are hardened by their climate and soil.

Their lands, however somewhat different in aspect, yet taken all together consist of gloomy forests or nasty marshes; lower and moister towards the confines of Gaul, more mountainous and windy towards Noricum and Pannonia; very apt to bear grain, but altogether unkindly to fruit trees; abounding in flocks and herds, but generally small of growth. Nor even in their oxen is found the usual stateliness, no more than the natural ornaments and grandeur of head. In the number of their herds they rejoice; and these are their only, these their most desirable riches. Silver and gold the Gods have denied them, whether in mercy or in wrath, I am unable to determine. Yet I would not venture to aver that in Germany no vein of gold or silver is produced; for who has ever searched? For the use and possession, it is certain they care not. Amongst them indeed are to be seen vessels of silver, such as have been presented to their Princes and Ambassadors, but holden in no other esteem than vessels made of earth. The Germans however adjoining to our frontiers value gold and silver for the purposes of commerce, and are wont to distinguish and prefer certain of our coins. They who live more remote are more primitive and simple in their dealings, and exchange one commodity for another. The money which they like is the old and long known, that indented,[2] or that impressed with a chariot and two horses. Silver too is what they seek more than gold, from no fondness or preference, but because small pieces are more ready in purchasing things cheap and common.

Neither in truth do they abound in iron, as from the

[2] With milled edges.

fashion of their weapons may be gathered. Swords they rarely use, or the larger spear. They carry javelins or, in their own language, *framms,* pointed with a piece of iron short and narrow, but so sharp and manageable, that with the same weapon they can fight at a distance or hand to hand, just as need requires. Nay, the horsemen also are content with a shield and a javelin. The foot throw likewise weapons missive, each particular is armed with many, and hurls them a mighty space, all naked or only wearing a light cassock. In their equipment they show no ostentation; only that their shields are diversified and adorned with curious colours. With coats of mail very few are furnished, and hardly upon any is seen a headpiece or helmet. Their horses are nowise signal either in fashion or in fleetness; nor taught to wheel and bound, according to the practice of the Romans: they only move them forward in a line, or turn them right about, with such compactness and equality that no one is ever behind the rest. To one who considers the whole it is manifest, that in their foot their principal strength lies, and therefore they fight intermixed with the horse: for such is their swiftness as to match and suit with the motions and engagements of the cavalry. So that the infantry are elected from amongst the most robust of their youth, and placed in front of the army. The number to be sent is also ascertained, out of every village *an hundred,* and by this very name they continue to be called at home, *those of the hundred band:* thus what was at first no more than a number, becomes thenceforth a title and distinction of honour. In arraying their army, they divide the whole into distinct battalions formed sharp in front. To recoil in battle, provided you return again to the attack, passes with them rather for policy than fear. Even when the combat is no more than doubtful, they bear away the bodies of their slain. The most glaring disgrace that can befall them, is to have quitted their shield; nor to one branded with such ignominy is it lawful to join in their sacrifices, or to enter into their assemblies; and many who had escaped in the day of battle, have hanged themselves to put an end to this their infamy.

In the choice of kings they are determined by the splendour of their race, in that of generals by their bravery. Neither is the power of their kings unbounded or arbitrary: and their generals procure obedience not so much by the force of their authority as by that of their example, when they appear enterprising and brave, when they signalise themselves by courage and prowess; and if they surpass all in admiration and pre-eminence, if they surpass all at the head of an army. But to none else but the Priests is it allowed to exercise correction, or to inflict bonds or stripes. Nor when the Priests do this, is the same considered as a punishment, or arising from the orders of the general, but from the immediate command of the Deity, Him whom they believe to accompany them in war. They therefore carry with them when going to fight, certain images and figures taken out of their holy groves. What proves the principal incentive to their valour is, that it is not at random nor by the fortuitous conflux of men that their troops and pointed battalions are formed, but by the conjunction of whole families, and tribes of relations. Moreover, close to the field of battle are lodged all the nearest and most interesting pledges of nature. Hence they hear the doleful howlings of their wives, hence the cries of their tender infants. These are to each particular the witnesses whom he most reverences and dreads; these yield him the praise which affect him most. Their wounds and maims they carry to their mothers, or to their wives, neither are their mothers or wives shocked in telling, or in sucking their bleeding sores.[8] Nay, to their husbands and sons whilst engaged in battle, they administer meat and encouragement.

In history we find, that some armies already yielding and ready to fly, have been by the women restored, through their inflexible importunity and entreaties, presenting their breasts, and showing their impending captivity; an evil to the Germans then by far most dreadful when it befalls their women. So that the spirit of such cities as amongst their hostages are enjoined to send their damsels of quality, is always engaged more effectually than that of others. They even believe them endowed with something celestial

[8] Nec illæ numerare aut exigere plagas pavent.

and the spirit of prophecy. Neither do they disdain to consult them, nor neglect the responses which they return. In the reign of the deified Vespasian, we have seen *Veleda* for a long time, and by many nations, esteemed and adored as a divinity. In times past they likewise worshipped *Aurinia* and several more, from no complaisance or effort of flattery, nor as Deities of their own creating.

Of all the Gods, Mercury is he whom they worship most. To him on certain stated days it is lawful to offer even human victims. Hercules and Mars they appease with beasts usually allowed for sacrifice. Some of the Suevians make likewise immolations to *Isis*. Concerning the cause and original of this foreign sacrifice I have found small light; unless the figure of her image formed like a galley, show that such devotion arrived from abroad. For the rest, from the grandeur and majesty of beings celestial, they judge it altogether unsuitable to hold the Gods enclosed within walls, or to represent them under any human likeness. They consecrate whole woods and groves, and by the names of the Gods they call these recesses; divinities these, which only in contemplation and mental reverence they behold.

To the use of lots and auguries, they are addicted beyond all other nations. Their method of divining by lots is exceeding simple. From a tree which bears fruit they cut a twig, and divide it into two small pieces. These they distinguish by so many several marks, and throw them at random and without order upon a white garment. Then the Priest of the community, if for the public the lots are consulted, or the father of a family if about a private concern, after he has solemnly invoked the Gods, with eyes lifted up to heaven, takes up every piece thrice, and having done thus forms a judgment according to the marks before made. If the chances have proved forbidding, they are no more consulted upon the same affair during the same day: even when they are inviting, yet, for confirmation, the faith of auguries too is tried. Yea, here also is the known practice of divining events from the voices and flight of birds. But to this nation it is peculiar, to learn presages and admonitions divine from horses also. These are nourished by the State in the same sacred woods and groves, all milk-white and employed in no earthly labour. These yoked in the holy chariot, are accompanied by the Priest and the King, or the Chief of the community, who both carefully observed his actions and neighing. Nor in any sort of augury is more faith and assurance reposed, not by the populace only, but even by the nobles, even by the Priests. These account themselves the ministers of the Gods, and the horses privy to his will. They have likewise another method of divination, whence to learn the issue of great and mighty wars. From the nation with whom they are at war they contrive, it avails not how, to gain a captive: him they engage in combat with one selected from amongst themselves, each armed after the manner of his country, and according as the victory falls to this or to the other, gather a presage of the whole.

Affairs of smaller moment the chiefs determine: about matters of higher consequence the whole nation deliberates; yet in such sort, that whatever depends upon the pleasure and decision of the people, is examined and discussed by the chiefs. Where no accident or emergency intervenes, they assemble upon stated days, either, when the moon changes, or is full: since they believe such seasons to be the most fortunate for beginning all transactions. Neither in reckoning of time do they count, like us, the number of days but that of nights. In this style their ordinances are framed, in this style their diets appointed; and with them the night seems to lead and govern the day. From their extensive liberty this evil and default flows, that they meet not at once, nor as men commanded and afraid to disobey; so that often the second day, nay often the third, is consumed through the slowness of the members in assembling. They sit down as they list, promiscuously, like a crowd, and all armed. It is by the Priests that silence is enjoined, and with the power of correction the Priests are then invested. Then the King or Chief is heard, as are others, each according to his precedence in age, or in nobility, or in warlike renown, or in eloquence; and the influence of every speaker proceeds rather from his ability to persuade than from any authority to command. If the proposition displease, they reject it by an inarticulate murmur: if it be pleasing, they brandish their javelins. The most honourable manner of signifying their assent, is to express their applause by the sound of their arms.

In the assembly it is allowed to present accusations, and to prosecute capital offences. Punishments vary according to the quality of the crime. Traitors and deserters they hang upon trees. Cowards, and sluggards, and unnatural prostitutes they smother in mud and bogs under an heap of hurdles. Such diversity in their executions has this view, that in punishing of glaring iniquities, it behoves likewise to display them to sight; but effeminacy and pollution must be buried and concealed. In lighter transgressions too the penalty is measured by the fault, and the delinquents upon conviction are condemned to pay a certain number of horses or cattle. Part of this mulct accrues to the King or to the community, part to him whose wrongs are vindicated, or to his next kindred. In the same assemblies are also chosen their chiefs or rulers, such as administer justice in their villages and boroughs. To each of these are assigned an hundred persons chosen from amongst the populace, to accompany and assist him, men who help him at once with their authority and their counsel.

Without being armed they transact nothing, whether of public or private concernment. But it is repugnant to their custom for any man to use arms, before the community has attested his capacity to wield them. Upon such testimonial, either one of the rulers, or his father, or some kinsman dignify the young man in the midst of the assembly, with a shield and javelin. This amongst them is the *manly robe,* this the first degree of honour conferred upon their youth. Before this they seem no more than part of a private family, but thenceforward part of the Commonweal. The princely dignity they confer even upon striplings, whose race is eminently noble, or whose fathers have done great and signal services to the State. For about the rest, who are more vigorous and long since tried, they crowd to attend: nor is it any shame to be seem amongst the followers of these. Nay, there are likewise degrees of followers, higher or lower, just as he whom they follow judges fit. Mighty too is the emulation amongst these followers, of each to be first in favour with his Prince; mighty also the emulation of the Princes, to excel in the number and valour of followers. This is their principal state, this their chief force, to be at all times surrounded with a huge band of chosen young men, for ornament and glory in peace, for security and defence in war. Nor is it amongst his own people only, but even from the neighbouring communities, that any of their Princes reaps so much renown and a name so great, when he surpasses in the number and magnanimity of his followers. For such are courted by Embassies, and distinguished with presents, and by the terror of their fame alone often dissipate wars.

In the day of battle, it is scandalous to the Prince to be surpassed in feats of bravery, scandalous to his followers to fail in matching the bravery of the Prince. But it is infamy during life, and indelible reproach, to return alive from a battle where their Prince was slain. To preserve their Prince, to defend him, and to ascribe to his glory all their own valorous deeds, is the sum and most sacred part of their oath. The Princes fight for victory; for the Prince his followers fight. Many of the young nobility, when their own community comes to languish in its vigour by long peace and inactivity, betake themselves through impatience to other States which then prove to be in war. For, besides that this people cannot brook repose, besides that by perilous adventures they more quickly blazon their fame, they cannot otherwise than by violence and war support their huge train of retainers. For from the liberality of their Prince, they demand and enjoy that *war-horse* of theirs, with that *victorious javelin* dyed in the blood of their enemies. In the place of pay, they are supplied with a daily table and repasts; though grossly prepared, yet very profuse. For maintaining such liberality and munificence, a fund is furnished by continual wars and plunder. Nor could you so easily persuade them to cultivate the ground, or to await the return of the seasons and produce of the year, as to provoke the foe and to risk wounds and death: since stupid and spiritless they account it, to acquire by their sweat what they can gain by their blood.

Upon any recess from war, they do not much attend the chase. Much more of their time they pass in indolence, resigned to sleep and repasts.[4] All the most brave, all the most warlike, apply to nothing at all; but to their wives, to the ancient men, and to every the most impotent domestic, trust all the care of their house, and of their lands and possessions. They themselves loiter.[5] Such is the amazing diversity of their nature, that in the same men is found so much delight in sloth, with so much enmity to tranquillity and repose. The communities are wont, of their own accord and man by man, to bestow upon their Princes a certain number of beasts, or a certain portion of grain; a contribution which passes indeed for a mark of reverence and honour, but serves also to supply their necessities. They chiefly rejoice in the gifts which come from the bordering countries, such as are sent not only by particulars but in the name of the State; curious horses, splendid armour, rich harness, with collars of silver and gold. Now too they have learnt, what we have taught them, to receive money.

That none of the several people in Germany live together in cities, is abundantly known; nay, that amongst them none of their dwellings are suffered to be contiguous. They inhabit apart and distinct, just as a fountain, or a field, or a wood happened to invite them to settle. They raise their villages in opposite rows, but not in our manner with the houses joined one to another. Every man has a vacant space quite round his own, whether for security against accidents from fire, or that they want the art of building. With them in truth, is unknown even the use of mortar and of tiles. In all their structures they employ materials quite gross and unhewn, void of fashion and comeliness. Some parts they besmear with an earth so pure and resplendent, that it resembles painting and colours. They are likewise wont to scoop caves deep in the ground, and over them to lay great heaps of dung. Thither they retire for shelter in the winter, and thither convey their grain: for by such close places they mollify the rigorous and ex-

[4] "Dediti somno, ciboque:" handed over to sloth and gluttony.
[5] Are rude and lazy.

cessive cold. Besides when at any time their enemy invades them, he can only ravage the open country, but either knows not such recesses as are invisible and subterraneous; or must suffer them to escape him, on this very account that he is uncertain where to find them.

For their covering a mantle is what they all wear, fastened with a clasp or, for want of it, with a thorn. As far as this reaches not they are naked, and lie whole days before the fire. The most wealthy are distinguished with a vest, not one large and flowing like those of Sarmatians and Parthians, but girt close about them and expressing the proportion of every limb. They likewise wear the skins of savage beasts, a dress which those bordering upon the Rhine use without any fondness or delicacy, but about which such who live further in the country are more curious, as void of all apparel introduced by commerce. They choose certain wild beasts, and, having flayed them, diversify their hides with many spots, as also with the skins of monsters from the deep, such as are engendered in the distant ocean and in seas unknown. Neither does the dress of the women differ from that of the men, save that the women are orderly attired in linen embroidered with purple, and use no sleeves, so that all their arms are bare. The upper part of their breast is withal exposed.

Yet the laws of matrimony are severely observed there; nor in the whole of their manners is aught more praiseworthy than this: for they are almost the only Barbarians contented with one wife, excepting a very few amongst them; men of dignity who marry divers wives, from no wantonness or lubricity, but courted for the lustre of their family into many alliances.

To the husband, the wife tenders no dowry; but the husband, to the wife. The parents and relations attend and declare their approbation of the presents, not presents adapted to feminine pomp and delicacy, nor such as serve to deck the new married woman; but oxen and horse accoutred, and a shield, with a javelin and sword. By virtue of these gifts, she is espoused. She too on her part brings her husband some arms. This they esteem the highest tie, these the holy mysteries, and matrimonial Gods. That the woman may not suppose herself free from the considerations of fortitude and fighting, or exempt from the casualties of war, the very first solemnities of her wedding serve to warn her, that she comes to her husband as a partner in his hazards and fatigues, that she is to suffer alike with him, to adventure alike, during peace or during war. This the oxen joined in the same yoke plainly indicate, this the horse ready equipped, this the present of arms. 'Tis thus she must be content to live, thus to resign life. The arms which she then receives she must preserve inviolate, and to her sons restore the same, as presents worthy of them, such as their wives may again receive, and still resign to her grandchildren.

They therefore live in a state of chastity well secured; corrupted by no seducing shows and public diversions, by no irritations from banqueting. Of learning and of any secret intercourse by letters, they are all equally ignorant, men and women. Amongst a people so numerous, adultery is exceeding rare; a crime instantly punished, and the punishment left to be inflicted by the husband. He, having cut off her hair, expells her from his house naked, in presence of her kindred, and pursues her with stripes throughout the village. For, to a woman who has prostituted her person, no pardon is ever granted. However beautiful she be, however young, however abounding in wealth, a husband she can never find. In truth, nobody turns vices into mirth there, nor is the practice of corrupting and of yielding to corruption, called the custom of the Age. Better still do those communities, in which none but virgins marry, and where to a single marriage all their views and inclinations are at once confined. Thus, as they have but one body and one life, they take but one husband, that beyond him they may have no thought, no further wishes, nor love him only as their husband but as their marriage.[6] To restrain generation and the increase of children, is esteemed an abominable sin, as also to kill infants newly born. And more powerful with them are good manners, than with other people are good laws.

In all their houses the children are reared naked and

[6] "Sed tamquam matrimonium ament."

nasty; and thus grow into those limbs, into that bulk, which with marvel we behold. They are all nourished with the milk of their own mothers, and never surrendered to handmaids and nurses. The lord you cannot discern from the slave, by any superior delicacy in rearing. Amongst the same cattle they promiscuously live, upon the same ground they without distinction lie, till at a proper age the free-born are parted from the rest, and their bravery recommend them to notice. Slow and late do the young men come to the use of women, and thus very long preserve the vigour of youth. Neither are the virgins hastened to wed. They must both have the same sprightly youth, the like stature, and marry when equal and able-bodied. Thus the robustness of the parents is inherited by the children. Children are holden in the same estimation with their mother's brother, as with their father. Some hold this tie of blood to be most inviolable and binding, and in receiving of hostages, such pledges are most considered and claimed, as they who at once possess affections the most unalienable, and the most diffuse interest in their family. To every man, however, his own children are heirs and successors: wills they make none: for want of children his next akin inherits; his own brothers, those of his father, or those of his mother. To ancient men, the more they abound in descendants, in relations and affinities, so much the more favour and reverence accrues. From being childless, no advantage nor estimation is derived.

All the enmities of your house, whether of your father or of your kindred, you must necessarily adopt; as well as all their friendships. Neither are such enmities unappeasable and permanent: since even for so great a crime as homicide, compensation is made by a fixed number of sheep and cattle, and by it the whole family is pacified to content. A temper this, wholesome to the State; because to a free nation, animosities and faction are always more menacing and perilous. In social feasts, and deeds of hospitality, no nation upon earth was ever more liberal and abounding. To refuse admitting under your roof any man whatsoever, is held wicked and inhuman. Every man receives every comer, and treats him with repasts as large as his ability can possibly furnish. When the whole stock is consumed, he who had treated so hospitably guides and accompanies his guest to a new scene of hospitality; and both proceed to the next house, though neither of them invited. Nor avails it, that they were not: they are there received, with the same frankness and humanity. Between a stranger and an acquaintance, in dispensing the rules and benefits of hospitality, no difference is made. Upon your departure, if you ask anything, it is the custom to grant it; and with the same facility, they ask of you. In gifts they delight, but neither claim merit from what they give, nor own any obligation for what they receive. Their manner of entertaining their guests is familiar and kind.

The moment they rise from sleep, which they generally prolong till late in the day, they bathe, most frequently in warm water; as in a country where the winter is very long and severe. From bathing, they sit down to meat; every man apart, upon a particular seat, and at a separate table. They then proceed to their affairs, all in arms; as in arms, they no less frequently go to banquet. To continue drinking night and day without intermission, is a reproach to no man. Frequent then are their broils, as usual amongst men intoxicated with liquor; and such broils rarely terminate in angry words, but for the most part in maimings and slaughter. Moreover in these their feasts, they generally deliberate about reconciling parties at enmity, about forming affinities, choosing of Princes, and finally about peace and war. For they judge, that at no season is the soul more open to thoughts that are artless and upright, or more fired with such as are great and bold. This people, of themselves nowise subtile or politic, from the freedom of the place and occasion acquire still more frankness to disclose the most secret motions and purposes of their hearts. When therefore the minds of all have been once laid open and declared, on the day following the several sentiments are revised and canvassed; and to both conjectures of time, due regard is had. They consult, when they know not how to dissemble; they determine, when they cannot mistake.

For their drink, they draw a liquor from barley or other grain; and ferment the same, so as to make it resemble wine. Nay, they who dwell upon the bank of the Rhine deal in wine. Their food is very simple; wild fruit, fresh venison, or coagulated milk. They banish hunger without formality, without curious dressing and curious fare. In extinguishing thirst, they use not equal temperance. If you will but humour their excess in drinking, and supply them with as much as they covet, it will be no less easy to vanquish them by vices than by arms.

Of public diversions they have but one sort, and in all their meetings the same is still exhibited. Young men, such as make it their pastime, fling themselves naked and dance amongst sharp swords and the deadly points of javelins. From habit they acquire their skill, and from their skill a graceful manner; yet from hence draw no gain or hire: though this adventurous gaiety has its reward, namely, that of pleasing the spectators. What is marvellous, playing at dice is one of their most serious employments; and even sober, they are gamesters: nay, so desperately do they venture upon the chance of winning or losing, that when their whole substance is played away, they stake their liberty and their persons upon one and the last throw. The loser goes calmly into voluntary bondage. However younger he be, however stronger, he tamely suffers himself to be bound and sold by the winner. Such is their perseverance in an evil course: they themselves call it honour.

Slaves of this class, they exchange away in commerce, to free themselves too from the shame of such a victory. Of their other slaves they make not such use as we do of ours, by distributing amongst them the several offices and employments of the family. Each of them has a dwelling of his own, each a household to govern. His lord uses him like a tenant, and obliges him to pay a quantity of grain, or of cattle, or of cloth. Thus far only the subserviency of the slave extends. All the other duties in a family, not the slaves, but the wives and children discharge. To inflict stripes upon a slave, or to put him in chains, or to doom him to severe labour, are things rarely seen. To kill them they sometimes are wont, not through correction or government, but in heat and rage, as they would an enemy, save that no vengeance or penalty follows. The freedmen very little surpass the slaves, rarely are of moment in the house; in the community never, excepting only such nations where arbitrary dominion prevails. For there they bear higher sway than the free-born, nay, higher than the nobles. In other countries the inferior condition of freedmen is a proof of public liberty.

To the practice of usury and of increasing money by interest, they are strangers; and hence is found a better guard against it, than if it were forbidden. They shift from land to land; and, still appropriating a portion suitable to the number of hands for manuring, anon parcel out the whole amongst particulars according to the condition and quality of each. As the plains are very spacious, the allotments are easily assigned. Every year they change, and cultivate a fresh soil; yet still there is ground to spare. For they strive not to bestow labour proportionable to the fertility and compass of their lands, by planting orchards, by enclosing meadows, by watering gardens. From the earth, corn only is exacted. Hence they quarter not the year into so many seasons. Winter, Spring, and Summer, they understand; and for each have proper appellations. Of the name and blessings of Autumn, they are equally ignorant.

In performing their funerals, they show no state or vainglory. This only is carefully observed, that with the corpses of their signal men certain woods be burned. Upon the funeral pile they accumulate neither apparel nor perfumes. Into the fire, are always thrown the arms of the dead, and sometimes his horse. With sods of earth only the sepulchre is raised. The pomp of tedious and elaborate monuments they contemn, as things grievous to the deceased. Tears and wailings they soon dismiss: their affliction and woe they long retain. In women, it is reckoned becoming to bewail their loss; in men, to remember it. This is what in general we have learned, in the original and customs of the whole people of Germany. I shall now deduce the institutions and usages of the several people, as far as they vary one from another; as also an account of what nations from thence removed, to settle themselves in Gaul.

That the Gauls were in times past more puissant and formidable, is related by the Prince of authors, the deified Julius;[7] and hence it is probable that they too have passed into Germany. For what a small obstacle must be a river, to restrain any nation, as each grew more potent, from seizing or changing habitations; when as yet all habitations were common, and not parted or appropriated by the founding and terror of Monarchies? The region therefore between the Hercynian Forest and the rivers Mœnus[8] and Rhine, was occupied by the Helvetians; as was that beyond it by the Boians, both nations of Gaul. There still remains a place called *Boiemum,* which denotes the primitive name and antiquity of the country, although the inhabitants have been changed. But whether the Araviscans are derived from the Osians, a nation of Germans passing into Pannonia, or the Osians from the Araviscans removing from thence into Germany, is a matter undecided; since they both still use the language, the same customs and the same laws. For, as of old they lived alike poor and alike free, equal proved the evils and advantages on each side the river, and common to both people. The Treverians and Nervians aspire passionately to the reputation of being descended from the Germans; since by the glory of this original, they would escape all imputation of resembling the Gauls in person and effeminacy. Such as dwell upon the bank of the Rhine, the Vangiones, the Tribocians, and the Nemetes, are without doubt all Germans. The Ubians are ashamed of their original; though they have a particular honour to boast, that of having merited an establishment as a Roman Colony, and still delight to be called *Agrippinensians,* after the name of their founder: they indeed formerly came from beyond the Rhine, and, for the many proofs of their fidelity, were settled upon the very bank of the river; not to be there confined or guarded themselves, but to guard and defend that boundary against the rest of the Germans.

Of all these nations, the Batavians are the most signal in bravery. They inhabit not much territory upon the Rhine, but possess an island in it. They were formerly part of the Cattans, and by means of feuds at home removed to these

[7] Julius Cæsar. [8] Main.

dwellings; whence they might become a portion of the Roman Empire. With them this honour still remains, as also the memorials of their ancient association with us: for they are not under the contempt of paying tribute, nor subject to be squeezed by the farmers of the revenue. Free from all impositions and payments, and only set apart for the purposes of fighting, they are reserved wholly for the wars, in the same manner as a magazine of weapons and armour. Under the same degree of homage are the nation of the Mattiacians. For such is the might and greatness of the Roman People, as to have carried the awe and esteem of their Empire beyond the Rhine and the ancient boundaries. Thus the Mattiacians, living upon the opposite banks, enjoy a settlement and limits of their own; yet in spirit and inclination are attached to us: in other things resembling the Batavians, save that as they still breathe their original air, still possess their primitive soil, they are thence inspired with superior vigour and keenness. Amongst the people of Germany I would not reckon those who occupy the lands which are under decimation, though they be such as dwell beyond the Rhine and the Danube. By several worthless and vagabond Gauls, and such as poverty rendered daring, that region was seized as one belonging to no certain possessor: afterwards it became a skirt of the Empire and part of a province, upon the enlargement of our bounds and the extending of our garrisons and frontier.

Beyond these are the Cattans, whose territories begin at the Hercynian Forest, and consist not of such wide and marshy plains, as those of the other communities contained within the vast compass of Germany; but produce ranges of hills, such as run lofty and contiguous for a long tract, then by degrees sink and decay. Moreover the Hercynian Forest attends for a while its native Cattans, then suddenly forsakes them. This people are distinguished with bodies more hardy and robust, compact limbs, stern countenances, and greater vigour of spirit. For Germans, they are men of much sense and address.[9] They dignify chosen men, listen to such as are set over them, know how to preserve their post, to discern occasions, to rebate their own ardour and

[9] "Leur intelligence et leur finesse étonnent, dans des Germains."

impatience; how to employ the day, how to entrench themselves by night. They account fortune amongst things slippery and uncertain, but bravery amongst such as are never-failing and secure; and, what is exceeding rare nor ever to be learnt but by a wholesome course of discipline, in the conduct of the general they repose more assurance than in the strength of the army. Their whole forces consist of foot, who besides their arms carry likewise instruments of iron and their provisions. You may see other Germans proceed equipped to battle, but the Cattans so as to conduct a war.[10] They rarely venture upon excursions or casual encounters. It is in truth peculiar to cavalry, suddenly to conquer, or suddenly to fly. Such haste and velocity rather resembles fear. Patience and deliberation are more akin to intrepidity.

Moreover a custom, practised indeed in other nations of Germany, yet very rarely and confined only to particulars more daring than the rest, prevails amongst the Cattans by universal consent. As soon as they arrive to maturity of years, they let their hair and beards continue to grow, nor till they have slain an enemy do they ever lay aside this form of countenance by vow sacred to valour. Over the blood and spoil of a foe they make bare their face. They allege, that they have now acquitted themselves of the debt and duty contracted by their birth, and rendered themselves worthy of their country, worthy of their parents. Upon the spiritless, cowardly and unwarlike, such deformity of visage still remains.[11] All the most brave likewise wear an iron ring (a mark of great dishonour this in that nation) and retain it as a chain; till by killing an enemy they become released. Many of the Cattans delight always to bear this terrible aspect; and, when grown white through age, become awful and conspicuous by such marks, both to the enemy and their own countrymen. By them in all engagements the first assault is made: of them the front of the battle is always composed, as men who in their looks are singular and tremendous. For even during peace they abate nothing in the grimness and horror of their countenance. They have no

[10] "Alios ad prœlium ire videas, Chattos ad bellum."
[11] "Manet squalor."

house to inhabit, no land to cultivate, nor any domestic charge or care. With whomsoever they come to sojourn, by him they are maintained; always very prodigal of the substance of others, always despising what is their own, till the feebleness of old age overtakes them, and renders them unequal to the efforts of such rigid bravery.

Next to the Cattans, dwell the Usipians and Tencterians; upon the Rhine now running in a channel uniform and certain, such as suffices for a boundary. The Tencterians, besides their wonted glory in war, surpass in the service and discipline of their cavalry. Nor do the Cattans derive higher applause from their foot, than the Tencterians from their horse. Such was the order established by their forefathers, and what their posterity still pursue. From riding and exercising of horses, their children borrow their pastimes; in this exercise the young men find matter for emulating one another, and in this the old men take pleasure to persevere. Horses are by the father bequeathed as part of his household and family, horses are conveyed amongst the rights of succession, and as such the son receives them; but not the eldest son, like other effects, by priority of birth, but he who happens to be signal in boldness and superior in war.

Contiguous to the Tencterians formerly dwelt the Bructerians, in whose room it is said the Chamavians and Angrivarians are now settled; they who expulsed and almost extirpated the Bructerians, with the concurrence of the neighbouring nations: whether in detestation of their arrogance, or allured by the love of spoil, or through the special favour of the Gods towards us Romans. They in truth even vouchsafed to gratify us with the sight of the battle. In it there fell above sixty thousand souls, without a blow struck by the Romans; but, what is a circumstance still more glorious, fell to furnish them with a spectacle of joy and recreation. May the Gods continue and perpetuate amongst these nations, if not any love for us, yet by all means this their animosity and hate towards each other: since whilst the destiny of the Empire thus urges it, fortune cannot more signally befriend us, than in sowing strife amongst our foes.

The Angrivarians and Chamavians are enclosed behind, by the Dulgibinians and Chasuarians; and by other nations not so much noted: before, the Frisians face them. The country of Frisia is divided into two; called the greater and lesser, according to the measure of their strength. Both nations stretch along the Rhine, quite to the ocean; and surround vast lakes such as once have borne Roman fleets. We have moreover even ventured out from thence into the ocean, and upon its coasts common fame has reported the pillars of Hercules to be still standing: whether it be that Hercules ever visited these parts, or that to his renowned name we are wont to ascribe whatever is grand and glorious everywhere. Neither did Drusus who made the attempt, want boldness to pursue it: but the roughness of the ocean withstood him, nor would suffer discoveries to be made about itself, no more than about Hercules. Thenceforward the enterprise was dropped: nay, more pious and reverential it seemed, to believe the marvellous feats of the Gods than to know and to prove them.[12]

Hitherto, I have been describing Germany towards the west. To the northward, it winds away with an immense compass. And first of all occurs the nation of the Chaucians: who though they begin immediately at the confines of the Frisians, and occupy part of the shore, extend so far as to border upon all the several people whom I have already recounted; till at last, by a Circuit, they reach quite to the boundaries of the Cattans. A region so vast, the Chaucians do not only possess but fill; a people of all the Germans the most noble, such as would rather maintain their grandeur by justice than violence. They live in repose, retired from broils abroad, void of avidity to possess more, free from a spirit of domineering over others. They provoke no wars, they ravage no countries, they pursue no plunder. Of their bravery and power, the chief evidence arises from hence, that, without wronging or oppressing others, they are come to be superior to all. Yet they are all ready to arm, and if an exigency require, armies are presently raised, powerful and abounding as they are in men and horses; and even when they are quiet and their weapons laid aside, their credit and name continue equally high.

Along the side of the Chaucians and Cattans dwell the

[12] "Cœlum ipsum petimus stultitia."

Cheruscans; a people who finding no enemy to rouse them, were enfeebled by a peace over lasting and uniform, but such as they failed not to nourish. A conduct which proved more pleasing than secure; since treacherous is that repose which you enjoy amongst neighbours that are very powerful and very fond of rule and mastership. When recourse is once had to the sword, modesty and fair dealing will be vainly pleaded by the weaker; names these which are always assumed by the stronger. Thus the Cheruscans, they who formerly bore the character of *good and upright,* are now called *cowards and fools;* and the fortune of the Cattans who subdued them, grew immediately to be wisdom. In the ruin of the Cheruscans, the Fosians, also their neighbours, were involved; and in their calamities bore an equal share, though in their prosperity they had been weaker and less considered.

In the same winding tract of Germany live the Cimbrians, close to the ocean; a community now very small, but great in fame. Nay, of their ancient renown, many and extensive are the traces and monuments still remaining; even their entrenchments upon either shore, so vast in compass that from thence you may even now measure the greatness and numerous bands of that people, and assent to the account of an army so mighty. It was on the six hundred and fortieth year of Rome, when of the arms of the Cimbrians the first mention was made, during the Consulship of Cæcilius Metellus and Papirius Carbo. If from that time we count to the second Consulship of the Emperor Trajan, the interval comprehends near two hundred and ten years; so long have we been conquering Germany. In a course of time, so vast between these two periods, many have been the blows and disasters suffered on each side. In truth neither from the Samnites, nor from the Carthaginians, nor from both Spains, nor from all the nations of Gaul, have we received more frequent checks and alarms; nor even from the Parthians: for, more vigorous and invincible is the liberty of the Germans than the monarchy of the Arsacides. Indeed, what has the power of the East to allege to our dishonour; but the fall of Crassus, that power which was itself overthrown and abased by Ventidius, with the loss of the great King Pacorus bereft of his life? But by the Germans the Roman People have been bereft of five armies, all commanded by Consuls; by the Germans, the commanders of these armies, Carbo, and Cassius, and Scaurus Aurelius, and Servilius Cæpio, as also Marcus Manlius, were all routed or taken: by the Germans even the Emperor Augustus was bereft of Varus and three legions. Nor without difficulty and loss of men were they defeated by Caius Marius in Italy, or by the deified Julius in Gaul, or by Drusus or Tiberius or Germanicus in their native territories. Soon after, the mighty menaces of Caligula against them ended in mockery and derision. Thenceforward they continued quiet, till taking advantage of our domestic division and civil wars, they stormed and seized the winter entrenchments of the legions, and aimed at the dominion of Gaul; from whence they were once more expulsed, and in the times preceding the present, we gained a triumph over them rather than a victory.

I must now proceed to speak of the Suevians, who are not, like the Cattans and Tencterians, comprehended in a single people; but divided into several nations all bearing distinct names, though in general they are entitled Suevians, and occupy the larger share of Germany. This people are remarkable for a peculiar custom, that of twisting their hair and binding it up in a knot. It is thus the Suevians are distinguished from the other Germans, thus the free Suevians from their slaves. In other nations, whether from alliance of blood with the Suevians, or, as is usual, from imitation, this practice is also found, yet rarely, and never exceeds the years of youth. The Suevians, even when their hair is white through age, continue to raise it backwards in a manner stern and staring; and often tie it upon the top of their head only. That of their Princes, is more accurately disposed, and so far they study to appear agreeable and comely; but without any culpable intention. For by it, they mean not to make love or to incite it: they thus dress when proceeding to war, and deck their heads so as to add to their height and terror in the eyes of the enemy.

Of all the Suevians, the Semnones recount themselves to be the most ancient and most noble. The belief of their antiquity is confirmed by religious mysteries. At a stated time of the year, all the several people descended from the same stock, assemble by their deputies in a wood; consecrated by the idolatries of their forefathers, and by superstitious awe in times of old. There by publicly sacrificing a man, they begin the horrible solemnity of their barbarous worship. To this grove another sort of reverence is also paid. No one enters it otherwise than bound with ligatures, thence professing his subordination and meanness, and the power of the Deity there. If he fall down, he is not permitted to rise or be raised, but grovels along upon the ground. And of all their superstition, this is the drift and tendency; that from this place the nation drew their original, that here God, the supreme Governor of the world, resides, and that all things else whatsoever are subject to him and bound to obey him. The potent condition of the Semnones has increased their influence and authority, as they inhabit an hundred towns; and from the largeness of their community it comes, that they hold themselves for the head of the Suevians.

What on the contrary ennobles the Langobards is the smallness of their number, for that they, who are surrounded with very many and very powerful nations, derive their security from no obsequiousness or plying; but from the dint of battle and adventurous deeds. There follow in order the Reudignians, and Aviones, and Angles, and Varinians, and Eudoses, and Suardones and Nuithones; all defended by rivers or forests. Nor in one of these nations docs aught remarkable occur, only that they universally join in the worship of *Herthum;* that is to say, the Mother Earth. Her they believe to interpose in the affairs of men, and to visit countries. In an island of the ocean stands the wood *Castum:* in it is a chariot dedicated to the Goddess, covered over with a curtain, and permitted to be touched by none but the Priest. Whenever the Goddess enters this her holy vehicle, he perceives her; and with profound veneration attends the motion of the chariot, which is always drawn by yoked cows. Then it is that days of rejoicing always ensue, and in all places whatsoever which she descends to honour with a visit and her company, feasts and recreation abound. They go not to war; they touch no arms; fast laid up is every hostile weapon; peace and repose are then only known, then only beloved, till to the temple the same priest reconducts the Goddess when well tired with the conversation of mortal beings. Anon the chariot is washed and purified in a secret lake, as also the curtains; nay, the Deity herself too, if you choose to believe it. In this office it is slaves who minister, and they are forthwith doomed to be swallowed up in the same lake. Hence all men are possessed with mysterious terror; as well as with a holy ignorance what that must be, which none see but such as are immediately to perish. Moreover this quarter of the Suevians stretches to the middle of Germany.

The community next adjoining, is that of the Hermondurians; (that I may now follow the course of the Danube, as a little before I did that of the Rhine) a people this, faithful to the Romans. So that to them alone of all the Germans, commerce is permitted; not barely upon the bank of the Rhine, but more extensively, and even in that glorious colony in the province of Rhœtia. They travel everywhere at their own discretion and without a guard; and when to other nations, we show no more than our arms and encampments, to this people we throw open our houses and dwellings, as to men who have no longing to possess them. In the territories of the Hermondurians rises the Elbe, a river very famous and formerly well known to us; at present we only hear it named.

Close by the Hermondurians reside the Nariscans, and next to them the Marcomanians and Quadians. Amongst these the Marcomanians are most signal in force and renown; nay, their habitation itself they acquired by their bravery, as from thence they formerly expulsed the Boians. Nor do the Nariscans or Quadians degenerate in spirit. Now this is as it were the frontier of Germany, as far as Germany is washed by the Danube. To the times within our memory the Marcomanians and Quadians were governed by kings, who were natives of their own, descended from the noble line of Maroboduus and Tudrus. At present they are even subject to such as are foreigners. But the whole strength and sway of their kings is derived from the authority of the Romans. From our arms, they rarely receive any aid; from our money very frequently.

Nor less powerful are the several people beyond them; namely, the Marsignians, the Gothinians, the Osians and the Burians, who altogether enclose the Marcomanians and Quadians behind. Of those, the Marsignians and the Burians in speech and dress resemble the Suevians. From the Gallic language spoken by the Gothinians, and from that of Pannonia by the Osians, it is manifest that neither of these people are Germans; as it is also from their bearing to pay tribute. Upon them as upon aliens their tribute is imposed, partly by the Sarmatians, partly by the Quadians. The Gothinians, to heighten their disgrace, are forced to labour in the iron mines. By all these several nations but little level country is possessed: they are seated amongst forests, and upon the ridges and declivities of mountains. For, Suevia is parted by a continual ridge of mountains; beyond which, live many distinct nations. Of these the Lygians are most numerous and extensive, and spread into several communities. It will suffice to mention the most puissant; even the Arians, Helvicones, Manimians; Elysians and Naharvalians. Amongst the Naharvalians is shown a grove, sacred to devotion extremely ancient. Over it a Priest presides apparelled like a woman; but according to the explication of the Romans, 'tis *Castor* and *Pollux* who are here worshipped. This Divinity is named *Alcis.* There are indeed no images here, no traces of an extraneous superstition: yet their devotion is addressed to young men and to brothers. Now the Aryans, besides their forces, in which they surpass the several nations just recounted, are in their persons stern and truculent; and even humour and improve their natural grimness and ferocity by art and time. They wear black shields, their bodies are painted black, they choose dark nights for engaging in battle; and by the very awe and ghastly hue of their army, strike the enemy with dread, as none can bear this their aspect so surprising and as it were quite infernal. For, in all battles the eyes are vanquished first.

Beyond the Lygians dwell the Gothones, under the rule of a King; and thence held in subjection somewhat stricter than the other German nations, yet not so strict as to extinguish all their liberty. Immediately adjoining are the Rugians and Lemovians upon the coast of the ocean, and of these several nations the characteristics are a round shield, a short sword and kingly government. Next occur the communities of the Suiones, situated in the ocean itself; and besides their strength in men and arms, very powerful at sea. The form of their vessels varies thus far from ours, that they have prows at each end, so as to be always ready to row to shore without turning nor are they moved by sails, nor on their sides have benches of oars placed, but the rowers ply here and there in all parts of the ship alike, as in some rivers is done, and change their oars from place to place, just as they shift their course hither or thither. To wealth also, amongst them, great veneration is paid, and thence a single ruler governs them, without all restriction of power, and exacting unlimited obedience. Neither here, as amongst other nations of Germany, are arms used indifferently by all, but shut up and warded under the care of a particular keeper, who in truth too is always a slave: since from all sudden invasions and attacks from their foes, the ocean protects them: besides that armed bands, when they are not employed, grow easily debauched and tumultuous. The truth is, it suits not the interest of an arbitrary Prince, to trust the care and power of arms either with a nobleman or with a freeman, or indeed with any man above the condition of a slave.

Beyond the Suiones is another sea, one very heavy and almost void of agitation; and by it the whole globe is thought to be bounded and environed, for that the reflection of the sun, after his setting, continues till his rising, so bright as to darken the stars. To this, popular opinion has added, that the tumult also of his emerging from the sea is heard, that forms divine are then seen, as likewise the rays about his head. Only thus far extend the limits of nature, if what fame says be true. Upon the right of the Suevian Sea the Æstyan nations reside, who use the same customs and attire with the Suevians; their language more resembles that of Britain. They worship the Mother of the Gods. As the characteristic of their national superstition, they wear the images of wild boars. This alone serves them for arms, this is the safeguard of all, and by this every worshipper of the Goddess is secured even amidst his foes. Rare amongst them is the use of weapons of iron, but frequent that of clubs. In producing of grain and the other fruits of the earth, they labour with more assiduity and patience than is suitable to the usual laziness of Germans. Nay, they even search the deep, and of all the rest are the only people who gather *amber*. They call it *glasing*, and find it amongst the shallows and upon the very shore. But, according to the ordinary incuriosity and ignorance of Barbarians, they have neither learnt, nor do they inquire, what is its nature, or from what cause it is produced. In truth it lay long neglected amongst the other gross discharges of the sea; till from our luxury, it gained a name and value. To themselves it is of no use: they gather it rough, they expose it in pieces coarse and unpolished, and for it receive a price with wonder. You would however conceive it to be a liquor issuing from trees, for that in the transparent substance are often seen birds and other animals, such as at first stuck in the soft gum, and by it, as it hardened, became quite enclosed. I am apt to believe that, as in the recesses of the East are found woods and groves dropping frankincense and balms, so in the isles and continent of the West such gums are extracted by the force and proximity of the sun; at first liquid and flowing into the next sea, then thrown by winds and waves upon the opposite shore. If you try the nature of amber by the application of fire, it kindles like a torch; and feeds a thick and unctuous flame very high scented, and presently becomes glutinous like pitch or rosin.

Upon the Suiones, border the people Sitones; and, agreeing with them in all other things, differ from them in one, that here the sovereignty is exercised by a woman. So notoriously do they degenerate not only from a state of liberty, but even below a state of bondage. Here end the territories of the Suevians.

Whether amongst the Sarmatians or the Germans I ought to account the Peucinians, the Venedians, and the Fennians, is what I cannot determine; though the Peucinians, whom some call Basstarnians, speak the same language with the

Germans, use the same attire, build like them, and live like them, in that dirtiness and sloth so common to all. Somewhat they are corrupted into the fashion of the Sarmatians by the inter-marriages of the principal sort with that nation: from whence the Venedians have derived very many of their customs and a great resemblance. For they are continually traversing and infesting with robberies all the forests and mountains lying between the Peucinians and Fennians. Yet they are rather reckoned amongst the Germans, for that they have fixed houses, and carry shields, and prefer travelling on foot, and excel in swiftness. Usages these, all widely differing from those of the Sarmatians, who live on horseback and dwell in waggons. In wonderful savageness live the nation of the Fennians, and in beastly poverty, destitute of arms, of horses, and of homes; their food, the common herbs; their apparel, skins; their bed, the earth; their only hope in their arrows, which for want of iron they point with bones. Their common support they have from the chase, women as well as men; for with these the former wander up and down, and crave a portion of the prey. Nor other shelter have they even for their babes, against the violence of tempests and ravening beasts, than to cover them with the branches of trees twisted together; this a reception for the old men, and hither resort the young. Such a condition they judge more happy than the painful occupation of cultivating the ground, than the labour of rearing houses, than the agitations of hope and fear attending the defence of their own property or the seizing that of others. Secure against the designs of men, secure against the malignity of the Gods, they have accomplished a thing of infinite difficulty; that to them nothing remains even to be wished.

What further accounts we have are fabulous: as that the Hellusians and Oxiones have the countenances and aspect of men, with the bodies and limbs of savage beasts. This, as a thing about which I have no certain information, I shall leave untouched.

SIR FRANCIS DRAKE REVIVED

INTRODUCTORY NOTE

Sir Francis Drake, *the greatest of the naval adventurers of England of the time of Elizabeth, was born in Devonshire about 1540. He went to sea early, was sailing to the Spanish Main by 1565, and commanded a ship under Hawkins in an expedition that was overwhelmed by the Spaniards in 1567. In order to recompense himself for the loss suffered in this disaster, he equipped the expedition against the Spanish treasure-house at Nombre de Dios in 1572, the fortunes of which are described in the first of the two following narratives. It was on this voyage that he was led by native guides to "that goodly and great high tree" on the isthmus of Darien, from which, first of Englishmen, he looked on the Pacific, and "besought Almighty God of His goodness to give him life and leave to sail once in an English ship in that sea."*

The fulfilment of this prayer is described in the second of the voyages here printed, in which it is told how, in 1578, Drake passed through the Straits of Magellan into waters never before sailed by his countrymen, and with a single ship rifled the Spanish settlements on the west coast of South America and plundered the Spanish treasure-ships; how, considering it unsafe to go back the way he came lest the enemy should seek revenge, he went as far north as the Golden Gate, then passed across the Pacific and round by the Cape of Good Hope, and so home, the first Englishman to circumnavigate the globe. Only Magellan's ship had preceded him in the feat, and Magellan had died on the voyage. The Queen visited the ship, "The Golden Hind," as she lay at Deptford and knighted the commander on board.

Drake's further adventures were of almost equal interest. Returning from a raid on the Spaniards in 1586, he brought home the despairing Virginian colony, and is said at the same time to have introduced from America tobacco and potatoes. Two years later he led the English fleet in the decisive engagement with the Great Armada. In 1595 he set out on another voyage to the Spanish Main; and in the January of the following year died off Porto Bello and was buried in the waters where he had made his name as the greatest seaman of his day and nation.

Sir FRANCIS DRAKE *revived;*

Calling upon this dull or effeminate Age, to follow his noble steps for gold and silver:

By this memorable Relation of the rare occurrences (never yet declared to the world) in a Third Voyage made by him into the West Indies, in the years [15]72 and [15]73; when Nombre de Dios was by him, and fifty-two others only in his company, surprised.

Faithfully taken out of the report of Master CHRISTOPHER CEELY, ELLIS HIXOM, and others, who were in the same Voyage with him;

By PHILIP NICHOLS, Preacher.

Reviewed also by Sir FRANCIS DRAKE himself, before his death; and much holpen and enlarged by divers notes, with his own hand, here and there inserted.

Set forth by Sir FRANCIS DRAKE, Baronet, (his nephew) now living.

LONDON:
Printed by E. A. for NICHOLAS BOURNE, dwelling at the South Entrance of the Royal Exchange. 1626.

Facsimile of Title-page of First Edition

TO THE HIGH AND MIGHTY

CHARLES THE FIRST, OF GREAT BRITAIN, FRANCE, and IRELAND, KING, all the blessings of this, and a better life.

MOST GRACIOUS SOVEREIGN,

THAT this brief Treatise is yours, both by right and by succession, will appear by the Author's and Actor's ensuing *Dedication.* To praise either the Mistress or the Servant, might justly incur the censure of *Quis eos unquam sanus vituperavit;* either's worth having sufficiently blazed their fame.

This Present loseth nothing, by glancing on former actions; and the observation of passed adventures may probably advantage future employments. CÆSAR wrote his own *Commentaries;* and this Doer was partly the Inditor.

Neither is there wanting living testimony to confirm its truth.

For his sake, then, cherish what is good! and I shall willingly entertain check for what is amiss. Your favourable acceptance may encourage my collecting of more neglected notes! However, though Virtue, as Lands, be not inheritable; yet hath he left of his Name, one that resolves, and therein joys to approve himself.

Your most humble and loyal subject,

FRANCIS DRAKE [Bart.]

The Dedicatory Epistle, intended to

QUEEN ELIZABETH

Written by SIR FRANCIS DRAKE, Deceased.

To the Queen's most excellent Majesty, my most dread Sovereign.

MADAM,

SEEING divers have diversely reported and written of these Voyages and Actions which I have attempted and made, every one endeavouring to bring to light whatsoever inklings or conjectures they have had; whereby many untruths have been published, and the certain truth concealed: as [*so*] I have thought it necessary myself, as in a Card [*chart*] to prick the principal points of the counsels taken, attempts made, and success had, during the whole course of my employment in these services against the Spaniard. Not as setting sail for maintaining my reputation in men's judgement, but only as sitting at helm, if occasion shall be, for conducting the like actions hereafter. So I have accounted it my duty, to present this Discourse to Your Majesty, as of right; either for itself being the firstfruits of your Servant's pen, or for the matter, being service done to Your Majesty by your poor vassal, against your great Enemy: at times, in such places, and after such sort as may seem strange to those that are not acquainted with the whole carriage thereof; but will be a pleasing remembrance to Your Highness, who take the apparent height of the Almighty's favour towards you, by these events, as truest instruments.

Humbly submitting myself to Your gracious censure, both in writing and presenting; that Posterity be not deprived of such help as may happily be gained hereby, and our present Age, at least, may be satisfied, in the rightfulness of these actions, which hitherto have been silenced: and Your Servant's labour not seem altogether lost, not only in travels by sea and land, but also in writing the Report thereof (a work to him no less troublesome) yet made pleasant and sweet, in that it hath been, is, and shall be for Your Majesty's content; to whom I have devoted myself [and] live or die.

FRANCIS DRAKE [Knight].

January 1, 1592 [*i.e.*, 1593].

TO THE COURTEOUS READER

HONEST READER,

WITHOUT apology, I desire thee, in this ensuing Discourse, to observe, with me, the power and justice of the LORD of Hosts, Who could enable so mean a person to right himself upon so mighty a Prince; together with the goodness and providence of GOD very observable in that it pleased Him to raise this man, not only from a low condition, but even from the state of persecution. His father suffered in it, being forced to fly from his house, near South Tavistock in Devon, into Kent: and there to inhabit in the hull of a ship, wherein many of his younger sons were born. He had twelve in all: and as it pleased GOD to give most of them a being upon the water, so the greatest part of them died at sea. The youngest, who though he was [*went*] as far as any, yet died at home; whose posterity inherits that, which by himself and this noble Gentleman the eldest brother, was hardly, yet worthily gotten.

I could more largely acquaint thee, that this Voyage was his Third he made into the West Indies; after that [of] his excellent service, both by sea and land, in Ireland, under WALTER, Earl of ESSEX; his next, about the World; another, wherein he took St. Jago, Cartagena, St. Domingo, St. Augustino; his doings at Cadiz; besides the first Carrack taught by him to sail into England; his stirrings in Eighty-seven; his remarkable actions in Eighty-eight; his endeavours in the Portugal employment; his last enterprise, determined by death; and his filling Plymouth with a plentiful stream of fresh water: but I pass by all these. I had rather thou shouldest inquire of others! then to seem myself a vainglorious man.

I intend not his praise! I strive only to set out the praise of his and our good GOD! that guided him in his truth! and protected him in his courses! My ends are to stir thee up to the worship of GOD, and service of our King and Country, by his example! If anything be worth thy consideration; conclude with me, that the LORD only, can do great things!

FRANCIS DRAKE [Bart.]

SIR FRANCIS DRAKE REVIVED

Calling upon this dull or effeminate Age, to follow his noble steps for gold and silver.

AS THERE is a general Vengeance which secretly pursueth the doers of wrong, and suffereth them not to prosper, albeit no man of purpose empeach them: so is there a particular Indignation, engraffed in the bosom of all that are wronged, which ceaseth not seeking, by all means possible, to redress or remedy the wrong received. Insomuch as those great and mighty men, in whom their prosperous estate hath bred such an overweening of themselves, that they do not only wrong their inferiors, but despise them being injured, seem to take a very unfit course for their own safety, and far unfitter for their rest. For as ESOP teacheth, even the fly hath her spleen, and the emmet [*ant*] is not without her choler; and both together many times find means whereby, though the eagle lays her eggs in JUPITER'S lap, yet by one way or other, she escapeth not requital of her wrong done [to] the emmet.

Among the manifold examples hereof, which former Ages have committed to memory, or our Time yielded to sight: I suppose, there hath not been any more notable then this in hand; either in respect of the greatness of the person by whom the first injury was offered, or the meanness of him who righted himself. The one being, in his own conceit, the mightiest Monarch of all the world! The other, an English Captain, a mean subject of her Majesty's! Who (besides the wrongs received at Rio de [la] Hacha with Captain JOHN LOVELL in the years [15]65 and [15]66) having been grievously endamaged at San Juan de Ulua in the Bay of Mexico, with Captain JOHN HAWKINS, in the years [15]67 and [15]68, not only in the loss of his goods of some value, but also of his kinsmen and friends, and that by the falsehood of DON MARTIN HENRIQUEZ then the Viceroy of Mexico; and finding that no recompense could be recovered out of Spain, by any of his own means, or by Her Majesty's letters; he used such helps as he might, by two several voyages into the West Indies (the first with two ships, the one called the *Dragon,* the other the *Swan,* in the year [15]70: the other in the *Swan* alone in the year [15]71), to gain such intelligences as might further him, to get some amends for his loss.

And having, in those two Voyages, gotten such certain notice of the persons and places aimed at, as he thought requisite, and thereupon with good deliberation resolved on a Third Voyage (the description whereof we have now in hand); he accordingly prepared his ships and company, and then taking the first opportunity of a good wind, had such success in his proceedings, as now follows further to be declared.

On Whitsunday Eve, being the 24th of May, in the year 1572, Captain DRAKE in the *Pascha* of Plymouth of 70 tons, his admiral [*flag-ship*]; with the *Swan* of the same port, of 25 tons, his vice-admiral, in which his brother JOHN DRAKE was Captain (having in both of them, of men and boys seventy-three, all voluntarily assembled; of which the eldest was fifty, all the rest under thirty: so divided that there were forty-seven in the one ship, and twenty-six in the other. Both richly furnished with victuals and apparel for a whole year; and no less heedfully provided of all manner of munition, artillery, artificers, stuff and tools, that were requisite for such a Man-of-war in such an attempt: but especially having three dainty pinnaces made in Plymouth, taken asunder all in pieces, and stowed aboard, to be set up as occasion served), set sail, from out of the Sound of Plymouth, with intent to land at Nombre de Dios.

The wind continued prosperous and favourable at northeast, and gave us a very good passage, without any alteration or change: so that albeit we had sight (3rd June) of Porto Santo, one of the Madeiras, and of the Canaries also within twelve days of our setting forth: yet we never struck sail, nor came to anchor, nor made any stay for any cause, neither there nor elsewhere, until twenty-five days after; when (28th June) we had sight of the island of Guadaloupe, one of the islands of the West Indies, goodly high land.

The next morning (29th June), we entered between Dominica and Guadaloupe, where we descried two canoes coming from a rocky island, three leagues off Dominica; which usually repair thither to fish, by reason of the great plenty thereof, which is there continually to be found.

We landed on the south side of it, remaining there three days to refresh our men; and to water our ships out of one of those goodly rivers, which fall down off the mountain. There we saw certain poor cottages; built with Palmito boughs and branches; but no inhabitants, at that time, civil or savage: the cottages it may be (for we could know no certain cause of the solitariness we found there) serving, not for continual inhabitation, but only for their uses, that came to that place at certain seasons to fish.

The third day after (1st July), about three in the afternoon, we set sail from thence, toward the continent of *Terra firma*.

And the fifth day after (6th July), we had sight of the high land of Santa Marta; but came not near the shore by ten leagues.

But thence directed our course, for a place called by us, Port Pheasant; for that our Captain had so named it in his former voyage, by reason of the great store of those goodly fowls, which he and his company did then daily kill and feed on, in that place. In this course notwithstanding we had two days calm, yet within six days after we arrived (12th July) at Port Pheasant, which is a fine round bay, of very safe harbour for all winds, lying between two high points, not past half a cable's length over at the mouth, but within, eight or ten cables' length every way, having ten or twelve fathoms of water more or less, full of good fish; the soil also very fruitful, which may appear by this, that our Captain having been in this place, within a year and few days before [*i. e., in July*, 1571] and having rid the place with many alleys and paths made; yet now all was so overgrown again, as that we doubted, at first, whether this was the same place or not.

At our entrance into this bay, our Captain having given order to his brother what to do, if any occasion should happen in his absence, was on his way, with intent to have gone aland with some few only in his company, because he knew there dwelt no Spaniards within thirty-five leagues of that place. [Santiago de] Tolou being the nearest to the eastwards, and Nombre de Dios to the westwards, where any of that nation dwelt.

But as we were rowing ashore, we saw a smoke in the woods, even near the place where our Captain had aforetime frequented; therefore thinking it fit to take more strength with us, he caused his other boat also to be manned, with certain muskets and other weapons, suspecting some enemy had been ashore.

When we landed, we found by evident marks, that there had been lately there, a certain Englishman of Plymouth, called JOHN GARRET, who had been conducted thither by certain English mariners which had been there with our Captain, in some of his former voyages. He had now left a plate of lead, nailed fast to a mighty great tree (greater than any four men joining hands could fathom about) on which were engraven these words, directed to our Captain.

CAPTAIN DRAKE

IF YOU fortune to come to this Port, make haste away! For the Spaniards which you had with you here, the last year, have bewrayed this place, and taken away all that you left here.

I depart from hence, this present 7th of July, 1572.

Your very loving friend,

John Garret.

The smoke which we saw, was occasioned by a fire, which the said GARRET and his company had made, before their departure, in a very great tree, not far from this which had the lead nailed on it, which had continued burning at least five days before our arrival.

This advertisement notwithstanding, our Captain meant

not to depart before he had built his pinnaces; which were yet aboard in pieces: for which purpose he knew this port to be a most convenient place.

And therefore as soon as we had moored our ships, our Captain commanded his pinnaces to be brought ashore for the carpenters to set up; himself employing all his other company in fortifying a place (which he had chosen out, as a most fit plot) of three-quarters of an acre of ground, to make some strength or safety for the present, as sufficiently as the means he had would afford. Which was performed by felling of great trees; bowsing and hauling them together, with great pulleys and hawsers, until they were enclosed to the water; and then letting others fall upon them, until they had raised with trees and boughs thirty feet in height round about, leaving only one gate to issue at, near the water side; which every night, that we might sleep in more safety and security, was shut up, with a great tree drawn athwart it.

The whole plot was built in pentagonal form, to wit, of five equal sides and angles, of which angles two were toward the sea, and that side between them was left open, for the easy launching of our pinnaces: the other four equal sides were wholly, excepting the gate before mentioned, firmly closed up.

Without, instead of a trench, the ground was rid [*laid bare*] for fifty feet space, round about. The rest was very thick with trees, of which many were of those kinds which are never without green leaves, till they are dead at the root: excepting only one kind of tree amongst them, much like to our Ash, which when the sun cometh right over them, causing great rains, suddenly casteth all its leaves, viz., within three days, and yet within six days after becomes all green again. The leaves of the other trees do also in part fall away, but so as the trees continue still green notwithstanding: being of a marvellous height, and supported as it were with five or six natural buttresses growing out of their bodies so far, that three men may so be hidden in each of them, that they which shall stand in the very next buttress shall not be able to see them. One of them specially was marked to have had seven of those stays or buttresses, for the supporting of his greatness and height, which being measured with a line close by the bark and near to the ground, as it was indented or extant, was found to be above thirty-nine yards about. The wood of those trees is as heavy or heavier than Brazil or *Lignum vitæ;* and is in colour white.

The next day after we had arrived (13th July), there came also into that bay, an English bark of the Isle of Wight, of Sir EDWARD HORSEY'S; *wherein* JAMES RANSE was Captain and JOHN OVERY, Master, with thirty men: of which, some had been with our Captain in the same place, the year before. They brought in with them a Spanish caravel of Seville, which he had taken the day before, athwart of that place; being a Caravel of *Adviso* [*Despatch boat*] bound for Nombre de Dios; and also one shallop with oars, which he had taken at Cape Blanc. This Captain RANSE understanding our Captain's purpose, was desirous to join in consort with him; and was received upon conditions agreed on between them.

Within seven days after his coming, having set up our pinnaces, and despatched all our business, in providing all things necessary, out of our ships into our pinnaces: we departed (20th July) from that harbour, setting sail in the morning towards Nombre de Dios, continuing our course till we came to the Isles of Pinos: where, being within three days arrived, we found (22nd July) two frigates of Nombre de Dios lading plank and timber from thence.

The Negroes which were in those frigates, gave us some particular understanding of the present state of the town; and besides, told us that they had heard a report, that certain soldiers should come thither shortly, and were daily looked for, from the Governor of Panama, and the country thereabout, to defend the town against the Cimaroons (a black people, which about eighty years past [*i. e.*, 1512] fled from the Spaniards their masters, by reason of their cruelty, and are since grown to a Nation, under two Kings of their own: the one inhabiteth to the West, and the other to the East of the Way from Nombre de Dios to Panama) which had nearly surprised it [*i. e., Nombre de Dios*], about six weeks before [*i. e., about 10th June, 1572*].

Our Captain willing to use those Negroes well (not hurting himself) set them ashore upon the Main, that they might perhaps join themselves to their countrymen the Cimaroons, and gain their liberty if they would; or if they would not, yet by reason of the length and troublesomeness of the way by land to Nombre de Dios, he might prevent any notice of his coming, which they should be able to give. For he was loath to put the town to too much charge (which he knew they would willingly bestow) in providing beforehand for his entertainment; and therefore he hastened his going thither, with as much speed and secrecy as possibly he could.

To this end, disposing of all his companies, according as they inclined most; he left the three ships and the caravel with Captain RANSE; and chose into his four pinnaces (Captain RANSE's shallop made the fourth) beside fifty-three of our men, twenty more of Captain RANSE's company; with which he seemed competently furnished, to achieve what he intended; especially having proportioned, according to his own purpose, and our men's disposition, their several arms, viz., six targets, six firepikes, twelve pikes, twenty-four muskets and calivers, sixteen bows, and six partisans, two drums, and two trumpets.

Thus having parted (23rd July) from our company: we arrived at the island of Cativaas, being twenty-five leagues distant, about five days afterward (28th July). There we landed all in the morning betimes: and our Captain trained his men, delivering them their several weapons and arms which hitherto he had kept very fair and safe in good caske [*casks*]: and exhorting them after his manner, he declared "the greatness of the hope of good things that was there! the weakness of the town, being unwalled! and the hope he had of prevailing to recompense his wrongs! especially now that he should come with such a crew, who were like-minded with himself; and at such a time, as he should be utterly undiscovered."

Therefore, even that afternoon, he causeth us to set sail for Nombre de Dios, so that before sunset we were as far as Rio Francisco. Thence, he led us hard aboard the shore, that we might not be descried of the Watch House, until that being come within two leagues of the point of the bay, he caused us to strike a hull, and cast our grappers [*grappling irons*], riding so until it was dark night.

Then we weighed again, and set sail, rowing hard aboard the shore, with as much silence as we could, till we recovered the point of the harbour under the high land. There, we stayed, all silent; purposing to attempt the town in the dawning of the day: after that we had reposed ourselves, for a while.

But our Captain with some other of his best men, finding that our people were talking of the greatness of the town, and what their strength might be; especially by the report of the Negroes that we took at the Isle of Pinos: thought it best to put these conceits out of their heads, and therefore to take the opportunity of the rising of the moon that night, persuading them that "it was the day dawning." By this occasion we were at the town a large hour sooner then first was purposed. For we arrived there by three of the clock after midnight. At what time it fortuned that a ship of Spain, of 60 tons, laden with Canary wines and other commodities, which had but lately come into the bay; and had not yet furled her sprit-sail (espying our four pinnaces, being an extraordinary number, and those rowing with many oars) sent away her gundeloe [? *gondola*] towards the town, to give warning. But our Captain perceiving it, cut betwixt her and the town, forcing her to go to the other side of the bay: whereby we landed without impeachment, although we found one gunner upon the Platform [*battery*] in the very place where we landed; being a sandy place and no key [*quay*] at all, not past twenty yards from the houses.

There we found six great pieces of brass ordnance, mounted upon their carriages, some Demy, some Whole-Culvering.

We presently dismounted them. The gunner fled. The town took alarm (being very ready thereto, by reason of their often disquieting by their near neighbours the Cimaroons); as we perceived, not only by the noise and cries of the people, but by the bell ringing out, and drums running up and down the town.

Our Captain, according to the directions which he had

given over night, to such as he had made choice of for the purpose, left twelve to keep the pinnaces; that we might be sure of a safe retreat, if the worst befell. And having made sure work of the Platform before he would enter the town, he thought best, first to view the Mount on the east side of the town: where he was informed, by sundry intelligences the year before, they had an intent to plant ordnance, which might scour round about the town.

Therefore, leaving one half of his company to make a stand at the foot of the Mount, he marched up presently unto the top of it, with all speed to try the truth of the report, for the more safety. There we found no piece of ordnance, but only a very fit place prepared for such use, and therefore we left it without any of our men, and with all celerity returned now down the Mount.

Then our Captain appointed his brother, with JOHN OXNAM [*or* OXENHAM] and sixteen other of his men, to go about, behind the King's Treasure House, and enter near the easter[n] end of the Market Place: himself with the rest, would pass up the broad street into the Market Place, with sound of drum and trumpet. The Firepikes, divided half to the one, and half to the other company, served no less for fright to the enemy than light of our men, who by his means might discern every place very well, as if it were near day: whereas the inhabitants stood amazed at so strange a sight, marvelling what the matter might be, and imagining, by reason of our drums and trumpets sounding in so sundry places, that we had been a far greater number then we were.

Yet, by means of the soldiers of which were in the town, and by reason of the time which we spent in marching up and down the Mount, the soldiers and inhabitants had put themselves in arms, and brought their companies in some order, at the south-east end of the Market Place, near the Governor's House, and not far from the gate of the town, which is the only one, leading towards Panama: having (as it seems) gathered themselves thither, either that in the Governor's sight they might shew their valour, if it might prevail; or else, that by the gate they might best take their *Vale,* and escape readiest.

And to make a shew of far greater numbers of shot, or else of a custom they had, by the like device to terrify the Cimaroons; they had hung lines with matches lighted, overthwart the wester[n] end of the Market Place, between the Church and the Cross; as though there had been in a readiness some company of shot, whereas indeed there were not past two or three that taught these lines to dance, till they themselves ran away, as soon as they perceived they were discovered.

But the soldiers and such as were joined with them, presented us with a jolly hot volley of shot, beating full upon the full egress of that street, in which we marched; and levelling very low, so as their bullets ofttimes grazed on the sand.

We stood not to answer them in like terms: but having discharged our first volley of shot, and feathered them with our arrows (which our Captain had caused to be made of purpose in England; not great sheaf arrows, but fine roving shafts, very carefully reserved for the service) we came to the push of pike, so that our firepikes being well armed and made of purpose, did us very great service.

For our men with their pikes and short weapons, in short time took such order among these gallants (some using the butt-end of their pieces instead of other weapons), that partly by reason of our arrows which did us there notable service, partly by occasion of this strange and sudden closing with them in this manner unlooked for, and the rather for that at the very instant, our Captain's brother, with the other company, with their firepikes, entered the Market Place by the easter[n] street: they casting down their weapons, fled all out of the town by the gate aforesaid, which had been built for a bar to keep out of the town the Cimaroons, who had often assailed it; but now served for a gap for the Spaniards to fly at.

In following, and returning; divers of our men were hurt with the weapons which the enemy had let fall as he fled; somewhat, for that we marched with such speed, but more for that they lay so thick and cross one on the other.

Being returned, we made our stand near the midst of the Market Place, where a tree groweth hard by the Cross;

whence our Captain sent some of our men to stay the ringing of the alarm bell, which had continued all this while: but the church being very strongly built and fast shut, they could not without firing (which our Captain forbade) get into the steeple where the bell rung.

In the meantime, our Captain having taken two or three Spaniards in their flight, commanded them to shew him the Governor's House, where he understood was the ordinary place of unlading the moiles [*mules*] of all the treasure which came from Panama by the King's appointment. Although the silver only was kept there; the gold, pearl, and jewels (being there once entered by the King's officer) was carried from thence to the King's Treasure House not far off, being a house very strongly built of lime and stone, for the safe keeping thereof.

At our coming to the Governor's House, we found the great door where the mules do usually unlade, even then opened, a candle lighted upon the top of the stairs; and a fair gennet ready saddled, either for the Governor himself, or some other of his household to carry it after him. By means of this light we saw a huge heap of silver in that nether [*lower*] room; being a pile of bars of silver of, as near as we could guess, seventy feet in length, of ten feet in breadth, and twelve feet in height, piled up against the wall, each bar was between thirty-five and forty pounds in weight.

At sight hereof, our Captain commanded straightly that none of us should touch a bar of silver; but stand upon our weapons, because the town was full of people, and there was in the King's Treasure House near the water side, more gold and jewels than all our four pinnaces could carry: which we would presently set some in hand to break open, notwithstanding the Spaniards report the strength of it.

We were no sooner returned to our strength, but there was a report brought by some of our men that our pinnaces were in danger to be taken; and that if we ourselves got not aboard before day, we should be oppressed with multitude both of soldiers and towns-people. This report had his ground from one DIEGO a Negro, who, in the time of the first conflict, came and called to our pinnaces, to know "whether they were Captain DRAKE'S?" And upon answer received, continued entreating to be taken aboard, though he had first three or four shot made at him, until at length they fetched him; and learned by him, that, not past eight days before our arrival, the King had sent thither some 150 soldiers to guard the town against the Cimaroons, and the town at this time was full of people beside: which all the rather believed, because it agreed with the report of the Negroes, which we took before at the Isle of Pinos. And therefore our Captain sent his brother and JOHN OXNAM to understand the truth thereof.

They found our men which we left in our pinnaces much frightened, by reason that they saw great troops and companies running up and down, with matches lighted, some with other weapons, crying *Que gente? que gente?* which not having been at the first conflict, but coming from the utter ends of the town (being at least as big as Plymouth), came many times near us; and understanding that we were English, discharged their pieces and ran away.

Presently after this, a mighty shower of rain, with a terrible storm of thunder and lightning, fell, which poured down so vehemently (as it usually doth in those countries) that before we could recover the shelter of a certain shade or penthouse at the western end of the King's Treasure House, (which seemeth to have been built there of purpose to avoid sun and rain) some of our bow-strings were wet, and some of our match and powder hurt! which while we were careful of, to refurnish and supply; divers of our men harping on the reports lately brought us, were muttering of the forces of the town, which our Captain perceiving, told them, that "He had brought them to the mouth of the Treasure of the World, if they would want it, they might henceforth blame nobody but themselves!"

And therefore as soon as the storm began to assuage of his fury (which was a long half hour) willing to give his men no longer leisure to demur of those doubts, nor yet allow the enemy farther respite to gather themselves together, he stept forward commanding his brother, with JOHN OXNAM and the company appointed them, to break the King's Treasure House: the rest to follow him to keep the strength of the Market Place, till they had despatched the business for which they came.

But as he stepped forward, his strength and sight and speech failed him, and he began to faint for want of blood, which, as then we perceived, had, in great quantity, issued upon the sand, out of a wound received in his leg in the first encounter, whereby though he felt some pain, yet (for that he perceived divers of the company, having already gotten many good things, to be very ready to take all occasions, of winding themselves out of that conceited danger) would he not have it known to any, till this his fainting, against his will, bewrayed it: the blood having first filled the very prints which our footsteps made, to the greater dismay of all our company, who thought it not credible that one man should be able to spare so much blood and live.

And therefore even they, which were willing to have adventured the most for so fair a booty, would in no case hazard their Captain's life; but (having given him somewhat to drink wherewith he recovered himself, and having bound his scarf about his leg, for the stopping of the blood) entreated him to be content to go with them aboard, there to have his wound searched and dressed, and then to return on shore again if he thought good.

This when they could not persuade him unto (as who knew it to be utterly impossible, at least very unlikely, that ever they should, for that time, return again, to recover the state in which they now were: and was of opinion, that it were more honourable for himself, to jeopard his life for so great a benefit, than to leave off so high an enterprise unperformed), they joined altogether and with force mingled with fair entreaty, they bare him aboard his pinnace, and so abandoned a most rich spoil for the present, only to preserve their Captain's life: and being resolved of him, that while they enjoyed his presence, and had him to command them, they might recover wealth sufficient; but if once they lost him, they should hardly be able to recover home. No, not with that which they had gotten already.

Thus we embarked by break of the day (29th July), having besides our Captain, many of our men wounded, though none slain but one Trumpeter: whereupon though our surgeons were busily employed, in providing remedies and salves for their wounds: yet the main care of our Captain was respected by all the rest; so that before we departed out of the harbour for the more comfort of our company, we took the aforesaid ship of wines without great resistance.

But before we had her free of the haven, they of the town had made means to bring one of their culverins, which we had dismounted, so as they made a shot at us, but hindered us not from carrying forth the prize to the Isle of *Bastimentos*, or the Isle of Victuals: which is an island that lieth without the bay to the westward, about a league off the town, where we stayed the two next days, to cure our wounded men, and refresh ourselves, in the goodly gardens which we there found abounding with great store of all dainty roots and fruits; besides great plenty of poultry and other fowls, no less strange then delicate.

Shortly upon our first arrival in this island, the Governor and the rest of his Assistants in the town, as we afterwards understood, sent unto our Captain, a proper gentleman, of mean stature, good complexion, and a fair spoken, a principal soldier of the late sent garrison, to view in what state we were. At his coming he protested "He came to us, of mere good will, for that we had attempted so great and incredible a matter with so few men: and that, at the first, they feared that we had been French, at whose hands they knew they should find no mercy: but after they perceived by our arrows, that we were Englishmen, their fears were the less, for that they knew, that though we took the treasure of the place, yet we would not use cruelty toward their persons. But albeit this his affection gave him cause enough, to come aboard such, whose virtue he so honoured: yet the Governor also had not only consented to his coming, but directly sent him, upon occasion that divers of the town affirmed, said he, 'that they knew our Captain, who the last two years had been often on our coast, and had always used their persons very well.' And therefore desired to know, first, Whether our Captain was the same Captain Drake or not? and next, Because many of their men were wounded with our arrows, whether they were poisoned or not? and how their wounds might best be cured? lastly, What victuals we wanted, or other necessaries? of which the Governor promised by him to supply and furnish us, as largely as he durst."

Our Captain, although he thought this soldier but a spy: yet used him very courteously, and answered him to his Governor's demands: that "He was the same DRAKE whom they meant! It was never his manner to poison his arrows! They might cure their wounded by ordinary surgery! As for wants, he knew the Island of *Bastimentos* had sufficient, and could furnish him if he listed! but he wanted nothing but some of that special commodity which that country yielded, to content himself and his company." And therefore he advised the Governor "to hold open his eyes! for before he departed, if GOD lent him life and leave, he meant to reap some of their harvest, which they get out of the earth, and send into Spain to trouble all the earth!"

To this answer unlooked for, this gentleman replied, "If he might, without offence, move such a question, what should then be the cause of our departing from that town at this time, where was above 360 tons of silver ready for the Fleet, and much more gold in value, resting in iron chests in the King's Treasure House?"

But when our Captain had shewed him the true cause of his unwilling retreat aboard, he acknowledged that "we had no less reason in departing, than courage in attempting": and no doubt did easily see, that it was not for the town to seek revenge of us, by manning forth such frigates or other vessels as they had; but better to content themselves and provide for their own defence.

Thus, with great favour and courteous entertainment, besides such gifts from our Captain as most contented him, after dinner, he was in such sort dismissed, to make report of that he had seen, that he protested, "he was never so much honoured of any in his life."

After his departure, the Negro formentioned, being examined more fully, confirmed this report of the gold and the silver; with many other intelligences of importance: especially how we might have gold and silver enough, if we would, by means of the Cimaroons, whom though he had betrayed divers times (being used thereto by his Masters) so that he knew they would kill him, if they got him: yet if our Captain would undertake his protection, he durst adventure his life, because he knew our Captain's name was most precious and highly honoured by them.

This report ministered occasion to further consultation: for which, because this place seemed not the safest; as being neither the healthiest nor quietest; the next day, in the morning, we all set our course for the Isle of *Pinos* or Port Plenty, where we had left our ships, continuing all that day, and the next till towards night, before we recovered it.

We were the longer in this course, for that our Captain sent away his brother and Ellis Hixom to the westward, to search the River of Chagres, where himself had been the year before, and yet was careful to gain more notice of; it being a river which trendeth to the southward, within six leagues of Panama, where is a little town called Venta Cruz [*Venta de Cruzes*], whence all the treasure, that was usually brought thither from Panama by mules, was embarked in frigates [sailing] down that river into the North sea, and so to Nombre de Dios.

It ebbeth and floweth not far into the land, and therefore it asketh three days' rowing with a fine pinnace to pass [up] from the mouth to Venta Cruz; but one day and a night serveth to return down the river.

At our return to our ships (1st August), in our consultation, Captain Ranse (forecasting divers doubts of our safe continuance upon that coast, being now discovered) was willing to depart; and our Captain no less willing to dismiss him: and therefore as soon as our pinnaces returned from Chagres (7th August) with such advertisement as they were sent for, about eight days before; Captain Ranse took his leave, leaving us at the isle aforesaid, where we had remained five or six days.

In which meantime, having put all things in a readiness, our Captain resolved, with his two ships and three pinnaces to go to Cartagena; whither in sailing, we spent some six days by reason of the calms which came often upon us:

but all this time we attempted nothing that we might have done by the way, neither at [Santiago de] Tolou nor otherwhere, because we would not be discovered.

We came to anchor with our two ships in the evening [13th August], in seven fathom water, between the island of Charesha [*the island of Cartagena, p.* 161] and St. Barnards [*San Bernardo*].

Our Captain led the three pinnaces about the island, into the harbour of Cartagena; where at the very entry, he found a frigate at anchor, aboard which was only one old man; who being demanded, "Where the rest of his company was?" answered, "That they were gone ashore in their gundel oe[? *gondola or ship's boat*], that evening, to fight about a mistress": and voluntarily related to our Captain that, "two hours before night, there past by them a pinnace, with sail and oars, as fast as ever they could row, calling to him 'Whether there had not been any English or Frenchmen there lately?' and upon answer that, 'There had been none!' they bid them 'look to themselves!' That, within an hour that this pinnace was come to the utterside [*outside*] of Cartagena, there were many great pieces shot off, whereupon one going to top, to descry what might be the cause? espied, over the land, divers frigates and small shipping bringing themselves within the Castle."

This report our Captain credited, the rather for that himself had heard the report of the ordnance at sea; and perceived sufficiently, that he was now descried. Notwithstanding in farther examination of this old mariner, having understood, that there was, within the next point, a great ship of Seville, which had here discharged her loading, and rid now with her yards across, being bound the next morning for Santo Domingo: our Captain took this old man into his pinnace to verify that which he had informed, and rowed towards this ship, which as we came near it, hailed us, asking, "Whence our shallops were?"

We answered, "From Nombre de Dios!"

Straightway they railed! and reviled! We gave no heed to their words, but every pinnace, according to our Captain's order, one on the starboard bow, the other on the starboard quarter, and the Captain in the midship on the larboard side, forthwith boarded her; though we had some difficulty to enter by reason of her height, being of 240 tons. But as soon as we entered upon the decks, we threw down the grates and spardecks, to prevent the Spaniards from annoying us with their close fights: who then perceiving that we were possessed of their ship, stowed themselves all in hold with their weapons, except two or three yonkers, which were found afore the beetes: when having light out of our pinnaces, we found no danger of the enemy remaining, we cut their cables at halse, and with our three pinnaces, towed her without the island into the sound right afore the town, without [*beyond the*] danger of their great shot.

Meanwhile, the town having intelligence hereof, or by their watch, took the alarm, rang out their bells, shot off about thirty pieces of great ordnance, put all their men in a readiness, horse and foot, came down to the very point of the wood, and discharged their calivers, to impeach us if they might, in going forth.

The next morning (14th August) our ships took two frigates, in which there were two, who called themselves King's *Scrivanos,* the one of Cartagena, the other of Veragua, with seven mariners and two Negroes: who had been at Nombre de Dios and were now bound for Cartagena with double [? duplicate] letters of advice, to certify them that Captain DRAKE had been at Nombre de Dios, had taken it; and had it not been that he was hurt with some blessed shot, by all likelihood he had sacked it. He was yet still upon the coast; they should therefore carefully prepare for him!

After that our Captain had brought all his fleet together, at the *Scrivanos'* entreaties, he was content to do them all favour, in setting them and all their companies on shore; and so bare thence with the islands of St. Bernards, about three leagues of the town: where we found great store of fish for our refreshing.

Here, our Captain considering that he was now discovered upon the chiefest places of all the coast, and yet not meaning to leave it till he had found the Cimaroons, and "made" his voyage, as he had conceived; which would require some length of time, and sure manning of his pinnaces: he determined with himself, to burn one of the ships, and make the other a Storehouse; that his pinnaces (which could not otherwise) might be thoroughly manned, and so he might be able to abide any time.

But knowing the affection of his company, how loath they were to leave either of their ships, being both so good sailers and so well furnished; he purposed in himself by some policy, to make them most willing to effect that he intended. And therefore sent for one THOMAS MOONE, who was Carpenter in the *Swan,* and taking him into his cabin, chargeth him to conceal for a time, a piece of service, which he must in any case consent to do aboard his own ship: that was, in the middle of the second watch, to go down secretly into the well of the ship, and with a spike-gimlet, to bore three holes, as near the keel as he could, and lay something against it, that the force of the water entering, might make no great noise, nor be discovered by a boiling up.

THOMAS MOONE at the hearing hereof, being utterly dismayed, desired to know "What cause there might be, to move him to sink so good a bark of his own, new and strong; and that, by *his* means, who had been in two so rich and gainful voyages in her with himself heretofore: If his brother, the Master, and the rest of the company [*numbering 26, see p. 134*] should know of such his fact, he thought verily they would kill him."

But when our Captain had imparted to him his cause, and had persuaded him with promise that it should not be known, till all of them should be glad of it: he understood it, and did it accordingly.

The next morning [15th August] our Captain took his pinnace very early, purposing to go a fishing, for that there is very great store on the coast; and falling aboard the *Swan,* calleth for his brother to go with him, who rising suddenly, answereth that "He would follow presently, or if it would please him to stay a very little, he would attend him."

Our Captain perceiving the feat wrought, would not hasten him; but in rowing away, demanded of them, "Why their bark was so deep?" as making no great account of it. But, by occasion of this demand, his brother sent one down to the Steward, to know "Whether there were any water in the ship? or what other cause might be?"

The Steward, hastily stepping down at his usual scuttle, was wet up to his waist, and shifting with more haste to come up again as if the water had followed him, cried out that "The ship was full of water!" There was no need to hasten the company, some to the pump, others to search for the leak, which the Captain of the bark seeing they did, on all hands, very willingly; he followed his brother, and certified him of "the strange chance befallen them that night; that whereas they had not pumped twice in six weeks before, now they had six feet of water in hold: and therefore he desireth leave from attending him in fishing, to intend the search and remedy of the leak." And when our Captain with his company preferred [*offered*] to go to help them; he answered, "They had men enough aboard, and prayed him to continue his fishing, that they might have some part of it for their dinner." Thus returning, he found his company had taken great pain, but had freed the water very little: yet such was their love to the bark, as our Captain well knew, that they ceased not, but to the utmost of their strength, laboured all that they might till three in the afternoon; by which time, the company perceiving, that (though they had been relieved by our Captain himself and many of his company) yet they were not able to free above a foot and a half of water, and could have no likelihood of finding the leak, had now a less liking of her than before, and greater content to hear of some means for remedy.

Whereupon our Captain (consulting them what they thought best to be done) found that they had more desire to have all as he thought fit, than judgement to conceive any means of remedy. And therefore he propounded, that himself would go in the pinnace, till he could provide him some handsome frigate; and that his brother should be Captain in the admiral [*flag-ship*] and the Master should also be there placed with him, instead of this: which seeing they could not save, he would have fired that the enemy might never recovor her: but first all the pinnaces should be brought aboard her, that every one might take out of her whatever they lacked or liked.

This, though the company at the first marvelled at; yet presently it was put in execution and performed that night.

Our Captain had his desire, and men enough for his pinnaces.

The next morning (16th August) we resolved to seek out some fit place, in the Sound of Darien, where we might safely leave our ship at anchor, not discoverable by the enemy, who thereby might imagine us quite departed from the coast, and we the meantime better follow our purposes with our pinnaces; of which our Captain would himself take two to Rio Grande [*Magdalena*], and the third leave with his brother to seek the Cimaroons.

Upon this resolution, we set sail presently for the said Sound; which within five days (21st August), we recovered: abstaining of purpose from all such occasion, as might hinder our determination, or bewray [*betray*] our being upon the coast.

As soon as we arrived where our Captain intended, and had chosen a fit and convenient road out of all trade [*to or from any Mart*] for our purpose; we reposed ourselves there, for some fifteen days, keeping ourselves close, that the bruit of our being upon the coast might cease.

But in the meantime, we were not idle: for beside such ordinary works, as our Captain, every month did usually inure us to, about the trimming and setting of his pinnaces, for their better sailing and rowing: he caused us to rid a large plot of ground, both of trees and brakes, and to build us houses sufficient for all our lodging, and one especially for all our public meetings; wherein the Negro which fled to us before, did us great service, as being well acquainted with the country, and their means of building. Our archers made themselves butts to shoot at, because we had many that delighted in that exercise, and wanted not a fletcher to keep our bows and arrows in order. The rest of the company, every one as he liked best, made his disport at bowls, quoits, keiles, &c. For our Captain allowed one half of the company to pass their time thus, every other day interchangeable; the other half being enjoined to the necessary works, about our ship and pinnaces, and the providing of fresh victuals, fish, fowl, hogs, deer, conies, &c., whereof there is great plenty. Here our smiths set up their forge, as they used, being furnished out of England, with anvil, iron, coals, and all manner of necessaries, which stood us in great stead.

At the end of these fifteen days (5th September), our Captain leaving his ship in his brother's charge, to keep all things in order; himself took with him, according to his former determination, two pinnaces for Rio Grande, and passing by Cartagena but out of sight, when we were within two leagues of the river, we landed (8th September), to the westward on the Main, where we saw great store of cattle. There we found some Indians, who asking us in friendly sort, in broken Spanish, "What we would have"? and understanding that we desired fresh victuals in traffic; they took such cattle for us as we needed, with ease and so readily, as if they had a special commandment over them, whereas they would not abide us to come near them. And this also they did willingly, because our Captain, according to his custom, contented them for their pains, with such things as they account greatly of; in such sort that they promised, we should have there, of them at any time what we would.

The same day, we departed thence to Rio Grande [*Magdalena*], where we entered about three of the clock in the afternoon. There are two entries into this river, of which we entered the wester[n] most called *Boca Chica.* The freshet [*current*] is so great, that we being half a league from the mouth of it, filled fresh water for our beverage.

From three o'clock till dark at night, we rowed up the stream; but the current was so strong downwards, that we got but two leagues, all that time. We moored our pinnaces to a tree that night: for that presently, with the closing of the evening, there fell a monstrous shower of rain, with such strange and terrible claps of thunder, and flashes of lightning, as made us not a little to marvel at, although our Captain had been acquainted with such like in that country, and told us that they continue seldom longer than three-quarters of an hour.

This storm was no sooner ceast, but it became very calm, and therewith there came such an innumerable multitude of a kind of flies of that country, called mosquitoes, like our gnats, which bite so spitefully, that we could not rest all that night, nor find means to defend ourselves from them, by reason of the heat of the country. The best remedy we then found against them, was the juice of lemons.

At the break of day (9th Sept.), we departed, rowing in the eddy, and hauling up by the trees where the eddy failed, with great labour, by spells, without ceasing, each company their half-hour glass: without meeting any, till about three o'clock in the afternoon, by which time we could get but five leagues ahead.

Then we espied a canoe, with two Indians fishing in the river; but we spake not to them, least so we might be descried: nor they to us, as taking us to be Spaniards. But within an hour after, we espied certain houses, on the other side of the river, whose channel is twenty-five fathom deep, and its breadth so great, that a man can scantly be discerned from side to side. Yet a Spaniard which kept those houses, had espied our pinnaces; and thinking we had been his countrymen, made a smoke, for a signal to turn that way, as being desirous to speak with us. After that, we espying this smoke, had made with it, and were half the river over, he wheaved [*waved*] to us, with his hat and his long hanging sleeves, to come ashore.

But as we drew nearer to him, and he discerned that we were not those he looked for; he took his heels, and fled from his houses, which we found to be, five in number, all full of white rusk, dried bacon, that country cheese (like Holland cheese in fashion, but far more delicate in taste, of which they send into Spain as special presents) many sorts of sweetmeats, and conserves; with great store of sugar: being provided to serve the Fleet returning to Spain.

With this store of victuals, we loaded our pinnaces; by the shutting in of the day, we were ready to depart; for that we hastened the rather, by reason of an intelligence given us by certain Indian women which we found in those houses: that the frigates (these are ordinarily thirty, or upwards, which usually transport the merchandise, sent out of Spain to Cartagena from thence to these houses, and so in great canoes up hence into Nuevo Reyno, for which the river running many hundred of leagues within the land serveth very fitly: and return in exchange, the gold and treasure, silver, victuals, and commodities, which that kingdom yields abundantly) were not yet returned from Cartagena, since the first alarm they took of our being there.

As we were going aboard our pinnaces from these Storehouses (10th Sept.), the Indians of a great town called Villa del Rey, some two miles distant from the water's side where we landed, were brought down by the Spaniards into the bushes, and shot arrows; but we rowed down the stream with the current (for that the wind was against us) only one league; and because it was night, anchored till the morning, when we rowed down to the mouth of the river, where we unloaded all our provisions, and cleansed our pinnaces, according to our Captain's custom, and took it in again, and the same day went to the Westward.

In this return, we descried a ship, a barque, and a frigate, of which the ship and frigate went for Cartagena, but the Barque was bound to the Northwards, with the wind easterly, so that we imagined she had some gold or treasure going for Spain: therefore we gave her chase, but taking her, and finding nothing of importance in her, understanding that she was bound for sugar and hides, we let her go; and having a good gale of wind, continued our former course to our ship and company.

In the way between Cartagena and Tolou, we took [11th September] five or six frigates, which were laden from Tolou, with live hogs, hens, and maize which we call Guinea wheat. Of these, having gotten what intelligence they could give, of their preparations for us, and divers opinions of us, we dismissed all the men; only staying two frigates with us, because they were so well stored with good victuals.

Within three days after, we arrived at the place which our Captain chose, at first, to leave his ship in, which was called by our Captain, Port Plenty; by reason we brought in thither continually all manner store of good victuals, which we took, going that way by sea, for the victualling of Cartagena and Nombre de Dios as also the Fleets going and coming out of Spain. So that if we had been two thousand, yea three thousand persons, we might with our pinnaces easily have provided them sufficient victuals of wine, meal, rusk; *cassavi* (a kind of bread made of a root called Yucca, whose juice is poison, but the substance good and wholesome), dried beef, dried fish, live sheep, live hogs, abundance of hens, besides the infinite store of dainty flesh fish, very easily to be taken every day; insomuch that we were forced to build four several magazines or store-houses, some ten, some twenty leagues asunder; some in islands, some in the Main, providing ourselves in divers places, that though the enemy should, with force, surprise any one, yet we might be sufficiently furnished, till we had "made" our voyage as we did hope. In building of these, our Negro's help was very much, as having a special skill, in the speedy erection of such houses.

This our store was much, as thereby we relieved not only ourselves and the Cimaroons while they were with us; but also two French ships in extreme want.

For in our absence, Captain JOHN DRAKE, having one of our pinnaces, as was appointed, went in with the Main, and as he rowed aloof the shore, where he was directed by DIEGO the Negro aforesaid, which willingly came unto us at Nombre de Dios, he espied certain of the Cimaroons; with whom he dealt so effectually, that in conclusion he left two of our men with their leader, and brought aboard two of theirs: agreeing that they should meet him again the next day, at a river midway between the Cabezas [*Cabeza is Spanish for Headland*] and our ships; which they named Rio Diego.

These two being very sensible men, chosen out by their commander [*chief*], did, with all reverence and respect, declare unto our Captain, that their nation conceited great joy of his arrival, because they knew him to be an enemy to the Spaniards, not only by his late being in Nombre de Dios, but also by his former voyages; and therefore were ready to assist and favour his enterprises against his and their enemies to the uttermost: and to that end their captain and company did stay at this present near the mouth of Rio Diego, to attend what answer and order should be given them; that they would have marched by land, even to this place, but that the way is very long, and more troublesome, by reason of many steep mountains, deep rivers, and thick brakes: desiring therefore, that it might please our Captain to take some order, as he thought best, with all convenient speed in this behalf.

Our Captain considering the speech of these persons, and weighing it with his former intelligences had not only by Negroes, but Spaniards also, whereof he was always very careful: as also conferring it with his brother's informations of the great kindness that they shewed him, being lately with them: after he had heard the opinions of those of best service with him, "what were fittest to be done presently?" resolved himself with his brother, and the two Cimaroons, in his two pinnaces, to go toward this river. As he did the same evening, giving order, that the ship and the rest of his fleet should the next morning follow him, because there was a place of as great safety and sufficiency, which his brother had found out near the river. The safety of it consisted, not only in that which is common all along that coast from Tolou to Nombre de Dios, being above sixty leagues, that it is a most goodly and plentiful country, and yet inhabited not with one Spaniard, or any for the Spaniards: but especially in that it lieth among a great many of goodly islands full of trees. Where, though there be channels, yet there are such rocks and shoals, that no man can enter by night without great danger; nor by day without discovery, whereas our ships might lie hidden within the trees.

The next day (14th September) we arrived at this river appointed, where we found the Cimaroons according to promise: the rest of their number were a mile up, in a wood by the river's side. There after we had given them entertainment, and received good testimonies of their joy and good will towards us, we took two more of them into our pinnace, leaving our two men with the rest of theirs, to march by land, to another river called Rio Guana, with intent there to meet with another company of Cimaroons which were now in the mountains.

So we departed that day from Rio Diego, with our pinnaces, towards our ship, as marvelling that she followed us not as was appointed.

But two days after (16th September), we found her in the place where we left her; but in far other state, being much spoiled and in great danger, by reason of a tempest she had in our absence.

As soon as we could trim our ship, being some two days, our Captain sent away (18th September) one of his pinnaces, towards the bottom of the bay, amongst the shoals and sandy islands, to sound out the channel, for the bringing in of our ship nearer the Main.

The next day (19th September) we followed, and were with wary pilotage, directed safely into the best channel, with much ado to recover the road, among so many flats and shoals. It was near about five leagues from the Cativaas, betwixt an island and the Main, where we moored our ship. The island was not above four cables in length from the Main, being in quantity some three acres of ground, flat and very full of trees and bushes.

We were forced to spend the best part of three days, after our departure from our Port Plenty, before we were quiet in this new found road [*on Rio Diego, see pp.* 157 *and* 158] (22nd September), which we had but newly entered, when our two men and the former troop of Cimaroons, with twelve others whom they had met in the mountains, came (23rd September) in sight over against our ship, on the Main. Whence we fet[ched] them all aboard, to their great comfort and our content: they rejoicing that they should have some fit opportunity to wreak their wrongs on the Spaniards; we hoping that now our voyage should be bettered.

At our first meeting, when our Captain had moved them, to shew him the means which they had to furnish him with gold and silver; they answered plainly, that "had they known gold had been his desire; they would have satisfied him with store, which, for the present, they could not do:

because the rivers, in which they sunk great store (which they had taken from the Spaniards, rather to despite them than for love of gold) were now so high, that they could not get it out of such depths for him; and because the Spaniards, in these rainy months, do not use [*are not accustomed*] to carry their treasure by land."

This answer although it were somewhat unlooked for; yet nothing discontented us, but rather persuaded us farther of their honest and faithful meaning toward us. Therefore our Captain to entertain these five months, commanded all our ordnance and artillery ashore, with all our other provisions: sending his pinnaces to the Main, to bring over great trees, to make a fort upon the same island, for the planting of all our ordnance therein, and for our safeguard, if the enemy, in all this time, should chance to come.

Our Cimaroons (24th September) cut down Palmito boughs and branches, and with wonderful speed raised up two large houses for all our company. Our fort was then made, by reason of the place, triangle-wise, with main timber, and earth of which the trench yielded us good store, so that we made it thirteen feet in height. [*Fort Diego.*]

But after we had continued upon this island fourteen days, our Captain having determined, with three pinnaces, to go for Cartagena left (7th October), his brother JOHN DRAKE, to govern these who remained behind with the Cimaroons to finish the fort which he had begun: for which he appointed him to fetch boards and planks, as many as his pinnaces would carry, from the prize we took at Rio Grande, and left at the Cativaas, where she drove ashore and wrecked in our absence: but now she might serve commodiously, to supply our use, in making platforms for our ordnance. Thus our Captain and his brother took their leave; the one to the Eastward, and the other to the Cativaas.

That night, we came to an isle, which he called Spur-kite land, because we found there great store of such a kind of bird in shape, but very delicate, of which we killed and roasted many; staying there till the next day midnoon (8th October), when we departed thence. And about four o'clock recovered a big island in our way, where we stayed all night, by reason that there was great store of fish, and especially of a great kind of shell-fish of a foot long. We called them Whelks.

The next morning (9th October), we were clear of these islands and shoals, and hauled off into the sea. About four days after (13th October), near the island of St. Bernards, we chased two frigates ashore; and recovering one of these islands, made our abode there some two days (14th-15th October) to wash our pinnaces and to take of the fish.

Thence we went towards Tolou, and that day (16th October) landed near the town in a garden, where we found certain Indians, who delivered us their bows and arrows, and gathered for us such fruit as the garden did yield, being many sorts of dainty fruits and roots, [we] still contenting them for what we received. Our Captain's principal intent in taking this and other places by the way, not being for any other cause, but only to learn true intelligence of the state of the country and of the Fleets.

Hence we departed presently, and rowed towards Charesha, the island of Cartagena; and entered in at Bocha Chica, and having the wind large, we sailed in towards the city, and let fall our grappers [*grappling irons*] betwixt the island and the Main, right over against the goodly Garden Island. In which, our Captain would not suffer us to land, notwithstanding our importunate desire, because he knew, it might be dangerous: for that they are wont to send soldiers thither, when they know of any Men-of-war on the coast; which we found accordingly. For within three hours after, passing by the point of the island, we had a volley of a hundred shot from them, and yet there was but one of our men hurt.

This evening (16th October) we departed to sea; and the day following (17th October), being some two leagues off the harbour, we took a bark, and found that the captain and his wife with the better sort of the passengers, had forsaken her, and were gone ashore in the Gundeloe [*ship's boat*]: by occasion whereof we boarded without resistance, though they were well provided with swords and targets and some small shot, besides four iron bases. She was 50 tons, having ten mariners, five or six Negroes, great store of soap and sweet meat, bound from St. Domingo to Cartagena. This Captain left behind him a silk ancient [*flag*] with his arms; as might be thought, in hasty departing.

The next day (18th October), we sent all the company ashore to seek their masters, saving a young Negro two or three years old, which we brought away; but kept the bark, and in her, bore into the mouth of Cartagena harbour, where we anchored.

That afternoon, certain horsemen came down to the point by the wood side, and with the *Scrivano* fore-mentioned, came towards our bark with a flag of truce, desiring of our Captain's safe conduct for his coming and going; the which being granted, he came aboard us, giving our Captain "great thanks for his manifold favours, etc., promising that night before daybreak, to bring as much victuals as they would desire, what shift so ever he made, or what danger soever incurred of law and punishment." But this fell out to be nothing but a device of the Governor forced upon the *Scrivano,* to delay time, till they might provide themselves of sufficient strength to entrap us: for which this fellow, by his smooth speech, was thought a fit means. So by sun rising, (19th October), when we perceived his words but words, we put to sea to the westward of the island, some three leagues off, where we lay at hull the rest of all that day and night.

The next day (20th October), in the afternoon, there came out of Cartagena, two frigates bound for St. Domingo, the one of 58, the other of 12 tons, having nothing in them but ballast. We took them within a league of the town, and came to anchor with them within sacre shot of the east Bulwark. There were in those frigates some twelve or thirteen common mariners, which entreated to be set ashore. To them our Captain gave the great[er] frigate's gundeloe, and dismissed them.

The next morning (21st October) when they came down to the wester[n] point with a flag of truce, our Captain manned one of his pinnaces and rowed ashore. When we were within a cable's length of the shore, the Spaniards fled hiding themselves in the woods, as being afraid of our ordnance; but indeed to draw us on to land confidently, and to presume of our strength. Our Captain commanding the grapnell to be cast out of the stern, veered the pinnace ashore, and as soon as she touched the sand, he alone leapt ashore in their sight, to declare that he durst set his foot a land: but stayed not among them, to let them know, that though he had not sufficient forces to conquer them, yet he had sufficient judgment to take heed of them.

And therefore perceiving their intent, as soon as our Captain was aboard, we hauled off upon our grapner and rid awhile.

They presently came forth upon the sand[s], and sent a youth, as with a message from the Governor, to know, "What our intent was, to stay upon the coast?"

Our Captain answered: "He meant to traffic with them; for he had tin, pewter, cloth, and other merchandise that they needed."

The youth swam back again with this answer, and was presently returned, with another message: that, "The King had forbidden to traffic with any foreign nation for any commodities, except powder and shot; of which, if he had any store, they would be his merchants."

He answered, that "He was come from his country, to exchange his commodities for gold and silver, and is not purposed to return without his errand. They are like, in his opinion, to have little rest, if that, by fair means, they would not traffic with him."

He gave this messenger a fair shirt for a reward, and so returned him: who rolled his shirt about his head and swam very speedily.

We heard no answer all that day; and therefore toward night we went aboard our frigates and reposed ourselves, setting and keeping very orderly all that night our watch, with great and small shot.

The next morning (22nd October) the wind, which had been westerly in the evening, altered to the Eastward.

About the dawning of the day, we espied two sails turning towards us, whereupon our Captain weighed with his pinnaces, leaving the two frigates unmanned. But when we were come somewhat nigh them, the wind calmed, and we were fain to row towards them, till that approaching very nigh, we saw many heads peering over board. For, as we perceived, these two frigates were manned and set forth out of Cartagena, to fight with us, and, at least, to impeach or busy us; whilst by some means or other they might recover the frigates from us.

But our Captain prevented both their drifts. For commanding JOHN OXNAM to stay with the one pinnace, to entertain these two Men-of-war; himself in the other made such speed, that he got to his frigates which he had left at anchor; and caused the Spaniards (who in the meantime had gotten aboard in a small canoe, thinking to have towed them within the danger of their shot) to make greater haste thence, than they did thither.

For he found that in shifting thence, some of them were fain to swim aland (the canoe not being able to receive them) and had left their apparel, some their rapiers and targets, some their flasks and calivers behind them; although they were towing away of one of them.

Therefore considering that we could not man them, we sunk the one, and burnt the other, giving them to understand by this, that we perceived their secret practices.

This being done, he returned to JOHN OXNAM; who all this while lay by the Men-of-war without proffering to fight. And as soon as our Captain was come up to these frigates, the wind blew much from the sea, so that, we being betwixt the shore and them, were in a manner forced to bear room into the harbour before them, to the great joy of the Spaniards; who beheld it; in supposing, that we would still have fled before them. But as soon as we were in the harbour, and felt smooth water, our pinnaces, as we were assured of, getting the wind, we sought with them upon the advantage, so that after a few shot exchanged, and a storm rising, they were contented to press no nearer. Therefore as they let fall their anchors, we presently let drop our grapner in the wind of them: which the Spanish soldiers seeing, considering the disadvantage of the wind, the likelihood of the storm to continue, and small hope of doing any good, they were glad to retire themselves to the town.

But by reason of the foul and tempestuous weather, we

rode therein four days, feeling great cold, by reason we had such sore rains with westerly wind, and so little succour in our pinnaces.

The fifth day (27th October) there came in a frigate from the sea, which seeing us make towards her, ran herself ashore, unhanging her rudder and taking away her sails, that she might not easily be carried away. But when we were come up to her, we perceived about a hundred horse and foot, with their furniture, come down to the point of the Main, where we interchanged some shot with them. One of our great shot passed so near a brave cavalier of theirs, that thereby they were occasioned to advise themselves, and retreat into the woods: where they might sufficiently defend and rescue the frigate from us, and annoy us also, if we stayed long about her.

Therefore we concluded to go to sea again, putting forth through *Boca Chica,* with intent to take down our masts, upon hope of fair weather, and to ride under the rocks called *Las Serenas,* which are two leagues off at sea, as we had usually done aforetime, so that they could not discern us from the rocks. But, there, the sea was mightily grown, that we were forced to take the harbour again; where we remained six days, notwithstanding the Spaniards grieved greatly at our abode there so long.

They put (2nd November) another device in practice to endanger us.

For they sent forth a great shallop, a fine gundeloe, and a great canoe, with certain Spaniards with shot, and many Indians with poisoned arrows, as it seemed, with intent to begin some fight, and then to fly. For as soon as we rowed toward them and interchanged shot, they presently retired and went ashore into the woods, where an ambush of some sixty shot were laid for us: besides two pinnaces and a frigate warping towards us, which were manned as the rest. They attempted us very boldly, being assisted by those others, which from out of the wood, had gotten aboard the gundeloe and canoe, and seeing us bearing from them (which we did in respect of the *ambuscado*), they encouraged themselves and assured their fellows of the day.

But our Captain weighing this their attempt, and being

out of danger of their shot from the land, commanding his other pinnace to be brought ahead of him, and to let fall their grapners each ahead the other, environed both the pinnaces with bonnets, as for a close fight, and then wheaved [*waved*] them aboard him.

They kept themselves upon their oars at caliver-shot distance, spending powder apace; as we did some two or three hours. We had only one of our men wounded in that fight. What they had is unknown to us, but we saw their pinnaces shot through in divers places, and the powder of one of them took fire; whereupon we weighed, intending to bear room to overrun them: which they perceiving, and thinking that we would have boarded them, rowed away amain to the defence they had in the wood, the rather because they were disappointed of their help that they expected from the frigate; which was warping towards us, but by reason of the much wind that blew, could not come to offend us or succour them.

Thus seeing that we were still molested, and no hope remained of any purchase to be had in this place any longer; because we were now so notably made known in those parts, and because our victuals grew scant: as soon as the weather waxed somewhat better (the wind continuing always westerly, so that we could not return to our ships) our Captain thought best to go (3rd November) to the Eastward, towards *Rio Grande* [Magdalena] long the coast, where we had been before, and found great store of victuals.

But when after two days' sailing, we were arrived (5th November) at the villages of store, where before we had furnished ourselves with abundance of hens, sheep, calves, hogs, &c.; now we found bare nothing, not so much as any people left: for that they, by the Spaniards' commandments, had fled to the mountains, and had driven away all their cattle, that we might not be relieved by them. Herewith being very sorry, because much of our victuals in our pinnaces was spoilt by the foul weather at sea and rains in harbour. A frigate being descried at sea revived us, and put us in some hope for the time, that in her we should find sufficient; and thereupon it may easily be guessed, how much we laboured to recover her: but when we had boarded her, and understood that she had neither meat nor money, but that she was bound for *Rio Grande* to take in provision upon bills, our great hope converted into grief.

We endured with our allowance seven or eight days more, proceeding to the Eastward, and bearing room for Santa Marta, upon hope to find some shipping in the road, or limpets on the rocks, or succour against the storm in that good harbour. Being arrived; and seeing no shipping; we anchored under the wester[n] point, where is high land, and, as we thought, free in safety from the town, which is in the bottom of the bay: not intending to land there, because we knew that it was fortified, and that they had intelligence of us.

But the Spaniards (knowing us to be Men-of-war, and misliking that we should shroud under their rocks without their leave) had conveyed some thirty or forty shot among the cliffs, which annoyed us so spitefully and so unrevengedly, for that they lay hidden behind the rocks, but we lay open to them, that we were soon weary of our harbour, and enforced (for all the storm without and want within) to put to sea. Which though these enemies of ours were well contented withal, yet for a farewell, as we came open of the town, they sent us a culverin shot; which made a near escape, for it fell between our pinnaces, as we were upon conference of what was best to be done.

The company advised that if it pleased him, they might put themselves a land, some place to the Eastward to get victuals, and rather hope for courtesy from the country-people, than continue at sea, in so long cold, and great a storm in so leaky a pinnace. But our Captain would in no wise like of that advice; he thought it better to bear up towards Rio de [la] Hacha, or Coriçao [*Curaçao*], with hope to have plenty without great resistance: because he knew, either of the islands were not very populous, or else it would be very likely that there would be found ships of victual in a readiness.

The company of the other pinnace answered, that "They would willingly follow him through the world; but in this they could not see how either their pinnaces should live in that sea, without being eaten up in that storm, or they themselves able to endure so long time, with so slender provision as they had, viz., only one gammon of bacon and thirty pounds of biscuit for eighteen men."

Our Captain replied, that "They were better provided than himself was, who had but one gammon of bacon, and forty pounds of biscuit for his twenty-four men; and therefore he doubted not but they would take such part as he did, and willingly depend upon GOD's Almighty providence, which never faileth them that trust in Him."

With that he hoisted his foresail, and set his course for Coriçao; which the rest perceiving with sorrowful hearts in respect of the weak pinnace, yet desirous to follow their Captain, consented to take the same course.

We had not sailed past three leagues, but we had espied a sail plying to the Westward, with her two courses, to our great joy: who vowed together, that we would have her, or else it should cost us dear.

Bearing with her, we found her to be a Spanish ship of above 90 tons, which being wheaved [*waved*] amain by us, despised our summons, and shot off her ordnance at us.

The sea went very high, so that it was not for us to attempt to board her, and therefore we made fit small sail to attend upon her, and keep her company to her small content, till fairer weather might lay the sea. We spent not past two hours in our attendance, till it pleased GOD, after a great shower, to send us a reasonable calm, so that we might use our pieces [*i. e., bases*] and approach her at pleasure, in such sort that in short time we had taken her; finding her laden with victuals well powdered [*salted*] and dried: which at that present we received as sent us of GOD's great mercy.

After all things were set in order, and that the wind increased towards night, we plied off and on, till day (13th November), at what time our Captain sent in ELLIS HIXOM, who had then charge of his pinnace, to search out some harbour along the coast; who having found out a little one, some ten or twelve leagues to the east of Santa Marta, where in sounding he had good ground and sufficient water, presently returned, and our Captain brought in his new prize. Then by promising liberty, and all the apparel to the

Spaniards which we had taken, if they would bring us to water and fresh victuals; the rather by their means, we obtained of the inhabitants (Indians) what they had, which was plentiful. These Indians were clothed and governed by a Spaniard, which dwelt in the next town, not past a league off. We stayed there all day, watering and wooding, and providing things necessary, by giving content and satisfaction of the Indians. But towards night our captain called all of us aboard (only leaving the Spaniards lately taken in the prize ashore, according to our promise made them, to their great content; who acknowledged that our Captain did them a far greater favour in setting them freely at liberty, than he had done them displeasure in taking their ship), and so set sail.

The sickness which had begun to kindle among us, two or three days before, did this day shew itself, in CHARLES GLUB, one of our Quarter-Masters, a very tall man, and a right good mariner; taken away, to the great grief both of Captain and company. What the cause of this malady was, we knew not of certainty, we imputed it to the cold which our men had taken, lying without succour in the pinnaces. But howsoever it was, thus it pleased GOD to visit us, and yet in favour to restore unto health all the rest of our company, that were touched with this disease; which were not a few.

The next morning (15th November) being fair weather, though the wind continued contrary, our Captain commanded the *Minion,* his lesser pinnace, to hasten away before him towards his ships at Fort Diego within the Cabeças [*Headlands*] to carry news of his coming, and to put all things in a readiness for our land journey, if they heard anything of the Fleet's arrival by the Cimaroons; giving the *Minion* charge if they wanted wine, to take St. Bernards in their way, and there take in some such portion as they thought good, of the wines which we had there hidden in the sand.

We plied to windwards, as near as we could, so that within seven-night after the *Minion* departed from us, we came (22nd November) to St. Bernards, finding but twelve *botijos* of wine of all the store we left, which had escaped the curious search of the enemy, who had been there; for they were deep in the ground.

Within four or five days after, we came (27th November) to our ship, where we found all other things in good order; but received very heavy news of the death of JOHN DRAKE, our Captain's brother, and another young man called RICHARD ALLEN, which were both slain at one time (9th October), as they attempted the boarding of a frigate, within two days after our departing from them.

The manner of it, as we learned by examination of the company, was this. When they saw this frigate at sea, as they were going towards their fort with planks to make the platforms, the company were very importunate on him, to give chase and set upon this frigate, which they deemed had been a fit booty for them. But he told them, that they "wanted weapons to assail; they knew not how the frigate was provided, they had their boats loaded with planks, to finish that his brother had commanded." But when this would not satisfy them, but that still they urged him with words and supposals: "If you will needs," said he, "adventure! it shall never be said that I will be hindmost, neither shall you report to my brother, that you lost your voyage by any cowardice you found in me!"

Thereupon every man shifted as they might for the time: and heaving their planks overboard, took them such poor weapons as they had: viz., a broken pointed rapier, one old visgee, and a rusty caliver: JOHN DRAKE took the rapier, and made a gauntlet of his pillow, RICHARD ALLEN the visgee, both standing at the head of the pinnace, called *Eion*. ROBERT took the caliver and so boarded. But they found the frigate armed round about with a close fight of hides, full of pikes and calivers, which were discharged in their faces, and deadly wounded those that were in the fore-ship, JOHN DRAKE in the belly, and RICHARD ALLEN in the head. But notwithstanding their wounds, they with oars shifted off the pinnace, got clear of the frigate, and with all haste recovered their ship: where within an hour after, this young man of great hope, ended his days, greatly lamented of all the company.

Thus having moored our ships fast, our Captain resolved to keep himself close without being descried, until he might hear of the coming of the Spanish Fleet; and therefore set no more to sea; but supplied his wants, both for his own company and the Cimaroons, out of his foresaid magazine, beside daily out of the woods, with wild hogs, pheasants, and guanas: continuing in health (GOD be praised) all the meantime, which was a month at least; till at length about the beginning of January, half a score of our company fell down sick together (3rd Jan. 1573), and the most of them died within two or three days. So long that we had thirty at a time sick of this *calenture,* which attacked our men, either by reason of the sudden change from cold to heat, or by reason of brackish water which had been taken in by our pinnace, through the sloth of their men in the mouth of the river, not rowing further in where the water was good.

Among the rest, JOSEPH DRAKE, another of his brethren, died in our Captain's arms, of the same disease: of which, that the cause might be the better discerned, and consequently remedied, to the relief of others, by our Captain's appointment he was ripped open by the surgeon, who found his liver swollen, his heart as it were sodden, and his guts all fair. This was the first and last experiment that our Captain made of anatomy in this voyage.

The Surgeon that cut him open, over-lived him not past four days, although he was not touched with that sickness, of which he had been recovered about a month before: but only of an over-bold practice which he would needs make upon himself, by receiving an over-strong purgation of his own device, after which taken, he never spake; nor his Boy recovered the health which he lost by tasting it, till he saw England.

The Cimaroons, who, as is before said, had been entertained by our Captain in September last, and usually repaired to our ship, during all the time of our absence, ranged the country up and down, between Nombre de Dios and us, to learn what they might for us; whereof they gave our Captain advertisement, from time to time; as now particularly, certain of them let him understand, that the Fleet had certainly arrived in Nombre de Dios.

Therefore he sent (30th January) the *Lion,* to the sea-most islands of the Cativaas, to descry the truth of the report: by reason it must needs be, that if the Fleet were in Nombre de Dios, all frigates of the country would repair thitherward with victuals.

The *Lion,* within a few days descried that she was sent for, espying a frigate, which she presently boarded and took, laden with maize, hens, and pompions from Tolou; who assured us of the whole truth of the arrival of the Fleet: in this frigate were taken one woman and twelve men, of whom one was the *Scrivano* of Tolou. These we used very courteously, keeping them diligently guarded from the deadly hatred of the Cimaroons; who sought daily by all means they could, to get them of our Captain, that they might cut their throats, to revenge their wrongs and injuries which the Spanish nation had done them: but our Captain persuaded them not to touch them, or give them ill countenance, while they were in his charge; and took order for their safety, not only in his presence, but also in his absence. For when he had prepared to take his journey for Panama, by land; he gave ELLIS HIXOM charge of his own ship and company, and especially of those Spaniards whom he had put into the great prize, which was hauled ashore to the island, which we termed Slaughter Island (because so many of our men died there), and used as a storehouse for ourselves, and a prison for our enemies.

All things thus ordered, our Captain conferring with his company, and the chiefest of the Cimaroons, what provisions were to be prepared for this great and long journey, what kind of weapons, what store of victuals, and what manner of apparel: was especially advised, to carry as great store of shoes as possible he might, by reason of so many rivers with stone and gravel as they were to pass. Which, accordingly providing, prepared his company for that journey, entering it upon Shrove-Tuesday (3rd February). At what time, there had died twenty-eight of our men, and a few whole men were left aboard with ELLIS HIXOM to keep the ship, and attend the sick, and guard the prisoners.

At his departure our Captain gave this Master straight charge, in any case not to trust any messenger, that should come in his name with any tokens, unless he brought his handwriting: which he knew could not be counterfeited by the Cimaroons or Spaniards.

We were in all forty-eight, of which eighteen only were English; the rest were Cimaroons, which beside their arms, bare every one of them, a great quantity of victuals and provision, supplying our want of carriage in so long a march, so that we were not troubled with anything but our furniture. And because they could not carry enough to suffice us altogether; therefore (as they promised before) so by the way with their arrows, they provided for us competent store from time to time.

They have every one of them two sorts of arrows: the one to defend himself and offend the enemy, the other to kill his victuals. These for fight are somewhat like the Scottish arrow; only somewhat longer, and headed with iron, wood, or fish bones. But the arrows for provision are of three sorts, the first serveth to kill any great beast near [at] hand, as ox, stag, or wild boar: this hath a head of iron of a pound and a half weight, shaped in form like the head of a javelin or boar-spear, as sharp as any knife, making so large and deep a wound as can hardly be believed of him that hath not seen it. The second serveth for lesser beasts, and hath a head of three-quarters of a pound: this he most usually shooteth. The third serveth for all manner of birds: it hath a head of an ounce weight. And these heads though they be of iron only, yet are they so cunningly tempered, that they will continue a very good edge a long time: and though they be turned sometimes, yet they will never or seldom break. The necessity in which they stand hereof continually causeth them to have iron in far greater account than gold: and no man among them is of greater estimation, than he that can most perfectly give this temper unto it.

Every day we were marching by sun-rising. We continued till ten in the forenoon: then resting (ever near some river) till past twelve, we marched till four, and then by some river's side, we reposed ourselves in such houses, as either we found prepared heretofore by them, when they travelled through these woods, or they daily built very readily for us in this manner.

As soon as we came to the place where we intended to lodge, the Cimaroons, presently laying down their burdens, fell to cutting of forks or posts, and poles or rafters, and palmito boughs, or plantain leaves; and with great speed set up to the number of six houses. For every of which, they first fastened deep into the ground, three or four great posts with forks: upon them, they laid one transom, which was commonly about twenty feet, and made the sides, in the manner of the roofs of our country houses, thatching it close with those aforesaid leaves, which keep out water a long time: observing always that in the lower ground, where greater heat was, they left some three or four feet open unthatched below, and made the houses, or rather roofs, so many feet the higher. But in the hills, where the air was more piercing and the nights cold, they made our rooms always lower, and thatched them close to the ground, leaving only one door to enter in, and a lover [*louvre*] hole for a vent, in the midst of the roof. In every [one] of these, they made four several lodgings, and three fires, one in the midst, and one at each end of every house: so that the room was most temperately warm, and nothing annoyed with smoke, partly by reason of the nature of the wood which they use to burn, yielding very little smoke, partly by reason of their artificial making of it: as firing the wood cut in length like our billets at the ends, and joining them together so close, that though no flame or fire did appear, yet the heat continued without intermission.

Near many of the rivers where we stayed or lodged, we found sundry sorts of fruits, which we might use with great pleasure and safety temperately: Mammeas, Guayvas, Palmitos, Pinos, Oranges, Lemons, and divers other; from eating of which, they dissuaded us in any case, unless we eat very few of them, and those first dry roasted, as Plantains, Potato[e]s, and such like.

In journeying, as oft as by chance they found any wild swine, of which those hills and valleys have store, they would ordinarily, six at a time, deliver their burdens to the rest of their fellows, pursue, kill and bring away after us, as much as they could carry, and time permitted. One day as we travelled, the Cimaroons found an otter, and prepared it to be drest: our Captain marvelling at it, PEDRO, our chief Cimaroon, asked him, "Are you a man of war, and in want; and yet doubt whether this be meat, that hath blood?"

Herewithal our Captain rebuked himself secretly, that he had so slightly considered of it before.

The third day of our journey (6th February), they brought us to a town of their own, seated near a fair river, on the side of a hill, environed with a dyke of eight feet broad, and a thick mud wall of ten feet high, sufficient to stop a sudden surpriser. It had one long and broad street, lying east and west, and two other cross streets of less breadth and length: there were in it some five or six and fifty households; which were kept so clean and sweet, that not only the houses, but the very streets were very pleasant to behold. In this town we saw they lived very civilly and cleanly. For as soon as we came thither, they washed themselves in the river; and changed their apparel, as also their women do wear, which was very fine and fitly made somewhat after the Spanish fashion, though nothing so costly. This town is distant thirty-five leagues from Nombre de Dios and forty-five from Panama. It is plentifully stored with many sorts of beasts and fowl, with plenty of maize and sundry fruits.

Touching their affection in religion, they have no kind of priests, only they held the Cross in great reputation. But at our Captain's persuasion, they were contented to leave their crosses, and to learn the *Lord's Prayer,* and to be instructed in some measure concerning GOD's true worship. They kept a continual watch in four parts, three miles off their town, to prevent the mischiefs, which the Spaniards intend against them, by the conducting of some of their own coats [*i.e., Cimaroons*], which having been taken by the Spaniards have been enforced thereunto: wherein, as we learned, sometimes the Spaniards have prevailed over them, especially when they lived less careful; but since, they [watch] against the Spaniards, whom they killed like beasts, as often as they take them in the woods; having aforehand understood of their coming.

We stayed with them that night, and the next day (7th

February) till noon; during which time, they related unto us divers very strange accidents, that had fallen out between them and the Spaniards, namely [*especially*] one. A gallant gentleman entertained by the Governors of the country, undertook, the year last past [1572], with 150 soldiers, to put this town to the sword, men, women, and children. Being conducted to it by one of them, that had been taken prisoner, and won by great gifts; he surprised it half an hour before day, by which occasion most of the men escaped, but many of their women and children were slaughtered, or taken: but the same morning by sun rising (after that their guide was slain, in following another man's wife, and that the Cimaroons had assembled themselves in their strength) they behaved themselves in such sort, and drove the Spaniards to such extremity, that what with the disadvantage of the woods (having lost their guide and thereby their way), what with famine and want, there escaped not past thirty of them, to return answer to those which sent them.

Their king [*chief*] dwelt in a city within sixteen leagues south-east of Panama; which is able to make 1,700 fighting men.

They all intreated our Captain very earnestly, to make his abode with them some two or three days; promising that by that time, they would double his strength if he thought good. But he thanking them for their offer, told them, that "He could stay no longer! It was more than time to prosecute his purposed voyage. As for strength, he would wish no more than he had, although he might have presently twenty times as much!" Which they took as proceeding not only from kindness, but also from magnanimity; and therefore, they marched forth, that afternoon, with great good will.

This was the order of our march. Four of those Cimaroons that best knew the ways, went about a mile distance before us, breaking boughs as they went, to be a direction to those that followed; but with great silence, which they also required us to keep.

Then twelve of them were as it were our Vanguard, other twelve, our Rearward. We with their two Captains in the midst.

All the way was through woods very cool and pleasant, by

reason of those goodly and high trees, that grow there so thick, that it is cooler travelling there under them in that hot region, than it is in the most parts of England in the summer time. This [also] gave a special encouragement unto us all, that we understood there was a great Tree about the midway, from which, we might at once discern the North Sea from whence we came, and the South Sea whither we were going.

The fourth day following (11th February) we came to the height of the desired hill, a very high hill, lying East and West, like a ridge between the two seas, about ten of the clock: where [PEDRO] the chiefest of these Cimaroons took our Captain by the hand, and prayed him to follow him, if he was desirous to see at once the two seas, which he had so long longed for.

Here was that goodly and great high Tree, in which they had cut and made divers steps, to ascend up near unto the top, where they had also made a convenient bower, wherein ten or twelve men might easily sit: and from thence we might, without any difficulty, plainly see the Atlantic Ocean whence now we came, and the South Atlantic [*i.e., Pacific Ocean*] so much desired. South and north of this Tree, they had felled certain trees, that the prospect might be the clearer; and near about the Tree there were divers strong houses, that had been built long before, as well by other Cimaroons as by these, which usually pass that way, as being inhabited in divers places in those waste countries.

After our Captain had ascended to this bower, with the chief Cimaroon, and having, as it pleased GOD, at that time, by reason of the brize [*breeze*], a very fair day, had seen that sea, of which he had heard such golden reports: he "besought Almighty GOD of His goodness, to give him life and leave to sail once in an English ship, in that sea!" And then calling up all the rest of our [17 *English*] men, he acquainted JOHN OXNAM especially with this his petition and purpose, if it would please GOD to grant him that happiness. Who understanding it, presently protested, that "unless our Captain did beat him from his company, he would follow him, by GOD's grace!"

Thus all, thoroughly satisfied with the sight of the seas,

descended; and after our repast, continued our ordinary march through woods, yet two days more as before: without any great variety. But then (13th February) we came to march in a champion country, where the grass groweth, not only in great lengths as the knot grass groweth in many places, but to such height, that the inhabitants are fain to burn it thrice in the year, that it may be able to feed the cattle, of which they have thousands.

For it is a kind of grass with a stalk, as big as a great wheaten reed, which hath a blade issuing from the top of it, on which though the cattle feed, yet it groweth every day higher, until the top be too high for an ox to reach. Then the inhabitants are wont to put fire to it, for the space of five or six miles together; which notwithstanding after it is thus burnt, within three days, springeth up fresh like green corn. Such is the great fruitfulness of the soil: by reason of the evenness of the day and night, and the rich dews which fall every morning.

In these three last days' march in the champion, as we past over the hills, we might see Panama five or six times a day; and the last day (14th February) we saw the ships riding in the road.

But after that we were come within a day's journey of Panama, our Captain (understanding by the Cimaroons that the Dames of Panama are wont to send forth hunters and fowlers for taking of sundry dainty fowl, which the land yieldeth; by whom if we marched not very heedfully, we might be descried) caused all his company to march out of all ordinary way, and that with as great heed, silence, and secrecy, as possibly they might, to the grove (which was agreed on four days before) lying within a league of Panama, where we might lie safely undiscovered near the highway, that leadeth from thence to Nombre de Dios.

Thence we sent a chosen Cimaroon, one that had served a master in Panama before time, in such apparel as the Negroes of Panama do use to wear, to be our espial, to go into the town, to learn the certain night, and time of the night, when the carriers laded the Treasure from the King's Treasure House to Nombre de Dios. For they are wont to take their journey from Panama to Venta Cruz, which is six leagues, ever by night; because the country is all champion, and consequently by day very hot. But from Venta Cruz to Nombre de Dios as oft as they travel by land with their treasure, they travel always by day and not by night, because all that way is full of woods, and therefore very fresh and cool; unless the Cimaroons happily encounter them, and made them sweat with fear, as sometimes they have done: whereupon they are glad to guard their *Recoes* [*i.e.,* Recuas, *the Spanish word for a drove of beasts of burden; meaning here, a mule train,*] with soldiers as they pass that way.

This last day, our Captain did behold and view the most of all that fair city, discerning the large street which lieth directly from the sea into the land, South and North.

By three of the clock, we came to this grove; passing for the more secrecy alongst a certain river, which at that time was almost dried up.

Having disposed of ourselves in the grove, we despatched our spy an hour before night, so that by the closing in of the evening, he might be in the city; as he was. Whence presently he returned unto us, that which very happily he understood by companions of his. That the Treasurer of Lima intending to pass into Spain in the first *Adviso* (which was a ship of 350 tons, a very good sailer), was ready that night to take his journey towards Nombre de Dios, with his daughter and family: having fourteen mules in company: of which eight were laden with gold, and one with jewels. And farther, that there were two other *Recuas,* of fifty mules in each, laden with victuals for the most part, with some little quantity of silver, to come forth that night after the other.

There are twenty-eight of these *Recuas;* the greatest of them is of seventy mules, the less of fifty; unless some particular man hire for himself, ten, twenty, or thirty, as he hath need.

Upon this notice, we forthwith marched four leagues, till we came within two leagues of Venta Cruz, in which march two of our Cimaroons which were sent before, by scent of his match, found and brought a Spaniard, whom they had found asleep by the way, by scent of the said match, and drawing near thereby, heard him taking his breath as he slept; and being but one, they fell upon him, stopped his mouth from crying, put out his match, and bound him so, that they well near strangled him by that time he was brought unto us.

By examining him, we found all that to be true, which our spy had reported to us, and that he was a soldier entertained with others by the Treasurer, for guard and conduct of this treasure, from Venta Cruz to Nombre de Dios.

This soldier having learned who our Captain was, took courage, and was bold to make two requests unto him. The one that "He would command his Cimaroons which hated the Spaniards, especially the soldiers extremely, to spare his life; which he doubted not but they would do at his charge." The other was, that "seeing he was a soldier, and assured him, that they should have that night more gold, besides jewels, and pearls of great price, then all they could carry (if not, then he was to be dealt with how they would); but if they all found it so, then it might please our Captain to give unto him, as much as might suffice for him and his mistress to live upon, as he had heard our Captain had done to divers others: for which he would make his name as famous as any of them which had received like favour."

Being at the place appointed, our Captain with half his men [8 *English and* 15 *Cimaroons*], lay on one side of the way, about fifty paces off in the long grass; JOHN OXNAM with the Captain of the Cimaroons, and the other half, lay on the other side of the way, at the like distance: but so far behind, that as occasion served, the former company might take the foremost mules by the heads, and the hindmost because the mules tied together, are always driven one after another; and especially that if we should have need to use our weapons that night, we might be sure not to endamage our fellows. We had not lain thus in ambush much above an hour, but we heard the *Recuas* coming both from the city to Venta Cruz, and from Venta Cruz to the city, which hath a very common and great trade, when the fleets are there. We heard them by reason they delight much to have deep-sounding bells, which, in a still night, are heard very far off.

Now though there were as great charge given as might be,

that none of our men should shew or stir themselves, but let all that came from Venta Cruz to pass quietly; yea, their *Recuas* also, because we knew that they brought nothing but merchandise from thence: yet one of our men, called Robert Pike, having drunken too much *aqua vitæ* without water, forgot himself, and enticing a Cimaroon forth with him was gone hard to the way, with intent to have shown his forwardness on the foremost mules. And when a cavalier from Venta Cruz, well mounted, with his page running at his stirrup, passed by, unadvisedly he rose up to see what he was: but the Cimaroon of better discretion pulled him down, and lay upon him, that he might not discover them any more. Yet by this, the gentleman had taken notice by seeing one half all in white: for that we had all put our shirts over our other apparel, that we might be sure to know our own men in the pell mell in the night. By means of this sight, the cavalier putting spurs to his horse, rode a false gallop; as desirous not only himself to be free of this doubt which he imagined, but also to give advertisement to others that they might avoid it.

Our Captain who had heard and observed by reason of the hardness of the ground and stillness of the night, the change of this gentleman's trot to a gallop, suspected that he was discovered, but could not imagine by whose fault, neither did the time give him leisure to search. And therefore considering that it might be, by reason of the danger of the place, well known to ordinary travellers: we lay still in expectation of the Treasurer's coming; and he had come forward to us, but that this horseman meeting him, and (as we afterwards learnt by the other *Recuas*) making report to him, what he had seen presently that night, what he heard of Captain Drake this long time, and what he conjectured to be most likely: *viz.*, that the said Captain Drake, or some for him, disappointed of his expectation, of getting any great treasure, both at Nombre de Dios and other places, was by some means or other come by land, in covert through the woods, unto this place, to speed of his purpose: and thereupon persuaded him to turn his *Recua* out of the way, and let the other *Recuas* which were coming after to pass on. They were whole *Recuas*, and loaded but with victuals for the most part, so that the loss of them were far less if the worst befell, and yet they should serve to discover them as well as the best.

Thus by the recklessness of one of our company, and by the carefulness of this traveller; we were disappointed of a most rich booty: which is to be thought GOD would not should be taken, for that, by all likelihood, it was well gotten by that Treasurer.

The other two *Recuas* were no sooner come up to us, but being stayed and seized on. One of the Chief Carriers, a very sensible fellow, told our Captain by what means we were discovered, and counselled us to shift for ourselves betimes, unless we were able to encounter the whole force of the city and country before day would be about us.

It pleased us but little, that we were defeated of our golden *Recua,* and that in these we could find not past some two horse-loads of silver: but it grieved our Captain much more, that he was discovered, and that by one of his own men. But knowing it bootless to grieve at things past, and having learned by experience, that all safety in extremity, consisteth in taking of time [*i. e., by the forelock, making an instant decision*]: after no long consultation with PEDRO the chief of our Cimaroons, who declared that "there were but two ways for him: the one to travel back again the same secret way they came, for four leagues space into the woods, or else to march forward, by the highway to Venta Cruz, being two leagues, and make a way with his sword through the enemies." He resolved, considering the long and weary marches that we had taken, and chiefly that last evening and day before: to take now the shortest and readiest way: as choosing rather to encounter his enemies while he had strength remaining, than to be encountered or chased when we should be worn out with weariness: principally now having the mules to ease them that would, some part of the way.

Therefore commanding all to refresh themselves moderately with such store of victuals as we had here in abundance: he signified his resolution and reason to them all: asking PEDRO by name, "Whether he would give his hand not to forsake him?" because he knew that the rest of the

Cimaroons would also then stand fast and firm, so faithful are they to their captain. He being very glad of his resolution, gave our Captain his hand, and vowed that "He would rather die at his foot, than leave him to the enemies, if he held this course."

So having strengthened ourselves for the time, we took our journey towards Venta Cruz, with help of the mules till we came within a mile of the town, where we turned away the *Recuas,* charging the conductors of them, not to follow us upon pain of their lives.

There, the way is cut through the woods, above ten or twelve feet broad, so as two *Recuas* may pass one by another. The fruitfulness of the soil, causeth that with often shredding and ridding the way, those woods grow as thick as our thickest hedges in England that are oftenest cut.

To the midst of this wood, a company of soldiers, which continually lay in that town, to defend it against the Cimaroons, were come forth, to stop us if they might on the way; if not, to retreat to their strength, and there to expect us. A Convent [*Monastery*] of Friars, of whom one was become a Leader, joined with these soldiers, to take such part as they did.

Our Captain understanding by our two Cimaroons, which with great heedfulness and silence, marched now, but about half a flight-shot before us, that it was time for us to arm and take us to our weapons, for they knew the enemy was at hand, by smelling of their match and hearing of a noise: had given us charge, that no one of us should make any shot, until the Spaniards had first spent their volley: which he thought they would not do before they had spoken, as indeed fell out.

For as soon as we were within hearing, a Spanish Captain cried out, "Hoo!" Our Captain answered him likewise, and being demanded *"Que gente?"* replied "Englishmen!" But when the said Commander charged him, "In the name of the King of Spain, his Master, that we should yield ourselves; promising in the word and faith of a Gentleman Soldier, that if we would so do, he would use us with all courtesy." Our Captain drawing somewhat near him said: "That for the honour of the Queen of England, his Mistress, he must have passage that way," and therewithal discharged his pistol towards him.

Upon this, they presently shot off their whole volley; which, though it lightly wounded our Captain, and divers of our men, yet it caused death to one only of our company called JOHN HARRIS, who was so powdered with hail-shot, (which they all used for the most part as it seemed, or else "quartered," for that our men were hurt with that kind) that we could not recover his life, though he continued all that day afterwards with us.

Presently as our Captain perceived their shot to come slacking, as the latter drops of a great shower of rain, with his whistle he gave us his usual signal, to answer them with our shot and arrows, and so march onwards upon the enemy, with intent to come to handy-strokes, and to have joined with them; whom when we found retired as to a place of some better strength, he increased his pace to prevent them if he might. Which the Cimaroons perceiving, although by terror of the shot continuing, they were for the time stept aside; yet as soon as they discerned by hearing that we marched onward, they all rushed forward one after another, traversing the way, with their arrows ready in their bows, and their manner of country dance or leap, very singing *Yó pehó! Yó pehó* and so got before us, where they continued their leap and song, after the manner of their own country wars, till they and we overtook some of the enemy, who near the town's end, had conveyed themselves within the woods, to have taken their stand at us, as before.

But our Cimaroons now thoroughly encouraged, when they saw our resolution, brake in through the thickets, on both sides of them, forcing them to fly, Friars and all!: although divers of our men were wounded, and one Cimaroon especially was run through with one of their pikes, whose courage and mind served him so well notwithstanding, that he revenged his own death ere he died, by killing him that had given him that deadly wound.

We, with all speed, following this chase, entered the town of Venta Cruz, being of about forty or fifty houses, which had both a Governor and other officers and some fair houses, with many storehouses large and strong for the wares, which brought thither from Nombre de Dios, by the river of Chagres, so to be transported by mules to Panama: beside the Monastery, where we found above a thousand bulls and pardons, newly sent from Rome.

In those houses we found three gentlewomen, which had lately been delivered of children there, though their dwellings were in Nombre de Dios; because it hath been observed of long time, as they reported to us, that no Spaniard or white woman could ever be delivered in Nombre de Dios with safety of their children but that within two or three days they died; notwithstanding that being born and brought up in this Venta Cruz or Panama five or six years, and then brought to Nombre de Dios, if they escaped sickness the first or second month, they commonly lived in it as healthily as in any other place: although no stranger (as they say) can endure there any long time, without great danger of death or extreme sickness.

Though at our first coming into the town with arms so suddenly, these ladies were in great fear, yet because our Captain had given straight charge to all the Cimaroons (that while they were in his company, they should never hurt any woman nor man that had not a weapon in his hand to do them hurt; which they earnestly promised, and no less faithfully performed) they had no wrong offered them, nor any thing taken from them, to the worth of a garter; wherein, albeit they had indeed sufficient safety and security, by those of his company, which our Captain sent unto them, of purpose to comfort them: yet they never ceased most earnestly entreating, that our Captain would vouchsafe to come to them himself for their more safety; which when he did, in their presence reporting the charge he had first given, and the assurance of his men, they were comforted.

While the guards which we had, not without great need, set, as well on the bridge which we had to pass over, as at the town's end where we entered (they have no other entrance into the town by land: but from the water's side there is one other to carry up and down their merchandise from their frigates) gained us liberty and quiet to stay in this town some hour and half: we had not only refreshed ourselves, but our company and Cimaroons had gotten some good pillage, which our Captain allowed and gave them (being not the thing he looked for) so that it were not too cumbersome or heavy in respect of our travel, or defence of ourselves.

A little before we departed, some ten or twelve horsemen came from Panama; by all likelihood, supposing that we were gone out of this town, for that all was so still and quiet, came to enter the town confidently: but finding their entertainment such as it was; they that could, rode faster back again for fear than they had ridden forward for hope.

Thus we having ended our business in this town, and the day beginning to spring, we marched over the bridge, observing the same order that we did before. There we were all safe in our opinion, as if we had been environed with wall and trench, for that no Spaniard without his extreme danger could follow us. The rather now, for that our Cimaroons were grown very valiant. But our Captain considering that he had a long way to pass, and that he had been now well near a fortnight from his ship, where he had left his company but weak by reason of their sickness, hastened his journeys as much as he might, refusing to visit the other Cimaroon towns (which they earnestly desired him) and encouraging his own company with such example and speech, that the way seemed much shorter. For he marched most cheerfully, and assured us that he doubted not but ere he left that coast, we should all be bountifully paid and recompensed for all those pains taken: but by reason of this our Captain's haste, and leaving of their towns, we marched many days with hungry stomachs, much against the will of our Cimaroons: who if we would have stayed any day from this continual journeying, would have killed for us victuals sufficient.

In our absence, the rest of the Cimaroons had built a little town within three leagues off the port where our ship lay. There our Captain was contented, upon their great and earnest entreaties to make some stay; for that they alleged, it was only built for his sake. And indeed he consented the rather, that the want of shoes might be supplied by means of the Cimaroons, who were a great help unto us: all our men complaining of the tenderness of their feet, whom our Captain would himself accompany in their complaint, some times without cause, but some times with cause indeed; which made the rest to bear the burden the more easily.

These Cimaroons, during all the time that we were with burden, did us continually very good service, and in particular in this journey, being unto us instead of intelligencers, to advertise us; of guides in our way to direct us; of purveyors, to provide victuals for us; of house-wrights to build our lodgings; and had indeed able and strong bodies carrying all our necessaries: yea, many times when some of our company fainted with sickness of weariness, two Cimaroons would carry him with ease between them, two miles together, and at other times, when need was, they would shew themselves no less valiant than industrious, and of good judgment.

From this town, at our first entrance in the evening, on Saturday (22nd February), our Captain despatched a Cimaroon with a token and certain order to the Master: who had, these three weeks, kept good watch against the enemy, and shifted in the woods for fresh victual, for the relief and recovery of our men left aboard.

As soon as this messenger was come to the shore, calling to our ship, as bringing some news, he was quickly fet[ched] aboard by those which longed to hear of our Captain's speeding: but when he showed the toothpike of gold, which he said our Captain had sent for a token to ELLIS HIXOM, with charge to meet him at such a river though the Master knew well the Captain's toothpike: yet by reason of his admonition and caveat [*warning*] given him at parting, he (though he bewrayed no sign of distrusting the Cimaroon) yet stood as amazed, least something had befallen our Captain otherwise than well. The Cimaroon perceiving this, told him, that it was night when he was sent away, so that our Captain could not send any letter, but yet with the point of his knife, he wrote something upon the toothpick, "which," he said, "should be sufficient to gain credit to the messenger."

Thereupon, the Master looked upon it, and saw written, *By me,* FRANCIS DRAKE: wherefore he believed, and according to the message, prepared what provision he could, and repaired to the mouth of the river of Tortugos, as the Cimaroons that went with him then named it.

That afternoon towards three a clock, we were come down to that river, not past half-an-hour before we saw our pinnace ready come to receive us: which was unto us all a double rejoicing: first that we saw them, and next, so soon. Our Captain with all our company praised GOD most heartily, for that we saw our pinnace and fellows again.

We all seemed to these, who had lived at rest and plenty all this while aboard, as men strangely changed (our Captain yet not much changed) in countenance and plight: and indeed our long fasting and sore travail might somewhat forepine and waste us; but the grief we drew inwardly, for that we returned without that gold and treasure we hoped for did no doubt show her print and footsteps in our faces.

The rest of our men which were then missed, could not travel so well as our Captain, and therefore were left at the Indian new town: and the next day (23rd February) we rowed to another river in the bottom of the bay and took them all aboard. Thus being returned from Panama, to the great rejoicing of our company, who were thoroughly revived with the report we brought from thence: especially understanding our Captain's purpose, that he meant not to leave off thus, but would once again attempt the same journey, whereof they also might be partakers.

Our Captain would not, in the meantime, suffer this edge and forwardness of his men to be dulled or rebated, by lying still idly unemployed, as knowing right well by continual experience, that no sickness was more noisome to impeach any enterprise than delay and idleness.

Therefore considering deeply the intelligences of other places of importance thereabouts, which he had gotten the former years; and particularly of Veragua, a rich town lying to the Westward, between Nombre de Dios and Nicaragua, where is the richest mine of fine gold that is on this North side: he consulted with his company touching their opinions, what was to be done in this meantime, and how they stood affected?

Some thought, that "It was most necessary to seek supply of victuals, that we might the better be able to keep our men close and in health till our time came: and this was easy to be compassed, because the frigates with victuals went without great defence, whereas the frigate and barks with treasure, for the most part were wafted with great ships and store of soldiers."

Others yet judged, "We might better bestow our time in intercepting the frigates of treasure; first, for that our magazines and storehouses of victuals were reasonably furnished, and the country itself was so plentiful, that every man might provide for himself if the worst befell: and victuals might hereafter be provided abundantly as well as now: whereas the treasure never floateth upon the sea, so ordinarily as at this time of the Fleets being there, which time in no wise may be neglected."

The Cimaroons being demanded also their opinion (for that they were experienced in the particularities of all the towns thereabouts, as in which some or other of them had served), declared that "by Veragua, Signior PEZORO (some time their master from whom they fled) dwelt; not in the town for fear of some surprise, but yet not far off from the town, for his better relief; in a very strong house of stone, where he had dwelt nineteen years at least, never travelling from home; unless happily once a year to Cartagena, or Nombre de Dios when the Fleets were there. He keepeth a hundred slaves at least in the mines, each slave being bound to bring in daily, clear gain (all charges deducted) three Pesos of Gold for himself and two for his women (8s. 3d. the Peso), amounting in the whole, to above £200 sterling [=£1,600 *now*] each day: so that he hath heaped a mighty mass of treasure together, which he keepeth in certain great chests, of two feet deep, three broad, and four long: being (notwithstanding all his wealth) bad and cruel not only to his slaves, but unto all men, and therefore never going abroad but with a guard of five or six men to defend his person from danger, which he feareth extraordinarily from all creatures."

"And as touching means of compassing this purpose, they would conduct him safely through the woods, by the same ways by which they fled, that he should not need to enter their havens with danger, but might come upon their backs altogether unlooked for. And though his house were of stone, so that it could not be burnt; yet if our Captain would undertake the attempt, they would undermine and overthrow, or otherwise break it open, in such sort, as we might have easy access to his greatest treasure."

Our Captain having heard all their opinions, concluded so that by dividing his company, the two first different sentences were both reconciled, both to be practised and put in use.

JOHN OXNAM appointed in the *Bear,* to be sent Eastward towards Tolou, to see what store of victuals would come athwart his half; and himself would to the Westward in the *Minion,* lie off and on the *Cabezas,* where was the greatest trade and most ordinary passage of those which transported treasure from Veragua and Nicaragua to the Fleet; so that no time might be lost, nor opportunity let slip either for victuals or treasure. As for the attempt of Veragua, or Signior PEZORO's house by land, by marching through the woods; he liked not of, lest it might overweary his men by continual labour; whom he studied to refresh and strengthen for his next service forenamed.

Therefore using our Cimaroons most courteously, dismissing those that were desirous to their wives, with such gifts and favours as were most pleasing, and entertaining those still aboard his ship, which were contented to abide with the company remaining; the pinnaces departed as we determined: the *Minion* to the West, the *Bear* to the East.

The *Minion* about the *Cabeças,* met with a frigate of Nicaragua, in which was some gold, and a Genoese Pilot (of which Nation there are many in those coasts), which had been at Veragua not past eight days before. He being very well entreated, certified our Captain of the state of the town, and of the harbour, and of a frigate that was there ready to come forth within few days, aboard which there was above a million of gold, offering to conduct him to it, if we would do him his right: for that he knew the channel very perfectly, so that he could enter by night safely without danger of the sands and shallows, though there be but little water, and utterly undescried; for that the town is five leagues within the harbour, and the way by land is so far about and difficult through the woods, that though we should by any casualty be discovered, about the point of the harbour, yet we might despatch our business and depart, before the town could have notice of our coming.

At his being there, he perceived they had heard of DRAKE's being on the coast, which had put them in great fear, as in all other places (PEZORO purposing to remove himself to the South Sea!): but there was nothing done to prevent him, their fear being so great, that, as it is accustomed in such cases, it excluded counsel and bred despair.

Our Captain, conferring with his own knowledge and former intelligences, was purposed to have returned to his ship, to have taken some of those Cimaroons which had dwelt with Signior PEZORO, to be the more confirmed in this point.

But when the Genoese Pilot was very earnest, to have the time gained, and warranted our Captain of good speed, if we delayed not; he dismissed the frigate, somewhat lighter to hasten her journey! and with this Pilot's advice, laboured with sail and oars to get this harbour and to enter it by night accordingly: considering that this frigate might now be gained, and PEZORO's house attempted hereafter notwithstanding.

But when we were come to the mouth of the harbour, we heard the report of two Chambers, and farther off about a league within the bay, two other as it were answering them: whereby the Genoese Pilot conjectured that we were discovered: for he assured us, that this order had been taken since his last being there, by reason of the advertisement and charge, which the Governor of Panama had sent to all the Coasts; which even in their beds lay in great and continual fear of our Captain, and therefore by all likelihood, maintained this kind of watch, at the charge of the rich Gnuffe PEZORO for their security.

Thus being defeated of this expectation, we found it was not GOD'S will that we should enter at that time: the rather for that the wind, which had all this time been Easterly, came up to the Westward, and invited us to return again to our ship; where, on Sheere Thursday (19th March), we met, according to appointment, with our *Bear,* and found that she had bestowed her time to more profit than we had done.

For she had taken a frigate in which there were ten men (whom they set ashore) great store of maize, twenty-eight fat hogs, and two hundred hens. Our Captain discharged (20th March) this frigate of her lading; and because she was new, strong, and of a good mould, the next day (21st March) he tallowed her to make her a Man-of-war: disposing all our ordnance and provisions that were fit for such use, in her. For we had heard by the Spaniards last taken, that there were two little galleys built in Nombre de Dios, to waft the Chagres Fleet to and fro, but were not yet both launched: wherefore he purposed now to adventure for that Fleet.

And to hearten his company he feasted them that Easter-Day (22nd March) with great cheer and cheerfulness, setting up his rest upon that attempt.

The next day (23rd March) with the new tallowed frigate of Tolou [*not of 20 tons, p. 203; one of the two frigates in which the Expedition returned to England*], and his *Bear,* we set sail towards the Cativaas, where about two days after we landed, and stayed till noon; at what time seeing a sail to the westward, as we deemed making to the island: we set sail and plied towards him, who descrying us, bare with us, till he perceived by our confidence, that we were no Spaniards, and conjectured we were those Englishmen, of whom he had heard long before. And being in great want, and desirous to be relieved by us: he bare up under our lee, and in token of amity, shot off his lee ordnance, which was not unanswered.

We understood that he was TETÛ, a French Captain of Newhaven [*Havre*] a Man-of-war as we were, desirous to be relieved by us. For at our first meeting, the French Captain cast abroad his hands, and prayed our Captain to help him to some water, for that he had nothing but wine and cider aboard him, which had brought his men into great sickness. He had sought us ever since he first heard of our being upon the coast, about this five weeks. Our Captain sent one aboard him with some relief for the present, willing him to follow us to the next port, where he should have both water and victuals.

At our coming to anchor, he sent our Captain a case of pistols, and a fair gilt scimitar (which had been the late King's of France [HENRY II.], whom Monsieur MONTGOMERY hurt in the eye, and was given him by Monsieur STROZZE). Our Captain requited him with a chain of gold, and a tablet which he wore.

This Captain reported unto us the first news of the Massacre of Paris, at the King of NAVARRE's marriage on Saint Bartholomew's Day last, [24 August, 1572]; of the Admiral of France slain in his chamber, and divers other murders: so that he "thought those Frenchmen the happiest which were farthest from France, now no longer France but Frensy, even as if all Gaul were turned into wormwood and gall: Italian practices having over-mastered the French simplicity." He showed what famous and often reports he had heard of our great riches. He desired to know of our Captain which way he might "compass" his voyage also.

Though we had seen him in some jealousy and distrust, for all his pretence; because we considered more the strength he had than the good-will he might bear us: yet upon consultation among ourselves, "Whether it were fit to receive him or not?" we resolved to take him and twenty of his men, to serve with our Captain for halves. In such sort as we needed not doubt of their forces, being but twenty; nor be hurt by their portions, being no greater than ours: and yet gratify them in their earnest suit, and serve our own purpose, which without more help we could very hardly have achieved. Indeed, he had 70 men, and we now but 31; his ship was above 80 tons, and our frigate not 20, or pinnace nothing near 10 tons. Yet our Captain thought this proportionable, in consideration that not numbers of men, but quality of their judgements and knowledge, were to be the principal actors herein: and the French ship could do no service, nor stand in any stead to this enterprise which we intended, and had agreed upon before, both touching the time when it should take beginning, and the place where we should meet, namely, at Rio Francisco.

Having thus agreed with Captain Tetû, we sent for the Cimaroons as before was decreed. Two of them were brought aboard our ships, to give the French assurance of this agreement.

And as soon as we could furnish ourselves and refresh the French company, which was within five or six days (by bringing them to the magazines which were the nearest, where they were supplied by us in such sort, as they protested they were beholding to us for all their lives) taking twenty of the French and fifteen of ours with our Cimaroons, leaving both our ships in safe road, we manned our frigate and two pinnaces (we had formerly sunk our *Lion,* shortly after our return from Panama, because we had not men sufficient to man her), and went towards Rio Francisco: which because it had not water enough for our frigate, caused us to leave her at the Cabeças, manned with English and French, in the charge of Robert Doble, to stay there without attempting any chase, until the return of our pinnaces.

And then bore to Rio Francisco, where both Captains landed (31st March) with such force as aforesaid [*i.e.,* 20 *French,* 15 *English, and the Cimaroons*], and charged them that had the charge of the pinnaces to be there the fourth day next following without any fail. And thus knowing that the carriages [*mule loads*] went now daily from Panama to Nombre de Dios; we proceeded in covert through the woods, towards the highway that leadeth between them.

It is five leagues accounted by sea, between Rio Francisco and Nombre de Dios; but that way which we march by land, we found it above seven leagues. We marched as in our former journey to Panama, both for order and silence; to the great wonder of the French Captain and company, who protested they knew not by any means how to recover the pinnaces, if the Cimaroons (to whom what our Captain commanded was a law; though they little regarded the French, as having no trust in them) should leave us: our Captain assured him, "There was no cause of doubt of them, of whom he had had such former trial."

When we were come within an English mile of the way, we stayed all night, refreshing ourselves, in great stillness, in a most convenient place: where we heard the carpenters, being many in number, working upon their ships, as they usually do by reason of the great heat of the day in Nombre de Dios; and might hear the mules coming from Panama, by reason of the advantage of the ground.

The next morning (1st April), upon hearing of that number of bells, the Cimaroons, rejoiced exceedingly, as though there could not have befallen them a more joyful accident chiefly having been disappointed before. Now they all assured us, "We should have more gold and silver than all of us could bear away": as in truth it fell out.

For there came three *Recuas,* one of 50 mules, the other two, of 70 each, every [one] of which carried 300 lbs. weight of silver; which in all amounted to near thirty tons [*i.e.,* 190 *mules, with* 300 *lbs. each=about* 57,000 *lbs. of silver*].

We putting ourselves in readiness, went down near the way to hear the bells; where we stayed not long, but we saw of what metal they were made; and took such hold on the heads of the foremost and hindmost mules, that all the rest stayed and lay down, as their manner is.

These three *Recuas* were guarded with forty-five soldiers or thereabouts, fifteen to each *Recua,* which caused some exchange of bullets and arrows for a time; in which conflict the French Captain was sore wounded with hail-shot in the belly, and one Cimaroon was slain: but in the end, these soldiers thought it the best way to leave their mules with us, and to seek for more help abroad.

In which meantime we took some pain to ease some of the mules which were heaviest loaden of their carriage. And because we ourselves were somewhat weary, we were contented with a few bars and quoits of gold, as we could well carry: burying about fifteen tons of silver, partly in the burrows which the great land crabs had made in the earth, and partly under old trees which were fallen thereabout, and partly in the sand and gravel of a river, not very deep of water.

Thus when about this business, we had spent some two hours, and had disposed of all our matters, and were ready to march back the very self-same way that we came, we heard both horse and foot coming as it seemed to the mules: for they never followed us, after we were once entered the woods, where the French Captain by reason of his wound, not able to travel farther, stayed, in hope that some rest would recover him better strength.

But after we had marched some two leagues, upon the French soldiers' complaint, that they missed one of their men also, examination being made whether he were slain or not: it was found that he had drunk much wine, and overlading himself with pillage, and hasting to go before us, had lost himself in the woods. And as we afterwards knew, he was taken by the Spaniards that evening; and upon torture, discovered unto them where we had hidden our treasure.

We continued our march all that and the next day (2nd and 3rd April) towards Rio Francisco, in hope to meet with our pinnaces; but when we came thither, looking out to sea, we saw seven Spanish pinnaces, which had been searching all the coast thereabouts: whereupon we mightily suspected that they had taken or spoiled our pinnaces, for that our Captain had given so straight charge, that they should repair to this place this afternoon; from the Cabeças where they rode; whence to our sight these Spaniards' pinnaces did come.

But the night before, there had fallen very much rain, with much westerly wind, which as it enforced the Spaniards to return home the sooner, by reason of the storm: so it kept our pinnaces, that they could not keep the appointment; because the wind was contrary, and blew so strong, that with their oars they could all that day get but half the way. Notwithstanding, if they had followed our Captain's direction in setting forth over night, while the wind served, they had arrived at the place appointed with far less labour, but with far more danger: because that very day at noon, the shallops manned out, of purpose, from Nombre de Dios, were come to this place to take our pinnaces: imagining where we were, after they had heard of our intercepting of the treasure.

Our Captain seeing the shallops, feared least having taken our pinnaces, they had compelled our men by torture to confess where his frigate and ships were. Therefore in this distress and perplexity, the company misdoubting that all means of return to their country were cut off, and that their treasure then served them to small purpose; our Captain comforted and encouraged us all, saying, "We should venture no farther than he did. It was no time now to fear: but rather to haste[n] to prevent that which was feared! If the enemy have prevailed against our pinnaces, which GOD forbid! yet they must have time to search them, time to examine the mariners, time to execute their resolution after it is determined. Before all these times be taken, we may get to our ships, if ye will! though not possibly by land, because of the hills, thickets, and rivers, yet by water. Let us, therefore, make a raft with the trees that are here in readiness, as offering themselves, being brought down the river, happily this last storm, and put ourselves to sea! I will be one, who will be the other?"

JOHN SMITH offered himself, and two Frenchmen that could swim very well, desired they might accompany our Captain, as did the Cimaroons likewise (who had been very earnest with our Captain to have marched by land, though it were sixteen days' journey, and in case the ship had been surprised, to have abode always with them), especially PEDRO, who yet was fain to be left behind, because he could not row.

The raft was fitted and fast bound; a sail of a biscuit sack prepared; an oar was shaped out of a young tree to serve instead of a rudder, to direct their course before the wind.

At his departure he comforted the company, by promising, that "If it pleased GOD, he should put his foot in safety aboard his frigate, he would, GOD willing, by one means or other get them all aboard, in despite of all the Spaniards in the Indies!"

In this manner pulling off to the sea, he sailed some three leagues, sitting up to the waist continually in water, and at every surge of the wave to the arm-pits, for the space of six hours, upon this raft: what with the parching of the sun and what with the beating of the salt water, they had all of them their skins much fretted away.

At length GOD gave them the sight of two pinnaces turning towards them with much wind; but with far greater joy to him than could easily conjecture, and did cheerfully declare to those three with him, that "they were our pinnaces! and that all was safe, so that there was no cause of fear!"

But see, the pinnaces not seeing this raft, nor suspecting any such matter, by reason of the wind and night growing on, were forced to run into a cove behind the point, to take succour, for that night: which our Captain seeing, and gathering (because they came not forth again), that they would anchor there, put his raft ashore, and ran by land about the point, where he found them; who, upon sight of him, made as much haste as they could to take him and his company aboard. For our Captain (of purpose to try what haste they could and would make in extremity), himself ran in great haste, and so willed the other three with him; as if they had been chased by the enemy: which they the rather suspected, because they saw so few with him.

And after his coming aboard, when they demanding "How all his company did?" he answered coldly, "Well!" They all doubted [*feared*] that all went scarce well. But he willing to rid all doubts, and fill them with joy, took out of his bosom a quoit of gold, thanking GOD that "our voyage was made!"

And to the Frenchmen he declared, how their Captain indeed was left behind, sore wounded and two of his company with him: but it should be no hindrance to them.

That night (4th April) our Captain with great pain of his company, rowed to Rio Francisco: where he took the rest in, and the treasure which we had brought with us: making such expedition, that by dawning of the day, we set sail back again to our frigate, and from thence directly to our ships: where, as soon as we arrived, our Captain divided by weight, the gold and silver into two even portions, between the French and the English.

About a fortnight after, when we had set all things in order, and taking out of our ship [*the* Pascha] all such necessaries as we needed for our frigate, had left and given her to the Spaniards, whom we had all this time detained, we put out of that harbour [*at Fort Diego, p.* 160] together with the French ship, riding some few days among the Cabeças.

In the meantime, our Captain made a secret composition with the Cimaroons, that twelve of our men and sixteen of theirs, should make another voyage, to get intelligence in what case the country stood; and if it might be, recover Monsieur TETU, the French Captain; at leastwise to bring away that which was hidden in our former surprise, and could not then be conveniently carried.

JOHN OXNAM and THOMAS SHERWELL were put in trust for his service, to the great content of the whole company, who conceived greatest hope of them next our Captain; whom by no means they would condescend to suffer to adventure again, this time: yet he himself rowed to set them ashore at Rio Francisco; finding his labour well employed both otherwise, and also in saving one of those two Frenchmen that had remained willingly to accompany their wounded captain.

For this gentleman, having escaped the rage of the Spaniards, was now coming towards our pinnace, where he fell down on his knees, blessing GOD for the time, "that ever our Captain was born; who now, beyond all his hopes, was become his deliverer."

He being demanded, "What was become of his Captain and other fellow?" shewed that within half an hour after our departure, the Spaniards had overgotten them, and took his Captain and other fellow: he only escaped by flight, having cast away all his carriage, and among the rest one box of jewels, that he might fly the swifter from the pursuers: but his fellow took it up and burdened himself so sore, that he could make no speed; as easily as he might otherwise, if he would have cast down his pillage, and laid aside his covetous mind. As for the silver, which we had hidden thereabout in the earth and the sands, he thought that it was all gone: for that he thought there had been near two thousand Spaniards and Negroes there to dig and search for it.

This report notwithstanding, our purpose held, and our men were sent to the said place, where they found that the earth, every way a mile distant had been digged and turned up in every place of any likelihood, to have anything hidden in it.

And yet nevertheless, for all that narrow search, all our men's labour was not quite lost, but so considered, that the third day after their departure, they all returned safe and cheerful, with as much silver as they and all the Cimaroons could find (*viz.*, thirteen bars of silver, and some few quoits of gold), with which they were presently embarked, without empeachment, repairing with no less speed than joy to our frigate.

Now was it high time to think of homewards, having sped ourselves as we desired: and therefore our Captain concluded to visit Rio Grande [*Magdelena*] once again, to see if he could meet with any sufficient ship or bark, to carry victuals enough to serve our turn homewards, in which we might in safety and security embark ourselves.

The Frenchmen having formerly gone from us, as soon as they had their shares, at our first return with the treasure; as being very desirous to return home into their country, and our Captain as desirous to dismiss them, as they were to be dismissed: for that he foresaw they could not in their ship avoid the danger of being taken by the Spaniards, if they should make out any Men-of-war for them, while they lingered on the coast; and having also been then again relieved with victuals by us.—Now at our meeting of them again, were very loath to leave us, and therefore accompanied us very kindly as far up as St. Bernards; and farther would, but that they durst not adventure so great danger; for that we had intelligence, that the Fleet was ready to set sail for Spain, riding at the entry of Cartagena.

Thus we departed from them, passing hard by Cartagena, in the sight of all the Fleet, with a flag of St. George in the main top of our frigate, with silk streamers and ancients down to the water, sailing forward with a large wind, till we came within two leagues of the river [*Magdalena*], being all low land, and dark night: where to prevent the over shooting of the river in the night, we lay off and on bearing small sail, till that about midnight the wind veering to the eastward, by two of the clock in the morning, a frigate from

Rio Grande [*Magdalena*] passed hard by us, bearing also but small sail. We saluted them with our shot and arrows, they answered us with bases; but we got aboard them, and took such order, that they were content against their wills to depart ashore and to leave us this frigate: which was of 25 tons, loaded with maize, hens, and hogs, and some honey, in very good time fit for our use; for the honey especially was notable reliever and preserver of our crazed [*sick*] people.

The next morning as soon as we set those Spaniards ashore on the Main, we set our course for the Cabeças without any stop, whither we came about five days after. And being at anchor, presently we hove out all the maize a land, saving three butts which we kept for our store: and carrying all our provisions ashore, we brought both our frigates on the careen, and new tallowed them.

Here we stayed about seven nights, trimming and rigging our frigates, boarding and stowing our provisions, tearing abroad and burning our pinnaces, that the Cimaroons might have the iron-work.

About a day or two before our departure, our Captain willed PEDRO and three of the chiefest of the Cimaroons to go through both his frigates, to see what they liked; promising to give it them, whatsoever it were, so it were not so necessary as that he could not return into England without it. And for their wives he would himself seek out some silks or linen that might gratify them; which while he was choosing out of his trunks, the scimitar which CAPTAIN TETÛ had given to our Captain, chanced to be taken forth in PEDRO's sight: which he seeing grew so much in liking thereof, that he accounted of nothing else in respect of it, and preferred it before all that could be given him. Yet imagining that it was no less esteemed of our Captain, durst not himself open his mouth to crave or commend it; but made one FRANCIS TUCKER to be his mean to break his mind, promising to give him a fine quoit of gold, which yet he had in store, if he would but move our Captain for it; and to our Captain himself, he would give four other great quoits which he had hidden, intending to have reserved them until another voyage.

Our Captain being accordingly moved by FRANCIS TUCKER, could have been content to have made no such exchange; but yet desirous to content him, that had deserved so well, he gave it him with many good words: who received it with no little joy, affirming that if he should give his wife and children which he loved dearly in lieu of it, he could not sufficient recompense it (for he would present his king with it, who he knew would make him a great man, even for this very gift's sake); yet in gratuity and stead of other requital of this jewel, he desired our Captain to accept these four pieces of gold, as a token of his thankfulness to him, and a pawn of his faithfulness during life.

Our Captain received it in most kind sort, but took it not to his own benefit, but caused it to be cast into the whole Adventure, saying, "If he had not been set forth to that place, he had not attained such a commodity, and therefore it was just that they which bare part with him of his burden in setting him to sea, should enjoy the proportion of his benefit whatsoever at his return."

Thus with good love and liking we took our leave of that people, setting over to the islands of [?], whence the next day after, we set sail towards Cape St. Antonio; by which we past with a large wind: but presently being to stand for the Havana, we were fain to ply to the windward some three or four days; in which plying we fortuned to take a small bark, in which were two or three hundred hides, and one most necessary thing, which stood us in great stead, viz., a pump! which we set in our frigate. Their bark because it was nothing fit for our service, our Captain gave them to carry them home.

And so returning to Cape St. Antonio, and landing there, we refreshed ourselves, and beside great store of turtle eggs, found by day in the [sand], we took 250 turtles by night. We powdered [salted] and dried some of them, which did us good service. The rest continued but a small time.

There were, at this time, belonging to Cartagena, Nombre de Dios, Rio Grande, Santa Marta, Rio de la Hacha, Venta Cruz, Veragua, Nicaragua, the Honduras, Jamaica &c., above 200 frigates; some of a 120 tons, others but of 10 or

12 tons, but the most of 30 or 40 tons, which all had intercourse between Cartagena and Nombre de Dios. The most of which, during our abode in those parts, we took; and some of them, twice or thrice each: yet never burnt nor sunk any, unless they were made out Men-of-war against us, or laid as stales to entrap us.

And of all the men taken in these several vessels, we never offered any kind of violence to any, after they were once come under our power; but either presently dismissed them in safety, or keeping them with us some longer time (as some of them we did), we always provided for their sustenance as for ourselves, and secured them from the rage of the Cimaroons against them: till at last, the danger of their discovering where our ships lay being over past, for which only cause we kept them prisoners, we set them also free.

Many strange birds, beasts, and fishes, besides fruits, trees, plants, and the like, were seen and observed of us in this journey, which willingly we pretermit as hastening to the end of our voyage: which from this Cape of St. Antonio, we intended to finish by sailing the directest and speediest way homeward; and accordingly, even beyond our own expectation, most happily performed.

For whereas our Captain had purposed to touch at Newfoundland, and there to have watered; which would have been some let unto us, though we stood in great want of water; yet GOD Almighty so provided for us, by giving us good store of rain water, that we were sufficiently furnished: and, within twenty-three days, we passed from the Cape of Florida, to the Isles of Scilly, and so arrived at Plymouth, on Sunday, about sermon time, August the 9th, 1573.

At what time, the news of our Captain's return brought unto his, did so speedily pass over all the church, and surpass their minds with desire and delight to see him, that very few or none remained with the Preacher. All hastened to see the evidence of GOD's love and blessing towards our Gracious Queen and country, by the fruit of our Captain's labour and success.

Soli DEO Gloria.

FINIS.

SIR FRANCIS DRAKE'S FAMOUS VOYAGE ROUND THE WORLD

BY

FRANCIS PRETTY

SIR FRANCIS DRAKE'S FAMOUS VOYAGE ROUND THE WORLD

NARRATIVE BY FRANCIS PRETTY,
ONE OF DRAKE'S GENTLEMEN AT ARMS.

The FAMOUS VOYAGE *of* SIR FRANCIS DRAKE *into the South Sea, and therehence about the whole Globe of the Earth, begun in the year of our Lord 1577.*

THE 15. day of November, in the year of our Lord 1577, Master *Francis Drake,* with a fleet of five ships and barks,[1] and to the number of 164 men, gentlemen and sailors, departed from *Plymouth,* giving out his pretended voyage for *Alexandria.* But the wind falling contrary, he was forced the next morning to put into *Falmouth* Haven, in *Cornwall,* where such and so terrible a tempest took us, as few men have seen the like, and was indeed so vehement that all our ships were like to have gone to wrack. But it pleased God to preserve us from that extremity, and to afflict us only for that present with these two particulars: the mast of our Admiral, which was the *Pelican,* was cut overboard for the safeguard of the ship, and the *Marigold* was driven ashore, and somewhat bruised. For the repairing of which damages we returned again to *Plymouth;* and having recovered those harms, and brought the ships again to good state, we set forth the second time from *Plymouth,* and set sail the 13. day of December following.

The 25. day of the same month we fell with the Cape

[1] The *Pelican,* 120 tons, commanded by Drake; the *Elizabeth,* a new Deptford-built ship of 80 tons, commanded by Winter, with her pinnace the *Benedict;* the *Marigold,* of 30 tons; and the *Swan,* a fly-boat of 50 tons.

Cantin, upon the coast of *Barbary;* and coasting along, the 27. day we found an island called *Mogador,* lying one mile distant from the main. Between which island and the main we found a very good and safe harbour for our ships to ride in, as also very good entrance, and void of any danger. On this island our General erected a pinnace, whereof he brought out of *England* with him four already framed. While these things were in doing, there came to the water's side some of the inhabitants of the country, shewing forth their flags of truce; which being seen of our General, he sent his ship's boat to the shore to know what they would. They being willing to come aboard, our men left there one man of our company for a pledge, and brought two of theirs aboard our ship; which by signs shewed our General that the next day they would bring some provision, as sheep, capons, and hens, and such like. Whereupon our General bestowed amongst them some linen cloth and shoes, and a javelin, which they very joyfully received, and departed for that time. The next morning they failed not to come again to the water's side. And our General again setting out our boat, one of our men leaping over-rashly ashore, and offering friendly to embrace them, they set violent hands on him, offering a dagger to his throat if he had made any resistance; and so laying him on a horse carried him away. So that a man cannot be too circumspect and wary of himself among such miscreants. Our pinnace being finished, we departed from this place the 30. and last day of December, and coasting along the shore we did descry, not contrary to our expectation, certain *canters,* which were Spanish fishermen;[2] to whom we gave chase and took three of them. And proceeding further we met with three carvels, and took them also.

The 17. day of January we arrived at *Cape Blanco,* where we found a ship riding at anchor, within the Cape, and but two simple mariners in her. Which ship we took and carried her further into the harbour, where we remained four days; and in that space our General mustered and trained his men on land in warlike manner, to make them fit for all occasions. In this place we took of the fishermen such necessaries as we wanted, and they could yield us;

[2] Old Sp. *cantera* (perhaps from *cantharus*).

and leaving here one of our little barks, called the *Benedict,* we took with us one of theirs which they called *canters,* being of the burden of 40 tons or thereabouts. All these things being finished we departed this harbour the 22. of January, carrying along with us one of the Portugal carvels, which was bound to the islands of *Cape Verde* for salt, whereof good store is made in one of those islands. The master or pilot of that carvel did advertise our General that upon one of those islands, called *Mayo,* there was great store of dried *cabritos,*[3] which a few inhabitants there dwelling did yearly make ready for such of the king's ships as did there touch, being bound for his country of *Brazil* or elsewhere. We fell with this island the 27. of January, but the inhabitants would in no case traffic with us, being thereof forbidden by the king's edict. Yet the next day our General sent to view the island, and the likelihoods that might be there of provision of victuals, about threescore and two men under the conduct and government of Master *Winter* and Master *Doughty.* And marching towards the chief place of habitation in this island (as by the Portugal we were informed), having travelled to the mountains the space of three miles, and arriving there somewhat before the daybreak, we arrested ourselves, to see day before us. Which appearing, we found the inhabitants to be fled; but the place, by reason that it was manured, we found to be more fruitful than the other part, especially the valleys among the hills.

Here we gave ourselves a little refreshing, as by very ripe and sweet grapes, which the fruitfulness of the earth at that season of the year yielded us; and that season being with us the depth of winter, it may seem strange that those fruits were then there growing. But the reason thereof is this, because they being between the tropic and the equinoctial, the sun passeth twice in the year through their zenith over their heads, by means whereof they have two summers; and being so near the heat of the line they never lose the heat of the sun so much, but the fruits have their increase and continuance in the midst of winter. The island is wonderfully stored with goats and wild hens; and it hath

[3] Goats.

salt also, without labour, save only that the people gather it into heaps; which continually in greater quantity is increased upon the sands by the flowing of the sea, and the receiving heat of the sun kerning the same. So that of the increase thereof they keep a continual traffic with their neighbours.

Amongst other things we found here a kind of fruit called *cocos,* which because it is not commonly known with us in *England,* I thought good to make some description of it. The tree beareth no leaves nor branches, but at the very top the fruit groweth in clusters, hard at the top of the stem of the tree, as big every several fruit as a man's head; but having taken off the uttermost bark, which you shall find to be very full of strings or sinews, as I may term them, you shall come to a hard shell, which may hold in quantity of liquor a pint commonly, or some a quart, and some less. Within that shell, of the thickness of half-an-inch good, you shall have a kind of hard substance and very white, no less good and sweet than almonds; within that again, a certain clear liquor, which being drunk, you shall not only find it very delicate and sweet, but most comfortable and cordial.

After we had satisfied ourselves with some of these fruits, we marched further into the island, and saw great store of *cabritos* alive, which were so chased by the inhabitants that we could do no good towards our provision; but they had laid out, as it were to stop our mouths withal, certain old dried *cabritos,* which being but ill, and small and few, we made no account of. Being returned to our ships, our General departed hence the 31. of this month, and sailed by the island of *Santiago,* but far enough from the danger of the inhabitants, who shot and discharged at us three pieces; but they all fell short of us, and did us no harm. The island is fair and large, and, as it seemeth, rich and fruitful, and inhabited by the Portugals; but the mountains and high places of the island are said to be possessed by the Moors, who having been slaves to the Portugals, to ease themselves, made escape to the desert places of the island, where they abide with great strength. Being before this island, we espied two ships under sail, to the one of which we gave chase, and in the end boarded her with a ship-boat without resistance; which we found to be a good prize, and she yielded unto us good store of wine. Which prize our General committed to the custody of Master *Doughty;* and retaining the pilot, sent the rest away with his pinnace, giving them a butt of wine and some victuals, and their wearing clothes, and so they departed. The same night we came with the island called by the Portugals *Ilha do Fogo,* that is, the burning island; in the north side whereof is a consuming fire. The matter is said to be of sulphur, but, notwithstanding, it is like to be a commodious island, because the Portugals have built, and do inhabit there. Upon the south side thereof lieth a most pleasant and sweet island, the trees whereof are always green and fair to look upon; in respect whereof they call it *Ilha Brava,* that is, the brave island. From the banks thereof into the sea do run in many places reasonable streams of fresh water easy to come by, but there was no convenient road for our ships; for such was the depth that no ground could be had for anchoring. And it is reported that ground was never found in that place; so that the tops of *Fogo* burn not so high in the air, but the roots of *Brava* are quenched as low in the sea.

Being departed from these islands, we drew towards the line, where we were becalmed the space of three weeks, but yet subject to divers great storms, terrible lightnings and much thunder. But with this misery we had the commodity of great store of fish, as dolphins, *bonitos,* and flying-fishes, whereof some fell into our ships; wherehence they could not rise again for want of moisture, for when their wings are dry they cannot fly.

From the first day of our departure from the islands of *Cape Verde,* we sailed 54 days without sight of land. And the first land that we fell with was the coast of *Brazil,* which we saw the fifth of April, in the height of 33 degrees towards the pole Antarctic. And being discovered at sea by the inhabitants of the country, they made upon the coast great fires for a sacrifice (as we learned) to the devils; about which they use conjurations, making heaps of sand, and other ceremonies, that when any ship shall go about to stay upon their coast, not only sands may be gathered together in shoals in every place, but also that storms and tempests may arise, to the casting away of ships and men, whereof, as it is reported, there have been divers experiments.

The 7. day in a mighty great storm, both of lightning, rain, and thunder, we lost the *canter,* which we called the *Christopher.* But the eleventh day after, by our General's great care in dispersing his ships, we found her again; and the place where we met our General called the *Cape of Joy,* where every ship took in some water. Here we found a good temperature and sweet air, a very fair and pleasant country with an exceeding fruitful soil, where were great store of large and mighty deer, but we came not to the sight of any people; but travelling further into the country we perceived the footing of people in the clay ground, shewing that they were men of great stature. Being returned to our ships we weighed anchor, and ran somewhat further, and harboured ourselves between the rock and the main; where by means of the rock that brake the force of the sea, we rid very safe. And upon this rock we killed for our provision certain sea-wolves, commonly called with us *seals.* From hence we went our course to 36 degrees, and entered the great river of *Plate,* and ran into 54 and 53 1-2 fathoms of fresh water, where we filled our water by the ship's side; but our General finding here no good harborough, as he thought he should, bare out again to sea the 27. of April, and in bearing out we lost sight of our fly-boat wherein Master *Doughty* was. But we, sailing along, found a fair and reasonable good bay, wherein were many and the same profitable islands; one whereof had so many seals as would at the least have laden all our ships, and the rest of the islands are, as it were, laden with fowls, which is wonderful to see, and they of divers sorts. It is a place very plentiful of victuals, and hath in it no want of fresh water. Our General, after certain days of his abode in this place, being on shore in an island, the people of the country shewed themselves unto him, leaping and dancing, and entered into traffic with him; but they would not receive anything at any man's hands, but the same must be cast upon the ground. They are of clean, comely, and strong bodies, swift on foot, and seem to be very active.

The 18. day of May, our General thought it needful to

have a care of such ships as were absent; and therefore endeavouring to seek the fly-boat wherein Master *Doughty* was, we espied her again the next day. And whereas certain of our ships were sent to discover the coast and to search an harbour, the *Marigold* and the *canter* being employed in that business, came unto us and gave us understanding of a safe harbour that they had found. Wherewith all our ships bare, and entered it; where we watered and made new provision of victuals, as by seals, whereof we slew to the number of 200 or 300 in the space of an hour. Here our General in the *Admiral* rid close aboard the fly-boat, and took out of her all the provision of victuals and what else was in her, and hauling her to the land, set fire to her, and so burnt her to save the iron work. Which being a-doing, there came down of the country certain of the people naked, saving only about their waist the skin of some beast, with the fur or hair on, and something also wreathed on their heads. Their faces were painted with divers colours, and some of them had on their heads the similitude of horns, every man his bow, which was an ell in length, and a couple of arrows. They were very agile people and quick to deliver, and seemed not to be ignorant in the feats of wars, as by their order of ranging a few men might appear. These people would not of a long time receive anything at our hands; yet at length our General being ashore, and they dancing after their accustomed manner about him, and he once turning his back towards them, one leaped suddenly to him, and took his cap with his gold band off his head, and ran a little distance from him, and shared it with his fellow, the cap to the one, and the band to the other. Having despatched all our business in this place, we departed and set sail. And immediately upon our setting forth we lost our *canter,* which was absent three of four days; but when our General had her again, he took out the necessaries, and so gave her over, near to the *Cape of Good Hope.* The next day after, being the 20. of June, we harboured ourselves again in a very good harborough, called by *Magellan, Port St. Julian,* where we found a gibbet standing upon the main; which we supposed to be the place where *Magellan* did execution upon some of his disobedient and rebellious company.

The two and twentieth day our General went ashore to the main, and in his company *John Thomas,* and *Robert Winterhie, Oliver* the master-gunner, *John Brewer, Thomas Hood,* and *Thomas Drake.* And entering on land, they presently met with two or three of the country people. And *Robert Winterhie* having in his hands a bow and arrows, went about to make a shoot of pleasure, and, in his draught, his bowstring brake; which the rude savages taking as a token of war, began to bend the force of their bows against our company, and drove them to their shifts very narrowly.

In this port our General began to enquire diligently of the actions of Master *Thomas Doughty,* and found them not to be such as he looked for, but tending rather of contention or mutiny, or some other disorder, whereby, without redress, the success of the voyage might greatly have been hazarded. Whereupon the company was called together and made acquainted with the particulars of the cause, which were found, partly by Master *Doughty's* own confession, and partly by the evidence of the fact, to be true. Which when our General saw, although his private affection to Master *Doughty,* as he then in the presence of us all sacredly protested, was great, yet the care he had of the state of the voyage, of the expectation of her Majesty, and of the honour of his country did more touch him, as indeed it ought, than the private respect of one man. So that the cause being throughly heard, and all things done in good order as near as might be to the course of our laws in *England,* it was concluded that Master *Doughty* should receive punishment according to the quality of the offence. And he, seeing no remedy but patience for himself, desired before his death to receive the communion, which he did at the hands of Master *Fletcher,* our minister, and our General himself accompanied him in that holy action. Which being done, and the place of execution made ready, he having embraced our General, and taken his leave of all the company, with prayers for the Queen's Majesty and our realm, in quiet sort laid his head to the block, where he ended his life. This being done, our General made divers speeches to the whole company, persuading us to unity, obedience, love, and regard of our voyage; and for the better confirmation thereof, willed every man the next Sunday following to prepare himself the communion, as Christian brethren and friends ought to do. Which was done in very reverent sort; and so with good contentment every man went about his business.

The 17. day of August we departed the port of *St. Julian,*[4] and the 20. day we fell with the Strait of *Magellan,* going into the South Sea; at the cape or headland whereof we found the body of a dead man, whose flesh was clean consumed. The 21. day we entered the Strait,[5] which we found to have many turnings, and as it were shuttings-up, as if there were no passage at all. By means whereof we had the wind often against us; so that some of the fleet recovering a cape or point of land, others should be forced to turn back again, and to come to an anchor where they could. In this Strait there be many fair harbours, with store of fresh water. But yet they lack their best commodity, for the water there is of such depth, that no man shall find ground to anchor in, except it be in some narrow river or corner, or between some rocks; so that if any extreme blasts or contrary winds do come, whereunto the place is much subject, it carrieth with it no small danger. The land on both sides is very huge and mountainous; the lower mountains whereof, although they be monstrous and wonderful to look upon for their height, yet there are others which in height exceed them in a strange manner, reaching themselves above their fellows so high, that between them did appear three regions of clouds. These mountains are covered with snow. At both the southerly and easterly parts of the Strait there are islands, among which the sea hath his indraught into the Straits, even as it hath in the main entrance of the frete.[6] This Strait is extreme cold, with frost and snow continually; the trees seem to stoop with the burden of the weather, and yet are green continually, and many good and sweet herbs do very plentifully grow and increase under them. The breadth of the Strait is in some places a league, in some other places two leagues and three leagues, and in some

[4] The squadron was now reduced to three ships, the *Swan* and the *Christopher,* as well as the Portuguese prize, having been condemned as unseaworthy, and burnt or abandoned.

[5] Drake here changed the name of the *Pelican* to the *Golden Hind,* the crest of Sir Christopher Hatton.

[6] Lat. *fretum.*

other four leagues; but the narrowest place hath a league over.

The 24. of August we arrived at an island in the Straits, where we found great store of fowl which could not fly, of the bigness of geese; whereof we killed in less than one day 3,000, and victualled ourselves throughly therewith. The 6. day of September we entered the South Sea at the cape or head shore. The 7. day we were driven by a great storm from the entering into the South Sea, 200 leagues and odd in longitude, and one degree to the southward of the Strait; in which height, and so many leagues to the westward, the 15. day of September, fell out the eclipse of the moon at the hour of six of the clock at night. But neither did the ecliptical conflict of the moon impair our state, nor her clearing again amend us a whit; but the accustomed eclipse of the sea continued in his force, we being darkened more than the moon sevenfold.[7]

From the bay which we called the *Bay of Severing of Friends,* we were driven back to the southward of the Straits in 57 degrees and a tierce; in which height we came to an anchor among the islands, having there fresh and very good water, with herbs of singular virtue. Not far from hence we entered another bay, where we found people, both men and women, in their canoes naked, and ranging from one island to another to seek their meat; who entered traffic with us for such things as they had. We returning hence northward again, found the third of October three islands, in one of which was such plenty of birds as is scant credible to report. The 8. day of October we lost sight of one of our consorts,[8] wherein Master *Winter* was; who, as then we supposed, was put by a storm into the Straits again. Which at our return home we found to be true, and he not perished, as some of our company feared. Thus being come into the height of the Straits again, we ran, supposing the coast of *Chili* to lie as the general maps have described it, namely north-west; which we found to lie and trend to the north-east and eastwards. Whereby it appeareth that this part of *Chili* hath not been truly hitherto discovered,

[7] In this storm the *Marigold* went down with all hands.

[8] The *Elizabeth.* Winter, having lost sight of the Admiral, sailed home. The *Golden Hind* was thus left to pursue her voyage alone.

or at the least not truly reported, for the space of twelve degrees at the least; being set down either of purpose to deceive, or of ignorant conjecture.

We continuing our course, fell the 29. of November with an island called *La Mocha,* where we cast anchor; and our General, hoisting out our boat, went with ten of our company to shore. Where we found people, whom the cruel and extreme dealings of the Spaniards have forced, for their own safety and liberty, to flee from the main, and to fortify themselves in this island. We being on land, the people came down to us to the water side with show of great courtesy, bringing to us potatoes, roots, and two very fat sheep; which our General received, and gave them other things for them, and had promised to have water there. But the next day repairing again to the shore, and sending two men a-land with barrels to fill water, the people taking them for Spaniards (to whom they use to show no favour if they take them) laid violent hands on them, and, as we think, slew them. Our General seeing this, stayed here no longer, but weighed anchor, and set sail towards the coast of *Chili.* And drawing towards it, we met near to the shore an Indian in a *canoa,* who thinking us to have been Spaniards, came to us and told us, that at a place called *Santiago,* there was a great Spanish ship laden from the kingdom of *Peru;* for which good news our General gave him divers trifles. Whereof he was glad, and went along with us and brought us to the place, which is called the port of *Valparaiso.* When we came thither we found, indeed, the ship riding at anchor, having in her eight Spaniards and three negroes; who, thinking us to have been Spaniards, and their friends, welcomed us with a drum, and made ready a *botija*[9] of wine of *Chili* to drink to us. But as soon as we were entered, one of our company called *Thomas Moon* began to lay about him, and struck one of the Spaniards, and said unto him, *Abaxo, perro!* that is in English. 'Go down, dog!' One of these Spaniards, seeing persons of that quality in those seas, all to crossed and blessed himself. But, to be short, we stowed them under hatches, all save one Spaniard, who suddenly and desperately leapt overboard into the sea, and swam

[9] Jar.

ashore to the town of *Santiago,* to give them warning of our arrival.

They of the town, being not above nine households, presently fled away and abandoned the town. Our General manned his boat and the Spanish ship's boat, and went to the town; and, being come to it, we rifled it, and came to a small chapel, which we entered, and found therein a silver chalice, two cruets, and one altar-cloth, the spoil whereof our General gave to Master *Fletcher,* his minister. We found also in this town a warehouse stored with wine of *Chili* and many boards of cedar-wood; all which wine we brought away with us, and certain of the boards to burn for firewood. And so, being come aboard, we departed the haven, having first set all the Spaniards on land, saving one *John Griego,* a Greek born, whom our General carried with him as pilot to bring him into the haven of *Lima.*

When we were at sea our General rifled the ship, and found in her good store of the wine of *Chili,* and 25,000 *pesos* of very pure and fine gold of *Valdivia,* amounting in value to 37,000 ducats of Spanish money, and above. So, going on our course, we arrived next at a place called *Coquimbo,* where our General sent fourteen of his men on land to fetch water. But they were espied by the Spaniards, who came with 300 horsemen and 200 footmen, and slew one of our men with a piece. The rest came aboard in safety, and the Spaniards departed. We went on shore again and buried our man, and the Spaniards came down again with a flag of truce; but we set sail, and would not trust them. From hence we went to a certain port called *Tarapaca;* where, being landed, we found by the sea side a Spaniard lying asleep, who had lying by him thirteen bars of silver, which weighed 4,000 ducats Spanish. We took the silver and left the man. Not far from hence, going on land for fresh water, we met with a Spaniard and an Indian boy driving eight *llamas* or sheep of *Peru,* which are as big as asses; every of which sheep had on his back two bags of leather, each bag containing 50 lb. weight of fine silver. So that, bringing both the sheep and their burthen to the ships, we found in all the bags eight hundred weight of silver.

Herehence we sailed to a place called *Arica;* and, being

entered the port, we found there three small barks, which we rifled, and found in one of them fifty-seven wedges of silver, each of them weighing about 20 lb. weight, and every of these wedges were of the fashion and bigness of a brickbat. In all these three barks, we found not one person. For they, mistrusting no strangers, were all gone a-land to the town, which consisteth of about twenty houses; which we would have ransacked if our company had been better and more in number. But our General, contented with the spoil of the ships, left the town and put off again to sea, and set sail for *Lima,* and, by the way, met with a small bark, which he boarded, and found in her good store of linen cloth. Whereof taking some quantity, he let her go.

To *Lima* we came the 13. of February; and, being entered the haven, we found there about twelve sail of ships lying fast moored at an anchor, having all their sails carried on shore; for the masters and merchants were here most secure, having never been assaulted by enemies, and at this time feared the approach of none such as we were. Our General rifled these ships, and found in one of them a chest full of reals of plate, and good store of silks and linen cloth; and took the chest into his own ship, and good store of the silks and linen. In which ship he had news of another ship called the *Cacafuego,*[10] which was gone towards *Payta,* and that the same ship was laden with treasure. Whereupon we stayed no longer here, but, cutting all the cables of the ships in the haven, we let them drive whither they would, either to sea or to the shore; and with all speed we followed the *Cacafuego* toward *Payta,* thinking there to have found her. But before we arrived there she was gone from thence towards *Panama;* whom our General still pursued, and by the way met with a bark laden with ropes and tackle for ships, which he boarded and searched, and found in her 80 lb. weight of gold, and a crucifix of gold with goodly great emeralds set in it, which he took, and some of the cordage also for his own ship. From hence we departed, still following the *Cacafuego;* and our General promised our company that whosoever should first descry her should have his chain of gold for his good news. It fortuned that

[10] 'Spitfire.'

John Drake, going up into the top, descried her about three of the clock. And about six of the clock we came to her and boarded her, and shot at her three pieces of ordnance, and strake down her mizen; and, being entered, we found in her great riches, as jewels and precious stones, thirteen chests full of reals of plate, fourscore pound weight of gold, and six-and-twenty ton of silver. The place where we took this prize was called *Cape de San Francisco,* about 150 leagues [south] from *Panama.* The pilot's name of this ship was *Francisco;* and amongst other plate that our General found in this ship he found two very fair gilt bowls of silver, which were the pilot's. To whom our General said, *Señor Pilot, you have here two silver cups, but I must needs have one of them;* which the pilot, because he could not otherwise choose, yielded unto, and gave the other to the steward of our General's ships. When this pilot departed from us, his boy said thus unto our General: *Captain, our ship shall be called no more the Cacafuego, but the Cacaplata, and your ship shall be called the Cacafuego.* Which pretty speech of the pilot's boy ministered matter of laughter to us, both then and long after. When our General had done what he would with this *Cacafuego,* he cast her off, and we went on our course still towards the west; and not long after met with a ship laden with linen cloth and fine *China* dishes of white earth, and great store of *China* silks, of all which things we took as we listed. The owner himself of this ship was in her, who was a Spanish gentleman,[11] from whom our General took a falcon of gold, with a great emerald in the breast thereof;[12] and the pilot of the ship he took also with him, and so cast the ship off.

This pilot brought us to the haven of *Guatulco,* the town whereof, as he told us, had but 17 Spaniards in it. As soon as we were entered this haven, we landed, and went presently to the town and to the town-house; where we found a judge sitting in judgment, being associated with three other officers, upon three negroes that had conspired the burning of the town. Both which judges and prisoners we took, and brought them a-shipboard, and caused the chief judge

[11] Don Francisco de Zarate.

[12] Drake presented him in return with a hanger and a silver brazier.

to write his letter to the town to command all the townsmen to avoid, that we might safely water there. Which being done, and they departed, we ransacked the town; and in one house we found a pot, of the quantity of a bushel, full of reals of plate, which we brought to our ship. And here one *Thomas Moon,* one of our company, took a Spanish gentleman as he was flying out of the town; and, searching him, he found a chain of gold about him, and other jewels, which he took, and so let him go. At this place our General, among other Spaniards, set ashore his Portugal pilot which he took at the islands of *Cape Verde* out of a ship of *St. Mary* port, of *Portugal.* And having set them ashore we departed hence, and sailed to the island of *Canno;* where our General landed, and brought to shore his own ship, and discharged her, mended and graved her, and furnished our ship with water and wood sufficiently.

And while we were here we espied a ship and set sail after her, and took her, and found in her two pilots and a Spanish governor, going for the islands of the *Philippinas.* We searched the ship, and took some of her merchandises, and so let her go. Our General at this place and time, thinking himself, both in respect of his private injuries received from the Spaniards, as also of their contempts and indignities offered to our country and prince in general, sufficiently satisfied and revenged; and supposing that her Majesty at his return would rest contented with this service, purposed to continue no longer upon the Spanish coast, but began to consider and to consult of the best way for his country.

He thought it not good to return by the Straits, for two special causes; the one, lest the Spaniards should there wait and attend for him in great number and strength, whose hands, he, being left but one ship, could not possibly escape. The other cause was the dangerous situation of the mouth of the Straits in the South Sea; where continual storms reigning and blustering, as he found by experience, besides the shoals and sands upon the coast, he thought it not a good course to adventure that way. He resolved, therefore, to avoid these hazards, to go forward to the Islands of the *Malucos,* and therehence to sail the course of the Portugals by the Cape of *Buena Esperanza.* Upon this resolution he began to think of his best way to the *Malucos,* and finding himself, where he now was, becalmed, he saw that of necessity he must be forced to take a Spanish course; namely, to sail somewhat northerly to get a wind. We therefore set sail, and sailed 600 leagues at the least for a good wind; and thus much we sailed from the 16. of April till the third of June.

The fifth of June, being in 43 degrees towards the pole Arctic, we found the air so cold, that our men being grievously pinched with the same, complained of the extremity thereof; and the further we went, the more the cold increased upon us. Whereupon we thought it best for that time to seek the land, and did so; finding it not mountainous, but low plain land, till we came within 38 degrees towards the line. In which height it pleased God to send us into a fair and good bay, with a good wind to enter the same. In this bay we anchored; and the people of the country, having their houses close by the water's side, shewed themselves unto us, and sent a present to our General. When they came unto us, they greatly wondered at the things that we brought. But our General, according to his natural and accustomed humanity, courteously intreated them, and liberally bestowed on them necessary things to cover their nakedness; whereupon they supposed us to be gods, and would not be persuaded to the contrary. The presents which they sent to our General, were feathers, and cauls of network. Their houses are digged round about with earth, and have from the uttermost brims of the circle, clifts of wood set upon them, joining close together at the top like a spire steeple, which by reason of that closeness are very warm. Their bed is the ground with rushes strowed on it; and lying about the house, [they] have the fire in the midst. The men go naked; the women take bulrushes, and kemb them after the manner of hemp, and thereof make their loose garments, which being knit about their middles, hang down about their hips, having also about their shoulders a skin of deer, with the hair upon it. These women are very obedient and serviceable to their husbands.

After they were departed from us, they came and visited

us the second time, and brought with them feathers and bags of *tabacco* for presents. And when they came to the top of the hill, at the bottom whereof we had pitched our tents, they stayed themselves; where one appointed for speaker wearied himself with making a long oration; which done, they left their bows upon the hill, and came down with their presents. In the meantime the women, remaining upon the hill, tormented themselves lamentably, tearing their flesh from their cheeks, whereby we perceived that they were about a sacrifice. In the meantime our General with his company went to prayer, and to reading of the Scriptures, at which exercise they were attentive, and seemed greatly to be affected with it; but when they were come unto us, they restored again unto us those things which before we bestowed upon them. The news of our being there being spread through the country, the people that inhabited round about came down, and amongst them the king himself, a man of a goodly stature, and comely personage, with many other tall and warlike men; before whose coming were sent two ambassadors to our General, to signify that their king was coming, in doing of which message, their speech was continued about half an hour. This ended, they by signs requested our General to send something by their hand to their king, as a token that his coming might be in peace. Wherein our General having satisfied them, they returned with glad tidings to their king, who marched to us with a princely majesty, the people crying continually after their manner; and as they drew near unto us, so did they strive to behave themselves in their actions with comeliness. In the fore-front was a man of a goodly personage, who bare the sceptre or mace before the king; whereupon hanged two crowns, a less and a bigger, with three chains of a marvellous length. The crowns were made of knit work, wrought artificially with feathers of divers colours. The chains were made of a bony substance, and few be the persons among them that are admitted to wear them; and of that number also the persons are stinted, as some ten, some twelve, &c. Next unto him which bare the sceptre, was the king himself, with his guard about his person, clad with coney skins, and other skins. After them followed the naked common sort of people, every one having his face painted, some with white, some with black, and other colours, and having in their hands one thing or another for a present. Not so much as their children, but they also brought their presents.

In the meantime our General gathered his men together, and marched within his fenced place, making, against their approaching, a very warlike show. They being trooped together in their order, and a general salutation being made, there was presently a general silence. Then he that bare the sceptre before the king, being informed by another, whom they assigned to that office, with a manly and lofty voice proclaimed that which the other spake to him in secret, continuing half an hour. Which ended, and a general *Amen,* as it were, given, the king with the whole number of men and women, the children excepted, came down without any weapon; who, descending to the foot of the hill, set themselves in order. In coming towards our bulwarks and tents, the sceptre-bearer began a song, observing his measures in a dance, and that with a stately countenance; whom the king with his guard, and every degree of persons, following, did in like manner sing and dance, saving only the women, which danced and kept silence. The General permitted them to enter within our bulwark, where they continued their song and dance a reasonable time. When they had satisfied themselves, they made signs to our General to sit down; to whom the king and divers others made several orations, or rather supplications, that he would take their province and kingdom into his hand, and become their king, making signs that they would resign unto him their right and title of the whole land, and become his subjects. In which, to persuade us the better, the king and the rest, with one consent, and with great reverence, joyfully singing a song, did set the crown upon his head, enriched his neck with all their chains, and offered him many other things, honouring him by the name of *Hioh,* adding thereunto, as it seemed, a sign of triumph; which thing our General thought not meet to reject, because he knew not what honour and profit it might be to our country. Wherefore in the name, and to the use of her Majesty, he took the sceptre, crown, and dignity of the said country into his hands, wishing that the riches and treasure thereof might so conveniently be transported to the enriching of her kingdom at home, as it aboundeth in the same.

The common sort of people, leaving the king and his guard with our General, scattered themselves together with their sacrifices among our people, taking a diligent view of every person: and such as pleased their fancy (which were the youngest), they enclosing them about offered their sacrifices unto them with lamentable weeping, scratching and tearing their flesh from their faces with their nails, whereof issued abundance of blood. But we used signs to them of disliking this, and stayed their hands from force, and directed them upwards to the living God, whom only they ought to worship. They shewed unto us their wounds, and craved help of them at our hands; whereupon we gave them lotions, plaisters, and ointments agreeing to the state of their griefs, beseeching God to cure their diseases. Every third day they brought their sacrifices unto us, until they understood our meaning, that we had no pleasure in them; yet they could not be long absent from us, but daily frequented our company to the hour of our departure, which departure seemed so grievous unto them, that their joy was turned into sorrow. They entreated us, that being absent we would remember them, and by stealth provided a sacrifice, which we misliked.

Our necessary business being ended, our General with his company travelled up into the country to their villages, where we found herds of deer by a thousand in a company, being most large, and fat of body. We found the whole country to be a warren of a strange kind of coneys; their bodies in bigness as be the *Barbary* coneys, their heads as the heads of ours, the feet of a want,[13] and the tail of a rat, being of great length. Under her chin is on either side a bag, into the which she gathereth her meat, when she hath filled her belly abroad. The people eat their bodies, and make great account of their skins, for their king's coat was made of them. Our General called this country *Nova Albion,* and that for two causes; the one in respect of the

[13] Mole.

white banks and cliffs, which lie towards the sea, and the other, because it might have some affinity with our country in name, which sometime was so called. There is no part of earth here to be taken up, wherein there is not some probable show of gold or silver.

At our departure hence our General set up a monument of our being there, as also of her Majesty's right and title to the same; namely a plate, nailed upon a fair great post, whereupon was engraved her Majesty's name, the day and year of our arrival there, with the free giving up of the province and people into her Majesty's hands, together with her Highness' picture and arms, in a piece of six pence of current English money, under the plate, whereunder was also written the name of our General.

It seemeth that the Spaniards hitherto had never been in this part of the country, neither did ever discover the land by many degrees to the southwards of this place.

After we had set sail from hence, we continued without sight of land till the 13. day of October following, which day in the morning we fell with certain islands eight degrees to the northward of the line, from which islands came a great number of *canoas,* having in some of them four, in some six, and in some also fourteen men, bringing with them cocos and other fruits. Their *canoas* were hollow within, and cut with great art and cunning, being very smooth within and without, and bearing a glass[14] as if it were a horn daintily burnished, having a prow and a stern of one sort, yielding inward circle-wise, being of a great height, and full of certain white shells for a bravery; and on each side of them lie out two pieces of timber about a yard and a half long, more or less, according to the smallness or bigness of the boat. These people have the nether part of their ears cut into a round circle, hanging down very low upon their cheeks, whereon they hang things of a reasonable weight. The nails of their hands are an inch long, their teeth are as black as pitch, and they renew them often, by eating of an herb with a kind of powder, which they always carry about them in a cane for the same purpose.

Leaving this island the night after we fell with it, the 18

[14] I. e., having a gloss.

of October we lighted upon divers others, some whereof made a great show of inhabitants. We continued our course by the islands of *Tagulanda,*[15] *Zelon,* and *Zewarra,* being friends to the Portugals, the first whereof hath growing in it great store of cinnamon. The 14. of November we fell in with the islands of *Maluco.* Which day at night (having directed our course to run with *Tidore*) in coasting along the island of *Mutyr,*[16] belonging to the king of *Ternate,* his deputy or vice-king seeing us at sea, came with his *canoa* to us without all fear, and came aboard; and after some conference with our General, willed him in any wise to run in with *Ternate,* and not with *Tidore,* assuring him that the king would be glad of his coming, and would be ready to do what he would require, for which purpose he himself would that night be with the king, and tell him the news. With whom if he once dealt, we should find that as he was a king, so his word should stand; adding further, that if he went to *Tidore* before he came to *Ternate,* the king would have nothing to do with us, because he held the Portugal as his enemy. Whereupon our General resolved to run with *Ternate.* Where the next morning early we came to anchor; at which time our General sent a messenger to the king, with a velvet cloak for a present and token of his coming to be in peace, and that he required nothing but traffic and exchange of merchandise, whereof he had good store, in such things as he wanted.

In the meantime the vice-king had been with the king according to his promise, signifying unto him what good things he might receive from us by traffic. Whereby the king was moved with great liking towards us, and sent to our General, with special message, that he should have what things he needed and would require, with peace and friendship; and moreover that he would yield himself and the right of his island to be at the pleasure and commandment of so famous a prince as we served. In token whereof he sent to our General a signet; and within short time after came in his own person, with boats and *canoas,* to our ship, to bring her into a better and safer road than she was in at

[15] Tagulandang, to the north-east of Celebes.
[16] Motir, one of the Ternate Moluccas.

that present. In the meantime, our General's messenger, being come to the Court, was met by certain noble personages with great solemnity, and brought to the king, at whose hands he was most friendly and graciously entertained.

The king, purposing to come to our ship, sent before four great and large *canoas,* in every one whereof were certain of his greatest states[17] that were about him, attired in white lawn of cloth of *Calicut,* having over their heads, from the one end of the *canoa* to the other, a covering of thin perfumed mats, borne up with a frame made of reeds for the same use; under which every one did sit in his order according to his dignity, to keep him from the heat of the sun; divers of whom being of good age and gravity, did make an ancient and fatherly show. There were also divers young and comely men attired in white, as were the others; the rest were soldiers, which stood in comely order round about on both sides. Without whom sat the rowers in certain galleries; which being three on a side all along the *canoas,* did lie off from the side thereof three or four yards, one being orderly builded lower than another, in every of which galleries were the number of fourscore rowers. These *canoas* were furnished with warlike munition, every man for the most part having his sword and target, with his dagger, beside other weapons, as lances, calivers, darts, bows and arrows; also every *canoa* had a small cast base mounted at the least one full yard upon a stock set upright. Thus coming near our ship, in order, they rowed about us one after another, and passing by, did their homage with great solemnity; the great personages beginning with great gravity and fatherly countenances, signifying that the king had sent them to conduct our ship into a better road. Soon after the king himself repaired, accompanied with six grave and ancient persons, who did their obeisance with marvellous humility. The king was a man of tall stature, and seemed to be much delighted with the sound of our music; to whom, as also to his nobility, our General gave presents, wherewith they were passing well contented.

At length the king craved leave of our General to depart, promising the next day to come aboard, and in the meantime

[17] States—men of property or estate.

to send us such victuals as were necessary for our provision. So that the same night we received of them meal, which they call *sagu,* made of the tops of certain trees, tasting in the mouth like sour curds, but melteth like sugar, whereof they make certain cakes, which may be kept the space of ten years, and yet then good to be eaten. We had of them store of rice, hens, unperfect and liquid sugar, sugar-canes, and a fruit which they call *figo,*[18] with store of cloves.

The king having promised to come aboard, brake his promise, but sent his brother to make his excuse, and to entreat our General to come on shore, offering himself pawn aboard for his safe return. Whereunto our General consented not, upon mislike conceived of the breach of his promise; the whole company also utterly refusing it. But to satisfy him, our General sent certain of his gentlemen to the Court, to accompany the king's brother, reserving the vice-king for their safe return. They were received of another brother of the king's, and other states, and were conducted with great honour to the castle. The place that they were brought unto was a large and fair house, where were at the least a thousand persons assembled.

The king being yet absent, there sat in their places 60 grave personages, all which were said to be of the king's council. There were besides four grave persons, apparelled all in red, down to the ground, and attired on their heads like the Turks; and these were said to be Romans[19] and ligiers[20] there to keep continual traffic with the people of *Ternate.* There were also two Turks ligiers in this place, and one Italian. The king at last came in guarded with twelve lances, covered over with a rich canopy with embossed gold. Our men, accompanied with one of their captains called *Moro,* rising to meet him, he graciously did welcome and entertain them. He was attired after the manner of the country, but more sumptuously than the rest. From his waist down to the ground was all cloth of gold, and the same very rich; his legs were bare, but on his feet were a pair of shoes, made of *Cordovan* skin. In the attire of his head were finely wreathed hooped rings of gold, and about his

[18] Plantains. [19] Probably Greeks (Arab. *Rumi*). [20] Resident agents.

neck he had a chain of perfect gold, the links whereof were great, and one fold double. On his fingers he had six very fair jewels; and sitting in his chair of state, at his right hand stood a page with a fan in his hand, breathing and gathering the air to the king. The same was in length two foot, and in breadth one foot, set with eight sapphires richly embroidered, and knit to a staff three foot in length, by the which the page did hold and move it. Our gentlemen having delivered their message and received order accordingly, were licensed to depart, being safely conducted back again by one of the king's council. This island is the chief of all the islands of *Maluco,* and the king hereof is king of 70 islands besides. The king with his people are Moors in religion, observing certain new moons, with fastings; during which fasts they neither eat nor drink in the day, but in the night.

After that our gentlemen were returned, and that we had here by the favour of the king received all necessary things that the place could yield us; our General considering the great distance, and how far he was yet off from his country, thought it not best here to linger the time any longer, but weighing his anchors, set out of the island, and sailed to a certain little island to the southwards of *Celebes,* where we graved our ship, and continued there, in that and other businesses, 26 days. This island is throughly grown with wood of a large and high growth, very straight, and without boughs, save only in the head or top, whose leaves are not much differing from our broom in *England.* Amongst these trees night by night, through the whole land, did shew themselves an infinite swarm of fiery worms flying in the air, whose bodies being no bigger than our common English flies, make such a show and light as if every twig or tree had been a burning candle. In this place breedeth also wonderful store of bats, as big as large hens. Of cray-fishes also here wanted no plenty, and they of exceeding bigness, one whereof was sufficient for four hungry stomachs at a dinner, being also very good and restoring meat, whereof we had experience: and they dig themselves holes in the earth like coneys.

When we had ended our business here we weighed, and set sail to run for the *Malucos.* But having at that time a bad wind, and being amongst the islands, with much difficulty we recovered to the northward of the island of *Celebes;* where by reason of contrary winds, not able to continue our course to run westwards, we were enforced to alter the same to the southward again, finding that course also to be very hard and dangerous for us, by reason of infinite shoals which lie off and among the islands; whereof we had too much trial, to the hazard and danger of our ship and lives. For, of all other days, upon the 9. of January, in the year 1579,[21] we ran suddenly upon a rock, where we stuck fast from eight of the clock at night till four of the clock in the afternoon the next day, being indeed out of all hope to escape the danger. But our General, as he had always hitherto shewed himself courageous, and of a good confidence in the mercy and protection of God, so now he continued in the same. And lest he should seem to perish wilfully, both he and we did our best endeavour to save ourselves; which it pleased God so to bless, that in the end we cleared ourselves most happily of the danger.

We lighted our ship upon the rocks of three ton of cloves, eight pieces of ordnance, and certain meal and beans; and then the wind, as it were in a moment by the special grace of God, changing from the starboard to the larboard of the ship, we hoised our sails, and the happy gale drove our ship off the rock into the sea again, to the no little comfort of all our hearts, for which we gave God such praise and thanks, as so great a benefit required.

The 8. of February following, we fell with the fruitful island of *Barateve,*[22] having in the mean time suffered many dangers by winds and shoals. The people of this island are comely in body and stature, and of a civil behaviour, just in dealing, and courteous to strangers; whereof we had the experience sundry ways, they being most glad of our presence, and very ready to relieve our wants in those things which their country did yield. The men go naked, saving their heads and loins, every man having something or other hanging at their ears. Their women are covered from the middle down to the foot, wearing a great number of bracelets upon their arms; for some had eight upon each arm,

[21] I. e. 1580. [22] BatJan.

being made some of bone, some of horn, and some of brass, the lightest whereof, by our estimation, weighed two ounces apiece. With this people linen-cloth is good merchandise, and of good request; whereof they make rolls for their heads, and girdles to wear about them. Their island is both rich and fruitful; rich in gold, silver, copper, and sulphur, wherein they seem skilful and expert, not only to try the same, but in working it also artificially into any form and fashion that pleaseth them. Their fruits be divers and plentiful; as nutmegs, ginger, long pepper, lemons, cucumbers, cocos, *figu, sagu,* with divers other sorts. And among all the rest we had one fruit, in bigness, form and husk, like a bay berry, hard of substance and pleasant of taste, which being sodden becometh soft, and is a most good and wholesome victual; whereof we took reasonable store, as we did also of the other fruits and spices. So that to confess a truth, since the time that we first set out of our own country of *England,* we happened upon no place, *Ternate* only excepted, wherein we found more comforts and better means of refreshing.

At our departure from *Barateve,* we set our course for *Java Major;*[28] where arriving, we found great courtesy, and honourable entertainment. This island is governed by five kings, whom they call *Rajah;* as *Rajah Donaw,* and *Rajah Mang Bange,* and *Rajah Cabuccapollo,* which live as having one spirit and one mind. Of these five we had four a-shipboard at once, and two or three often. They are wonderfully delighted in coloured clothes, as red and green; the upper part of their bodies are naked, save their heads, whereupon they wear a Turkish roll as do the *Maluccians.* From the middle downward they wear a *pintado* of silk, trailing upon the ground, in colour as they best like. The *Maluccians* hate that their women should be seen of strangers; but these offer them of high courtesy, yea, the kings themselves. The people are of goodly stature and warlike, well provided of swords and targets, with daggers, all being of their own work, and most artificially done, both in tempering their metal, as also in the form; whereof we bought reasonable store. They have an house in every village for their common assembly; every day they meet twice, men, women, and

[28] Java.

children, bringing with them such victuals as they think good, some fruits, some rice boiled, some hens roasted, some *sagu,* having a table made three foot from the ground, whereon they set their meat, that every person sitting at the table may eat, one rejoicing in the company of another. They boil their rice in an earthen pot, made in form of a sugar loaf, being full of holes, as our pots which we water our gardens withal, and it is open at the great end, wherein they put their rice dry, without any moisture. In the mean time they have ready another great earthen pot, set fast in a furnace, boiling full of water, whereinto they put their pot with rice, by such measure, that they swelling become soft at the first, and by their swelling stopping the holes of the pot, admit no more water to enter, but the more they are boiled, the harder and more firm substance they become. So that in the end they are a firm and good bread, of the which with oil, butter, sugar, and other spices, they make divers sorts of meats very pleasant of taste, and nourishing to nature. * * * Not long before our departure, they told us that not far off there were such great ships as ours, wishing us to beware; upon this our captain would stay no longer. From *Java Major* we sailed for the Cape of *Good Hope,* which was the first land we fell withal; neither did we touch with it, or any other land, until we came to *Sierra Leona,* upon the coast of *Guinea;* notwithstanding we ran hard aboard the cape, finding the report of the Portugals to be most false, who affirm that it is the most dangerous cape of the world, never without intolerable storms and present danger to travellers which come near the same. This cape is a most stately thing, and the fairest cape we saw in the whole circumference of the earth, and we passed by it the 18. of June. From thence we continued our course to *Sierra Leona,* on the coast of *Guinea,* where we arrived the 22. of July, and found necessary provisions, great store of elephants, oysters upon trees of one kind,[24] spawning and increasing infinitely, the oyster suffering no bud to grow. We departed thence the four and twentieth day.

We arrived in *England* the third of November, 1580, being the third year of our departure.

[24] The mangrove.

DRAKE'S GREAT ARMADA

NEARLY five years elapsed between Drake's return from his Famous Voyage and the despatch of the formidable armament commemorated in the following pages. During the last of these years the march of events had been remarkably rapid. Gilbert, who had been empowered by Elizabeth, in the year of Frobisher's last expedition, to found colonies in America, had sailed for that purpose to Newfoundland (1583), and had perished at sea on his way homeward. Raleigh, who had succeeded to his half-brother's enterprises, had despatched his exploring expedition to 'Virginia,' under Amadas and Barlow, in 1584, and had followed it up in the next year (1585) by an actual colony. In April Sir Richard Greenville sailed from Plymouth, and at Raleigh's expense established above a hundred colonists on the island of Roanoak. Drake's Great Armada left Plymouth in September of the same year. It marked a turning-point in the relations between the English and Spanish monarchs. Elizabeth, knowing that the suppression of the insurrection in the Netherlands would be followed by an attack upon England, was treating with the insurgents. Philip deemed it prudent to lay an embargo on all her subjects, together with their ships and goods, that might be found in his dominions. Elizabeth at once authorized general reprisals on the ships and goods of Spaniards. A company of adventurers was quickly formed for taking advantage of this permission on a scale commensurate with the national resources. They equipped an armada of twenty-five vessels, manned by 2,300 men, and despatched it under the command of Drake to plunder Spanish America. Frobisher was second in command. Two-thirds of the booty were to belong to the adventurers; the remaining third was to be divided among the men employed in the expedition.

Drake's armament of 1585 was the greatest that had ever crossed the Atlantic. After plundering some vessels at the Vigo river, he sailed for the West Indies by way of the Canaries and Cape Verde Islands, hoisted the English flag over Santiago and burnt the town, crossed the Atlantic in eighteen days, and arrived at Dominica. At daybreak, on New Year's Day, 1586, Drake's soldiers landed in Española, a few miles to the west of the capital, and before evening Carlile and Powell had entered the city, which the colonists only saved from destruction by the payment of a heavy ransom. Drake's plan was to do exactly the same at Carthagena and Nombre de Dios, and thence to strike across the isthmus and secure the treasure that lay waiting for transport at Panama. Drake held St. Domingo for a month, and Carthagena for six weeks. He was compelled to forego the further prosecution of his enterprise. A deadly fever, which had attacked the men during the sojourn at Santiago, still continued its ravages. In existing circumstances, even had Nombre de Dios been successfully attacked, the march to Panama was out of the question; and after consultation with the military commanders, Drake resolved on sailing home at once by way of Florida. He brought back with him all the colonists who had been left by Sir Richard Greenville in 'Virginia.' Drake had offered either to furnish them with stores, and to leave them a ship, or to take them home. The former offer was accepted: but a furious storm which ensued caused them to change their minds. They recognized in it the hand of God, whose will it evidently was that they should no longer be sojourners in the American wilderness; and the first English settlement of 'Virginia' was abandoned accordingly.

Ten years afterwards (1595) Drake was again at the head of a similar expedition. The second command was given to his old associate Hawkins, Frobisher, his Vice-Admiral in 1585, having recently died of the wound received at Crozon. This time Nombre de Dios was taken and burnt, and 750 soldiers set out under Sir Thomas Baskerville to march to Panama: but at the first of the three forts which the Spaniards had by this time constructed, the march had to be abandoned. Drake did not long survive this second failure of his favourite scheme. He was attacked by dysentery a fortnight afterwards, and in a month he died. When he felt the hand of death upon him, he rose, dressed himself, and endeavoured to make a farewell speech to those around him. Exhausted by the effort, he was lifted to his berth, and within an hour breathed his last. Hawkins had died off Puerto Rico six weeks previously.

The following narrative is in the main the composition of

Walter Biggs, who commanded a company of musketeers under Carlile. Biggs was one of the five hundred and odd men who succumbed to the fever. He died shortly after the fleet sailed from Carthagena; and the narrative was completed by some comrade. The story of this expedition, which had inflicted such damaging blows on the Spaniards in America, was eminently calculated to inspire courage among those who were resisting them in Europe. Cates, one of Carlile's lieutenants, obtained the manuscript and prepared it for the press, accompanied by illustrative maps and plans. The publication was delayed by the Spanish Armada; but a copy found its way to Holland, where it was translated into Latin, and appeared at Leyden, in a slightly abridged form, in 1588. The original English narrative duly appeared in London in the next year. The document called the 'Resolution of the Land-Captains' was inserted by Hakluyt when he reprinted the narrative in 1600.

DRAKE'S GREAT ARMADA

[NARRATIVE MAINLY BY CAPTAIN WALTER BIGGS]

A Summary and True Discourse of SIR FRANCIS DRAKE'S *West Indian Voyage, begun in the year 1585. Wherein were taken the cities of* SANTIAGO, SANTO DOMINGO, CARTHAGENA, *and the town of* ST. AUGUSTINE, *in* FLORIDA. *Published by* MASTER THOMAS CATES.

THIS worthy knight, for the service of his prince and country, having prepared his whole fleet, and gotten them down to *Plymouth,* in *Devonshire,* to the number of five and twenty sail of ships and pinnaces, and having assembled of soldiers and mariners to the number of 2,300 in the whole, embarked them and himself at *Plymouth* aforesaid, the 12. day of September, 1585, being accompanied with these men of name and charge which hereafter follow: Master *Christopher Carlile,* Lieutenant-General, a man of long experience in the wars as well by sea as land, who had formerly carried high offices in both kinds in many fights, which he discharged always very happily, and with great good reputation; *Anthony Powell,* Sergeant-Major; Captain *Matthew Morgan,* and Captain *John Sampson,* Corporals of the Field. These officers had commandment over the rest of the land-captains, whose names hereafter follow: Captain *Anthony Platt,* Captain *Edward Winter,* Captain *John Goring,* Captain *Robert Pew,* Captain *George Barton,* Captain *John Merchant,* Captain *William Cecil,* Captain *Walter Biggs,*[1] Captain *John Hannam,* Captain *Richard Stanton.* Captain *Martin Frobisher,* Vice-Admiral, a man of great experience in seafaring actions, who had carried the chief charge of many ships himself, in sundry voyages before, being now shipped in the *Primrose;* Captain *Francis Knolles,* Rear-Admiral in the galleon *Leicester;* Master *Thomas Venner,* captain in the *Elizabeth Bonadventure,* under the

[1] The writer of the first part of the narrative.

General; Master *Edward Winter,* captain in the *Aid;* Master *Christopher Carlile,* the Lieutenant-General, captain of the *Tiger; Henry White,* captain of the *Sea-Dragon; Thomas Drake,*[2] captain of the *Thomas; Thomas Seeley,* captain of the *Minion; Baily,* captain of the *Talbot; Robert Cross,* captain of the bark *Bond; George Fortescue,* captain of the bark *Bonner; Edward Careless,* captain of the *Hope; James Erizo,* captain of the *White Lion; Thomas Moon,* captain of the *Francis; John Rivers,* captain of the *Vantage; John Vaughan,* captain of the *Drake; John Varney,* captain of the *George; John Martin,* captain of the *Benjamin; Edward Gilman,* captain of the *Scout; Richard Hawkins,* captain of the galliot called the *Duck; Bitfield,* captain of the *Swallow.*

After our going hence, which was the 14. of September, in the year of our Lord 1585, and taking our course towards *Spain,* we had the wind for a few days somewhat scant, and sometimes calm. And being arrived near that part of *Spain* which is called the *Moors,*[3] we happened to espy divers sails, which kept their course close by the shore, the weather being fair and calm. The General caused the Vice-Admiral to go with the pinnaces well manned to see what they were; who upon sight of the said pinnaces approaching near unto them, abandoned for the most part all their ships, being Frenchmen, laden all with salt, and bound homewards into *France.* Amongst which ships, being all of small burthen, there was one so well liked, which also had no man in her, as being brought unto the General, he thought good to make stay of her for the service, meaning to pay for her, as also accordingly he performed at our return; which bark was called the *Drake.* The rest of these ships, being eight or nine, were dismissed without anything at all taken from them. Who being afterwards put somewhat farther off from the shore, by the contrariety of the wind, we happened to meet with some other French ships, full laden with *Newland* fish, being upon their return homeward from the said *Newfoundland;* whom the General after some speech had with them, and seeing plainly that they were Frenchmen, dismissed, without once suffering any man to go aboard of them.

The day following, standing in with the shore again, we

[2] Francis Drake's brother. [3] Muros, S. of Cape Finisterre.

described another tall ship of twelve score tons or thereabouts, upon whom *Master Carlile,* the Lieutenant-General, being in the *Tiger,* undertook the chase; whom also anon after the Admiral followed. And the *Tiger* having caused the said strange ship to strike her sails, kept her there without suffering anybody to go aboard until the Admiral was come up; who forthwith sending for the master, and divers others of their principal men, and causing them to be severally examined, found the ship and goods to be belonging to the inhabitants of *St. Sebastian,* in *Spain,* but the mariners to be for the most part belonging to *St. John de Luz,* and the *Passage.*[4] In this ship was great store of dry *Newland* fish, commonly called with us *Poor John;* whereof afterwards, being thus found a lawful prize, there was distribution made into all the ships of the fleet, the same being so new and good, as it did very greatly bestead us in the whole course of our voyage. A day or two after the taking of this ship we put in within the Isles of *Bayon,*[5] for lack of favourable wind. Where we had no sooner anchored some part of the fleet, but the General commanded all the pinnaces with the shipboats to be manned, and every man to be furnished with such arms as were needful for that present service; which being done, the General put himself into his galley, which was also well furnished, and rowing towards the city of *Bayon,* with intent, and the favour of the Almighty, to surprise it. Before we had advanced one half-league of our way there came a messenger, being an English merchant, from the governor, to see what strange fleet we were; who came to our General, conferred a while with him, and after a small time spent, our General called for Captain *Sampson,* and willed him to go to the governor of the city, to resolve him of two points. The first to know *if there were any wars between Spain and England;* the second, *why our merchants with their goods were embarged or arrested?* Thus departed Captain *Sampson* with the said messenger to the city, where he found the governor and people much amazed of such a sudden accident. The General, with the advice and counsel of Master *Carlile,* his Lieutenant-General, who was in the galley with him,

4 Passages, E. of San Sebastian.
5 The Cies Islets, at the mouth of the Vigo River.

Now seeing the expectation of this attempt frustrated by the causes aforesaid, we thought it meeter to fall with the Isle *Ferro,* to see if we could find any better fortune; and coming to the island we landed a thousand men in a valley under a high mountain, where we stayed some two or three hours. In which time the inhabitants, accompanied with a young fellow born in *England,* who dwelt there with them, came unto us, shewing their state to be so poor that they were all ready to starve, which was not untrue; and therefore without anything gotten, we were all commanded presently to embark, so as that night we put off to sea south-south-east along towards the coast of *Barbary.*

Upon Saturday in the morning, being the 13. of November, we fell with *Cape Blank,* which is a low land and shallow water, where we catched store of fish; and doubling the cape, we put into the bay, where we found certain French ships of war, whom we entertained with great courtesy, and there left them. This afternoon the whole fleet assembled, which was a little scattered about their fishing, and put from thence to the Isles of *Cape Verde,* sailing till the 16. of the same month in the morning; on which day we descried the Island of *Santiago.* And in the evening we anchored the fleet between the town called the *Playa* or *Praya* and *Santiago;* where we put on shore 1000 men or more, under the leading of Master *Christopher Carlile,* Lieutenant-General, who directed the service most like a wise commander. The place where we had first to march did afford no good order, for the ground was mountainous and full of dales, being a very stony and troublesome passage; but such was his industrious disposition, as he would never leave, until we had gotten up to a fair plain, where we made stand for the assembling of the army. And when we were all gathered together upon the plain, some two miles from the town, the Lieutenant-General thought good not to make attempt till daylight, because there was not one that could serve for guide or giving knowledge at all of the place. And therefore after having well rested, even half an hour before day, he commanded the army to be divided into three special parts, such as he appointed, whereas before we had marched by several companies, being thereunto forced by the badness of the way as is aforesaid. Now by the time we were thus ranged into a very brave order, daylight began to appear. And being advanced hard to the wall, we saw no enemy to resist. Whereupon the Lieutenant-General appointed Captain *Sampson* with thirty shot,[6] and Captain *Barton* with other thirty, to go down into the town, which stood in the valley under us, and might very plainly be viewed all over from that place where the whole army was now arrived; and presently after these captains was sent the great ensign, which had nothing in it but the plain English cross, to be placed towards the sea, that our fleet might see *St. George's* cross flourish in the enemy's fortress. Order was given that all the ordnance throughout the town and upon all the platforms, which were about fifty pieces all ready charged, should be shot off in honour of the Queen's Majesty's coronation day, being the 17. of November, after the yearly custom of *England,* which was so answered again by the ordnance out of all the ships in the fleet, which now was come near, as it was strange to hear such a thundering noise last so long together. In this mean while the Lieutenant-General held still the most part of his force on the hilltop, till such time as the town was quartered out for the lodging of the whole army. Which being done, every captain took his own quarter; and in the evening was placed such a sufficient guard upon every part of the town that we had no cause to fear any present enemy. Thus we continued in the city the space of fourteen days, taking such spoils as the place yielded, which were, for the most part, wine, oil, meal, and some other such like things for victual as vinegar, olives, and some other trash, as merchandise for their Indian trades. But there was not found any treasure at all, or anything else of worth besides.

The situation of *Santiago* is somewhat strange; in form like a triangle, having on the east and west sides two mountains of rock and cliff, as it were hanging over it; upon the top of which two mountains were builded certain fortifications to preserve the town from any harm that might be offered, as in a plot is plainly shewed. From thence on the south side of the town is the main sea; and on the north side,

[6] Musketeers.

the valley lying between the aforesaid mountains, wherein the town standeth. The said valley and town both do grow very narrow; insomuch that the space between the two cliffs of this end of the town is estimated not to be above ten or twelve score [yards] over. In the midst of the valley cometh down a riveret, rill, or brook of fresh water, which hard by the seaside maketh a pond or pool, whereout our ships were watered with very great ease and pleasure. Somewhat above the town on the north side, between the two mountains, the valley waxeth somewhat larger than at the town's end; which valley is wholly converted into gardens and orchards, well replenished with divers sorts of fruits, herbs, and trees, as lemons, oranges, sugar-canes, *cocars* or cocos nuts, plantains, potato-roots, cucumbers, small and round onions, garlic, and some other things not now remembered. Amongst which the cocos nuts and plantains are very pleasant fruits; the said cocos hath a hard shell and a green husk over it as hath our walnut, but it far exceedeth in greatness, for this cocos in his green husk is bigger than any man's two fists. Of the hard shell many drinking cups are made here in *England,* and set in silver as I have often seen. Next within this hard shell is a white rind resembling in show very much, even as any thing may do, to the white of an egg when it is hard boiled. And within this white of the nut lieth a water, which is whitish and very clear, to the quantity of half a pint or thereabouts; which water and white rind before spoken of are both of a very cool fresh taste, and as pleasing as anything may be. I have heard some hold opinion that it is very restorative. The plantain groweth in cods, somewhat like to beans, but is bigger and longer, and much more thick together on the stalk; and when it waxeth ripe, the meat which filleth the rind of the cod becometh yellow, and is exceeding sweet and pleasant.

In this time of our being there happened to come a Portugal to the western fort, with a flag of truce. To whom Captain *Sampson* was sent with Captain *Goring;* who coming to the said messenger, he first asked them, *What nation they were?* they answered *Englishmen.* He then required to know *if wars were between England and Spain;* to which they answered, *that they knew not, but if he would go to their General he could best resolve him of such particulars.* And for his assurance of passage and repassage these captains made offer to engage their credits, which he refused for that he was not sent from his governor. Then they told him if his governor did desire to take a course for the common benefit of the people and country his best way were to come and present himself unto our noble and merciful governor, Sir *Francis Drake,* whereby he might be assured to find favour, both for himself and the inhabitants. Otherwise within three days we should march over the land, and consume with fire all inhabited places, and put to the sword all such living souls as we should chance upon. So thus much he took for the conclusion of his answer. And departing, he promised to return the next day; but we never heard more of him.

Upon the 24. of November, the General, accompanied with the Lieutenant-General and 600 men, marched forth to a village twelve miles within the land, called *Saint Domingo,* where the governor and the bishop, with all the better sort, were lodged; and by eight of the clock we came to it, finding the place abandoned, and the people fled into the mountains. So we made stand a while to ease ourselves, and partly to see if any would come to speak to us. After we had well rested ourselves, the General commanded the troops to march away homewards. In which retreat the enemy shewed themselves, both horse and foot, though not such force as durst encounter us; and so in passing some time at the gaze with them, it waxed late and towards night before we could recover home to *Santiago.*

On Monday, the 26. of November, the General commanded all the pinnaces with the boats to use all diligence to embark the army into such ships as every man belonged. The Lieutenant-General in like sort commanded Captain *Goring* and Lieutenant *Tucker,* with one hundred shot, to make a stand in the marketplace until our forces were wholly embarked; the Vice-Admiral making stay with his pinnace and certain boats in the harbour, to bring the said last company aboard the ships. Also the General willed forthwith the galley with two pinnaces to take into them the company of Captain *Barton,* and the company of Captain *Biggs,* under the leading of Captain *Sampson,* to seek out such munition as was hidden in the ground, at the town of *Praya,* or *Playa,* having been promised to be shewed it by a prisoner which was taken the day before.

The captains aforesaid coming to the *Playa,* landed their men; and having placed the troop in their best strength, Captain *Sampson* took the prisoner, and willed him to show that he had promised. The which he could not, or at least would not; but they searching all suspected places, found two pieces of ordnance, one of iron, another of brass. In the afternoon the General anchored with the rest of the fleet before the *Playa,* coming himself ashore, willing us to burn the town and make all haste aboard; the which was done by six of the clock the same day, and ourselves embarked again the same night. And so we put off to sea south-west.

But before our departure from the town of *Santiago,* we established orders for the better government of the army. Every man mustered to his captain, and oaths were ministered, to acknowledge her Majesty supreme Governor, as also every man to do his uttermost endeavour to advance the service of the action, and to yield due obedience unto the directions of the General and his officers. By this provident counsel, and laying down this good foundation beforehand, all things went forward in a due course, to the achieving of our happy enterprise.

In all the time of our being here, neither the governor for the said King of *Spain,* which is a Portugal, neither the bishop, whose authority is great, neither the inhabitants of the town, or island, ever came at us; which we expected they should have done, to entreat us to leave them some part of their needful provisions, or at the least to spare the ruining of their town at our going away. The cause of this their unreasonable distrust, as I do take it, was the fresh remembrance of the great wrongs that they had done to old Master *William Hawkins,* of *Plymouth,* in the voyage he made four or five years before, whenas they did both break their promise, and murdered many of his men; whereof I judge you have understood, and therefore it is needless to be repeated. But since they came not at us, we left written in sundry places, as also in the Spital House (which building was only appointed to be spared), the great discontentment and scorn we took at this their refraining to come unto us, as also at the rude manner of killing, and savage kind of handling the dead body of one of our boys found by them straggling all alone, from whom they had taken his head and heart, and had straggled the other bowels about the place, in a most brutish and beastly manner. In revenge whereof at our departing we consumed with fire all the houses, as well in the country which we saw, as in the town of *Santiago*.

From hence putting off to the *West Indies,* we were not many days at sea but there began among our people such mortality as in a few days there were dead above two or three hundred men. And until some seven or eight days after our coming from *Santiago,* there had not died any one man of sickness in all the fleet. The sickness showed not his infection, wherewith so many were strucken, until we were departed thence; and then seized our people with extreme hot burning and continual agues, whereof very few escaped with life, and yet those for the most part not without great alteration and decay of their wits and strength for a long time after. In some that died were plainly shown the small spots which are often found upon those that be infected with the plague. We were not above eighteen days in passage between the sight of *Santiago* aforesaid, and the island of *Dominica,* being the first island of the *West Indies* that we fell withal; the same being inhabited with savage people, which go all naked, their skin coloured with some painting of a reddish tawny, very personable and handsome strong men, who do admit little conversation with the Spaniards; for, as some of our people might understand them, they had a Spaniard or twain prisoners with them. Neither do I think that there is any safety for any of our nation, or any other, to be within the limits of their commandment; albeit they used us very kindly for those few hours of time which we spent with them, helping our folks to fill and carry on their bare shoulders fresh water from the river to our ships' boats, and fetching from their houses great store of *tabacco,* as also a kind of bread which they fed on, called *cassavi,* very white and savoury, made of the roots of *cassavi.* In recompense whereof we bestowed liberal rewards of glass, coloured beads, and other things, which we had found at *Santiago;* wherewith, as it seemed, they rested very greatly satisfied, and shewed some sorrowful countenance when they perceived that we would depart.

From hence we went to another island westward of it, called *Saint Christopher's* Island; wherein we spent some days of Christmas, to refresh our sick people, and to cleanse and air our ships. In which island were not any people at all that we could hear of.

In which time by the General it was advised and resolved, with the consent of the Lieutenant-General, the Vice-Admiral, and all the rest of the captains, to proceed to the great island of *Hispaniola,* as well for that we knew ourselves then to be in our best strength, as also the rather allured thereunto by the glorious fame of the city of *St. Domingo,* being the ancientest and chief inhabited place in all the tract of country thereabouts. And so proceeding in this determination, by the way we met a small frigate, bound for the same place, the which the Vice-Admiral took; and having duly examined the men that were in her, there was one found by whom we were advertised the haven to be a barred haven, and the shore or land thereof to be well fortified, having a castle thereupon furnished with great store of artillery, without the danger whereof was no convenient landing-place within ten English miles of the city, to which the said pilot took upon him to conduct us.

All things being thus considered on, the whole forces were commanded in the evening to embark themselves in pinnaces, boats, and other small barks appointed for this service. Our soldiers being thus embarked, the General put himself into the bark *Francis* as Admiral; and all this night we lay on the sea, bearing small sail until our arrival to the landing-place, which was about the breaking of the day. And so we landed, being New Year's Day, nine or ten miles to the westwards of that brave city of *St. Domingo;* for at that time nor yet is known to us any landing-place, where the sea-surge doth not threaten to overset a pinnace or boat. Our General having seen us all landed in safety, returned to his fleet, bequeathing us to God, and the good conduct of

Master *Carlile,* our Lieutenant-General; at which time, being about eight of the clock, we began to march. And about noon-time, or towards one of the clock, we approached the town; where the gentlemen and those of the better sort, being some hundred and fifty brave horses, or rather more, began to present themselves. But our small shot played upon them, which were so sustained with good proportion of pikes in all parts, as they finding no part of our troop unprepared to receive them (for you must understand they viewed all round about) they were thus driven to give us leave to proceed towards the two gates of the town which were the next to the seaward. They had manned them both, and planted their ordnance for that present and sudden alarm without the gate, and also some troops of small shot in *ambuscado* upon the highway side. We divided our whole force, being some thousand or twelve hundred men, into two parts, to enterprise both the gates at one instant; the Lieutenant-General having openly vowed to Captain *Powell,* who led the troop that entered the other gate, that with God's good favour he would not rest until our meeting in the market-place.

Their ordnance had no sooner discharged upon our near approach, and made some execution amongst us, though not much, but the Lieutenant-General began forthwith to advance both his voice of encouragement and pace of marching; the first man that was slain with the ordnance being very near unto himself; and thereupon hasted all that he might, to keep them from the recharging of the ordnance. And notwithstanding their *ambuscados,* we marched or rather ran so roundly into them, as pell-mell we entered the gates, and gave them more care every man to save himself by flight, than reason to stand any longer to their broken fight. We forthwith repaired to the market-place, but to be more truly understood, a place of very spacious square ground; whither also came, as had been agreed, Captain *Powell* with the other troop. Which place with some part next unto it, we strengthened with *barricados,* and there as the most convenient place assured ourselves, the city being far too spacious for so small and weary a troop to undertake to guard. Somewhat after midnight, they who had the guard of the castle, hearing us busy about the gates of the said castle, abandoned the same; some being taken prisoners, and some fleeing away by the help of boats to the other side of the haven, and so into the country.

The next day we quartered a little more at large, but not into the half part of the town; and so making substantial trenches, and planting all the ordnance, that each part was correspondent to other, we held this town the space of one month.

In the which time happened some accidents, more than are well remembered for the present. But amongst other things, it chanced that the General sent on his message to the Spaniards a negro boy with a flag of white, signifying truce, as is the Spanish ordinary manner to do there, when they approach to speak to us; which boy unhappily was first met withal by some of those who had been belonging as officers for the king in the Spanish galley, which with the town was lately fallen into our hands. Who, without all order or reason, and contrary to that good usage wherewith we had entertained their messengers, furiously struck the poor boy through the body with one of their horsemen's staves; with which wound the boy returned to the General, and after he had declared the manner of this wrongful cruelty, died forthwith in his presence. Wherewith the General being greatly passioned, commanded the provost-marshal to cause a couple of friars, then prisoners, to be carried to the same place where the boy was strucken, accompanied with sufficient guard of our soldiers, and there presently to be hanged, despatching at the same instant another poor prisoner, with this reason wherefore this execution was done, and with this message further, that until the party who had thus murdered the General's messenger were delivered into our hands to receive condign punishment, there should no day pass wherein there should not two prisoners be hanged, until they were all consumed which were in our hands. Whereupon the day following, he that had been captain of the king's galley brought the offender to the town's end, offering to deliver him into our hands. But it was thought to be a more honourable revenge to make them there, in our sight, to perform the execution themselves; which was done accordingly.

During our being in this town, as formerly also at *Santiago* there had passed justice upon the life of one of our own company for an odious matter, so here likewise was there an Irishman hanged for the murdering of his corporal.

In this time also passed many treaties between their commissioners and us, for ransom of their city; but upon disagreements we still spent the early mornings in firing the outmost houses; but they being built very magnificently of stone, with high lofts, gave us no small travail to ruin them. And albeit for divers days together we ordained each morning by daybreak, until the heat began at nine of the clock, that two hundred mariners did naught else but labour to fire and burn the said houses without our trenches, whilst the soldiers in a like proportion stood forth for their guard; yet did we not, or could not in this time consume so much as one-third part of the town, which town is plainly described and set forth in a certain map. And so in the end, what wearied with firing, and what hastened by some other respects, we were contented to accept of 25,000 ducats of five shillings six-pence the piece, for the ransom of the rest of the town.

Amongst other things which happened and were found at *St. Domingo,* I may not omit to let the world know one very notable mark and token of the unsatiable ambition of the Spanish king and his nation, which was found in the king's house, wherein the chief governor of that city and country is appointed always to lodge, which was this. In the coming to the hall or other rooms of this house, you must first ascend up by a fair large pair of stairs, at the head of which stairs is a handsome spacious place to walk in, somewhat like unto a gallery. Wherein, upon one of the walls, right over against you as you enter the said place, so as your eye cannot escape the sight of it, there is described and painted in a very large scutcheon the arms of the King of *Spain;* and in the lower part of the said scutcheon their is likewise described a globe, containing in it the whole circuit of the sea and the earth, whereupon is a horse standing on his hinder part within the globe, and the other forepart without the globe, lifted up as it were to leap, with a scroll painted in his mouth, wherein was written these words in Latin, NON SUFFICIT ORBIS, which is as much to say as, *The world sufficeth not.* Whereof the meaning was required to be known of some of those of the better sort that came in commission to treat upon the ransom of the town; who would shake their heads and turn aside their countenance, in some smiling sort, without answering anything, as greatly ashamed thereof. For by some of our company it was told them, that if the Queen of *England* would resolutely prosecute the wars against the King of *Spain,* he should be forced to lay aside that proud and unreasonable reaching vein of his; for he should find more than enough to do to keep that which he had already, as by the present example of their lost town they might for a beginning perceive well enough.

Now to the satisfying of some men, who marvel greatly that such a famous and goodly-builded city, so well inhabited of gallant people, very brave in their apparel (whereof our soldiers found good store for their relief), should afford no greater riches than was found there. Herein it is to be understood that the Indian people, which were the natives of this whole island of *Hispaniola* (the same being near hand as great as *England*), were many years since clean consumed by the tyranny of the Spaniards; which was the cause that, for lack of people to work in the mines, the gold and silver mines of this island are wholly given over. And thereby they are fain in this island to use copper money, whereof was found very great quantity. The chief trade of this place consisteth of sugar and ginger, which groweth in the island, and of hides of oxen and kine, which in this waste country of the island are bred in infinite numbers, the soil being very fertile. And the said beasts are fed up to a very large growth, and so killed for nothing so much as for their hides aforesaid. We found here great store of strong wine, sweet oil, vinegar, olives, and other such-like provisions, as excellent wheat-meal packed up in wine-pipes and other cask, and other commodities likewise, as woollen and linen cloth and some silks; all which provisions are brought out of *Spain,* and served us for great relief. There was but a little plate or vessel of silver, in comparison of the great pride in other things of this town, because in these hot countries they use much of those earthen dishes finely painted or varnished, which they call *porcellana,* which is had out of the East *India;* and for their drinking they use glasses altogether, whereof they make excellent good and fair in the same place. But yet some plate we found, and many other good things, as their household garniture, very gallant and rich, which had cost them dear, although unto us they were of small importance.

From *St. Domingo* we put over to the main or firm land, and, going all along the coast, we came at last in sight of *Carthagena,* standing upon the seaside, so near as some of our barks in passing alongst approached within the reach of their culverin shot, which they had planted upon certain platforms. The harbour-mouth lay some three miles toward the westward of the town, whereinto we entered at about three or four of the clock in the afternoon without any resistance of ordnance or other impeachment planted upon the same. In the evening we put ourselves on land towards the harbour-mouth, under the leading of Master *Carlile,* our Lieutenant-General. Who, after he had digested us to march forward about midnight, as easily as foot might fall, expressly commanded us to keep close by the sea-wash of the shore for our best and surest way; whereby we were like to go through, and not to miss any more of the way, which once we had lost within an hour after our first beginning to march, through the slender knowledge of him that took upon him to be our guide, whereby the night spent on, which otherwise must have been done by resting. But as we came within some two miles of the town, their horsemen, which were some hundred, met us, and, taking the alarm, retired to their townward again upon the first volley of our shot that was given them; for the place where we encountered being woody and bushy, even to the waterside, was unmeet for their service.

At this instant we might hear some pieces of artillery discharged, with divers small shot, towards the harbour; which gave us to understand, according to the order set down in the evening before by our General, that the Vice-Admiral, accompanied with Captain *Venner,* Captain *White,* and Captain *Cross,* with other sea captains, and with divers pinnaces and boats, should give some attempt unto the little fort standing on the entry of the inner haven, near adjoining to the town, though to small purpose, for that the place was strong, and the entry, very narrow, was chained over; so as there could be nothing gotten by the attempt more than the giving of them an alarm on that other side of the haven, being a mile and a-half from the place we now were at. In which attempt the Vice-Admiral had the rudder of his skiff strucken through with a saker[7] shot, and a little or no harm received elsewhere.

The troops being now in their march, half-a-mile behither the town or less, the ground we were on grew to be strait, and not above fifty paces over, having the main sea on the one side of it and the harbour-water or inner sea (as you may term it) on the other side, which in the plot is plainly shewed. This strait was fortified clean over with a stone wall and a ditch without it, the said wall being as orderly built, with flanking in every part, as can be set down. There was only so much of this strait unwalled as might serve for the issuing of the horsemen or the passing of carriage in time of need. But this unwalled part was not without a very good *barricado* of wine-butts or pipes, filled with earth, full and thick as they might stand on end one by another, some part of them standing even within the main sea. This place of strength was furnished with six great pieces, demiculverins[8] and sakers, which shot directly in front upon us as we approached. Now without this wall, upon the inner side of the strait, they had brought likewise two great galleys with their prows to the shore, having planted in them eleven pieces of ordnance, which did beat all cross the strait, and flanked our coming on. In these two galleys were planted three or four hundred small shot, and on the land, in the guard only of this place, three hundred shot and pikes.

They, in this their full readiness to receive us, spared not their shot both great and small. But our Lieutenant-General, taking the advantage of the dark (the daylight as yet not broken out) approached by the lowest ground, according to the express direction which himself had for-

[7] Bore 3½ inches, shot 5 lb. [8] Bore 4½ inches, shot 9 lb.

merly given, the same being the sea-wash shore, where the water was somewhat fallen, so as most of all their shot was in vain. Our Lieutenant-General commanded our shot to forbear shooting until we were come to the wall-side. And so with pikes roundly together we approached the place, where we soon found out the *barricados* of pipes or butts to be the meetest place for our assault; which, notwithstanding it was well furnished with pikes and shots, was without staying attempted by us. Down went the butts of earth, and pell-mell came our swords and pikes together, after our shot had first given their volley, even at the enemy's nose. Our pikes were somewhat longer than theirs, and our bodies better armed; for very few of them were armed. With which advantage our swords and pikes grew too hard for them, and they driven to give place. In this furious entry the Lieutenant-General slew with his own hands the chief ensign-bearer of the Spaniards, who fought very manfully to his life's end.

We followed into the town with them, and, giving them no leisure to breathe, we won the market-place, albeit they made head and fought awhile before we got it. And so we being once seized and assured of that, they were content to suffer us to lodge within their town, and themselves to go to their wives, whom they had carried into other places of the country before our coming thither. At every street's end they had raised very fine *barricados* of earth-works, with trenches without them, as well made as ever we saw any work done; at the entering whereof was some little resistance, but soon overcome it was, with few slain or hurt. They had joined with them many Indians, whom they had placed in corners of advantage, all bowmen, with their arrows most villainously empoisoned, so as if they did but break the skin, the party so touched died without great marvel. Some they slew of our people with their arrows; some they likewise mischiefed to death with certain pricks of small sticks sharply pointed, of a foot and a-half long, the one end put into the ground, the other empoisoned, sticking fast up, right against our coming in the way as we should approach from our landing towards the town, whereof they had planted a wonderful number in the ordinary way; but our keeping the sea-wash shore missed the greatest part of them very happily.

I overpass many particular matters, as the hurting of Captain *Sampson* at sword blows in the first entering, unto whom was committed the charge of the pikes of the vant-guard by his lot and turn; as also of the taking of *Alonzo Bravo,* the chief commander of that place, by Captain *Goring,* after the said captain had first hurt him with his sword; unto which captain was committed the charge of the shot of the said vant-guard. Captain *Winter* was likewise by his turn of the vant-guard in this attempt, where also the Lieutenant-General marched himself; the said Captain *Winter,* through a great desire to serve by land, having now exchanged his charge at sea with Captain *Cecil* for his band of footmen. Captain *Powell,* the Sergeant-Major, had by his turn the charge of the four companies which made the battle. Captain *Morgan,* who at *St. Domingo* was of the vant-guard, had now by turn his charge upon the companies of the rearward. Every man, as well of one part as of another, came so willingly on to the service, as the enemy was not able to endure the fury of such hot assault.

We stayed here six weeks, and the sickness with mortality before spoken of still continued among us, though not with the same fury as at the first; and such as were touched with the said sickness, escaping death, very few or almost none could recover their strength. Yea, many of them were much decayed in their memory, insomuch that it was grown an ordinary judgment, when one was heard to speak foolishly, to say he had been sick of the *calentura,* which is the Spanish name of their burning ague; for, as I told you before, it is a very burning and pestilent ague. The original cause thereof is imputed to the evening or first night air, which they term *la serena;* wherein they say and hold very firm opinion that whoso is then abroad in the open air shall certainly be infected to the death, not being of the Indian or natural race of those country people. By holding their watch our men were thus subjected to the infectious air, which at *Santiago* was most dangerous and deadly of all other places.

With the inconvenience of continual mortality we were forced to give over our intended enterprise to go with

Nombre de Dios, and so overland to *Panama,* where we should have strucken the stroke for the treasure, and full recompense of our tedious travails. And thus at *Carthagena* we took our first resolution to return homewards, the form of which resolution I thought good here to put down under the principal captains' hands as followeth:—

A RESOLUTION *of the* LAND-CAPTAINS, *what course they think most expedient to be taken. Given at* CARTHAGENA, *the 27. of February, 1585.*

WHEREAS it hath pleased the General to demand the opinions of his captains what course they think most expedient to be now undertaken, the land-captains being assembled by themselves together, and having advised hereupon, do in three points deliver the same.

THE FIRST, touching the keeping of the town against the force of the enemy, either that which is present, or that which may come out of Spain, is answered thus:—

'We hold opinion, that with this troop of men which we have presently with us in land service, being victualled and munitioned, we may well keep the town, albeit that of men able to answer present service we have not above 700. The residue, being some 150 men, by reason of their hurts and sickness, are altogether unable to stand us in any stead: wherefore hereupon the sea-captains are likewise to give their resolution, how they will undertake the safety and service of the ships upon the arrival of any Spanish fleet.'

THE SECOND point we make to be this, whether it be meet to go presently homeward, or else to continue further trial of our fortune in undertaking such like enterprises as we have done already, and thereby to seek after that bountiful mass of treasure for recompense of our travails, which was generally expected at our coming forth of *England:* wherein we answer:—

That it is well known how both we and the soldiers are entered into this action as voluntary men, without any impress or gage from her Majesty or anybody else. And forasmuch as we have hitherto discharged the parts of honest men, so that now by the great blessing and favour of our good God there have been taken three such notable towns, wherein by the estimation of all men would have been found some very great treasures, knowing that *Santiago* was the chief city of all the islands and traffics thereabouts, *St. Domingo* the chief city of Hispaniola, and the head government not only of that island, but also of *Cuba,* and of all the islands about it, as also of such inhabitations of the firm land, as were next unto it, and a place that is both magnificently built and entertaineth great trades of merchandise; and now lastly the city of *Carthagena,* which cannot be denied to be one of the chief places of most especial importance to the Spaniard of all the cities which be on this side of the *West India:* we do therefore consider, that since all these cities, with their goods and prisoners taken in them, and the ransoms of the said cities, being all put together, are found far short to satisfy that expectation which by the generality of the enterprisers was first conceived; and being further advised of the slenderness of our strength, whereunto we be now reduced, as well in respect of the small number of able bodies, as also not a little in regard of the slack disposition of the greater part of those which remain, very many of the better minds and men being either consumed by death or weakened by sickness and hurts; and lastly, since that as yet there is not laid down to our knowledge any such enterprise as may seem convenient to be undertaken with such few as we are presently able to make, and withal of such certain likelihood, as with God's good success which it may please him to bestow upon us, the same may promise to yield us any sufficient contentment: we do therefore conclude hereupon, that it is better to hold sure as we may the honour already gotten, and with the same to return towards our gracious sovereign and country, from whence, if it shall please her Majesty to set us forth again with her orderly means and entertainment, we are most ready and willing to go through with anything that the uttermost of our strength and endeavour shall be able to reach unto. But therewithal we do advise and protest that it is far from our thoughts, either to refuse, or so much as to seem to be weary of anything, which for the present shall be further required or directed to be done by us from our General.'

THE THIRD and last point is concerning the ransom of this city of *Carthagena*, for the which, before it was touched with any fire, there was made an offer of some £27,000 or £28,000 sterling:—

'Thus much we utter herein as our opinions, agreeing, so it be done in good sort, to accept this offer aforesaid, rather than to break off by standing still upon our demands of £100,000; which seems a matter impossible to be performed for the present by them. And to say truth, we may now with much honour and reputation better be satisfied with that sum offered by them at the first, if they will now be contented to give it, than we might at that time with a great deal more; inasmuch as we have taken our full pleasure, both in the uttermost sacking and spoiling of all their household goods and merchandise, as also in that we have consumed and ruined a great part of their town with fire. And thus much further is considered herein by us; that as there be in the voyage a great many poor men, who have willingly adventured their lives and travails, and divers amongst them having spent their apparel and such other little provisions as their small means might have given them leave to prepare, which being done upon such good and allowable intention as this action hath always carried with it (meaning, against the Spaniard, our greatest and most dangerous enemy), so surely we cannot but have an inward regard, so far as may lie in us, to help them in all good sort towards the satisfaction of this their expectation; and be procuring them some little benefit to encourage them, and to nourish this ready and willing disposition of theirs, both in them and in others by their example, against any other time of like occasion. But because it may be supposed that herein we forget not the private benefit of ourselves, and are thereby the rather moved to incline ourselves to this composition, we do therefore think good for the clearing ourselves of all such suspicion, to declare hereby, that what part or portion soever it be of this ransom or composition for *Carthagena* which should come unto us, we do freely give and bestow the same wholly upon the poor men who have remained with us in the voyage (meaning as well the sailor as the soldier), wishing with all our hearts it were such or so much as might see a sufficient reward for their painful endeavour. And for the firm confirmation thereof, we have thought meet to subsign these presents with our own hands in the place and time aforesaid.

'Captain *Christopher Carlile,* Lieutenant-General; Captain *Goring,* Captain *Sampson,* Captain *Powell,* &c.

But while we were yet there, it happened one day that our watch called the sentinel, upon the church-steeple, had discovered in the sea a couple of small barks or boats, making in with the harbour of *Carthagena.* Whereupon Captain *Moon* and Captain *Varney,* with *John Grant,* the master of the *Tiger*, and some other seamen, embarked themselves in a couple of small pinnaces, to take them before they should come nigh the shore, at the mouth of the harbour, lest by some straggling Spaniards from the land, they might be warned by signs from coming in. Which fell out accordingly, notwithstanding all the diligence that our men could use: for the Spanish boats, upon the sight of our pinnaces coming towards them, ran themselves ashore, and so their men presently hid themselves in bushes hard by the sea-side, amongst some others that had called them by signs thither. Our men presently without any due regard had to the quality of the place, and seeing no man of the Spaniards to shew themselves, boarded the Spanish barks or boats, and so standing all open in them, were suddenly shot at by a troop of Spaniards out of the bushes; by which volley of shot there were slain Captain *Varney,* which died presently, and Captain *Moon,* who died some few days after, besides some four or five others that were hurt: and so our folks returned without their purpose, not having any sufficient number of soldiers with them to fight on shore. For those men they carried were all mariners to row, few of them armed, because they made account with their ordnance to have taken the barks well enough at sea; which they might full easily have done, without any loss at all, if they had come in time to the harbour mouth, before the Spaniards' boats had gotten so near the shore.

During our abode in this place, as also at *St. Domingo,* there passed divers courtesies between us and the Spaniards, as feasting, and using them with all kindness and favour; so as amongst others there came to see the General the governor of *Carthagena,* with the bishop of the same, and divers other gentlemen of the better sort. This town of *Carthagena* we touched in the out parts, and consumed much with fire, as we had done *St. Domingo,* upon discontentments, and for want of agreeing with us in their first treaties touching their ransom; which at the last was concluded between us should be 110,000 ducats for that which was yet standing, the ducat valued at five shillings sixpence sterling.

This town, though not half so big as *St. Domingo,* gives, as you see, a far greater ransom, being in very deed of far more importance, by reason of the excellency of the harbour, and the situation thereof to serve the trade of *Nombre de Dios* and other places, and is inhabited with far more richer merchants. The other is chiefly inhabited with lawyers and brave gentlemen, being the chief or highest appeal of their suits in law of all the islands about it and of the mainland coast next unto it. And it is of no such account as *Carthagena,* for these and some like reasons which I could give you, over long to be now written.

The warning which this town received of our coming towards them from *St. Domingo,* by the space of 20 days before our arrival here, was cause that they had both fortified and every way prepared for their best defence. As also that they had carried and conveyed away all their treasure and principal substance.

The ransom of 110,000 ducats thus concluded on, as is aforesaid, the same being written, and expressing for nothing more than the town of *Carthagena,* upon the payment of the said ransom we left the said town and drew some part of our soldiers into the priory or abbey, standing a quarter of an English mile below the town upon the harbour water-side, the same being walled with a wall of stone; which we told the Spaniards was yet ours, and not redeemed by their composition. Whereupon they, finding the defect of their contract, were contented to enter into another ransom for all places, but specially for the said house, as also the blockhouse or castle, which is upon the mouth of the inner harbour. And when we asked as much for the one as for the other, they yielded to give a thousand crowns for the abbey, leaving us to take our pleasure upon the blockhouse, which they said they were not able to ransom, having stretched themselves to the uttermost of their powers; and therefore the said blockhouse was by us undermined, and so with gunpowder blown up in pieces. While this latter contract was in making, our whole fleet of ships fell down towards the harbour-mouth, where they anchored the third time and employed their men in fetching of fresh water aboard the ships for our voyage homewards, which water was had in a great well that is in the island by the harbour-mouth. Which island is a very pleasant place as hath been seen, having in it many sorts of goodly and very pleasant fruits, as the orange-trees and others, being set orderly in walks of great length together. Insomuch as the whole island, being some two or three miles about, is cast into grounds of gardening and orchards.

After six weeks' abode in this place, we put to sea the last of March; where, after two or three days, a great ship which we had taken at *St. Domingo,* and thereupon was called *The New Year's Gift,* fell into a great leak, being laden with ordnance, hides, and other spoils, and in the night she lost the company of our fleet. Which being missed the next morning by the General, he cast about with the whole fleet, fearing some great mischance to be happened unto her, as in very deed it so fell out; for her leak was so great that her men were all tired with pumping. But at the last, having found her, and the bark *Talbot* in her company, which stayed by great hap with her, they were ready to take their men out of her for the saving of them. And so the General, being fully advertised of their great extremity, made sail directly back again to *Carthagena* with the whole fleet; where, having staid eight or ten days more about the unlading of this ship and the bestowing thereof and her men into other ships, we departed once again to sea, directing our course toward the Cape *St. Anthony,* being the westermost part of *Cuba,* where we arrived the 27. of April. But because fresh water could not presently be found, we weighed anchor and departed, thinking in few days to recover the *Matanzas,* a place to the eastward of *Havana.*

After we had sailed some fourteen days we were brought to Cape *St. Anthony* again through lack of favourable wind; but then our scarcity was grown such as need make us look a little better for water, which we found in sufficient quantity, being indeed, as I judge, none other than rain-water newly fallen and gathered up by making pits in a plot of marish ground some three hundred paces from the seaside.

I do wrong if I should forget the good example of the General at this place, who, to encourage others, and to hasten the getting of fresh water aboard the ships, took no less pain himself than the meanest; as also at *St. Domingo, Carthagena,* and all other places, having always so vigilant a care and foresight in the good ordering of his fleet, accompanying them, as it is said, with such wonderful travail of body, as doubtless had he been the meanest person, as he was the chiefest, he had yet deserved the first place of honour; and no less happy do we account him for being associated with Master *Carlile,* his Liuetenant-General, by whose experience, prudent counsel, and gallant performance he achieved so many and happy enterprises of the war, by whom also he was very greatly assisted in setting down the needful orders, laws, and course of justice, and the due administration of the same upon all occasions.

After three days spent in watering our ships, we departed now the second time from this Cape of *St. Anthony* the 13. of May. And proceeding about the Cape of *Florida,* we never touched anywhere; but coasting alongst *Florida,* and keeping the shore still in sight, the 28. of May, early in the morning, we descried on the shore a place built like a beacon, which was indeed a scaffold upon four long masts raised on end for men to discover to the seaward, being in the latitude of thirty degrees, or very near thereunto. Our pinnaces manned and coming to the shore, we marched up alongst the river-side to see what place the enemy held there; for none amongst us had any knowledge thereof at all.

Here the General took occasion to march with the companies himself in person, the Lieutenant-General having the vant-guard; and, going a mile up, or somewhat more, by the river-side, we might discern on the other side of the river over against us a fort which newly had been built by the Spaniards; and some mile, or thereabout, above the fort was a little town or village without walls, built of wooden houses, as the plot doth plainly shew. We forthwith prepared to have ordnance for the battery; and one piece was a little before the evening planted, and the first shot being made by the Lieutenant-General himself at their ensign, strake through the ensign, as we afterwards understood by a Frenchman which came unto us from them. One shot more was then made, which struck the foot of the fort wall, which was all massive timber of great trees like masts. The Lieutenant-General was determined to pass the river this night with four companies, and there to lodge himself entrenched as near the fort as that he might play with his muskets and smallest shot upon any that should appear, and so afterwards to bring and plant the battery with him; but the help of mariners for that sudden to make trenches could not be had, which was the cause that this determination was remitted until the next night.

In the night the Lieutenant-General took a little rowing skiff and half a dozen well armed, as Captain *Morgan* and Captain *Sampson,* with some others, besides the rowers, and went to view what guard the enemy kept, as also to take knowledge of the ground. And albeit he went as covertly as might be, yet the enemy, taking the alarm, grew fearful that the whole force was approaching to the assault, and therefore with all speed abandoned the place after the shooting of some of their pieces. They thus gone, and he being returned unto us again, but nothing knowing of their flight from their fort, forthwith came a Frenchman,[9] being a fifer (who had been prisoner with them) in a little boat, playing

[9] Nicolas Borgoignon. The 'Prince of Orange's Song' was a popular ditty in praise of William Prince of Orange (assassinated 1584), the leader of the Dutch Protestant insurgents.

sent thither the year before by Sir *Walter Raleigh,* and brought them aboard; by whose direction we proceeded along to the place which they make their port. But some of our ships being of great draught, unable to enter, anchored without the harbour in a wild road at sea, about two miles from shore. From whence the General wrote letters to Master *Ralph Lane,* being governor of those English in *Virginia,* and then at his fort about six leagues from the road in an island which they called *Roanoac;* wherein especially he shewed how ready he was to supply his necessities and wants, which he understood of by those he had first talked withal.

The morrow after, Master *Lane* himself and some of his company coming unto him, with the consent of his captains he gave them the choice of two offers, that is to say: either he would leave a ship, a pinnace, and certain boats with sufficient masters and mariners, together furnished with a month's victual, to stay and make further discovery of the country and coasts, and so much victual likewise as might be sufficient for the bringing of them all (being an hundred and three persons) into *England,* if they thought good after such time, with any other thing they would desire, and that he might be able to spare: or else, if they thought they had made sufficient discovery already, and did desire to return into *England,* he would give them passage. But they, as it seemed, being desirous to stay, accepted very thankfully and with great gladness that which was offered first. Whereupon the ship being appointed and received into charge by some of their own company sent into her by Master *Lane,* before they had received from the rest of the fleet the provision appointed them, there arose a great storm (which they said was extraordinary and very strange) that lasted three days together, and put all our fleet in great danger to be driven from their anchoring upon the coast; for we brake many cables, and lost many anchors; and some of our fleet which had lost all, of which number was the ship appointed for Master *Lane* and his company, were driven to put to sea in great danger, in avoiding the coast, and could never see us again until we met in *England.* Many also of our small pinnaces and boats were lost in this storm.

Notwithstanding, after all this, the General offered them, with consent of his captains, another ship with some provisions, although not such a one for their turns as might have been spared them before, this being unable to be brought into their harbour: or else, if they would, to give them passage into *England,* although he knew he should perform it with greater difficulty than he might have done before. But Master *Lane,* with those of the chiefest of his company which he had then with him, considering what should be best for them to do, made request unto the General under their hands, that they might have passage for *England:* the which being granted, and the rest sent for out of the country and shipped, we departed from that coast the 18. of June. And so, God be thanked, both they and we in good safety arrived at *Portsmouth* the 28. of July, 1586, to the great glory of God, and to no small honour to our Prince, our country, and ourselves. The total value of that which was got in this voyage is esteemed at three score thousand pounds, whereof the companies which have travailed in the voyage were to have twenty thousand pounds, the adventurers the other forty. Of which twenty thousand pounds (as I can judge) will redound some six pounds to the single share. We lost some 750 men in the voyage; above three parts of them only by sickness. The men of name that died and were slain in this voyage, which I can presently call to remembrance, are these:—Captain *Powell,* Captain *Varney,* Captain *Moon,* Captain *Fortescue,* Captain *Biggs,* Captain *Cecil,* Captain *Hannam,* Captain *Greenfield; Thomas Tucker,* a lieutenant; *Alexander Starkey,* a lieutenant; Master *Escot,* a lieutenant; Master *Waterhouse,* a lieutenant; Master *George Candish,* Master *Nicholas Winter,* Master *Alexander Carlile,* Master *Robert Alexander,* Master *Scroope,* Master *James Dyer,* Master *Peter Duke.* With some other, whom for haste I cannot suddenly think on.

The ordnance gotten of all sorts, brass and iron, were about two hundred and forty pieces, whereof the two hundred and some more were brass, and were thus found and gotten:—At *Santiago* some two or three and fifty pieces. In *St. Domingo* about four score, whereof was very much great ordnance, as whole cannon,[10] demi-cannon, culverins, and such like. In *Carthagena* some sixty and three pieces, and good store likewise of the greater sort. In the Fort of *St. Augustine* were fourteen pieces. The rest was iron ordnance, of which the most part was gotten at *St. Domingo*, the rest at *Carthagena.*

[10] The 'whole cannon' had a bore of 8 inches, and carried a shot of 60 ℔; the 'demi-cannon' 6½ inches, shot 30 ℔; the culverin 5½ inches, shot 18 ℔.

SIR HUMPHREY GILBERT'S VOYAGE TO NEWFOUNDLAND

BY

EDWARD HAYES

INTRODUCTORY NOTE

Sir Humphrey Gilbert, *the founder of the first English colony in North America, was born about 1539, the son of a Devonshire gentleman, whose widow afterward married the father of Sir Walter Raleigh. He was educated at Eton and Oxford, served under Sir Philip Sidney's father in Ireland, and fought for the Netherlands against Spain. After his return he composed a pamphlet urging the search for a northwest passage to Cathay, which led to Frobisher's license for his explorations to that end.*

In 1578 Gilbert obtained from Queen Elizabeth the charter he had long sought, to plant a colony in North America. His first attempt failed, and cost him his whole fortune; but, after further service in Ireland, he sailed again in 1583 for Newfoundland. In the August of that year he took possession of the harbor of St. John and founded his colony, but on the return voyage he went down with his ship in a storm south of the Azores.

The following narrative is an account of this last voyage of Gilbert's, told by Edward Hayes, commander of "The Golden Hind," the only one to reach England of the three ships which set out from Newfoundland with Gilbert.

The settlement at St. John was viewed by its promoter as merely the beginning of a scheme for ousting Spain from America in favor of England. The plan did not progress as he hoped; but after long delays, and under far other impulses than Gilbert ever thought of, much of his dream was realized.

SIR HUMPHREY GILBERT'S
VOYAGE TO NEWFOUNDLAND

A REPORT *of the* VOYAGE *and success thereof, attempted in the year of our Lord* 1583, *by* SIR HUMFREY GILBERT, KNIGHT, *with other gentlemen assisting him in that action, intended to discover and to plant Christian inhabitants in place convenient, upon those large and ample countries extended northward from the Cape of* FLORIDA, *lying under very temperate climes, esteemed fertile and rich in minerals, yet not in the actual possession of any Christian prince. Written by* MR. EDWARD HAYES, gentleman, *and principal actor in the same voyage*[1], *who alone continued unto the end, and, by God's special assistance, returned home with his retinue safe and entire.*

MANY voyages have been pretended, yet hitherto never any thoroughly accomplished by our nation, of exact discovery into the bowels of those main, ample, and vast countries extended infinitely into the north from thirty degrees, or rather from twenty-five degrees, of septentrional latitude, neither hath a right way been taken of planting a Christian habitation and regiment[2] upon the same, as well may appear both by the little we yet do actually possess therein, and by our ignorance of the riches and secrets within those lands, which unto this day we know chiefly by the travel and report of other nations, and most of the French, who albeit they cannot challenge such right and interest unto the said countries as we, neither these many years have had opportunity nor means so great to discover and to plant, being vexed with the calamities of intestine wars, as we have had by the inestimable benefit of our long and happy peace, yet have they both ways performed

[1] Hayes was captain and owner of the *Golden Hind*, Gilbert's Rear-Admiral.

[2] Government.

more, and had long since attained a sure possession and settled government of many provinces in those northerly parts of *America,* if their many attempts into those foreign and remote lands had not been impeached by their garboils at home.

The first discovery of these coasts, never heard of before, was well begun by *John Cabot* the father and *Sebastian* his son, an Englishman born, who were the first finders out of all that great tract of land stretching from the Cape of *Florida* unto those islands which we now call the *Newfoundland;* all which they brought and annexed unto the crown of *England.* Since when, if with like diligence the search of inland countries had been followed, as the discovery upon the coast and outparts thereof was performed by those two men, no doubt her Majesty's territories and revenue had been mightily enlarged and advanced by this day; and, which is more, the seed of Christian religion had been sowed amongst those pagans, which by this time might have brought forth a most plentiful harvest and copious congregation of Christians; which must be the chief intent of such as shall make any attempt that way; or else whatsoever is builded upon other foundation shall never obtain happy success nor continuance.

And although we cannot precisely judge (which only belongeth to God) what have been the humours of men stirred up to great attempts of discovering and planting in those remote countries, yet the events do shew that either God's cause hath not been chiefly preferred by them, or else God hath not permitted so abundant grace as the light of His word and knowledge of Him to be yet revealed unto those infidels before the appointed time. But most assuredly, the only cause of religion hitherto hath kept back, and will also bring forward at the time assigned by God, an effectual and complete discovery and possession by Christians both of those ample countries and the riches within them hitherto concealed; whereof, notwithstanding, God in His wisdom hath permitted to be revealed from time to time a certain obscure and misty knowledge, by little and little to allure the minds of men that way, which else will be dull enough in the zeal of His cause, and thereby to prepare us unto a readiness for the execution of His will, against the due time ordained of calling those pagans unto Christianity.

In the meanwhile it behoveth every man of great calling, in whom is any instinct of inclination unto this attempt, to examine his own motions, which, if the same proceed of ambition or avarice, he may assure himself it cometh not of God, and therefore cannot have confidence of God's protection and assistance against the violence (else irresistible) both of sea and infinite perils upon the land; whom God yet may use [as] an instrument to further His cause and glory some way, but not to build upon so bad a foundation. Otherwise, if his motives be derived from a virtuous and heroical mind, preferring chiefly the honour of God, compassion of poor infidels captived by the devil, tyrannising in most wonderful and dreadful manner over their bodies and souls; advancement of his honest and well-disposed countrymen, willing to accompany him in such honourable actions; relief of sundry people within this realm distressed; all these be honourable purposes, imitating the nature of the munificent God, wherewith He is well pleased, who will assist such an actor beyond expectation of man. And the same, who feeleth this inclination in himself, by all likelihood may hope, or rather confidently repose in the preordinance of God, that in this last age of the world (or likely never) the time is complete of receiving also these gentiles into His mercy, and that God will raise Him an instrument to effect the same; it seeming probable by event of precedent attempts made by the Spaniards and French sundry times, that the countries lying north of *Florida* God hath reserved the same to be reduced unto Christian civility by the English nation. For not long after that *Christopher Columbus* had discovered the islands and continent of the *West Indies* for *Spain, John and Sebastian Cabot* made discovery also of the rest from *Florida* northwards to the behoof of *England.*

And whensoever afterwards the Spaniards, very prosperous in all their southern discoveries, did attempt anything into *Florida* and those regions inclining towards the north, they proved most unhappy, and were at length discouraged utterly by the hard and lamentable success of many both religious and valiant in arms, endeavouring to bring those northerly regions also under the Spanish jurisdiction, as if God had prescribed limits unto the Spanish nation which they might not exceed; as by their own gests recorded may be aptly gathered.

The French, as they can pretend less title unto these northern parts than the Spaniard, by how much the Spaniard made the first discovery of the same continent so far northward as unto *Florida,* and the French did but review that before discovered by the English nation, usurping upon our right, and imposing names upon countries, rivers, bays, capes, or headlands as if they had been the first finders of those coasts; which injury we offered not unto the Spaniards, but left off to discover when we approached the Spanish limits; even so God hath not hitherto permitted them to establish a possession permanent upon another's right, notwithstanding their manifold attempts, in which the issue hath been no less tragical than that of the Spaniards, as by their own reports is extant.

Then, seeing the English nation only hath right unto these countries of *America* from the Cape of *Florida* northward by the privilege of first discovery, unto which *Cabot* was authorised by regal authority, and set forth by the expense of our late famous King *Henry* the Seventh; which right also seemeth strongly defended on our behalf by the powerful hand of Almighty God withstanding the enterprises of other nations; it may greatly encourage us upon so just ground, as is our right, and upon so sacred an intent, as to plant religion (our right and intent being meet foundations for the same), to prosecute effectually the full possession of those so ample and pleasant countries appertaining unto the crown of *England;* the same, as is to be conjectured by infallible arguments of the world's end approaching, being now arrived unto the time by God prescribed of their vocation, if ever their calling unto the knowledge of God may be expected. Which also is very probable by the revolution and course of God's word and religion, which from the beginning hath moved from the east towards, and at last unto, the west, where it is like to end, unless the same begin again where it did in the east, which were to expect a like world again. But we are assured of the contrary by the prophecy of *Christ,* whereby we gather that after His word preached throughout the world shall be the end. And as the Gospel when it descended westward began in the south, and afterward spread into the north of *Europe;* even so, as the same hath begun in the south countries of *America,* no less hope may be gathered that it will also spread into the north.

These considerations may help to suppress all dreads rising of hard events in attempts made this way by other nations, as also of the heavy success and issue in the late enterprise made by a worthy gentleman our countryman, Sir *Humfrey Gilbert,* Knight, who was the first of our nation that carried people to erect an habitation and government in those northerly countries of *America.* About which albeit he had consumed much substance, and lost his life at last, his people also perishing for the most part: yet the mystery thereof we must leave unto God, and judge charitably both of the cause, which was just in all pretence, and of the person, who was very zealous in prosecuting the same, deserving honourable remembrance for his good mind and expense of life in so virtuous an enterprise. Whereby nevertheless, lest any man should be dismayed by example of other folks' calamity, and misdeem that God doth resist all attempts intended that way, I thought good, so far as myself was an eye-witness, to deliver the circumstance and manner of our proceedings in that action; in which the gentleman was so unfortunately encumbered with wants, and worse matched with many ill-disposed people, that his rare judgment and regiment premeditated for those affairs was subjected to tolerate abuses, and in sundry extremities to hold on a course more to uphold credit than likely in his own conceit happily to succeed.

The issue of such actions, being always miserable, not guided by God, who abhorreth confusion and disorder, hath left this for admonition, being the first attempt by our nation to plant, unto such as shall take the same cause in hand hereafter, not to be discouraged from it; but to make men well advised how they handle His so high and excellent matters, as the carriage is of His word into those very mighty and vast countries. An action doubtless not to be intermeddled with base purposes, as many have made the same but a colour to shadow actions otherwise scarce justifiable; which doth excite God's heavy judgments in the end, to the terrifying of weak minds from the cause, without pondering His just proceedings; and doth also incense foreign princes against our attempts, how just soever, who cannot but deem the sequel very dangerous unto their state (if in those parts we should grow to strength), seeing the very beginnings are entered with spoil.

And with this admonition denounced upon zeal towards God's cause, also towards those in whom appeareth disposition honourable unto this action of planting Christian people and religion in those remote and barbarous nations of *America* (unto whom I wish all happiness), I will now proceed to make relation briefly, yet particularly, of our voyage undertaken with Sir *Humfrey Gilbert,* begun, continued, and ended adversely.

When first Sir *Humfrey Gilbert* undertook the western discovery of *America,* and had procured from her Majesty a very large commission to inhabit and possess at his choice all remote and heathen lands not in the actual possession of any Christian prince, the same commission exemplified with many privileges, such as in his discretion he might demand, very many gentlemen of good estimation drew unto him, to associate him in so commendable an enterprise, so that the preparation was expected to grow unto a puissant fleet, able to encounter a king's power by sea. Nevertheless, amongst a multitude of voluntary men, their dispositions were diverse, which bred a jar, and made a division in the end, to the confusion of that attempt even before the same was begun. And when the shipping was in a manner prepared, and men ready upon the coast to go aboard, at that time some brake consort, and followed courses degenerating from the voyage before pretended. Others failed of their promises contracted, and the greater number were dispersed, leaving the General with few of his assured friends, with whom he adventured to sea; where, having tasted of no less misfortune, he was shortly driven to retire home with the loss of a tall ship and, more to his grief, of a valiant gentleman, *Miles Morgan.*

Having buried, only in a preparation, a great mass of substance, whereby his estate was impaired, his mind yet not dismayed, he continued his former designment, and purposed to revive this enterprise, good occasion serving. Upon which determination standing long without means to satisfy his desire, at last he granted certain assignments out of his commission to sundry persons of mean ability, desiring the privilege of his grant, to plant and fortify in the north parts of *America* about the river of *Canada;* to whom if God gave good success in the north parts (where then no matter of moment was expected), the same, he thought, would greatly advance the hope of the south, and be a furtherance unto his determination that way. And the worst that might happen in that course might be excused, without prejudice unto him, by the former supposition that those north regions were of no regard. But chiefly, a possession taken in any parcel of those heathen countries, by virtue of his grant, did invest him of territories extending every way 200 leagues; which induced Sir *Humfrey Gilbert* to make those assignments, desiring greatly their expedition, because his commission did expire after six years, if in that space he had not gotten actual possession.

Time went away without anything done by his assigns; insomuch that at last he must resolve himself to take a voyage in person, for more assurance to keep his patent in force, which then almost was expired or within two years. In furtherance of his determination, amongst others, Sir *George Peckham,* Knight, shewed himself very zealous to the action, greatly aiding him both by his advice and in the charge. Other gentlemen to their ability joined unto him, resolving to adventure their substance and lives in the same cause. Who beginning their preparation from that time, both of shipping, munition, victual, men, and things requisite, some of them continued the charge two years complete without intermission. Such were the difficulties and cross accidents opposing these proceedings, which took not end in less than two years; many of which circumstances I will omit.

The last place of our assembly, before we left the coast of England, was in *Cawset* Bay, near unto *Plymouth,* then resolved to put unto the sea with shipping and provision such as we had, before our store yet remaining, but chiefly the time and season of the year, were too far spent. Nevertheless, it seemed first very doubtful by what way to shape our course, and to begin our intended discovery, either from the south northward or from the north southward. The first, that is, beginning south, without all controversy was the likeliest; wherein we were assured to have commodity of the current which from the Cape of *Florida* setteth northward, and would have furthered greatly our navigation, discovering from the foresaid cape along towards Cape *Breton,* and all those lands lying to the north. Also, the year being far spent, and arrived to the month of June, we were not to spend time in northerly courses, where we should be surprised with timely winter, but to covet the south, which we had space enough then to have attained, and there might with less detriment have wintered that season, being more mild and short in the south than in the north, where winter is both long and rigorous. These and other like reasons alleged in favour of the southern course first to be taken, to the contrary was inferred that forasmuch as both our victuals and many other needful provisions were diminished and left insufficient for so long a voyage and for the wintering of so many men, we ought to shape a course most likely to minister supply; and that was to take the *Newfoundland* in our way, which was but 700 leagues from our English coast. Where being usually at that time of the year, and until the fine of August, a multitude of ships repairing thither for fish, we should be relieved abundantly with many necessaries, which, after the fishing ended, they might well spare and freely impart unto us. Not staying long upon that *Newland* coast, we might proceed southward, and follow still the sun, until we arrived at places more temperate to our content.

By which reasons we were the rather induced to follow this northerly course, obeying unto necessity, which must be supplied. Otherwise, we doubted that sudden approach of winter, bringing with it continual fog and thick mists, tempest and rage of weather, also contrariety of currents descending from the Cape of *Florida* unto Cape *Breton* and Cape *Race,* would fall out to be great and irresistible impediments unto our further proceeding for that year, and compel us to winter in those north and cold regions. Wherefore, suppressing all objections to the contrary, we resolved to begin our course northward, and to follow, directly as we might, the trade way unto *Newfoundland;* from whence, after our refreshing and reparation of wants, we intended without delay, by God's permission, to proceed into the south, not omitting any river or bay which in all that large tract of land appeared to our view worthy of search. Immediately we agreed upon the manner of our course and orders to be observed in our voyage; which were delivered in writing, unto the captains and masters of every ship a copy, in manner following.

Every ship had delivered two bullets or scrolls, the one sealed up in wax, the other left open; in both which were included several watchwords. That open, serving upon our own coast or the coast of Ireland; the other sealed, was promised on all hands not to be broken up until we should be clear of the Irish coast; which from thenceforth did serve until we arrived and met all together in such harbours of the *Newfoundland* as were agreed for our *rendez-vous.* The said watchwords being requisite to know our consorts whensoever by night, either by fortune of weather, our fleet dispersed should come together again; or one should hail another; or if by ill watch and steerage one ship should chance to fall aboard of another in the dark.

The reason of the bullet sealed was to keep secret that watchword while we were upon our own coast, lest any of the company stealing from the fleet might bewray the same; which known to an enemy, he might board us by night without mistrust, having our own watchword.

ORDERS *agreed upon by the* CAPTAINS *and* MASTERS *to be observed by the fleet of Sir* HUMFREY GILBERT.

FIRST, The Admiral to carry his flag by day, and his light by night.

2. Item, if the Admiral shall shorten his sail by night, then to shew two lights until he be answered again by every ship shewing one light for a short time.

3. Item, if the Admiral after his shortening of sail, as aforesaid, shall make more sail again; then he to shew three lights one above another.

4. Item, if the Admiral shall happen to hull in the night, then to make a wavering light over his other light, wavering the light upon a pole.

5. Item, if the fleet should happen to be scattered by weather, or other mishap, then so soon as one shall descry another, to hoise both topsails twice, if the weather will serve, and to strike them twice again; but if the weather serve not, then to hoise the maintopsail twice, and forthwith to strike it twice again.

6. Item, if it shall happen a great fog to fall, then presently every ship to bear up with the Admiral, if there be wind; but if it be a calm, then every ship to hull, and so to lie at hull till it clear. And if the fog do continue long, then the Admiral to shoot off two pieces every evening, and every ship to answer it with one shot; and every man bearing to the ship that is to leeward so near as he may.

7. Item, every master to give charge unto the watch to look out well, for laying aboard one of another in the night, and in fogs.

8. Item, every evening every ship to hail the Admiral, and so to fall astern him, sailing thorough the ocean; and being on the coast, every ship to hail him both morning and evening.

9. Item, if any ship be in danger in any way, by leak or otherwise, then she to shoot off a piece, and presently to hang out one light; whereupon every man to bear towards her, answering her with one light for a short time, and so to put it out again; thereby to give knowledge that they have seen her token.

10. Item, whensoever the Admiral shall hang out her ensign in the main shrouds, then every man to come aboard her as a token of counsel.

11. Item, if there happen any storm or contrary wind to the fleet after the discovery, whereby they are separated; then every ship to repair unto their last good port, there to meet again.

Our Course *agreed upon.*

The course first to be taken for the discovery is to bear directly to Cape *Race,* the most southerly cape of *Newfoundland;* and there to harbour ourselves either in *Rogneux* or *Fermous,* being the first places appointed for our *rendez-vous,* and the next harbours unto the northward of Cape *Race:* and therefore every ship separated from the fleet to repair to that place so fast as God shall permit, whether you shall fall to the southward or to the northward of it, and there to stay for the meeting of the whole fleet the space of ten days; and when you shall depart, to leave marks.

Beginning our course from *Scilly,* the nearest is by west-south-west (if the wind serve) until such time as we have brought ourselves in the latitude of 43 or 44 degrees, because the ocean is subject much to southerly winds in June and July. Then to take traverse from 45 to 47 degrees of latitude, if we be enforced by contrary winds; and not to go to the northward of the height of 47 degrees of septentrional latitude by no means, if God shall not enforce the contrary; but to do your endeavour to keep in the height of 46 degrees, so near as you can possibly, because Cape *Race* lieth about that height.

Note.

If by contrary winds we be driven back upon the coast of *England,* then to repair unto *Scilly* for a place of our assembly or meeting. If we be driven back by contrary winds that we cannot pass the coast of *Ireland,* then the place of our assembly to be at *Bere* haven or *Baltimore* haven. If we shall not happen to meet at Cape *Race,* then the place of *rendez-vous* to be at Cape *Breton,* or the nearest harbour unto the westward of Cape *Breton.* If by means of other shipping we may not safely stay there, then to rest at the very next safe port to the westward; every ship leaving their marks behind them for the more certainty of the after comers to know where to find them. The marks that every man ought to leave in such a case, were of the General's private device written by himself, sealed also in close wax, and delivered unto every ship one scroll, which was not to be opened until occasion required, whereby every man was certified what to leave for instruction of after comers; that every of us coming into any harbour or river might know who had been there, or whether any were still there up higher into the river, or departed, and which way.

Orders thus determined, and promises mutually given to be observed, every man withdrew himself unto his charge; the anchors being already weighed, and our ships under sail, having a soft gale of wind, we began our voyage upon Tuesday, the 11. day of June, in the year of our Lord 1583, having in our fleet (at our departure from *Cawset* Bay) these ships, whose names and burthens, with the names of the captains and masters of them, I have also inserted, as followeth:—1. The *Delight, alias* the *George,* of burthen 120 tons, was Admiral; in which went the General, and *William Winter,* captain in her and part owner, and *Richard Clarke,* master. 2. The bark *Raleigh,* set forth by Master *Walter Raleigh,* of the burthen of 200 tons, was then Vice-Admiral; in which went Master *Butler,* captain, and *Robert Davis,* of *Bristol,* master. 3. The *Golden Hind,* of burthen 40 tons, was then Rear-Admiral; in which went *Edward Hayes,* captain and owner, and *William Cox,* of *Limehouse,* master. 4. The *Swallow,* of burthen 40 tons; in her was captain *Maurice Browne.* 5. The *Squirrel,* of burthen 10 tons; in which went captain *William Andrews,* and one *Cade,* master. We were in number in all about 260 men; among whom we had of every faculty good choice, as shipwrights, masons, carpenters, smiths, and such like, requisite to such an action; also mineral men and refiners. Besides, for solace of our people, and allurement of the savages, we were provided of music in good variety; not omitting the least toys, as morris-dancers, hobby-horse, and May-like conceits to delight the savage people, whom we intended to win by all fair means possible. And to that end we were indifferently furnished of all petty haberdashery wares to barter with those simple people.

In this manner we set forward, departing (as hath been said) out of *Cawset* Bay the 11. day of June, being Tuesday, the weather and wind fair and good all day; but a great storm of thunder and wind fell the same night. Thursday following, when we hailed one another in the evening, according to the order before specified, they signified unto us out of the Vice-Admiral, that both the captain, and very many of the men, were fallen sick. And about midnight the Vice-Admiral forsook us, notwithstanding we had the wind east, fair and good. But it was after credibly reported that they were infected with a contagious sickness, and arrived greatly distressed at *Plymouth;* the reason I could never understand. Sure I am, no cost was spared by their owner, Master *Raleigh,* in setting them forth; therefore I leave it unto God. By this time we were in 48 degrees of latitude, not a little grieved with the loss of the most puissant ship in our fleet; after whose departure the *Golden Hind* succeeded in the place of Vice-Admiral, and removed her flag from the mizen into the foretop. From Saturday, the 15. of June, until the 28., which was upon a Friday, we never had fair day without fog or rain, and winds bad, much to the west-north-west, whereby we were driven southward unto 41 degrees scarce.

About this time of the year the winds are commonly west towards the *Newfoundland,* keeping ordinarily within two points of west to the south or to the north; whereby the course thither falleth out to be long and tedious after June, which in March, April, and May, hath been performed out of England in 22 days and less. We had wind always so scant from west-north-west, and from west-south-west again, that our traverse was great, running south unto 41 degrees almost, and afterwards north into 51 degrees. Also we were encumbered with much fog and mists in manner palpable, in which we could not keep so well together, but were dissevered, losing the company of the *Swallow* and the *Squirrel* upon the 20. day of July, whom we met again at several places upon the *Newfoundland* coast the 3. of August, as shall be declared in place convenient. Saturday, the 27. July, we might descry, not far from us, as it were mountains of ice driven upon the sea, being then in 50 degrees, which were carried southward to the weather of us; whereby may be conjectured that some current doth set that way from the north.

Before we come to *Newfoundland,* about 50 leagues on this side, we pass the bank, which are high grounds rising within the sea and under water, yet deep enough and without danger, being commonly not less than 25 and 30 fathom water upon them; the same, as it were some vein of mountains within the sea, do run along and from the *Newfoundland,* beginning northward about 52 or 53 degrees of latitude, and do extend into the south infinitely. The breadth of this bank is somewhere more, and somewhere less; but we found the same about ten leagues over, having sounded both on this side thereof, and the other toward *Newfoundland,* but found no ground with almost 200 fathom of line, both before and after we had passed the bank. The Portugals, and French chiefly, have a notable trade of fishing upon this bank, where are sometimes an hundred or more sails of ships, who commonly begin the fishing in April, and have ended by July. That fish is large, always wet, having no land near to dry, and is called *cod* fish. During the time of fishing, a man shall know without sounding when he is upon the bank, by the incredible multitude of sea-fowl hovering over the same, to prey upon the offals and garbage of fish thrown out by fishermen, and floating upon the sea.

Upon Tuesday, the 11. of June we forsook the coast of England. So again [on] Tuesday, the 30. of July, seven weeks after, we got sight of land, being immediately embayed in the *Grand Bay,* or some other great bay; the certainty whereof we could not judge, so great haze and fog did hang upon the coast, as neither we might discern the land well, nor take the sun's height. But by our best computation we were then in the 51 degrees of latitude. Forsaking this bay and uncomfortable coast (nothing appearing unto us but hideous rocks and mountains, bare of trees, and void of any green herb) we followed the coast to the south, with weather fair and clear. We had sight of an island named *Penguin,* of a fowl there breeding in abundance almost incredible, which cannot fly, their wings not able to carry their body, being very large (not much less than a goose) and exceeding fat, which the Frenchmen use to take without difficulty upon that island, and to barrel them up with salt. But for lingering of time, we had made us there the like provision.

Trending this coast, we came to the island called *Baccalaos,* being not past two leagues from the main; to the south thereof lieth Cape *St. Francis,* five leagues distant from *Baccalaos,* between which goeth in a great bay, by the vulgar sort called the Bay of *Conception.* Here we met with the *Swallow* again, whom we had lost in the fog, and all her men altered into other apparel; whereof it seemed their store was so amended, that for joy and congratulation of our meeting, they spared not to cast up into the air and overboard their caps and hats in good plenty. The captain, albeit himself was very honest and religious, yet was he not appointed of men to his humour and desert; who for the most part were such as had been by us surprised upon the narrow seas of *England,* being pirates, and had taken at that instant certain Frenchmen laden, one bark with wines, and another with salt. Both which we rescued, and took the man-of-war with all her men, which was the same ship now called the *Swallow;* following still their kind so oft as, being separated from the General, they found opportunity to rob and spoil. And because God's justice did follow the same company, even to destruction, and to the overthrow also of the captain (though not consenting to their misdemeanour) I will not conceal anything that maketh to the manifestation and approbation of His judgments, for examples of others; persuaded that God more sharply took revenge upon them, and hath tolerated longer as great outrage in others, by how much these went under protection of His cause and religion, which was then pretended.

Therefore upon further enquiry it was known how this company met with a bark returning home after the fishing with his freight; and because the men in the *Swallow* were very near scanted of victuals, and chiefly of apparel, doubtful withal where or when to find and meet with their Admiral, they besought the captain that they might go aboard this *Newlander,* only to borrow what might be spared, the rather because the same was bound homeward. Leave given, not without charge to deal favourably, they came aboard the fisherman, whom they rifled of tackle, sails, cables. victuals, and the men of their apparel; not sparing by torture, winding cords about their heads, to draw out else what they thought good. This done with expedition, like men skilful in such mischief, as they took their cockboat to go aboard their own ship, it was overwhelmed in the sea, and certain of these men there drowned; the rest were preserved even by those silly souls whom they had before spoiled, who saved and delivered them aboard the *Swallow*. What became afterwards of the poor *Newlander,* perhaps destitute of sails and furniture sufficient to carry them home, whither they had not less to run than 700 leagues, God alone knoweth; who took vengeance not long after of the rest that escaped at this instant, to reveal the fact, and justify to the world God's judgments inflicted upon them, as shall be declared in place convenient.

Thus after we had met with the *Swallow,* we held on our course southward, until we came against the harbour called *St. John,* about five leagues from the former Cape of *St. Francis,* where before the entrance into the harbour, we found also the frigate or *Squirrel* lying at anchor; whom the English merchants, that were and always be Admirals by turns interchangeably over the fleets of fishermen within the same harbour, would not permit to enter into the harbour. Glad of so happy meeting, both of the *Swallow* and frigate in one day, being Saturday, the third of August, we made ready our fights,[3] and prepared to enter the harbour, any resistance to the contrary notwithstanding, there being within of all nations to the number of 36 sails. But first the General despatched a boat to give them knowledge of his coming for no ill intent, having commission from her Majesty for his voyage he had in hand; and immediately we followed with a slack gale, and in the very entrance, which is but narrow, not above two butts' length,[4] the Admiral fell upon a rock on the larboard side by great oversight, in that the weather was fair, the rock much above water fast by the shore, where neither went any sea-gate.[5] But we found such readiness in the English merchants to help us in that danger, that without delay there were brought a number of boats, which towed off the ship, and cleared her of danger.

Having taken place convenient in the road, we let fall anchors, the captains and masters repairing aboard our

[3] See First Series, p. liii. [4] Bow-shot. [5] Current.

Admiral; whither also came immediately the masters and owners of the fishing fleet of Englishmen, to understand the General's intent and cause of our arrival there. They were all satisfied when the General had shewed his commission, and purpose to take possession of those lands to the behalf of the crown of *England,* and the advancement of the Christian religion in those paganish regions, requiring but their lawful aid for repairing of his fleet, and supply of some necessaries, so far as conveniently might be afforded him, both out of that and other harbours adjoining. In lieu whereof he made offer to gratify them with any favour and privilege, which upon their better advice they should demand, the like being not to be obtained hereafter for greater price. So craving expedition of his demand, minding to proceed further south without long detention in those parts, he dismissed them, after promise given of their best endeavour to satisfy speedily his so reasonable request. The merchants with their masters departed, they caused forthwith to be discharged all the great ordnance of their fleet in token of our welcome.

It was further determined that every ship of our fleet should deliver unto the merchants and masters of that harbour a note of all their wants: which done, the ships, as well English as strangers, were taxed at an easy rate to make supply. And besides, commissioners were appointed, part of our own company and part of theirs, to go into other harbours adjoining (for our English merchants command all there) to levy our provision: whereunto the Portugals, above other nations, did most willingly anl liberally contribute. In so much as we were presented, above our allowance, with wines, marmalades, most fine rusk[6] or biscuit, sweet oils, and sundry delicacies. Also we wanted not of fresh salmons, trouts, lobsters, and other fresh fish brought daily unto us. Moreover as the manner is in their fishing, every week to choose their Admiral anew, or rather they succeed in orderly course, and have weekly their Admiral's feast solemnized: even so the General, captains, and masters of our fleet were continually invited and feasted. To grow short in our abundance at home the entertainment had been delightful; but

[6] Rusk (Sp. *rosca*)=ship's biscuit.

after our wants and tedious passage through the ocean, it seemed more acceptable and of greater contentation, by how much the same was unexpected in that desolate corner of the world; where, at other times of the year, wild beasts and birds have only the fruition of all those countries, which now seemed a place very populous and much frequented.

The next morning being Sunday, and the fourth of August, the General and his company were brought on land by English merchants, who shewed unto us their accustomed walks unto a place they call the *Garden.* But nothing appeared more than nature itself without art: who confusedly hath brought forth roses abundantly, wild, but odoriferous, and to sense very comfortable. Also the like plenty of raspberries, which do grow in every place.

Monday following, the General had his tent set up; who, being accompanied with his own followers, summoned the merchants and masters, both English and strangers, to be present at his taking possession of those countries. Before whom openly was read, and interpreted unto the strangers, his commission: by virtue whereof he took possession in the same harbour of *St. John,* and 200 leagues every way, invested the Queen's Majesty with the title and dignity thereof, had delivered unto him, after the custom of England, a rod, and a turf of the same soil, entering possession also for him, his heirs and assigns for ever; and signified unto all men, that from that time forward, they should take the same land as a territory appertaining to the Queen of *England,* and himself authorised under her Majesty to possess and enjoy it, and to ordain laws for the government thereof, agreeable, so near as conveniently might be, unto the laws of *England,* under which all people coming thither hereafter, either to inhabit, or by way of traffic, should be subjected and governed. And especially at the same time for a beginning, he proposed and delivered three laws to be in force immediately. That is to say the first for religion, which in public exercise should be according to the Church of *England.* The second, for maintenance of her Majesty's right and possession of those territories, against which if any thing were attempted prejudicial, the party or parties offending should be adjudged and executed as in case of high treason, according to the laws of *England.* The third, if any person should utter words sounding to the dishonour of her Majesty, he should lose his ears, and have his ship and goods confiscate.

These contents published, obedience was promised by general voice and consent of the multitude, as well of Englishmen as strangers, praying for continuance of this possession and government begun; after this, the assembly was dismissed. And afterwards were erected not far from that place the arms of *England* engraven in lead, and infixed upon a pillar of wood. Yet further and actually to establish this possession taken in the right of her Majesty, and to the behoof of Sir *Humfrey Gilbert,* knight, his heirs and assigns for ever, the General granted in fee-farm divers parcels of land lying by the water-side, both in this harbour of *St. John,* and elsewhere, which was to the owners a great commodity, being thereby assured, by their proper inheritance, of grounds convenient to dress and to dry their fish; whereof many times before they did fail, being prevented by them that came first into the harbour. For which grounds they did covenant to pay a certain rent and service unto Sir *Humfrey Gilbert,* his heirs or assigns for ever, and yearly to maintain possession of the same, by themselves or their assigns.

Now remained only to take in provision granted, according as every ship was taxed, which did fish upon the coast adjoining. In the meanwhile, the General appointed men unto their charge: some to repair and trim the ships, others to attend in gathering together our supply and provisions: others to search the commodities and singularities of the country, to be found by sea or land, and to make relation unto the General what either themselves could know by their own travail and experience, or by good intelligence of Englishmen or strangers, who had longest frequented the same coast. Also some observed the elevation of the pole, and drew plots of the country exactly graded. And by that I could gather by each man's several relation, I have drawn a brief description of the *Newfoundland,* with the commodities by sea or land already made, and such also as are in possibility and great likelihood to be made. Nevertheless the cards and plots that were drawn, with the due gradation of the harbours, bays, and capes, did perish with the Admiral: wherefore in the description following, I must omit the particulars of such things.

That which we do call the *Newfoundland,* and the Frenchmen *Baccalaos,* is an island, or rather, after the opinion of some, it consisteth of sundry islands and broken lands, situate in the north regions of *America,* upon the gulf and entrance of a great river called *St. Lawrence* in *Canada;* into the which, navigation may be made both on the south and north side of this island. The land lieth south and north, containing in length between 300 and 400 miles, accounting from Cape *Race,* which is in 46 degrees 25 minutes, unto the *Grand Bay* in 52 degrees, of septentrional latitude. The land round about hath very many goodly bays and harbours, safe roads for ships, the like not to be found in any part of the known world.

The common opinion that is had of intemperature and extreme cold that should be in this country, as of some part it may be verified, namely the north, where I grant it is more cold than in countries of *Europe,* which are under the same elevation: even so it cannot stand with reason and nature of the clime, that the south parts should be so intemperate as the bruit hath gone. For as the same do lie under the climes of *Bretagne, Anjou, Poictou* in *France,* between 46 and 49 degrees, so can they not so much differ from the temperature of those countries: unless upon the out-coast lying open unto the ocean and sharp winds, it must indeed be subject to more cold than further within the land, where the mountains are interposed as walls and bulwarks, to defend and to resist the asperity and rigour of the sea and weather. Some hold opinion that the *Newfoundland* might be the more subject to cold, by how much it lieth high and near unto the middle region. I grant that not in *Newfoundland* alone, but in *Germany, Italy* and *Afric,* even under the equinoctial line, the mountains are extreme cold, and seldom uncovered of snow, in their culm and highest tops, which cometh to pass by the same reason that they are extended towards the middle region: yet in the countries lying beneath them, it is found quite contrary. Even so, all hills having their descents, the valleys also and low grounds must be likewise hot or temperate, as the clime doth give in *Newfoundland:* though I am of opinion that the sun's reflection is much cooled, and cannot be so forcible in *Newfoundland,* nor generally throughout *America,* as in *Europe* or *Afric:* by how much the sun in his diurnal course from east to west, passeth over, for the most part, dry land and sandy countries, before he arriveth at the west of *Europe* or *Afric,* whereby his motion increaseth heat, with little or no qualification by moist vapours. Where[as], on the contrary, he passeth from *Europe* and *Afric* unto *America* over the ocean, from whence he draweth and carrieth with him abundance of moist vapours, which do qualify and enfeeble greatly the sun's reverberation upon this country chiefly of *Newfoundland,* being so much to the northward. Nevertheless, as I said before, the cold cannot be so intolerable under the latitude of 46, 47, and 48, especial within land, that it should be unhabitable, as some do suppose, seeing also there are very many people more to the north by a great deal. And in these south parts there be certain beasts, ounces or leopards, and birds in like manner, which in the summer we have seen, not heard of in countries of extreme and vehement coldness. Besides, as in the months of June, July, August and September, the heat is somewhat more than in England at those seasons: so men remaining upon the south parts near unto Cape *Race,* until after holland-tide,[7] have not found the cold so extreme, nor much differing from the temperature of *England.* Those which have arrived there after November and December have found the snow exceeding deep, whereat no marvel, considering the ground upon the coast is rough and uneven, and the snow is driven into the places most declining, as the like is to be seen with us. The like depth of snow happily shall not be found within land upon the plainer countries, which also are defended by the mountains, breaking off the violence of winds and weather. But admitting extraordinary cold in those south parts, above that with us here, it cannot be so great as in *Swedeland,* much less in *Moscovia* or *Russia:* yet are the same countries very populous, and the rigour of cold is dis-

[7] All-hallow-tide (November 1).

pensed with by the commodity of stoves, warm clothing, meats and drinks: all of which need not to be wanting in the *Newfoundland,* if we had intent there to inhabit.

In the south parts we found no inhabitants, which by all likelihood have abandoned those coasts, the same being so much frequented by Christians; but in the north are savages altogether harmless. Touching the commodities of this country, serving either for sustentation of inhabitants or for maintenance of traffic, there are and may be made divers; so that it seemeth that nature hath recompensed that only defect and incommodity of some sharp cold, by many benefits; namely, with incredible quantity, and no less variety, of kinds of fish in the sea and fresh waters, as trouts, salmons, and other fish to us unknown; also cod, which alone draweth many nations thither, and is become the most famous fishing of the world; abundance of whales, for which also is a very great trade in the bays of *Placentia* and the *Grand Bay,* where is made train oil of the whale; herring, the largest that have been heard of, and exceeding the *Marstrand* herring of *Norway;* but hitherto was never benefit taken of the herring fishing. There are sundry other fish very delicate, namely, the *bonito,* lobsters, turbot, with others infinite not sought after; oysters having pearl but not orient in colour; I took it, by reason they were not gathered in season.

Concerning the inland commodities, as well to be drawn from this land, as from the exceeding large countries adjoining, there is nothing which our east and northerly countries of *Europe* do yield, but the like also may be made in them as plentifully, by time and industry; namely, resin, pitch, tar, soap-ashes, deal-board, masts for ships, hides, furs, flax, hemp, corn, cables, cordage, linen cloth, metals, and many more. All which the countries will afford, and the soil is apt to yield. The trees for the most in those south parts are fir-trees, pine, and cypress, all yielding gum and turpentine. Cherry trees bearing fruit no bigger than a small pease. Also pear-trees, but fruitless. Other trees of some sort to us unknown. The soil along the coast is not deep of earth, bringing forth abundantly peasen small, yet good feeding for cattle. Roses passing sweet, like unto our musk roses in form; raspises; a berry which we call whorts, good and wholesome to eat. The grass and herb doth fat sheep in very short space, proved by English merchants which have carried sheep thither for fresh victual and had them raised exceeding fat in less than three weeks. Peasen which our countrymen have sown in the time of May, have come up fair, and been gathered in the beginning of August, of which our General had a present acceptable for the rareness, being the first fruits coming up by art and industry in that desolate and dishabited land. Lakes or pools of fresh water, both on the tops of mountains and in the valleys; in which are said to be muscles not unlike to have pearl, which I had put in trial, if by mischance falling unto me I had not been letted from that and other good experiments I was minded to make. Fowl both of water and land in great plenty and diversity. All kind of green fowl; others as big as bustards, yet not the same. A great white fowl called of some a gaunt. Upon the land divers sort of hawks, as falcons, and others by report. Partridges most plentiful, larger than ours, grey and white of colour, and rough-footed like doves, which our men after one flight did kill with cudgels, they were so fat and unable to fly. Birds, some like blackbirds, linnets, canary birds, and other very small. Beasts of sundry kinds; red deer, buffles, or a beast as it seemeth by the tract and foot very large, in manner of an ox. Bears, ounces or leopards, some greater and some lesser; wolves, foxes, which to the northward a little further are black, whose fur is esteemed in some countries of *Europe* very rich. Otters, beavers, marterns; and in the opinion of most men that saw it, the General had brought unto him a sable alive, which he sent unto his brother, Sir *John Gilbert,* Knight, of *Devonshire,* but it was never delivered, as after I understood. We could not observe the hundredth part of creatures in those unhabited lands; but these mentioned may induce us to glorify the magnificent God, who hath super-abundantly replenished the earth with creatures serving for the use of man, though man hath not used the fifth part of the same, which the more doth aggravate the fault and foolish sloth in many of our nation, choosing rather to live indirectly, and very miserably to live and die within this realm pestered with inhabitants, than to adventure as becometh men, to obtain an habitation in those remote lands, in which nature very prodigally doth minister unto men's endeavours, and for art to work upon. For besides these already recounted and infinite more, the mountains generally make shew of mineral substance; iron very common, lead, and somewhere copper. I will not aver of richer metals; albeit by the circumstances following, more than hope may be conceived thereof.

For amongst other charges given to enquire out the singularities of this country, the General was most curious in the search of metals, commanding the mineral-man and refiner especially to be diligent. The same was a *Saxon*[8] born, honest, and religious, named *Daniel.* Who after search brought at first some sort of ore, seeming rather to be iron than other metal. The next time he found ore, which with no small show of contentment he delivered unto the General, using protestation that if silver were the thing which might satisfy the General and his followers, there it was, advising him to seek no further; the peril whereof he undertook upon his life (as dear unto him as the crown of *England* unto her Majesty, that I may use his own words) if it fell not out accordingly.

Myself at this instant liker to die than to live, by a mischance, could not follow this confident opinion of our refiner to my own satisfaction; but afterward demanding our Genreal's opinion therein, and to have some part of the ore, he replied, *Content yourself, I have seen enough; and were it but to satisfy my private humour, I would proceed no further. The promise unto my friends, and necessity to bring also the south countries within compass of my patent near expired, as we have already done these north parts, do only persuade me further. And touching the ore, I have sent it aboard, whereof I would have no speech to be made so long as we remain within harbour; here being both Portugals, Biscayans, and Frenchmen, not far off, from whom must be kept any bruit or muttering of such matter. When we are at sea, proof shall be made; if it be our desire, we may return the sooner hither again.* Whose answer I judged reasonable, and contenting me well; wherewith I will conclude this nar-

[8] Probably from the mining district of Lower Saxony.

ration and description of the *Newfoundland,* and proceed to the rest of our voyage, which ended tragically.

While the better sort of us were seriously occupied in repairing our wants, and contriving of matters for the commodity of our voyage, others of another sort and disposition were plotting of mischief; some casting to steal away our shipping by night, watching opportunity by the General's and captains' lying on the shore; whose conspiracies discovered, they were prevented. Others drew together in company, and carried away out of the harbours adjoining a ship laden with fish, setting the poor men on shore. A great many more of our people stole into the woods to hide themselves, attending time and means to return home by such shipping as daily departed from the coast. Some were sick of fluxes, and many dead; and in brief, by one means or other our company was diminished, and many by the General licensed to return home. Insomuch as after we had reviewed our people, resolved to see an end of our voyage, we grew scant of men to furnish all our shipping; it seemed good therefore unto the General to leave the *Swallow* with such provision as might be spared for transporting home the sick people.

The captain of the *Delight,* or Admiral, returned into *England,* in whose stead was appointed captain *Maurice Browne,* before captain of the *Swallow;* who also brought with him into the *Delight* all his men of the *Swallow,* which before have been noted of outrage perpetrated and committed upon fishermen there met at sea.

The General made choice to go in his frigate the *Squirrel,* whereof the captain also was amongst them that returned into *England;* the same frigate being most convenient to discover upon the coast, and to search into every harbour or creek, which a great ship could not do. Therefore the frigate was prepared with her nettings and fights, and overcharged with bases and such small ordnance, more to give a show, than with judgment to foresee unto the safety of her and the men, which afterward was an occasion also of their overthrow.

Now having made ready our shipping, that is to say, the *Delight,* the *Golden Hind,* and the *Squirrel,* we put aboard our provision, which was wines, bread or rusk, fish wet and dry, sweet oils, besides many other, as marmalades, figs, limons barrelled, and such like. Also we had other necessary provisions for trimming our ships, nets and lines to fish withal, boats or pinnaces fit for discovery. In brief, we were supplied of our wants commodiously, as if we had been in a country or some city populous and plentiful of all things.

We departed from this harbour of *St. John's* upon Tuesday, the 20. of August, which we found by exact observation to be in 47 degrees 40 minutes; and the next day by night we were at Cape *Race,* 25 leagues from the same harborough. This cape lieth south-south-west from *St. John's;* it is a low land, being off from the cape about half a league; within the sea riseth up a rock against the point of the cape, which thereby is easily known. It is in latitude 46 degrees 25 minutes. Under this cape we were becalmed a small time, during which we laid out hooks and lines to take cod, and drew in less than two hours fish so large and in such abundance, that many days after we fed upon no other provision. From hence we shaped our course unto the island of *Sablon,* if conveniently it would so fall out, also directly to Cape *Breton.*

Sablon lieth to the seaward of Cape *Breton* about 25 leagues, whither we were determined to go upon intelligence we had of a Portugal, during our abode in *St. John's,* who was himself present when the Portugals, above thirty years past, did put into the same island both neat and swine to breed, which were since exceedingly multiplied. This seemed unto us very happy tidings, to have in an island lying so near unto the main, which we intended to plant upon, such store of cattle, whereby we might at all times conveniently be relieved of victual, and served of store for breed.

In this course we trended along the coast, which from Cape *Race* stretcheth into the north-west, making a bay which some called *Trepassa.*[9] Then it goeth out again towards the west, and maketh a point, which with Cape *Race* lieth in manner east and west. But this point inclineth to the north, to the west of which goeth in the Bay of *Placentia.* We sent men on land to take view of the soil along this coast, whereof

[9] From the Baie des Trépassés at the Pointe du Raz in Brittany, from which Cape Race itself is named.

they made good report, and some of them had will to be planted there. They saw pease growing in great abundance everywhere.

The distance between Cape *Race* and Cape *Breton* is 87 leagues; in which navigation we spent eight days, having many times the wind indifferent good, yet could we never attain sight of any land all that time, seeing we were hindered by the current. At last we fell into such flats and dangers, that hardly any of us escaped; where nevertheless we lost our Admiral[10] with all the men and provisions, not knowing certainly the place. Yet for inducing men of skill to make conjecture, by our course and way we held from Cape *Race* thither, that thereby the flats and dangers may be inserted in sea cards, for warning to others that may follow the same course hereafter, I have set down the best reckonings that were kept by expert men, *William Cox,* Master of the *Hind,* and *John Paul,* his mate, both of *Limehouse* . . . . Our course we held in clearing us of these flats was east-south-east, and south-east, and south, fourteen leagues, with a marvellous scant wind.

Upon Tuesday, the 27. of August, toward the evening, our General caused them in his frigate to sound, who found white sand at 35 fathom, being then in latitude about 44 degrees. Wednesday, toward night, the wind came south, and we bare with the land all that night, west-north-west, contrary to the mind of Master *Cox;* nevertheless we followed the Admiral, deprived of power to prevent a mischief, which by no contradiction could be brought to hold another course, alleging they could not make the ship to work better, nor to lie otherways. The evening was fair and pleasant, yet not without token of storm to ensue, and most part of this Wednesday night, like the swan that singeth before her death, they in the Admiral, or *Delight,* continued in sounding of trumpets, with drums and fifes; also winding the cornets and hautboys, and in the end of their jollity, left with the battle and ringing of doleful knells. Towards the evening also we caught in the *Golden Hind* a very mighty porpoise with a harping iron, having first stricken divers of them, and brought away part of their flesh sticking upon the iron, but

[10] The *Delight.*

could recover only that one. These also, passing through the ocean in herds, did portend storm. I omit to recite frivolous reports by them in the frigate, of strange voices the same night, which scared some from the helm.

Thursday, the 29. of August, the wind rose, and blew vehemently at south and by east, bringing withal rain and thick mist, so that we could not see a cable length before us; and betimes in the morning we were altogether run and folded in amongst flats and sands, amongst which we found shoal and deep in every three or four ships' length, after we began to sound: but first we were upon them unawares, until Master *Cox* looking out, discerned, in his judgment, white cliffs, crying *Land!* withal; though we could not afterward descry any land, it being very likely the breaking of the sea white, which seemed to be white cliffs, through the haze and thick weather.

Immediately tokens were given unto the *Delight,* to cast about to seaward, which, being the greater ship, and of burthen 120 tons, was yet foremost upon the breach, keeping so ill watch, that they knew not the danger, before they felt the same, too late to recover it; for presently the Admiral struck aground, and had soon after her stern and hinder parts beaten in pieces; whereupon the rest (that is to say, the frigate, in which was the General, and the *Golden Hind*) cast about east-south-east, bearing to the south, even for our lives, into the wind's eye, because that way carried us to the seaward. Making out from this danger, we sounded one while seven fathom, then five fathom, then four fathom and less, again deeper, immediately four fathom, then but three fathom, the sea going mightily and high. At last we recovered, God be thanked, in some despair, to sea room enough.

In this distress, we had vigilant eye unto the Admiral, whom we saw cast away, without power to give the men succour, neither could we espy any of the men that leaped overboard to save themselves, either in the same pinnace, or cock, or upon rafters, and such like means presenting themselves to men in those extremities, for we desired to save the men by every possible means. But all in vain, sith God had determined their ruin; yet all that day, and part of the next, we beat up and down as near unto the wrack as was possible for us, looking out if by good hap we might espy any of them.

This was a heavy and grievous event, to lose at one blow our chief ship freighted with great provision, gathered together with much travail, care, long time, and difficulty; but more was the loss of our men, which perished to the number almost of a hundred souls. Amongst whom was drowned a learned man, a Hungarian,[11] born in the city of *Buda,* called thereof *Budæus,* who, of piety and zeal to good attempts, adventured in this action, minding to record in the Latin tongue the gests and things worthy of remembrance, happening in this discovery, to the honour of our nation, the same being adorned with the eloquent style of this orator and rare poet of our time.

Here also perished our Saxon refiner and discoverer of inestimable riches, as it was left amongst some of us in undoubted hope. No less heavy was the loss of the captain, *Maurice Brown,* a virtuous, honest, and discreet gentleman, overseen only in liberty given late before to men that ought to have been restrained, who showed himself a man resolved, and never unprepared for death, as by his last act of this tragedy appcared, by report of them that escaped this wrack miraculously, as shall be hereafter declared. For when all hope was past of recovering the ship, and that men began to give over, and to save themselves, the captain was advised before to shift also for his life, by the pinnace at the stern of the ship; but refusing that counsel, he would not give example with the first to leave the ship, but used all means to exhort his people not to despair, nor so to leave off their labour, choosing rather to die than to incur infamy by forsaking his charge, which then might be thought to have perished through his default, showing an ill precedent unto his men, by leaving the ship first himself. With this mind he mounted upon the highest deck, where he attended imminent death, and unavoidable; how long, I leave it to God, who withdraweth not his comfort from his servants at such times.

In the mean season, certain, to the number of fourteen

[11] Stephen Parmenius.

persons, leaped into a small pinnace, the bigness of a Thames barge, which was made in the *Newfoundland,* cut off the rope wherewith it was towed, and committed themselves to God's mercy, amidst the storm, and rage of sea and winds, destitute of food, not so much as a drop of fresh water. The boat seeming overcharged in foul weather with company, *Edward Headly,* a valiant soldier, and well reputed of his company, preferring the greater to the lesser, thought better that some of them perished than all, made this motion, to cast lots, and them to be thrown overboard upon whom the lots fell, thereby to lighten the boat, which otherways seemed impossible to live, [and] offered himself with the first, content to take his adventure gladly: which nevertheless *Richard Clarke,* that was master of the Admiral, and one of this number, refused, advising to abide God's pleasure, who was able to save all, as well as a few. The boat was carried before the wind, continuing six days and nights in the ocean, and arrived at last with the men, alive, but weak, upon the *Newfoundland,* saving that the foresaid *Headly,* who had been late sick, and another called of us *Brazil,* of his travel into those countries, died by the way, famished, and less able to hold out than those of better health . . . . Thus whom God delivered from drowning, he appointed to be famished; who doth give limits to man's times, and ordaineth the manner and circumstance of dying: whom, again, he will preserve, neither sea nor famine can confound. For those that arrived upon the *Newfoundland* were brought into *France* by certain Frenchmen, then being upon the coast.

After this heavy chance, we continued in beating the sea up and down, expecting when the weather would clear up that we might yet bear in with the land, which we judged not far off either the continent or some island. For we many times, and in sundry places found ground at 50, 45, 40 fathoms, and less. The ground coming upon our lead, being sometime oozy sand and other while a broad shell, with a little sand about it.

Our people lost courage daily after this ill success, the weather continuing thick and blustering, with increase of cold, winter drawing on, which took from them all hope of amendment, settling an assurance of worse weather to grow upon us every day. The leeside of us lay full of flats and dangers, inevitable if the wind blew hard at south. Some again doubted we were ingulfed in the Bay of *St. Lawrence,* the coast full of dangers, and unto us unknown. But above all, provision waxed scant, and hope of supply was gone with loss of our Admiral. Those in the frigate were already pinched with spare allowance, and want of clothes chiefly: whereupon they besought the General to return to *England,* before they all perished. And to them of the *Golden Hind* they made signs of distress, pointing to their mouths, and to their clothes thin and ragged: then immediately they also of the *Golden Hind* grew to be of the same opinion and desire to return home.

The former reasons having also moved the General to have compassion of his poor men, in whom he saw no want of good will, but of means fit to perform the action they came for, [he] resolved upon retire: and calling the captain and master of the *Hind,* he yielded them many reasons, enforcing this unexpected return, withal protesting himself greatly satisfied with that he had seen and knew already, reiterating these words: *Be content, we have seen enough, and take no care of expense past: I will set you forth royally the next spring, if God send us safe home. Therefore I pray you let us no longer strive here, where we fight against the elements.* Omitting circumstance, how unwillingly the captain and master of the *Hind* condescended to this motion, his own company can testify; yet comforted with the General's promise of a speedy return at spring, and induced by other apparent reasons, proving an impossibility to accomplish the action at that time, it was concluded on all hands to retire.

So upon Saturday in the afternoon, the 31. of August, we changed our course, and returned back for *England.* At which very instant, even in winding about, there passed along between us and towards the land which we now forsook a very lion to our seeming, in shape, hair, and colour, not swimming after the manner of a beast by moving of his feet, but rather sliding upon the water with his whole body, excepting the legs, in sight, neither yet diving under, and again rising above the water, as the manner is of whales, dolphins, tunnies, porpoises, and all other fish: but confidently showing himself above water without hiding: notwithstanding, we presented ourselves in open view and gesture to amaze him, as all creatures will be commonly at a sudden gaze and sight of men. Thus he passed along turning his head to and fro, yawing and gaping wide, with ugly demonstration of long teeth, and glaring eyes; and to bid us a farewell, coming right against the *Hind,* he sent forth a horrible voice, roaring or bellowing as doth a lion, which spectacle we all beheld so far as we were able to discern the same, as men prone to wonder at every strange thing, as this doubtless was, to see a lion in the ocean sea, or fish in shape of a lion. What opinion others had thereof, and chiefly the General himself, I forbear to deliver: but he took it for *bonum omen,* rejoicing that he was to war against such an enemy, if it were the devil. The wind was large for *England* at our return, but very high, and the sea rough, insomuch as the frigate, wherein the General went, was almost swallowed up.

Monday in the afternoon we passed in sight of Cape *Race,* having made as much way in little more than two days and nights back again, as before we had done in eight days from Cape *Race* unto the place where our ship perished. Which hindrance thitherward, and speed back again, is to be imputed unto the swift current, as well as to the winds, which we had more large in our return. This Monday the General came aboard the *Hind,* to have the surgeon of the *Hind* to dress his foot, which he hurt by treading upon a nail: at which time we comforted each other with hope of hard success to be all past, and of the good to come. So agreeing to carry out lights always by night, that we might keep together, he departed into his frigate, being by no means to be entreated to tarry in the *Hind,* which had been more for his security. Immediately after followed a sharp storm, which we overpassed for that time, praised be God.

The weather fair, the General came aboard the *Hind* again, to make merry together with the captain, master, and company, which was the last meeting, and continued there from morning until night. During which time there passed sundry discourses touching affairs past and to come, lamenting greatly the loss of his great ship, more of the men, but most of all his books and notes, and what else I know not, for which he was out of measure grieved, the same doubtless being some matter of more importance than his books, which I could not draw from him: yet by circumstance I gathered the same to be the ore which *Daniel* the Saxon had brought unto him in the *Newfoundland.* Whatsoever it was, the remembrance touched him so deep as, not able to contain himself, he beat his boy in great rage, even at the same time, so long after the miscarrying of the great ship, because upon a fair day, when we were becalmed upon the coast of the *Newfoundland* near unto Cape *Race,* he sent his boy aboard the *Admiral* to fetch certain things: amongst which, this being chief, was yet forgotten and left behind. After which time he could never conveniently send again aboard the great ship, much less he doubted her ruin so near at hand.

Herein my opinion was better confirmed diversely, and by sundry conjectures, which maketh me have the greater hope of this rich mine. For whereas the General had never before good conceit of these north parts of the world, now his mind was wholly fixed upon the *Newfoundland.* And as before he refused not to grant assignments liberally to them that required the same into these north parts, now he became contrarily affected, refusing to make any so large grants, especially of *St. John's,* which certain English merchants made suit for, offering to employ their money and travail upon the same yet neither by their own suit, nor of others of his own company, whom he seemed willing to pleasure, it could be obtained. Also laying down his determination in the spring following for disposing of his voyage then to be re-attempted: he assigned the captain and master of the *Golden Hind* unto the south discovery, and reserved unto himself the north, affirming that this voyage had won his heart from the south, and that he was now become a northern man altogether.

Last, being demanded what means he had, at his arrival in *England,* to compass the charges of so great preparation as he intended to make the next spring, having determined upon two fleets, one for the south, another for the north;

Leave that to me, he replied, *I will ask a penny of no man. I will bring good tidings unto her Majesty, who will be so gracious to lend me* £10,000; willing us therefore to be of good cheer; for *he did thank God,* he said, *with all his heart for that he had seen, the same being enough for us all, and that we needed not to seek any further.* And these last words he would often repeat, with demonstration of great fervency of mind, being himself very confident and settled in belief of inestimable good by this voyage; which the greater number of his followers nevertheless mistrusted altogether, not being made partakers of those secrets, which the General kept unto himself. Yet all of them that are living may be witnesses of his words and protestations, which sparingly I have delivered.

Leaving the issue of this good hope unto God, who knoweth the truth only, and can at His good pleasure bring the same to light, I will hasten to the end of this tragedy, which must be knit up in the person of our General. And as it was God's ordinance upon him, even so the vehement persuasion and entreaty of his friends could nothing avail to divert him of a wilful resolution of going through in his frigate; which was overcharged upon the decks with fights, nettings, and small artillery, too cumbersome for so small a boat that was to pass through the ocean sea at that season of the year, when by course we might expect much storm of foul weather. Whereof, indeed, we had enough.

But when he was entreated by the captain, master, and other his well-willers of the *Hind* not to venture in the frigate, this was his answer: *I will not forsake my little company going homeward, with whom I have passed so many storms and perils.* And in very truth he was urged to be so over hard by hard reports given of him that he was afraid of the sea; albeit this was rather rashness than advised resolution, to prefer the wind of a vain report to the weight of his own life. Seeing he would not bend to reason, he had provision out of the *Hind,* such as was wanting aboard his frigate. And so we committed him to God's protection, and set him aboard his pinnace, we being more than 300 leagues onward of our way home.

By that time we had brought the Islands of *Azores* south

of us; yet we then keeping much to the north, until we had got into the height and elevation of *England,* we met with very foul weather and terrible seas, breaking short and high, pyramid-wise. The reason whereof seemed to proceed either of hilly grounds high and low within the sea, as we see hills and vales upon the land, upon which the seas do mount and fall, or else the cause proceedeth of diversity of winds, shifting often in sundry points, all which having power to move the great ocean, which again is not presently settled, so many seas do encounter together, as there had been diversity of winds. Howsoever it cometh to pass, men which all their lifetime had occupied the sea never saw more outrageous seas. We had also upon our mainyard an apparition of a little fire by night, which seamen do call *Castor* and *Pollux.* But we had only one, which they take an evil sign of more tempest; the same is usual in storms.

Monday, the 9. of September, in the afternoon, the frigate was near cast away, oppressed by waves, yet at that time recovered; and giving forth signs of joy, the General, sitting abaft with a book in his hand, cried out to us in the *Hind,* so oft as we did approach within hearing, *We are as near to heaven by sea as by land!* Reiterating the same speech, well beseeming a soldier, resolute in Jesus Christ, as I can testify he was.

The same Monday night, about twelve of the clock, or not long after, the frigate being ahead of us in the *Golden Hind,* suddenly her lights were out, whereof as it were in a moment we lost the sight, and withal our watch cried *the General was cast away,* which was too true. For in that moment the frigate was devoured and swallowed up of the sea. Yet still we looked out all that night, and ever after until we arrived upon the coast of *England;* omitting no small sail at sea, unto which we gave not the tokens between us agreed upon to have perfect knowledge of each other, if we should at any time be separated.

In great torment of weather and peril of drowning it pleased God to send safe home the *Golden Hind,* which arrived in *Falmouth* the 22. of September, being Sunday, not without as great danger escaped in a flaw coming from the south-east, with such thick mist that we could not discern land to put in right with the haven. From *Falmouth* we went to *Dartmouth,* and lay there at anchor before the Range, while the captain went aland to enquire if there had been any news of the frigate, which, sailing well, might happily have been before us; also to certify Sir *John Gilbert,* brother unto the General, of our hard success, whom the captain desired, while his men were yet aboard him, and were witnesses of all occurrences in that voyage, it might please him to take the examination of every person particularly, in discharge of his and their faithful endeavour. Sir *John Gilbert* refused so to do, holding himself satisfied with report made by the captain, and not altogether despairing of his brother's safety, offered friendship and courtesy to the captain and his company, requiring to have his bark brought into the harbour; in furtherance whereof a boat was sent to help to tow her in.

Nevertheless, when the captain returned aboard his ship, he found his men bent to depart every man to his home; and then the wind serving to proceed higher upon the coast, they demanded money to carry them home, some to *London,* others to *Harwich,* and elsewhere, if the barque should be carried into *Dartmouth* and they discharged so far from home, or else to take benefit of the wind, then serving to draw nearer home, which should be a less charge unto the captain, and great ease unto the men, having else far to go. Reason accompanied with necessity persuaded the captain, who sent his lawful excuse and cause of this sudden departure unto Sir *John Gilbert,* by the boat of *Dartmouth,* and from thence the *Golden Hind* departed and took harbour at *Weymouth.* All the men tired with the tediousness of so unprofitable a voyage to their seeming, in which their long expense of time, much toil and labour, hard diet, and continual hazard of life was unrecompensed; their captain nevertheless by his great charges impaired greatly thereby, yet comforted in the goodness of God, and His undoubted providence following him in all that voyage, as it doth always those at other times whosoever have confidence in Him alone. Yet have we more near feeling and perseverance of His powerful hand and protection when God doth bring us together with others into one same peril, in which He leaveth them and delivereth us, making us thereby the beholders, but not partakers, of their ruin. Even so, amongst very many difficulties, discontentments, mutinies, conspiracies, sicknesses, mortality, spoilings, and wracks by sea, which were afflictions more than in so small a fleet or so short a time may be supposed, albeit true in every particularity, as partly by the former relation may be collected, and some I suppressed with silence for their sakes living, it pleased God to support this company, of which only one man died of a malady inveterate, and long infested, the rest kept together in reasonable contentment and concord, beginning, continuing, and ending the voyage, which none else did accomplish, either not pleased with the action, or impatient of wants, or prevented by death.

Thus have I delivered the contents of the enterprise and last action of Sir *Humfrey Gilbert,* Knight, faithfully, for so much as I thought meet to be published; wherein may always appear, though he be extinguished, some sparks of his virtues, he remaining firm and resolute in a purpose by all pretence honest and godly, as was this, to discover, possess, and to reduce unto the service of God and Christian piety those remote and heathen countries of *America* not actually possessed by Christians, and most rightly appertaining unto the crown of *England,* unto the which as his zeal deserveth high commendation, even so he may justly be taxed of temerity, and presumption rather, in two respects. First, when yet there was only probability, not a certain and determinate place of habitation selected, neither any demonstration if commodity there *in esse,* to induce his followers; nevertheless, he both was too prodigal of his own patrimony and too careless of other men's expenses to employ both his and their substance upon a ground imagined good. The which falling, very like his associates were promised, and made it their best reckoning, to be salved some other way, which pleased not God to prosper in his first and great preparation. Secondly, when by his former preparation he was enfeebled of ability and credit to perform his designments, as it were impatient to abide in expectation better opportunity, and means which God might raise, he thrust himself again into the action, for which he was not fit, presuming the cause pretended on God's behalf would carry him to the desired end. Into which having thus made re-entry, he could not yield again to withdraw, though he saw no encouragement to proceed; lest his credit, foiled in his first attempt, in a second should utterly be disgraced. Between extremities he made a right adventure, putting all to God and good fortune; and, which was worst, refused not to entertain every person and means whatsoever, to furnish out this expedition, the success whereof hath been declared.

But such is the infinite bounty of God, who from every evil deriveth good. For besides that fruit may grow in time of our travelling into those north-west lands, the crosses, turmoils, and afflictions, both in the preparation and execution of this voyage, did correct the intemperate humours which before we noted to be in this gentleman, and made unsavoury and less delightful his other manifold virtues. Then as he was refined, and made nearer drawing unto the image of God, so it pleased the Divine will to resume him unto Himself, whither both his and every other high and noble mind have always aspired.

THE DISCOVERY OF GUIANA

BY

SIR WALTER RALEIGH

INTRODUCTORY NOTE

Sir Walter Raleigh *may be taken as the great typical figure of the age of Elizabeth. Courtier and statesman, soldier and sailor, scientist and man of letters, he engaged in almost all the main lines of public activity in his time, and was distinguished in them all.*

His father was a Devonshire gentleman of property, connected with many of the distinguished families of the south of England. Walter was born about 1552 and was educated at Oxford. He first saw military service in the Huguenot army in France in 1569, and in 1578 engaged, with his half-brother, Sir Humphrey Gilbert, in the first of his expeditions against the Spaniards. After some service in Ireland, he attracted the attention of the Queen, and rapidly rose to the perilous position of her chief favorite. With her approval, he fitted out two expeditions for the colonization of Virginia, neither of which did his royal mistress permit him to lead in person, and neither of which succeeded in establishing a permanent settlement.

After about six years of high favor, Raleigh found his position at court endangered by the rivalry of Essex, and in 1592, on returning from convoying a squadron he had fitted out against the Spanish, he was thrown into the Tower by the orders of the Queen, who had discovered an intrigue between him and one of her ladies whom he subsequently married. He was ultimately released, engaged in various naval exploits, and in 1594 sailed for South America on the voyage described in the following narrative.

On the death of Elizabeth, Raleigh's misfortunes increased. He was accused of treason against James I, condemned, reprieved, and imprisoned for twelve years, during which he wrote his "History of the World," and engaged in scientific researches. In 1616 he was liberated, to make another attempt to find the gold mine in Venezuela; but the expedition was disastrous, and, on his return, Raleigh was executed on the old charge in 1618. In his vices as in his virtues, Raleigh is a thorough representative of the great adventurers who laid the foundations of the British Empire.

RALEIGH'S DISCOVERY OF GUIANA

The DISCOVERY *of the large, rich, and beautiful* EMPIRE *of* GUIANA; *with a Relation of the great and golden* CITY *of* MANOA, *which the Spaniards call* EL DORADO, *and the* PROVINCES *of* EMERIA, AROMAIA, AMAPAIA, *and other Countries, with their rivers, adjoining. Performed in the year 1595 by* SIR WALTER RALEIGH, KNIGHT, CAPTAIN *of her Majesty's* GUARD, *Lord Warden of the* STANNARIES, *and her Highness'* LIEUTENANT-GENERAL *of the* COUNTY *of* CORNWALL.

To the Right Honourable my singular good Lord and kinsman, CHARLES HOWARD, *Knight of the Garter, Baron, and Councillor, and of the Admirals of* ENGLAND *the most renowned; and to the Right Honourable* SIR ROBERT CECIL, KNIGHT, *Councillor in her Highness' Privy Councils.*

FOR your Honours' many honourable and friendly parts, I have hitherto only returned promises; and now, for answer of both your adventures, I have sent you a bundle of papers, which I have divided between your Lordship and Sir *Robert Cecil,* in these two respects chiefly; first, for that it is reason that wasteful factors, when they have consumed such stocks as they had in trust, do yield some colour for the same in their account; secondly, for that I am assured that whatsoever shall be done, or written, by me, shall need a double protection and defence. The trial that I had of both your loves, when I was left of all, but of malice and revenge, makes me still presume that you will be pleased (knowing what little power I had to perform aught, and the great advantage of forewarned enemies) to answer that out of knowledge, which others shall but object out of malice. In my more happy times as I did especially honour you both, so I found that your loves sought me out in the darkest shadow of adversity, and the same affection which accompanied my better fortune soared not away from me in my many miseries; all which though I cannot requite, yet I shall ever acknowledge; and the great debt which I have no power to pay, I can do no more for a time but confess to be due. It is true that as my errors were great, so they have yielded very grievous effects; and if aught might have been deserved in former times, to have counterpoised any part of offences, the fruit thereof, as it seemeth, was long before fallen from the tree, and the dead stock only remained. I did therefore, even in the winter of my life, undertake these travails, fitter for bodies less blasted with misfortunes, for men of greater ability, and for minds of better encouragement, that thereby, if it were possible, I might recover but the moderation of excess, and the least taste of the greatest plenty formerly possessed. If I had known other way to win, if I had imagined how greater adventures might have regained, if I could conceive what farther means I might yet use but even to appease so powerful displeasure, I would not doubt but for one year more to hold fast my soul in my teeth till it were performed. Of that little remain I had, I have wasted in effect all herein. I have undergone many constructions; I have been accompanied with many sorrows, with labour, hunger, heat, sickness, and peril; it appeareth, notwithstanding, that I made no other bravado of going to the sea, than was meant, and that I was never hidden in *Cornwall,* or elsewhere, as was supposed. They have grossly belied me that forejudged that I would rather become a servant to the Spanish king than return; and the rest were much mistaken, who would have persuaded that I was too easeful and sensual to undertake a journey of so great travail. But if what I have done receive the gracious construction of a painful pilgrimage, and purchase the least remission, I shall think all too little, and that there were wanting to the rest many miseries. But if both the times past, the present, and what may be in the future, do all by one grain of gall continue in eternal distaste, I do not then know whether I should bewail myself, either for my too much travail and expense, or condemn myself for doing less than that which can deserve nothing. From myself I have deserved no thanks, for I am returned a beggar, and withered; but that I might have bettered my poor estate, it shall appear from the following discourse, if I had not only respected her Majesty's future honour and riches.

It became not the former fortune, in which I once lived, to go journeys of picory;[1] it had sorted ill with the offices of honour,

[1] Fr. *picorée* (marauding).

which by her Majesty's grace I hold this day in *England,* to run from cape to cape and from place to place, for the pillage of ordinary prizes. Many years since I had knowledge, by relation, of that mighty, rich, and beautiful empire of *Guiana,* and of that great and golden city, which the Spaniards call *El Dorado,* and the naturals *Manoa,* which city was conquered, re-edified, and enlarged by a younger son of *Guayna-capac,* Emperor of *Peru,* at such time as *Francisco Pizarro* and others conquered the said empire from his two elder brethren, *Guascar* and *Atabalipa,* both then contending for the same, the one being favoured by the *orejones* of *Cuzco,* the other by the people of *Caxamalca.* I sent my servant *Jacob Whiddon,* the year before, to get knowledge of the passages, and I had some light from Captain *Parker,* sometime my servant, and now attending on your Lordship, that such a place there was to the southward of the great bay of *Charuas,* or *Guanipa:* but I found that it was 600 miles farther off than they supposed, and many impediments to them unknown and unheard. After I had displanted *Don Antonio de Berreo,* who was upon the same enterprise, leaving my ships at *Trinidad,* at the port called *Curiapan,* I wandered 400 miles into the said country by land and river; the particulars I will leave to the following discourse.

The country hath more quantity of gold, by manifold, than the best parts of the *Indies,* or *Peru.* All the most of the kings of the borders are already become her Majesty's vassals, and seem to desire nothing more than her Majesty's protection and the return of the English nation. It hath another ground and assurance of riches and glory than the voyages of the *West Indies;* an easier way to invade the best parts thereof than by the common course. The king of *Spain* is not so impoverished by taking three or four port towns in *America* as we suppose; neither are the riches of *Peru* or *Nueva España* so left by the sea side as it can be easily washed away with a great flood, or spring tide, or left dry upon the sands on a low ebb. The port towns are few and poor in respect of the rest within the land, and are of little defence, and are only rich when the fleets are to receive the treasure for *Spain;* and we might think the Spaniards very simple, having so many horses and slaves, if they could not upon two days' warning carry all the gold they have into the land, and far enough from the reach of our footmen, especially the *Indies* being, as they are for the most part, so mountainous, full of woods, rivers, and marishes. In the port towns of the province of *Venezuela*, as *Cumana, Coro,* and *St. Iago* (whereof *Coro* and *St. Iago* were taken by Captain *Preston,* and *Cumana* and *St. Josepho* by us) we found not the value of one real of plate in either. But the cities of *Barquasimeta, Valencia, St. Sebastian, Cororo, St. Lucia, Laguna, Maracaiba,* and *Truxillo,* are not so easily invaded. Neither doth the burning of those on the coast impoverish the king of *Spain* any one ducat; and if we sack the *River of Hacha, St. Martha,* and *Carthagena,* which are the ports of *Nuevo Reyno* and *Popayan,* there are besides within the land, which are indeed rich and prosperous, the towns and cities of *Merida, Lagrita, St. Christophoro,* the great cities of *Pamplona, Santa Fé de Bogota, Tunxa,* and *Mozo,* where the emeralds are found, the towns and cities of *Marequita, Velez, la Villa de Leiva, Palma, Honda, Angostura,* the great city of *Timana, Tocaima, St. Aguila, Pasto,* [*St.*] *Jago,* the great city of *Popayan* itself, *Los Remedios,* and the rest. If we take the ports and villages within the bay of *Uraba* in the kingdom or rivers of *Darien* and *Caribana,* the cities and towns of *St. Juan de Rodas,* of *Cassaris,* of *Antiochia, Caramanta, Cali,* and *Anserma* have gold enough to pay the king's part, and are not easily invaded by way of the ocean. Or if *Nombre de Dios* and *Panama* be taken, in the province of *Castilla del Oro,* and the villages upon the rivers of *Cenu* and *Chagre; Peru* hath, besides those, and besides the magnificent cities of *Quito* and *Lima,* so many islands, ports, cities, and mines as if I should name them with the rest it would seem incredible to the reader. Of all which, because I have written a particular treatise of the *West Indies,* I will omit the repetition at this time, seeing that in the said treatise I have anatomized the rest of the sea towns as well of *Nicaragua, Yucatan, Nueva España,* and the islands, as those of the inland, and by what means they may be best invaded, as far as any mean judgment may comprehend.

But I hope it shall appear that there is a way found to answer every man's longing; a better *Indies* for her Majesty than the king of *Spain* hath any; which if it shall please her Highness to undertake, I shall most willingly end the rest of my days in following the same. If it be left to the spoil and sackage of common persons, if the love and service of so many nations be despised, so great riches and so mighty an empire refused; I hope her Majesty will yet take my humble desire and my labour therein in gracious part, which, if it had not been in respect of her Highness' future honour and riches, could have laid hands on and ransomed many of the kings and *caciqui* of the country, and have had a reasonable proportion of gold for their redemption. But I have chosen rather to bear the burden of poverty than reproach; and rather to endure a second travail, and the chances thereof, than to have defaced an enterprise of so great assurance, until I knew whether it pleased God to put a disposition in her princely and royal heart either to follow or forslow[2] the same. I will therefore leave it to His ordinance that hath only power in all things; and do humbly pray that your honours will excuse such errors as, without the defence of art, overrun in every part the following discourse, in which I have neither studied phrase, form, nor fashion; that you will be pleased to esteem me as your own, though over dearly bought, and I shall ever remain ready to do you all honour and service.

[2] Neglect, decline (lose through sloth).

TO THE READER

BECAUSE there have been divers opinions conceived of the gold ore brought from *Guiana,* and for that an alderman of *London* and an officer of her Majesty's mint hath given out that the same is of no price, I have thought good by the addition of these lines to give answer as well to the said malicious slander as to other objections. It is true that while we abode at the island of *Trinidad* I was informed by an Indian that not far from the port where we anchored there were found certain mineral stones which they esteemed to be gold, and were thereunto persuaded the rather for that they had seen both English and Frenchmen gather and embark some quantities thereof. Upon this likelihood I sent forty men, and gave order that each one should bring a stone of that mine, to make trial of the goodness; which being performed, I assured them at their return that the same was *marcasite,* and of no riches or value. Notwithstanding, divers, trusting more to their own sense than to my opinion, kept of the said *marcasite,* and have tried thereof since my return, in divers places. In *Guiana* itself I never saw *marcasite;* but all the rocks, mountains, all stones in the plains, woods, and by the rivers' sides, are in effect thorough-shining, and appear marvellous rich; which, being tried to be no *marcasite,* are the true signs of rich minerals, but are no other than *El madre del oro,* as the Spaniards term them, which is the mother of gold, or, as it is said by others, the scum of gold. Of divers sorts of these many of my company brought also into *England,* every one taking the fairest for the best, which is not general. For mine own part, I did not countermand any man's desire or opinion, and I could have afforded them little if I should have denied them the pleasing of their own fancies therein; but I was resolved that gold must be found either in grains, separate from the stone, as it is in most of the rivers in *Guiana,* or else in a kind of hard stone, which we call the *white spar,* of which I saw divers hills, and in sundry places, but had neither time nor men, nor instruments fit for labour. Near unto one of the rivers I found of the said *white spar* or flint a very great ledge or bank, which I endeavoured to break by all the means I could, because there appeared on the outside some small grains of gold; but finding no mean to work the same upon the upper part, seeking the sides and circuit of the said rock, I found a clift in the same, from whence with daggers, and with the head of an axe, we got out some small quantity thereof; of which kind of white stone, wherein gold is engendered, we saw divers hills and rocks in every part of Guiana wherein we travelled. Of this there have been made many trials; and in *London* it was first assayed by Master *Westwood,* a refiner dwelling in *Wood Street,* and it held after the rate of twelve or thirteen thousand pounds a ton. Another sort was afterward tried by Master *Bulmar,* and Master *Dimock,* assay-master; and it held after the rate of three and twenty thousand pounds a ton. There was some of it again tried by Master *Palmer,* Comptroller of the *Mint,* and Master *Dimock* in *Goldsmith's Hall,* and it held after six and twenty thousand and nine hundred pounds a ton. There was also at the same time, and by the same persons, a trial made of the dust of the said mine; which held eight pounds and six ounces weight of gold in the hundred. There was likewise at the same time a trial of an image of copper made in *Guiana,* which held a third part of gold, besides divers trials made in the country, and by others in *London.* But because there came ill with the good, and belike the said alderman was not presented with the best, it hath pleased him therefore to scandal all the rest, and to deface the enterprise as much as in him lieth. It hath also been concluded by divers that if there had been any such ore in *Guiana,* and the same discovered, that I would have brought home a greater quantity thereof. First, I was not bound to satisfy any man of the quantity, but only such as adventured, if any store had been returned thereof; but it is very true that had all their mountains been of massy gold it was impossible for us to have made any longer stay to have wrought the same; and whosoever hath seen with what strength of stone the best gold ore is environed, he will not think it easy to be had out in heaps, and especially by us, who had neither men, instruments, nor time, as it is said before, to perform the same.

There were on this discovery no less than an hundred persons, who can all witness that when we passed any branch of the river to view the land within, and stayed from our boats but six hours, we were driven to wade to the eyes at our return; and if we attempted the same the day following, it was impossible either to ford it, or to swim it, both by reason of the swiftness, and also for that the borders were so pestered with fast woods, as neither boat nor man could find place either to land or to embark; for in June, July, August, and September it is impossible to navigate any of those rivers; for such is the fury of the current, and there are so many trees and woods overflown, as if any boat but touch upon any tree or stake it is impossible to save any one person therein. And ere we departed the land it ran with such swiftness as we drave down, most commonly against the wind, little less than an hundred miles a day. Besides, our vessels were no other than wherries, one little barge, a small cock-boat, and a bad *galiota* which we framed in haste for that purpose at *Trinidad;* and those little boats had nine or ten men apiece, with all their victuals and arms. It is further true that we were about four hundred miles from our ships, and had been a month from them, which also we left weakly manned in an open road, and had promised our return in fifteen days.

Others have devised that the same ore was had from *Barbary,* and that we carried it with us into *Guiana.* Surely the singularity of that device I do not well comprehend. For mine own part, I am not so much in love with these long voyages as to devise thereby to cozen myself, to lie hard, to fare worse, to be subjected to perils, to diseases, to ill savours, to be parched and withered, and withal to sustain the care and labour of such an enterprise, except the same had more comfort than the fetching of *marcasite* in *Guiana,* or buying of gold ore in *Barbary.* But I hope the better sort will judge me by themselves, and that the way of deceit is not the way of honour or good opinion. I have herein consumed much time, and many crowns; and I had no other respect or desire than to serve her Majesty and my country thereby. If the Spanish nation had been of like belief to these detractors we should little have feared or doubted their attempts, wherewith we now are daily threatened. But if we now consider of the actions both of *Charles the Fifth,* who had the maidenhead of *Peru* and the abundant treasures of *Atabalipa,* together with the affairs of the Spanish king now living, what territories he hath purchased, what he hath added to the acts of his predecessors, how many kingdoms he hath endangered, how many armies, garrisons, and navies he hath, and doth maintain, the great losses which he hath repaired, as in Eighty-eight above an hundred sail of great ships with their artillery, and that no year is less infortunate, but that many vessels, treasures, and people are devoured, and yet notwithstanding he beginneth again like a storm to threaten shipwrack to us all; we shall find that these abilities rise not from the trades of sacks and *Seville* oranges, nor from aught else that either *Spain, Portugal,* or any of his other provinces produce; it is his Indian gold that endangereth and disturbeth all the nations of *Europe;* it purchaseth intelligence, creepeth into counsels, and setteth bound loyalty at liberty in the greatest monarchies of *Europe.* If the Spanish king can keep us from foreign enterprises, and from the impeachment of his trades, either by offer of invasion, or by besieging us in *Britain, Ireland,* or elsewhere, he hath then brought the work of our peril in great forwardness.

Those princes that abound in treasure have great advantages over the rest, if they once constrain them to a defensive war, where they are driven once a year or oftener to cast lots for their own garments; and from all such shall all trades and intercourse be taken away, to the general loss and impoverishment of the kingdom and commonweal so reduced. Besides, when our men are constrained to fight, it hath not the like hope as when they are pressed and enccuraged by the desire of spoil and riches. Farther, it is to be doubted how those that in time of victory seem to affect their neighbour nations will remain after the first view of misfortunes or ill success; to trust, also, to the doubtfulness of a battle is but a fearful and uncertain adventure, seeing therein fortune is as likely to prevail as virtue. It shall not be necessary to allege all that might be said, and therefore I will thus conclude; that whatsoever kingdom shall be enforced to defend itself may be compared to a body dangerously diseased, which for a season may be preserved with vulgar medicines, but in a short time, and by little and little, the same must needs fall to the ground and be dissolved. I have therefore laboured all my life, both according to my small power and persuasion, to advance all those attempts that might either promise return of profit to ourselves, or at least be a let and impeachment to the quiet course and plentiful trades of the Spanish nation; who, in my weak judgement, by such a war were as easily endangered and brought from his powerfulness as any prince in *Europe,* if it be considered from how many kingdoms and nations his revenues are gathered, and those so weak in their own beings and so far severed from mutual succour. But because such a preparation and resolution is not to be hoped for in haste, and that the time which our enemies embrace cannot be had again to advantage, I will hope that these provinces, and that empire now by me discovered, shall suffice to enable her Majesty and the whole kingdom with no less quantities of treasure than the king of *Spain* hath in all the *Indies, East* and *West,* which he possesseth; which if the same be considered and followed, ere the Spaniards enforce the same, and if her Majesty will undertake it, I will be contented to lose her Highness' favour and good opinion for ever, and my life withal, if the same be not found rather to exceed than to equal whatsoever is in this discourse promised and declared. I will now refer the reader to the following discourse, with the hope that the perilous and chargeable labours and endeavours of such as thereby seek the profit and honour of her Majesty, and the English nation, shall by men of quality and virtue receive such construction and good acceptance as themselves would like to be rewarded withal in the like.

THE DISCOVERY[3] OF GUIANA[4]

ON Thursday, the sixth of February, in the year 1595, we departed *England,* and the Sunday following had sight of the north cape of *Spain,* the wind for the most part continuing prosperous; we passed in sight of the *Burlings,* and the Rock, and so onwards for the *Canaries,* and fell with *Fuerteventura* the 17. of the same month, where we spent two or three days, and relieved our companies with some fresh meat. From thence we coasted by the *Grand Canaria,* and so to *Teneriffe,* and stayed there for the *Lion's Whelp,* your Lordship's ship, and for Captain *Amyas Preston* and the rest. But when after seven or eight days we found them not, we departed and directed our course for *Trinidad,* with mine own ship, and a small barque of Captain *Cross's* only; for we had before lost sight of a small *galego* on the coast of *Spain,* which came with us from *Plymouth.* We arrived at *Trinidad* the 22. of March, casting anchor at Point *Curiapan,* which the Spaniards call *Punta de Gallo,* which is situate in eight degrees or thereabouts. We abode there four or five days, and in all that time we came not to the speech of any Indian or Spaniard. On the coast we saw a fire, as we sailed from the Point *Carao* towards *Curiapan,* but for fear of the Spaniards none durst come to speak with us. I myself coasted it in my barge close aboard the shore and landed in every cove, the better to know the island, while the ships kept the channel. From *Curiapan* after a few days we turned up north-east to recover that place which the Spaniards call *Puerto de los Españoles,*[5] and the inhabitants *Conquerabia;* and as before, revictualling my barge, I left the ships and kept by the shore, the better to come to speech with some of the inhabitants, and also to

[3] Exploration.
[4] The name is derived from the Guayano Indians, on the Orinoco.
[5] Now Port of Spain.

understand the rivers, watering-places, and ports of the island, which, as it is rudely done, my purpose is to send your Lordship after a few days. From *Curiapan* I came to a port and seat of Indians called *Parico,* where we found a fresh water river, but saw no people. From thence I rowed to another port, called by the naturals *Piche,* and by the Spaniards *Tierra de Brea.* In the way between both were divers little brooks of fresh water, and one salt river that had store of oysters upon the branches of the trees, and were very salt and well tasted. All their oysters grow upon those boughs and sprays, and not on the ground; the like is commonly seen in other places of the *West Indies,* and elsewhere. This tree is described by *Andrew Thevet,* in his *France Antarctique,* and the form figured in the book as a plant very strange; and by *Pliny* in his twelfth book of his *Natural History.* But in this island, as also in *Guiana,* there are very many of them.

At this point, called *Tierra de Brea* or *Piche,* there is that abundance of stone pitch that all the ships of the world may be therewith laden from thence; and we made trial of it in trimming our ships to be most excellent good, and melteth not with the sun as the pitch of *Norway,* and therefore for ships trading the south parts very profitable. From thence we went to the mountain foot called *Annaperima,* and so passing the river *Carone,* on which the Spanish city was seated, we met with our ships at *Puérto de los Españoles* or *Conquerabia.*

This island of *Trinidad* hath the form of a sheephook, and is but narrow; the north part is very mountainous; the soil is very excellent, and will bear sugar, ginger, or any other commodity that the *Indies* yield. It hath store of deer, wild porks, fruit, fish, and fowl; it hath also for bread sufficient maize, *cassavi,* and of those roots and fruits which are common everywhere in the *West Indies.* It hath divers beasts which the *Indies* have not; the Spaniards confessed that they found grains of gold in some of the rivers; but they having a purpose to enter *Guiana,* the magazine of all rich metals, cared not to spend time in the search thereof any further. This island is called by the people thereof *Cairi,* and in it are divers nations. Those about *Parico* are called *Jajo,* those at *Punta de Carao* are of the *Arwacas,*[6] and between *Carao* and *Curiapan* they are called *Salvajos.* Between *Carao* and *Punta de Galera* are the *Nepojos,* and those about the Spanish city term themselves *Carinepagotes.*[7] Of the rest of the nations, and of other ports and rivers, I leave to speak here, being impertinent to my purpose, and mean to describe them as they are situate in the particular plot and description of the island, three parts whereof I coasted with my barge, that I might the better describe it.

Meeting with the ships at *Puerto de los Españoles,* we found at the landing-place a company of Spaniards who kept a guard at the descent; and they offering a sign of peace, I sent Captain *Whiddon* to speak with them, whom afterwards to my great grief I left buried in the said island after my return from *Guiana,* being a man most honest and valiant. The Spaniards seemed to be desirous to trade with us, and to enter into terms of peace, more for doubt of their own strength than for aught else; and in the end, upon pledge, some of them came aboard. The same evening there stale also aboard us in a small *canoa* two Indians, the one of them being a *cacique* or lord of the people, called *Cantyman,* who had the year before been with Captain *Whiddon,* and was of his acquaintance. By this *Cantyman* we understood what strength the Spaniards had, how far it was to their city, and of *Don Antonio de Berreo,* the governor, who was said to be slain in his second attempt of *Guiana,* but was not.

While we remained at *Puerto de los Españoles* some Spaniards came aboard us to buy linen of the company, and such other things as they wanted, and also to view our ships and company, all which I entertained kindly and feasted after our manner. By means whereof I learned of one and another as much of the estate of *Guiana* as I could, or as they knew; for those poor soldiers having been many years without wine, a few draughts made them merry, in which mood they vaunted of *Guiana* and the riches thereof, and all what they knew of the ways and passages; myself seeming to purpose nothing less than the entrance or discovery thereof, but bred in them an opinion that I was bound only for

[6] Arawaks. [7] Carib-people.

the relief of those English which I had planted in *Virginia,* whereof the bruit was come among them; which I had performed in my return, if extremity of weather had not forced me from the said coast.

I found occasions of staying in this place for two causes. The one was to be revenged of *Berreo,* who the year before, 1594, had betrayed eight of Captain *Whiddon's* men, and took them while he departed from them to seek the *Edward Bonaventure,* which arrived at *Trinidad* the day before from the *East Indies*: in whose absence *Berreo* sent a *canoa* aboard the pinnace only with Indians and dogs inviting the company to go with them into the woods to kill a deer. Who, like wise men, in the absence of their captain followed the *Indians,* but were no sooner one arquebus shot from the shore, but *Berreo's* soldiers lying in ambush had them all, notwithstanding that he had given his word to Captain *Whiddon* that they should take water and wood safely. The other cause of my stay was, for that by discourse with the Spaniards I daily learned more and more of *Guiana,* of the rivers and passages, and of the enterprise of *Berreo,* by what means or fault he failed, and how he meant to prosecute the same.

While we thus spent the time I was assured by another *cacique* of the north side of the island, that *Berreo* had sent to *Margarita* and *Cumana* for soldiers, meaning to have given me a *cassado*[8] at parting, if it had been possible. For although he had given order through all the island that no Indian should come aboard to trade with me upon pain of hanging and quartering (having executed two of them for the same, which I afterwards found), yet every night there came some with most lamentable complaints of his cruelty: how he had divided the island and given to every soldier a part; that he made the ancient *caciques,* which were lords of the country, to be their slaves; that he kept them in chains, and dropped their naked bodies with burning bacon, and such other torments, which I found afterwards to be true. For in the city, after I entered the same, there were five of the lords or little kings, which they call *caciques* in the *West Indies,* in one chain, almost dead of famine, and

[8] *Cachado* (*cachada*)=a blow.

wasted with torments. These are called in their own language *acarewana,* and now of late since English, French, and Spanish, are come among them, they call themselves *captains,* because they perceive that the chiefest of every ship is called by that name. Those five *captains* in the chain were called *Wannawanare, Carroaori, Maquarima, Tarroopanama,* and *Aterima.* So as both to be revenged of the former wrong, as also considering that to enter *Guiana* by small boats, to depart 400 or 500 miles from my ships, and to leave a garrison in my back interested in the same enterprise, who also daily expected supplies out of *Spain,* I should have savoured very much of the ass; and therefore taking a time of most advantage, I set upon the *Corps du garde* in the evening, and having put them to the sword, sent Captain *Caulfield* onwards with sixty soldiers, and myself followed with forty more, and so took their new city, which they called *St. Joseph,* by break of day. They abode not any fight after a few shot, and all being dismissed, but only *Berreo* and his companion,[9] I brought them with me aboard, and at the instance of the Indians I set their new city of *St. Joseph* on fire. The same day arrived Captain *George Gifford* with your lordship's ship, and Captain *Keymis,* whom I lost on the coast of *Spain,* with the *galego,* and in them divers gentlemen and others, which to our little army was a great comfort and supply.

We then hasted away towards our purposed discovery, and first I called all the captains of the island together that were enemies to the Spaniards; for there were some which *Berreo* had brought out of other countries, and planted there to eat out and waste those that were natural of the place. And by my Indian interpreter, which I carried out of *England,* I made them understand that I was the servant of a queen who was the great *cacique* of the north, and a virgin, and had more *caciqui* under her than there were trees in that island; that she was an enemy to the *Castellani* in respect of their tyranny and oppression, and that she delivered all such nations about her, as were by them oppressed; and having freed all the coast of the northern world from their servitude, had sent me to free them also, and withal to de-

[9] The Portuguese captain Alvaro Jorge (see p. 369).

fend the country of *Guiana* from their invasion and conquest. I shewed them her Majesty's picture, which they so admired and honoured, as it had been easy to have brought them idolatrous thereof. The like and a more large discourse I made to the rest of the nations, both in my passing to *Guiana* and to those of the borders, so as in that part of the world her Majesty is very famous and admirable; whom they now call EZRABETA CASSIPUNA AQUEREWANA, which is as much as 'Elizabeth, the Great Princess, or Greatest Commander.' This done, we left *Puerto de los Españoles,* and returned to *Curiapan,* and having *Berreo* my prisoner, I gathered from him as much of *Guiana* as he knew. This *Berreo* is a gentleman well descended, and had long served the Spanish king in *Milan, Naples,* the *Low Countries,* and elsewhere, very valiant and liberal, and a gentleman of great assuredness, and of a great heart. I used him according to his estate and worth in all things I could, according to the small means I had.

I sent Captain *Whiddon* the year before to get what knowledge he could of *Guiana:* and the end of my journey at this time was to discover and enter the same. But my intelligence was far from truth, for the country is situate about 600 English miles further from the sea than I was made believe it had been. Which afterwards understanding to be true by *Berreo,* I kept it from the knowledge of my company, who else would never have been brought to attempt the same. Of which 600 miles I passed 400, leaving my ships so far from me at anchor in the sea, which was more of desire to perform that discovery than of reason, especially having such poor and weak vessels to transport ourselves in. For in the bottom of an old *galego* which I caused to be fashioned like a galley, and in one barge, two wherries, and a ship-boat of the *Lion's Whelp,* we carried 100 persons and their victuals for a month in the same, being all driven to lie in the rain and weather in the open air, in the burning sun, and upon the hard boards, and to dress our meat, and to carry all manner of furniture in them. Wherewith they were so pestered and unsavoury, that what with victuals being most fish, with the wet clothes of so many men thrust together, and the heat of the sun, I will undertake there was never any prison in *England* that could be found more unsavoury and loathsome, especially to myself, who had for many years before been dieted and cared for in a sort far more differing.

If Captain *Preston* had not been persuaded that he should have come too late to *Trinidad* to have found us there (for the month was expired which I promised to tarry for him there ere he could recover the coast of *Spain*) but that it had pleased God he might have joined with us, and that we had entered the country but some ten days sooner ere the rivers were overflown, we had adventured either to have gone to the great city of *Manoa,* or at least taken so many of the other cities and towns nearer at hand, as would have made a royal return. But it pleased not God so much to favour me at this time. If it shall be my lot to prosecute the same, I shall willingly spend my life therein. And if any else shall be enabled thereunto, and conquer the same, I assure him thus much; he shall perform more than ever was done in *Mexico* by *Cortes,* or in *Peru* by *Pizarro,* whereof the one conquered the empire of *Mutezuma,* the other of *Guascar* and *Atabalipa.* And whatsoever prince shall possess it, that prince shall be lord of more gold, and of a more beautiful empire, and of more cities and people, than either the king of *Spain* or the *Great Turk.*

But because there may arise many doubts, and how this empire of *Guiana* is become so populous, and adorned with so many great cities, towns, temples, and treasures, I thought good to make it known, that the emperor now reigning is descended from those magnificent princes of *Peru,* of whose large territories, of whose policies, conquests, edifices, and riches, *Pedro de Cieza, Francisco Lopez,* and others have written large discourses. For when *Francisco Pizarro, Diego Almagro* and others conquered the said empire of *Peru,* and had put to death *Atabalipa,* son to *Guayna Capac,* which *Atabalipa* had formerly caused his eldest brother *Guascar* to be slain, one of the younger sons of *Guayna Capac* fled out of *Peru,* and took with him many thousands of those soldiers of the empire called *orejones,*[10] and with

[10] *Orejones*='having large ears,' the name given by the Spaniards to the Peruvian warriors, who wore ear-pendants.

those and many others which followed him, he vanquished all that tract and valley of *America* which is situate between the great river of *Amazons* and *Baraquan,* otherwise called *Orenoque* and *Marañon.*[11]

The empire of *Guiana* is directly east from *Peru* towards the sea, and lieth under the equinoctial line; and it hath more abundance of gold than any part of *Peru,* and as many or moe[12] great cities than ever *Peru* had when it flourished most. It is governed by the same laws, and the emperor and people observe the same religion, and the same form and policies in government as were used in *Peru,* not differing in any part. And I have been assured by such of the Spaniards as have seen *Manoa,* the imperial city of *Guiana,* which the Spaniards call *El Dorado,* that for the greatness, for the riches, and for the excellent seat, it far exceedeth any of the world, at least of so much of the world as is known to the Spanish nation. It is founded upon a lake of salt water of 200 leagues long, like unto *Mare Caspium.* And if we compare it to that of *Peru,* and but read the report of *Francisco Lopez* and others, it will seem more than credible; and because we may judge of the one by the other, I thought good to insert part of the 120. chapter of *Lopez* in his *General History of the Indies,* wherein he describeth the court and magnificence of *Guayna Capac,* ancestor to the emperor of *Guiana,* whose very words are these:—

'Todo el servicio de su casa, mesa, y cocina era de oro y de plata, y cuando menos de plata y cobre, por mas recio. Tenia en su recamara estatuas huecas de oro, que parescian gigantes, y las figuras al propio y tamaño de cuantos animales, aves, arboles, y yerbas produce la tierra, y de cuantos peces cria la mar y agua de sus reynos. Tenia asimesmo sogas, costales, cestas, y troxes de oro y plata; rimeros de palos de oro, que pareciesen leña rajada para quemar. En fin no habia cosa en su tierra, que no la tuviese de oro contrahecha; y aun dizen, que tenian los Ingas un verjel en una isla cerca de la Puna, donde se iban a holgar, cuando querian

[11] Baraquan is the alternative name to Orenoque, Marañon to Amazons.
[12] More.

mar, que tenia la hortaliza, las flores, y arboles de oro y plata; invencion y grandeza hasta entonces nunca vista. Allende de todo esto, tenia infinitisima cantidad de plata y oro por labrar en el Cuzco, que se perdio por la muerte de Guascar; ca los Indios lo escondieron, viendo que los Españoles se lo tomaban, y enviaban a España.' That is, 'All the vessels of his house, table, and kitchen, were of gold and silver, and the meanest of silver and copper for strength and hardness of metal. He had in his wardrobe hollow statues of gold which seemed giants, and the figures in proportion and bigness of all the beasts, birds, trees, and herbs, that the earth bringeth forth; and of all the fishes that the sea or waters of his kingdom breedeth. He had also ropes, budgets, chests, and troughs of gold and silver, heaps of billets of gold, that seemed wood marked out[13] to burn. Finally, there was nothing in his country whereof he had not the counterfeit in gold. Yea, and they say, the *Ingas* had a garden of pleasure in an island near *Puna,* where they went to recreate themselves, when they would take the air of the sea, which had all kinds of garden-herbs, flowers, and trees of gold and silver; an invention and magnificence till then never seen. Besides all this, he had an infinite quantity of silver and gold unwrought in *Cuzco,* which was lost by the death of *Guascar,* for the Indians hid it, seeing that the Spaniards took it, and sent it into *Spain.*

And in the 117. chapter; *Francisco Pizarro* caused the gold and silver of *Atabalipa* to be weighed after he had taken it, which *Lopez* setteth down in these words following:— 'Hallaron cincuenta y dos mil marcos de buena plata, y un millon y trecientos y veinte y seis mil y quinientos pesos de oro.' Which is, 'They found 52,000 marks of good silver, and 1,326,500 *pesos* of gold.' Now, although these reports may seem strange, yet if we consider the many millions which are daily brought out of *Peru* into *Spain,* we may easily believe the same. For we find that by the abundant treasure of that country the Spanish king vexes all the princes of *Europe,* and is become, in a few years, from a poor king of *Castile,* the greatest monarch of this part of

[13] Rather, 'split into logs.'

the world, and likely every day to increase if other princes forslow the good occasions offered, and suffer him to add this empire to the rest, which by far exceedeth all the rest. If his gold now endanger us, he will then be unresistible. Such of the Spaniards as afterwards endeavoured the conquest thereof, whereof there have been many, as shall be declared hereafter, thought that this *Inga,* of whom this emperor now living is descended, took his way by the river of *Amazons,* by that branch which is called *Papamene.*[14] For by that way followed *Orellana,* by the commandment of *Gonzalo Pizarro,* in the year 1542, whose name the river also beareth this day. Which is also by others called *Marañon,* although *Andrew Thevet* doth affirm that between *Marañon* and *Amazons* there are 120 leagues; but sure it is that those rivers have one head and beginning, and the *Marañon,* which *Thevet* describeth, is but a branch of *Amazons* or *Orellana,* of which I will speak more in another place. It was attempted by *Ordas*; but it is now little less than 70 years since that *Diego Ordas,* a Knight of the Order of *Santiago,* attempted the same; and it was in the year 1542 that *Orellana* discovered the river of *Amazons;* but the first that ever saw *Manoa* was *Juan Martinez,* master of the munition to *Ordas.* At a port called *Morequito,*[15] in *Guiana,* there lieth at this day a great anchor of *Ordas* his ship. And this port is some 300 miles within the land, upon the great river of *Orenoque.* I rested at this port four days, twenty days after I left the ships at *Curiapan.*

The relation of this *Martinez,* who was the first that discovered *Manoa,* his success, and end, is to be seen in the Chancery of *St. Juan de Puerto Rico,* whereof *Berreo* had a copy, which appeared to be the greatest encouragement as well to *Berreo* as to others that formerly attempted the discovery and conquest. *Orellana,* after he failed of the discovery of *Guiana* by the said river of *Amazons,* passed into *Spain,* and there obtained a patent of the king for the invasion and conquest, but died by sea about the islands; and his fleet being severed by tempest, the action for that time proceeded not. *Diego Ordas* followed the enterprise, and departed

[14] The Papamene is a tributary not of the Amazon river but of the Meta, one of the principal tributaries of the Orinoco.

[15] Probably San Miguel.

Spain with 600 soldiers and thirty horse. Who, arriving on the coast of *Guiana,* was slain in a mutiny, with the most part of such as favoured him, as also of the rebellious part, insomuch as his ships perished and few or none returned; neither was it certainly known what became of the said *Ordas* until *Berreo* found the anchor of his ship in the river of *Orenoque;* but it was supposed, and so it is written by *Lopez,* that he perished on the seas, and of other writers diversely conceived and reported. And hereof it came that *Martinez* entered so far within the land, and arrived at that city of *Inga* the emperor; for it chanced that while *Ordas* with his army rested at the port of *Morequito* (who was either the first or second that attempted *Guiana*), by some negligence the whole store of powder provided for the service was set on fire, and *Martinez,* having the chief charge, was condemned by the General *Ordas* to be executed forthwith. *Martinez,* being much favoured by the soldiers, had all the means possible procured for his life; but it could not be obtained in other sort than this, that he should be set into a *canoa* alone, without any victual, only with his arms, and so turned loose into the great river. But it pleased God that the *canoa* was carried down the stream, and certain of the *Guianians* met it the same evening; and, having not at any time seen any Christian nor any man of that colour, they carried *Martinez* into the land to be wondered at, and so from town to town, until he came to the great city of *Manoa,* the seat and residence of *Inga* the emperor. The emperor, after he had beheld him, knew him to be a Christian, for it was not long before that his brethren *Guascar* and *Atabalipa* were vanquished by the Spaniards in *Peru:* and caused him to be lodged in his palace, and well entertained. He lived seven months in *Manoa,* but was not suffered to wander into the country anywhere. He was also brought thither all the way blindfold, led by the Indians, until he came to the entrance of *Manoa* itself, and was fourteen or fifteen days in the passage. He avowed at his death that he entered the city at noon, and then they uncovered his face; and that he travelled all that day till night thorough the city, and the next day from sun rising to sun setting, yere[13]

[13] Ere.

he came to the palace of *Inga*. After that *Martinez* had lived seven months in *Manoa,* and began to understand the language of the country, *Inga* asked him whether he desired to return into his own country, or would willingly abide with him. But *Martinez,* not desirous to stay, obtained the favour of *Inga* to depart; with whom he sent divers *Guianians* to conduct him to the river of *Orenoque,* all loaden with as much gold as they could carry, which he gave to *Martinez* at his departure. But when he was arrived near the river's side, the borderers which are called *Orenoqueponi*[17] robbed him and his *Guianians* of all the treasure (the borderers being at that time at wars, which *Inga* had not conquered) save only of two great bottles of gourds, which were filled with beads of gold curiously wrought, which those *Orenoqueponi* thought had been no other thing than his drink or meat, or grain for food, with which *Martinez* had liberty to pass. And so in *canoas* he fell down from the river of *Orenoque* to *Trinidad,* and from thence to *Margarita*; and so to *St. Juan de Puerto Rico;* where, remaining a long time for passage into *Spain,* he died. In the time of his extreme sickness, and when he was without hope of life, receiving the sacrament at the hands of his confessor, he delivered these things, with the relation of his travels, and also called for his *calabazas* or gourds of the gold beads, which he gave to the church and friars, to be prayed for.

This *Martinez* was he that christened the city of *Manoa* by the name of *El Dorado,* and, as *Berreo* informed me, upon this occasion, those *Guianians,* and also the borderers, and all other in that tract which I have seen, are marvellous great drunkards; in which vice I think no nation can compare with them; and at the times of their solemn feasts, when the emperor carouseth with his captains, tributaries, and governors, the manner is thus. All those that pledge him are first stripped naked and their bodies anointed all over with a kind of white *balsamum* (by them called *curca*), of which there is great plenty, and yet very dear amongst them, and it is of all other the most precious, whereof we have had good experience. When they are anointed all over, certain servants of the emperor, having prepared gold made

17 'On the Orinoco.' *Poni* is a Carib postposition meaning 'on.'

into fine powder, blow it thorough hollow canes upon their naked bodies, until they be all shining from the foot to the head; and in this sort they sit drinking by twenties and hundreds, and continue in drunkenness sometimes six or seven days together.[18] The same is also confirmed by a letter written into *Spain* which was intercepted, which Master *Robert Dudley* told me he had seen. Upon this sight, and for the abundance of gold which he saw in the city, the images of gold in their temples, the plates, armours, and shields of gold which they use in the wars, he called it *El Dorado.*

After the death of *Ordas* and *Martinez,* and after *Orellana,* who was employed by *Gonzalo Pizarro,* one *Pedro de Orsúa,* a knight of *Navarre,* attempted *Guiana,* taking his way into *Peru,* and built his brigandines upon a river called *Oia,* which riseth to the southward of *Quito,* and is very great. This river falleth into *Amazons,* by which *Orsúa* with his companies descended, and came out of that province which is called *Motilones;*[19] and it seemeth to me that this empire is reserved for her Majesty and the English nation, by reason of the hard success which all these and other Spaniards found in attempting the same, whereof I will speak briefly, though impertinent in some sort to my purpose. This *Pedro de Orsúa* had among his troops a Biscayan called *Aguirre,* a man meanly born, who bare no other office than a sergeant or *alferez:*[20] but after certain months, when the soldiers were grieved with travels and consumed with famine, and that no entrance could be found by the branches or body of *Amazons,* this *Aguirre* raised a mutiny, of which he made himself the head, and so prevailed as he put *Orsúa* to the sword and all his followers, taking on him the whole charge and commandment, with a purpose not only to make himself emperor of *Guiana,* but also of *Peru* and of all that side of the *West Indies.* He had of his party 700 soldiers, and of those many promised to draw in other captains and companies, to deliver up towns and forts in *Peru;* but neither

[18] The substance of this report is in the end of the 'Navigation of the Great River of Marañon,' written by Gonzalo Fernando de Oviedo to Cardinal Bembo (Ramusio, vol. iii. fol. 416). (Note by Hakluyt.)

[19] 'Friars' (Indians so named from their cropped heads).

[20] *Al-faris* (Arab.), horseman, mounted officer.

finding by the said river any passage into *Guiana,* nor any possibility to return towards *Peru* by the same *Amazons,* by reason that the descent of the river made so great a current, he was enforced to disemboque at the mouth of the said *Amazons,* which cannot be less than 1,000 leagues from the place where they embarked. From thence he coasted the land till he arrived at *Margarita* to the north of *Mompatar,* which is at this day called *Puerto de Tyranno,* for that he there slew *Don Juan de Villa Andreda,* Governor of *Margarita,* who was father to *Don Juan Sarmiento,* Governor of *Margarita* when Sir *John Burgh* landed there and attempted the island. *Aguirre* put to the sword all other in the island that refused to be of his party, and took with him certain *cimarrones*[21] and other desperate companions. From thence he went to *Cumana* and there slew the governor, and dealt in all as at *Margarita.* He spoiled all the coast of *Caracas* and the province of *Venezuela* and of *Rio de la Hacha;* and, as I remember, it was the same year that Sir *John Hawkins* sailed to *St. Juan de Ullua* in the *Jesus* of *Lubeck;*[22] for himself told me that he met with such a one upon the coast, that rebelled, and had sailed down all the river of *Amazons.* *Aguirre* from thence landed about *Santa Marta* and sacked it also, putting to death so many as refused to be his followers, purposing to invade *Nuevo Reyno de Granada* and to sack *Pamplona, Merida, Lagrita, Tunja,* and the rest of the cities of *Nuevo Reyno,* and from thence again to enter *Peru;* but in a fight in the said *Nuevo Reyno* he was overthrown, and, finding no way to escape, he first put to the sword his own children, foretelling them that they should not live to be defamed or upbraided by the Spaniards after his death, who would have termed them the children of a traitor or tyrant; and that, sithence he could not make them princes, he would yet deliver them from shame and reproach. These were the ends and tragedies of *Ordas, Martinez, Orellana, Orsúa,* and *Aguirre.* Also soon after *Ordas* followed *Jeronimo Ortal de Saragosa,* with 130 soldiers; who failing his entrance by sea, was cast with the current on the coast of *Paria,* and peopled about *S. Miguel de Neveri.* It was then attempted by *Don Pedro de Silva,* a Portuguese of the family of *Ruy*

[21] Fugitive slaves. [22] 1567-68.

Gomez de Silva, and by the favour which *Ruy Gomes* had with the king he was set out. But he also shot wide of the mark; for being departed from *Spain* with his fleet, he entered by *Marañon* or *Amazons,* where by the nations of the river and by the *Amazons,* he was utterly overthrown, and himself and all his army defeated; only seven escaped, and of those but two returned.

After him came *Pedro Hernandez de Serpa,* and landed at *Cumana,* in the *West Indies,* taking his journey by land towards *Orenoque,* which may be some 120 leagues; but yere he came to the borders of the said river, he was set upon by a nation of the Indians, called *Wikiri,* and overthrown in such sort, that of 300 soldiers, horsemen, many Indians, and negroes, there returned but eighteen. Others affirm that he was defeated in the very entrance of *Guiana,* at the first civil town of the empire called *Macureguarai.* Captain *Preston,* in taking *Santiago de Leon* (which was by him and his companies very resolutely performed, being a great town, and far within the land) held a gentleman prisoner, who died in his ship, that was one of the company of *Hernandez de Serpa,* and saved among those that escaped; who witnessed what opinion is held among the Spaniards thereabouts of the great riches *of Guiana,* and *El Dorado,* the city of *Inga.* Another Spaniard was brought aboard me by Captain *Preston,* who told me in the hearing of himself and divers other gentlemen, that he met with *Berreo's* camp-master at *Caracas,* when he came from the borders of *Guiana,* and that he saw with him forty of most pure plates of gold, curiously wrought, and swords of *Guiana* decked and inlaid with gold, feathers garnished with gold, and divers rarities, which he carried to the Spanish king.

After *Hernandez de Serpa,* it was undertaken by the *Adelantado, Don Gonzalez Ximenes de Quesada,* who was one of the chiefest in the conquest of *Nuevo Reyno,* whose daughter and heir *Don Antonio de Berreo* married. *Gonzalez* sought the passage also by the river called *Papamene,* which riseth by *Quito,* in *Peru,* and runneth south-east 100 leagues, and then falleth into *Amazons.* But he also, failing the entrance, returned with the loss of much labour and cost. I took one Captain *George,* a Spaniard, that followed *Gonzalez* in this enterprise. *Gonzalez* gave his daughter to *Berreo,* taking his oath and honour to follow the enterprise to the last of his substance and life. Who since, as he hath sworn to me, hath spent 300,000 ducats in the same, and yet never could enter so far into the land as myself with that poor troop, or rather a handful of men, being in all about 100 gentlemen, soldiers, rowers, boat-keepers, boys, and of all sorts; neither could any of the forepassed undertakers, nor *Berreo* himself, discover the country, till now lately by conference with an ancient king, called *Carapana,*[23] he got the true light thereof. For *Berreo* came about 1,500 miles yere he understood aught, or could find any passage or entrance into any part thereof; yet he had experience of all these fore-named, and divers others, and was persuaded of their errors and mistakings. *Berreo* sought it by the river *Cassanar,* which falleth into a great river called *Pato: Pato* falleth into *Meta,* and *Meta* into *Baraquan,* which is also called *Orenoque.* He took his journey from *Nuevo Reyno de Granada,* where he dwelt, having the inheritance of *Gonzalez Ximenes* in those parts; he was followed with 700 horse, he drove with him 1,000 head of cattle, he had also many women, Indians, and slaves. How all these rivers cross and encounter, how the country lieth and is bordered, the passage of *Ximenes* and *Berreo,* mine own discovery, and the way that I entered, with all the rest of the nations and rivers, your lordship shall receive in a large chart or map, which I have not yet finished, and which I shall most humbly pray your lordship to secrete, and not to suffer it to pass your own hands; for by a draught thereof all may be prevented by other nations; for I know it is this very year sought by the French, although by the way that they now take, I fear it not much. It was also told me yere I departed *England,* that *Villiers,* the Admiral, was in preparation for the planting of *Amazons,* to which river the French have made divers voyages, and returned[24] much gold and other rarities. I spake with a captain of a French ship that came

[23] Carapana (=Caribana, Carib land) was an old European name for the Atlantic coast near the mouth of the Orinoco, and hence was applied to one of its chiefs (see p. 207). Berrio called this district 'Emeria.'
[24] Brought back.

from thence, his ship riding in *Falmouth* the same year that my ships came first from Virginia; there was another this year in *Helford,* that also came from thence, and had been fourteen months at an anchor in *Amazons;* which were both very rich.

Although, as I am persuaded, *Guiana* cannot be entered that way, yet no doubt the trade of gold from thence passeth by branches of rivers into the river of *Amazons,* and so it doth on every hand far from the country itself; for those Indians of *Trinidad* have plates of gold from *Guiana,* and those cannibals of *Dominica* which dwell in the islands by which our ships pass yearly to the *West Indies,* also the Indians of *Paria,* those Indians called *Tucaris, Chochi, Apotomios, Cumanagotos,* and all those other nations inhabiting near about the mountains that run from *Paria* thorough the province of *Venezuela,* and in *Maracapana,* and the cannibals of *Guanipa,* the Indians called *Assawai, Coaca, Ajai,* and the rest (all which shall be described in my description as they are situate) have plates of gold of *Guiana.* And upon the river of *Amazons, Thevet* writeth that the people wear *croissants* of gold, for of that form the *Guianians* most commonly make them; so as from *Dominica* to *Amazons,* which is above 250 leagues, all the chief Indians in all parts wear of those plates of *Guiana.* Undoubtedly those that trade [with] *Amazons* return much gold, which (as is aforesaid) cometh by trade from *Guiana,* by some branch of a river that falleth from the country into *Amazons,* and either it is by the river which passeth by the nations called *Tisnados,* or by *Caripuna.*

I made enquiry amongst the most ancient and best travelled of the *Orenoqueponi,* and I had knowledge of all the rivers between *Orenoque* and *Amazons,* and was very desirous to understand the truth of those warlike women, because of some it is believed, of others not. And though I digress from my purpose, yet I will set down that which hath been delivered me for truth of those women, and I spake with a *cacique,* or lord of people, that told me he had been in the river, and beyond it also. The nations of these women are on the south side of the river in the provinces of *Topago,* and their chiefest strengths and retracts are in the islands situate on the south side of the entrance, some 60 leagues within the mouth of the said river. The memories of the like women are very ancient as well in *Africa* as in *Asia*. In *Africa* those that had *Medusa* for queen; others in *Scythia,* near the rivers of *Tanais* and *Thermodon.* We find, also, that *Lampedo* and *Marthesia* were queens of the *Amazons.* In many histories they are verified to have been, and in divers ages and provinces; but they which are not far from *Guiana* do accompany with men but once in a year, and for the time of one month, which I gather by their relation, to be in April; and that time all kings of the borders assemble, and queens of the *Amazons;* and after the queens have chosen, the rest cast lots for their valentines. This one month they feast, dance, and drink of their wines in abundance; and the moon being done they all depart to their own provinces. * * * * They are said to be very cruel and bloodthirsty, especially to such as offer to invade their territories. These *Amazons* have likewise great store of these plates of gold, which they recover by exchange chiefly for a kind of green stones, which the Spaniards call *piedras hijadas,* and we use for spleen-stones;[25] and for the disease of the stone we also esteem them. Of these I saw divers in *Guiana;* and commonly every king or *cacique* hath one, which their wives for the most part wear, and they esteem them as great jewels.

But to return to the enterprise of *Berreo,* who, as I have said, departed from *Nueva Reyno* with 700 horse, besides the provisions above rehearsed. He descended by the river called *Cassanar,* which riseth in *Nuevo Reyno* out of the mountains by the city of *Tunja,* from which mountain also springeth *Pato;* both which fall into the great river of *Meta,* and *Meta* riseth from a mountain joining to *Pamplona,* in the same *Nuevo Reyno de Granada.* These, as also *Guaiare,* which issueth out of the mountains by *Timana,* fall all into *Baraquan,* and are but of his heads; for at their coming together they lose their names, and *Baraquan* farther down is also rebaptized by the name of *Orenoque.* On the other side of the city and hills of *Timana* riseth *Rio Grande,*

[25] Stones reduced to powder and taken internally to cure maladies of the spleen.

which falleth into the sea by *Santa Marta*. By *Cassanar* first, and so into *Meta*, *Berreo* passed, keeping his horsemen on the banks, where the country served them for to march; and where otherwise, he was driven to embark them in boats which he builded for the purpose, and so came with the current down the river of *Meta*, and so into *Baraquan*. After he entered that great and mighty river, he began daily to lose of his companies both men and horse; for it is in many places violently swift, and hath forcible eddies, many sands, and divers islands sharp pointed with rocks. But after one whole year, journeying for the most part by river, and the rest by land, he grew daily to fewer numbers; for both by sickness, and by encountering with the people of those regions thorough which he travelled, his companies were much wasted, especially by divers encounters with the *Amapaians*.[26] And in all this time he never could learn of any passage into *Guiana*, nor any news or fame thereof, until he came to a further border of the said *Amapaia*, eight days' journey from the river *Caroli*,[27] which was the furthest river that he entered. Among those of *Amapaia*, *Guiana* was famous; but few of these people accosted *Berreo*, or would trade with him the first three months of the six which he sojourned there. This *Amapaia* is also marvellous rich in gold, as both *Berreo* confessed and those of *Guiana* with whom I had most conference; and is situate upon *Orenoque* also. In this country *Berreo* lost sixty of his best soldiers, and most of all his horse that remained in his former year's travel. But in the end, after divers encounters with those nations, they grew to peace, and they presented *Berreo* with ten images of fine gold among divers other plates and *croissants*, which, as he sware to me, and divers other gentlemen, were so curiously wrought, as he had not seen the like either in *Italy*, *Spain*, or the *Low Countries*; and he was resolved that when they came to the hands of the Spanish king, to whom he had sent them by his camp-master, they would appear very admirable, especially being wrought by such a nation as had no iron instruments at all, nor any

[26] Amapaia was Berrio's name for the Orinoco valley above the Caura river.

[27] The Caroni river, the first great affluent of the Orinoco on the south, about 180 miles from the sea.

of those helps which our goldsmiths have to work withal. The particular name of the people in *Amapaia* which gave him these pieces, are called *Anebas,* and the river of *Orenoque* at that place is about twelve English miles broad, which may be from his outfall into the sea 700 or 800 miles.

This province of *Amapaia* is a very low and a marish ground near the river; and by reason of the red water which issueth out in small branches thorough the fenny and boggy ground, there breed divers poisonful worms and serpents. And the Spaniards not suspecting, nor in any sort foreknowing the danger, were infected with a grievous kind of flux by drinking thereof, and even the very horses poisoned therewith; insomuch as at the end of the six months that they abode there, of all their troops there were not left above 120 soldiers, and neither horse nor cattle. For *Berreo* hoped to have found *Guiana* by 1,000 miles nearer than it fell out to be in the end; by means whereof they sustained much want, and much hunger, oppressed with grievous diseases, and all the miseries that could be imagined, I demanded of those in *Guiana* that had travelled *Amapaia,* how they lived with that tawny or red water when they travelled thither; and they told me that after the sun was near the middle of the sky, they used to fill their pots and pitchers with that water, but either before that time or towards the setting of the sun it was dangerous to drink of, and in the night strong poison. I learned also of divers other rivers of that nature among them, which were also, while the sun was in the meridian, very safe to drink, and in the morning, evening, and night, wonderful dangerous and infective. From this province *Berreo* hasted away as soon as the spring and beginning of summer appeared, and sought his entrance on the borders of *Orenoque* on the south side; but there ran a ledge of so high and impassable mountains, as he was not able by any means to march over them, continuing from the east sea into which *Orenoque* falleth, even to *Quito* in *Peru.* Neither had he means to carry victual or munition over those craggy, high, and fast hills, being all woody, and those so thick and spiny, and so full of prickles, thorns, and briars, as it is impossible to creep thorough them. He had also neither friendship among the people, nor any interpreter to persuade or treat with them; and more, to his disadvantage, the *caciques* and kings of *Amapaia* had given knowledge of his purpose to the *Guianians,* and that he sought to sack and conquer the empire, for the hope of their so great abundance and quantities of gold. He passed by the mouths of many great rivers which fell into *Orenoque* both from the north and south, which I forbear to name, for tediousness, and because they are more pleasing in describing than reading.

Berreo affirmed that there fell an hundred rivers into *Orenoque* from the north and south: whereof the least was as big as *Rio Grande,*[28] that passed between *Popayan* and *Nuevo Reyno de Granada, Rio Grande* being esteemed one of the renowned rivers in all the *West Indies,* and numbered among the great rivers of the world. But he knew not the names of any of these, but *Caroli* only; neither from what nations they descended, neither to what provinces they led, for he had no means to discourse with the inhabitants at any time; neither was he curious in these things, being utterly unlearned, and not knowing the east from the west. But of all these I got some knowledge, and of many more, partly by mine own travel, and the rest by conference; of some one I learned one, of others the rest, having with me an Indian that spake many languages, and that of *Guiana*[29] naturally. I sought out all the aged men, and such as were greatest travellers. And by the one and the other I came to understand the situations, the rivers, the kingdoms from the east sea to the borders of *Peru,* and from *Orenoque* southward as far as *Amazons* or *Marañon,* and the regions of *Marinatambal,*[30] and of all the kings of provinces, and captains of towns and villages, how they stood in terms of peace or war, and which were friends or enemies the one with the other; without which there can be neither entrance nor conquest in those parts, nor elsewhere. For by the dissension between *Guascar* and *Atabalipa, Pizarro* conquered *Peru,* and by the hatred that the *Tlaxcallians* bare to *Mutezuma, Cortes* was victorious over *Mexico;* without which both the one and the other had failed of their enterprise, and of the great honour and riches which they attained unto.

[28] The Magdalena. [29] The Carib. [30] North coasts of Brazil.

Now *Berreo* began to grow into despair, and looked for no other success than his predecessor in this enterprise; until such time as he arrived at the province of *Emeria* towards the east sea and mouth of the river, where he found a nation of people very favourable, and the country full of all manner of victual. The king of this land is called *Carapana,* a man very wise, subtle, and of great experience, being little less than an hundred years old. In his youth he was sent by his father into the island of *Trinidad,* by reason of civil war among themselves, and was bred at a village in that island, called *Parico.* At that place in his youth he had seen many Christians, both French and Spanish, and went divers times with the Indians of *Trinidad* to *Margarita* and *Cumaná,* in the *West Indies,* for both those places have ever been relieved with victual from *Trinidad:* by reason whereof he grew of more understanding, and noted the difference of the nations, comparing the strength and arms of his country with those of the Christians, and ever after temporised so as whosoever else did amiss, or was wasted by contention, *Carapana* kept himself and his country in quiet and plenty. He also held peace with the *Caribs* or cannibals, his neighbours, and had free trade with all nations, whosoever else had war.

Berreo sojourned and rested his weak troop in the town of *Carapana* six weeks, and from him learned the way and passage to *Guiana,* and the riches and magnificence thereof. But being then utterly unable to proceed, he determined to try his fortune another year, when he had renewed his provisions, and regathered more force, which he hoped for as well out of *Spain* as from *Nuevo Reyno,* where he had left his son *Don Antonio Ximenes* to second him upon the first notice given of his entrance; and so for the present embarked himself in *canoas,* and by the branches of *Orenoque* arrived at *Trinidad,* having from *Carapana* sufficient pilots to conduct him. From *Trinidad* he coasted *Paria,* and so recovered *Margarita*; and having made relation to *Don Juan Sarmiento,* the Governor, of his proceeding, and persuaded him of the riches of *Guiana,* he obtained from thence fifty soldiers, promising presently to return to *Carapana,* and so into *Guiana.* But *Berreo* meant nothing less at that time; for he wanted many provisions necessary for such an enterprise, and therefore departed from *Margarita,* seated himself in *Trinidad,* and from thence sent his camp-master and his sergeant-major back to the borders to discover the nearest passage into the empire, as also to treat with the borderers, and to draw them to his party and love; without which, he knew he could neither pass safely, nor in any sort be relieved with victual or aught else. *Carapana* directed his company to a king called *Morequito,* assuring them that no man could deliver so much of *Guiana* as *Morequito* could, and that his dwelling was but five days' journey from *Macureguarai,* the first civil town of *Guiana.*

Now your lordship shall understand that this *Morequito,* one of the greatest lords or kings of the borders of *Guiana,* had two or three years before been at *Cumaná* and at *Margarita,* in the *West Indies,* with great store of plates of gold, which he carried to exchange for such other things as he wanted in his own country, and was daily feasted, and presented by the governors of those places, and held amongst them some two months. In which time one *Vides,* Governor of *Cumaná,* won him to be his conductor into *Guiana,* being allured by those *croissants* and images of gold which he brought with him to trade, as also by the ancient fame and magnificence of *El Dorado*; whereupon *Vides* sent into *Spain* for a patent to discover and conquer *Guiana,* not knowing of the precedence of *Berreo's* patent; which, as *Berreo* affirmeth, was signed before that of *Vides.* So as when *Vides* understood of *Berreo* and that he had made entrance into that territory, and foregone his desire and hope, it was verily thought that *Vides* practised with *Morequito* to hinder and disturb *Berreo* in all he could, and not to suffer him to enter through his seignory, nor any of his companies; neither to victual, nor guide them in any sort. For *Vides,* Governor of *Cumaná,* and *Berreo,* were become mortal enemies, as well for that *Berreo* had gotten *Trinidad* into his patent with *Guiana,* as also in that he was by *Berreo* prevented in the journey of *Guiana* itself. Howsoever it was, I know not, but *Morequito* for a time dissembled his disposition, suffered ten Spaniards and a friar, which *Berreo* had sent to discover *Manoa,* to travel through his country, gave them a guide for *Macureguarai,* the first town of civil and apparelled people, from whence they had other guides to bring them to *Manoa,* the great city of *Inga;* and being furnished with those things which they had learned of *Carapana* were of most price in *Guiana,* went onward, and in eleven days arrived at *Manoa,* as *Berreo* affirmeth for certain; although I could not be assured thereof by the lord which now governeth the province of *Morequito,* for he told me that they got all the gold they had in other towns on this side *Manoa,* there being many very great and rich, and (as he said) built like the towns of Christians, with many rooms.

When these ten Spaniards were returned, and ready to put out of the border of *Aromaia,*[31] the people of *Morequito* set upon them, and slew them all but one that swam the river, and took from them to the value of 40,000 *pesos* of gold; and one of them only lived to bring the news to *Berreo,* that both his nine soldiers and holy father were benighted in the said province. I myself spake with the captains of *Morequito* that slew them, and was at the place where it was executed. *Berreo,* enraged herewithal, sent all the strength he could make into *Aromaia,* to be revenged of him, his people, and country. But *Morequito,* suspecting the same, fled over *Orenoque,* and thorough the territories of the *Saima* and *Wikiri* recovered *Cumaná,* where he thought himself very safe, with *Vides* the governor. But *Berreo* sending for him in the king's name, and his messengers finding him in the house of one *Fajardo,* on the sudden, yere he was suspected, so as he could not then be conveyed away, *Vides* durst not deny him, as well to avoid the suspicion of the practice, as also for that an holy father was slain by him and his people. *Morequito* offered *Fajardo* the weight of three quintals in gold, to let him escape; but the poor *Guianian,* betrayed on all sides, was delivered to the camp-master of *Berreo,* and was presently executed.

After the death of this *Morequito,* the soldiers of *Berreo* spoiled his territory and took divers prisoners. Among

[31] The district below the Caroni river.

others they took the uncle of *Morequito,* called *Topiawari,* who is now king of *Aromaia,* whose son I brought with me into *England,* and is a man of great understanding and policy; he is above an hundred years old, and yet is of a very able body. The Spaniards led him in a chain seventeen days, and made him their guide from place to place between his country and *Emeria,* the province of *Carapana* aforesaid, and he was at last redeemed for an hundred plates of gold, and divers stones called *piedras hijadas,* or spleen-stones. Now *Berreo* for executing of *Morequito,* and other cruelties, spoils, and slaughters done in *Aromaia,* hath lost the love of the *Orenoqueponi,* and of all the borderers, and dare not send any of his soldiers any further into the land than to *Carapana,* which he called the port of *Guiana;* but from thence by the help of *Carapana* he had trade further into the country, and always appointed ten Spaniards to reside in *Carapana's* town,[32] by whose favour, and by being conducted by his people, those ten searched the country thereabouts, as well for mines as for other trades and commodities.

They also have gotten a nephew of *Morequito,* whom they have christened and named *Don Juan,* of whom they have great hope, endeavouring by all means to establish him in the said province. Among many other trades, those Spaniards used *canoas* to pass to the rivers of *Barema, Pawroma,* and *Dissequebe,*[33] which are on the south side of the mouth of *Orenoque,* and there buy women and children from the cannibals, which are of that barbarous nature, as they will for three or four hatchets sell the sons and daughters of their own brethren and sisters, and for somewhat more even their own daughters. Hereof the Spaniards make great profit; for buying a maid of twelve or thirteen years for three or four hatchets, they sell them again at *Margarita* in the *West Indies* for fifty and an hundred *pesos,* which is so many crowns.

The master of my ship, *John Douglas,* took one of the *canoas* which came laden from thence with people to be sold, and the most of them escaped; yet of those he brought,

[32] The Spanish settlement of Santo Tomé de la Guyana, founded by Berrio in 1591 or 1592, but represented by Raleigh as an Indian pueblo.
[33] Essequibo.

there was one as well favoured and as well shaped as ever I saw any in *England;* and afterwards I saw many of them, which but for their tawny colour may be compared to any in *Europe.* They also trade in those rivers for bread of *cassavi,* of which they buy an hundred pound weight for a knife, and sell it at *Margarita* for ten *pesos.* They also recover great store of cotton, *Brazil* wood, and those beds which they call *hamacas* or *Brazil* beds, wherein in hot countries all the Spaniards use to lie commonly, and in no other, neither did we ourselves while we were there. By means of which trades, for ransom of divers of the *Guianians,* and for exchange of hatchets and knives, *Berreo* recovered some store of gold plates, eagles of gold, and images of men and divers birds, and dispatched his camp-master for *Spain,* with all that he had gathered, therewith to levy soldiers, and by the show thereof to draw others to the love of the enterprise. And having sent divers images as well of men as beasts, birds, and fishes, so curiously wrought in gold, he doubted not but to persuade the king to yield to him some further help, especially for that this land hath never been sacked, the mines never wrought, and in the *Indies* their works were well spent, and the gold drawn out with great labour and charge. He also despatched messengers to his son in *Nuevo Reyno* to levy all the forces he could, and to come down the river *Orenoque* to *Emeria,* the province of *Carapana,* to meet him; he had also sent to *Santiago de Leon* on the coast of the *Caracas,* to buy horses and mules.

After I had thus learned of his proceedings past and purposed, I told him that I had resolved to see *Guiana,* and that it was the end of my journey, and the cause of my coming to *Trinidad,* as it was indeed, and for that purpose I sent *Jacob Whiddon* the year before to get intelligence: with whom *Berreo* himself had speech at that time, and remembered how inquisitive *Jacob Whiddon* was of his proceedings, and of the country of *Guiana. Berreo* was stricken into a great melancholy and sadness, and used all the arguments he could to dissuade me; and also assured the gentlemen of my company that it would be labour lost, and that they should suffer many miseries if they proceeded. And first he delivered that I could not enter any of the rivers with any bark or pinnace, or hardly with any ship's boat, it was so low, sandy, and full of flats, and that his companies were daily grounded in their canoes, which drew but twelve inches water. He further said that none of the country would come to speak with us, but would all fly; and if we followed them to their dwellings, they would burn their own towns. And besides that, the way was long, the winter at hand, and that the rivers beginning once to swell, it was impossible to stem the current; and that we could not in those small boats by any means carry victuals for half the time, and that (which indeed most discouraged my company) the kings and lords of all the borders of *Guiana* had decreed that none of them should trade with any Christians for gold, because the same would be their own overthrow, and that for the love of gold the Christians meant to conquer and dispossess them of all together.

Many and the most of these I found to be true; but yet I resolving to make trial of whatsoever happened, directed Captain *George Gifford,* my Vice-Admiral, to take the *Lion's Whelp,* and Captain *Caulfield* his bark, [and] to turn to the eastward, against the mouth of a river called *Capuri,* whose entrance I had before sent Captain *Whiddon* and *John Douglas* the master to discover. Who found some nine foot water or better upon the flood, and five at low water; to whom I had given instructions that they should anchor at the edge of the shoal, and upon the best of the flood to thrust over, which shoal *John Douglas* buoyed and beckoned[34] for them before. But they laboured in vain; for neither could they turn it up altogether so far to the east, neither did the flood continue so long, but the water fell yere they could have passed the sands. As we after found by a second experience: so as now we must either give over our enterprise, or leaving our ships at adventure 400 mile behind us, must run up in our ship's boats, one barge, and two wherries. But being doubtful how to carry victuals for so long a time in such baubles, or any strength of men, especially for that *Berreo* assured us that his son must be by that time come down with many soldiers, I sent away one *King,* master of

[34] Beaconed, i. e. placed a beacon or signal upon the buoy.

the *Lion's Whelp,* with his ship-boat, to try another branch of the river in the bottom of the Bay of *Guanipa,* which was called *Amana,* to prove if there were water to be found for either of the small ships to enter. But when he came to the mouth of *Amana,* he found it as the rest, but stayed not to discover it thoroughly, because he was assured by an Indian, his guide, that the cannibals of *Guanipa* would assail them with many *canoas,* and that they shot poisoned arrows; so as if he hasted not back, they should all be lost.

In the meantime, fearing the worst, I caused all the carpenters we had to cut down a *galego* boat, which we meant to cast off, and to fit her with banks to row on, and in all things to prepare her the best they could, so as she might be brought to draw but five foot: for so much we had on the bar of *Capuri* at low water. And doubting of *King's* return, I sent *John Douglas* again in my long barge, as well to relieve him, as also to make a perfect search in the bottom of the bay; for it hath been held for infallible, that whatsoever ship or boat shall fall therein can never disemboque again, by reason of the violent current which setteth into the said bay, as also for that the breeze and easterly wind bloweth directly into the same. Of which opinion I have heard *John Hampton,*[35] of *Plymouth,* one of the greatest experience of *England,* and divers other besides that have traded to *Trinidad.*

I sent with *John Douglas* an old *cacique* of *Trinidad* for a pilot, who told us that we could not return again by the bay or gulf, but that he knew a by-branch which ran within the land to the eastward, and he thought by it we might fall into *Capuri,* and so return in four days. *John Douglas* searched those rivers, and found four goodly entrances, whereof the least was as big as the *Thames* at *Woolwich,* but in the bay thitherward it was shoal and but six foot water; so as we were now without hope of any ship or bark to pass over, and therefore resolved to go on with the boats, and the bottom of the *galego,* in which we thrust 60 men. In the *Lion's Whelp's* boat and wherry we carried twenty, Captain *Caulfield* in his wherry carried ten more, and in my barge other ten, which made up a hundred; we had no other means

[35] Captain of the *Minion* in the third voyage of Hawkins.

but to carry victual for a month in the same, and also to lodge therein as we could, and to boil and dress our meat. Captain *Gifford* had with him Master *Edward Porter,* Captain *Eynos,* and eight more in his wherry, with all their victual, weapons, and provisions. Captain *Caulfield* had with him my cousin *Butshead Gorges,* and eight more. In the galley, of gentlemen and officers myself had Captain *Thyn,* my cousin *John Greenvile,* my nephew *John Gilbert,* Captain *Whiddon,* Captain *Keymis, Edward Hancock,* Captain *Clarke,* Lieutenant *Hughes, Thomas Upton,* Captain *Facy, Jerome Ferrar, Anthony Wells, William Connock,* and above fifty more. We could not learn of *Berreo* any other way to enter but in branches so far to windward as it was impossible for us to recover; for we had as much sea to cross over in our wherries, as between *Dover* and *Calice,* and in a great bollow, the wind and current being both very strong. So as we were driven to go in those small boats directly before the wind into the bottom of the Bay of *Guanipa,* and from thence to enter the mouth of some one of those rivers which *John Douglas* had last discovered; and had with us for pilot an Indian of *Barema,* a river to the south of *Orenoque,* between that and *Amazons,* whose *canoas* we had formerly taken as he was going from the said *Barema,* laden with *cassavi* bread to sell at *Margarita.* This *Arwacan* promised to bring me into the great river of *Orenoque;* but indeed of that which he entered he was utterly ignorant, for he had not seen it in twelve years before, at which time he was very young, and of no judgment. And if God had not sent us another help, we might have wandered a whole year in that labyrinth of rivers, yere we had found any way, either out or in, especially after we were past ebbing and flowing, which was in four days. For I know all the earth doth not yield the like confluence of streams and branches, the one crossing the other so many times, and all so fair and large, and so like one to another, as no man can tell which to take: and if we went by the sun or compass, hoping thereby to go directly one way or other, yet that way we were also carried in a circle amongst multitudes of islands, and every island so bordered with high trees as no man could see any further than the breadth of the river, or length of the breach. But this it chanced, that entering into a river (which because it had no name, we called the *River of the Red Cross,* ourselves being the first Christians that ever came therein), the 22. of May, as we were rowing up the same, we espied a small *canoa* with three Indians, which by the swiftness of my barge, rowing with eight oars, I overtook yere they could cross the river. The rest of the people on the banks, shadowed under the thick wood, gazed on with a doubtful conceit what might befall those three which we had taken. But when they perceived that we offered them no violence, neither entered their *canoa* with any of ours, nor took out of the *canoa* any of theirs, they then began to show themselves on the bank's side, and offered to traffic with us for such things as they had. And as we drew near, they all stayed; and we came with our barge to the mouth of a little creek which came from their town into the great river.

As we abode here awhile, our Indian pilot, called *Ferdinando,* would needs go ashore to their village to fetch some fruits and to drink of their artificial wines, and also to see the place and know the lord of it against another time, and took with him a brother of his which he had with him in the journey. When they came to the village of these people the lord of the island offered to lay hands on them, purposing to have slain them both; yielding for reason that this Indian of ours had brought a strange nation into their territory to spoil and destroy them. But the pilot being quick and of a disposed body, slipt their fingers and ran into the woods, and his brother, being the better footman of the two, recovered the creek's mouth, where we stayed in our barge, crying out that his brother was slain. With that we set hands on one of them that was next us, a very old man, and brought him into the barge, assuring him that if we had not our pilot again we would presently cut off his head. This old man, being resolved that he should pay the loss of the other, cried out to those in the woods to save *Ferdinando,* our pilot; but they followed him notwithstanding, and hunted after him upon the foot with their deer-dogs, and with so main a cry that all the woods echoed with the shout they made. But at the last this poor chased Indian recovered the river side and got upon a tree, and, as we were coasting, leaped down and swam to the barge half dead with fear. But our good hap was that we kept the other old Indian, which we handfasted to redeem our pilot withal; for, being natural of those rivers, we assured ourselves that he knew the way better than any stranger could. And, indeed, but for this chance, I think we had never found the way either to *Guiana* or back to our ships; for *Ferdinando* after a few days knew nothing at all, nor which way to turn; yea, and many times the old man himself was in great doubt which river to take. Those people which dwell in these broken islands and drowned lands are generally called *Tivitivas.* There are of them two sorts; the one called *Ciawani,* and the other *Waraweete.*

The great river of *Orenoque* or *Baraquan* hath nine branches which fall out on the north side of his own main mouth. On the south side it hath seven other fallings into the sea, so it disemboqueth by sixteen arms in all, between islands and broken ground; but the islands are very great, many of them as big as the *Isle of Wight,* and bigger, and many less. From the first branch on the north to the last of the south it is at least 100 leagues, so as the river's mouth is 300 miles wide at his entrance into the sea, which I take to be far bigger than that of *Amazons.* All those that inhabit in the mouth of this river upon the several north branches are these *Tivitivas,* of which there are two chief lords which have continual wars one with the other. The islands which lie on the right hand are called *Pallamos,* and the land on the left, *Hororotomaka;* and the river by which *John Douglas* returned within the land from *Amana* to *Capuri* they call *Macuri.*

These *Tivitivas* are a very goodly people and very valiant, and have the most manly speech and most deliberate that ever I heard of what nation soever. In the summer they have houses on the ground, as in other places; in the winter they dwell upon the trees, where they build very artificial towns and villages, as it is written in the Spanish story of the *West Indies* that those people do in the low lands near the gulf of *Uraba.* For between May and September the river of *Orenoque* riseth thirty foot upright, and then are those islands overflown twenty foot high above the level of the ground, saving some few raised grounds in the middle of them; and for this cause they are enforced to live in this manner. They never eat of anything that is set or sown; and as at home they use neither planting nor other manurance, so when they come abroad they refuse to feed of aught but of that which nature without labour bringeth forth. They use the tops of *palmitos* for bread, and kill deer, fish, and porks for the rest of their sustenance. They have also many sorts of fruits that grow in the woods, and great variety of birds and fowls; and if to speak of them were not tedious and vulgar, surely we saw in those passages of very rare colours and forms not elsewhere to be found, for as much as I have either seen or read.

Of these people those that dwell upon the branches of *Orenoque,* called *Capuri* and *Macureo,* are for the most part carpenters of *canoas*; for they make the most and fairest *canoas,* and sell them into *Guiana* for gold and into *Trinidad* for *tabacco,* in the excessive taking whereof they exceed all nations. And notwithstanding the moistness of the air in which they live, the hardness of their diet, and the great labours they suffer to hunt, fish, and fowl for their living, in all my life, either in the *Indies* or in *Europe,* did I never behold a more goodly or better-favoured people or a more manly. They were wont to make war upon all nations, and especially on the *Cannibals,* so as none durst without a good strength trade by those rivers; but of late they are at peace with their neighbours, all holding the Spaniards for a common enemy. When their commanders die they use great lamentation; and when they think the flesh of their bodies is putrified and fallen from their bones, then they take up the carcase again and hang it in the *cacique's* house that died, and deck his skull with feathers of all colours, and hang all his gold plates about the bones of his arms, thighs, and legs. Those nations which are called *Arwacas,* which dwell on the south of *Orenoque,* of which place and nation our Indian pilot was, are dispersed in many other places, and do use to beat the bones of their lords into powder, and their wives and friends drink it all in their several sorts of drinks.

After we departed from the port of these *Ciawani* we passed up the river with the flood and anchored the ebb, and in this sort we went onward. The third day that we entered the river, our galley came on ground; and stuck so fast as we thought that even there our discovery had ended, and that we must have left four-score and ten of our men to have inhabited, like rooks upon trees, with those nations. But the next morning, after we had cast out all her ballast, with tugging and hauling to and fro we got her afloat and went on. At four days' end we fell into as goodly a river as ever I beheld, which was called the great *Amana,* which ran more directly without windings and turnings than the other. But soon after the flood of the sea left us; and, being enforced either by main strength to row against a violent current, or to return as wise as we went out, we had then no shift but to persuade the companies that it was but two or three days' work, and therefore desired them to take pains, every gentleman and others taking their turns to row, and to spell one the other at the hour's end. Every day we passed by goodly branches of rivers, some falling from the west, others from the east, into *Amana*; but those I leave to the description in the chart of discovery, where every one shall be named with his rising and descent. When three days more were overgone, our companies began to despair, the weather being extreme hot, the river bordered with very high trees that kept away the air, and the current against us every day stronger than other. But we evermore commanded our pilots to promise an end the next day, and used it so long as we were driven to assure them from four reaches of the river to three, and so to two, and so to the next reach. But so long we laboured that many days were spent, and we driven to draw ourselves to harder allowance, our bread even at the last, and no drink at all; and our men and ourselves so wearied and scorched, and doubtful withal whether we should ever perform it or no, the heat increasing as we drew towards the line; for we were now in five degrees.

The further we went on, our victual decreasing and the air breeding great faintness, we grew weaker and weaker, when we had most need of strength and ability. For hourly the river ran more violently than other against us, and the barge, wherries, and ship's boat of Captain *Gifford* and Captain *Caulfield* had spent all their provisions; so as we were brought into despair and discomfort, had we not persuaded all the company that it was but only one day's work more to attain the land where we should be relieved of all we wanted, and if we returned, that we were sure to starve by the way, and that the world would also laugh us to scorn. On the banks of these rivers were divers sorts of fruits good to eat, flowers and trees of such variety as were sufficient to make ten volumes of *Herbals*; we relieved ourselves many times with the fruits of the country, and sometimes with fowl and fish. We saw birds of all colours, some carnation, some crimson, orange-tawny, purple, watchet,[36] and of all other sorts, both simple and mixed, and it was unto us a great good-passing of the time to behold them, besides the relief we found by killing some store of them with our fowling-pieces; without which, having little or no bread, and less drink, but only the thick and troubled water of the river, we had been in a very hard case.

Our old pilot of the *Ciawani,* whom, as I said before, we took to redeem *Ferdinando,* told us, that if we would enter a branch of a river on the right hand with our barge and wherries, and leave the galley at anchor the while in the great river, he would bring us to a town of the *Arwacas,* where we should find store of bread, hens, fish, and of the country wine; and persuaded us, that departing from the galley at noon we might return yere night. I was very glad to hear this speech, and presently took my barge, with eight musketeers, Captain *Gifford's* wherry, with himself and four musketeers, and Captain *Caulfield* with his wherry, and as many; and so we entered the mouth of this river; and because we were persuaded that it was so near, we took no victual with us at all. When we had rowed three hours, we marvelled we saw no sign of any dwelling, and asked the pilot where the town was; he told us, a little further. After three hours more, the sun being almost set, we began to suspect that he led us that way to betray us; for he confessed that those Spaniards which fled from

[36] Pale blue.

Trinidad, and also those that remained with *Carapana* in *Emeria,* were joined together in some village upon that river. But when it grew towards night, and we demanded where the place was, he told us but four reaches more. When we had rowed four and four, we saw no sign; and our poor watermen, even heart-broken and tired, were ready to give up the ghost; for we had now come from the galley near forty miles.

At the last we determined to hang the pilot; and if we had well known the way back again by night, he had surely gone. But our own necessities pleaded sufficiently for his safety; for it was as dark as pitch, and the river began so to narrow itself, and the trees to hang over from side to side, as we were driven with arming swords to cut a passage thorough those branches that covered the water. We were very desirous to find this town hoping of a feast, because we made but a short breakfast aboard the galley in the morning, and it was now eight o'clock at night, and our stomachs began to gnaw apace; but whether it was best to return or go on, we began to doubt, suspecting treason in the pilot more and more; but the poor old Indian ever assured us that it was but a little further, but this one turning and that turning; and at the last about one o'clock after midnight we saw a light, and rowing towards it we heard the dogs of the village. When we landed we found few people; for the lord of that place was gone with divers *canoas* above 400 miles off, upon a journey towards the head of *Orenoque,* to trade for gold, and to buy women of the *Cannibals,* who afterwards unfortunately passed by us as we rode at an anchor in the port of *Morequito* in the dark of the night, and yet came so near us as his *canoas* grated against our barges; he left one of his company at the port of *Morequito,* by whom we understood that he had brought thirty young women, divers plates of gold, and had great store of fine pieces of cotton cloth, and cotton beds. In his house we had good store of bread, fish, hens, and Indian drink, and so rested that night; and in the morning, after we had traded with such of his people as came down, we returned towards our galley, and brought with us some quantity of bread, fish, and hens.

On both sides of this river we passed the most beautiful country that ever mine eyes beheld; and whereas all that we had seen before was nothing but woods, prickles, bushes, and thorns, here we beheld plains of twenty miles in length, the grass short and green, and in divers parts groves of trees by themselves, as if they had been by all the art and labour in the world so made of purpose; and still as we rowed, the deer came down feeding by the water's side as if they had been used to a keeper's call. Upon this river there were great store of fowl, and of many sorts; we saw in it divers sorts of strange fishes, and of marvellous bigness; but for *lagartos*[37] it exceeded, for there were thousands of those ugly serpents; and the people call it, for the abundance of them, the *River of Lagartos,* in their language. I had a negro, a very proper young fellow, who leaping out of the galley to swim in the mouth of this river, was in all our sights taken and devoured with one of those *lagartos.* In the meanwhile our companies in the galley thought we had been all lost, for we promised to return before night; and sent the *Lion's Whelp's* ship's boat with Captain *Whiddon* to follow us up the river. But the next day, after we had rowed up and down some fourscore miles, we returned, and went on our way up the great river; and when we were even at the last cast for want of victuals, Captain *Gifford* being before the galley and the rest of the boats, seeking out some place to land upon the banks to make fire, espied four *canoas* coming down the river; and with no small joy caused his men to try the uttermost of their strengths, and after a while two of the four gave over and ran themselves ashore, every man betaking himself to the fastness of the woods. The two other lesser got away, while he landed to lay hold on these; and so turned into some by-creek, we knew not whither. Those *canoas* that were taken were loaden with bread, and were bound for *Margarita* in the *West Indies,* which those Indians, called *Arwacas,* proposed to carry thither for exchange; but in the lesser there were three Spaniards, who having heard of the defeat of their Governor in *Trinidad,* and that we purposed to enter *Guiana,*

[37] Alligators and caymans.

came away in those *canoas;* one of them was a *cavallero,* as the captain of the *Arwacas* after told us, another a soldier and the third a refiner.

In the meantime, nothing on the earth could have been more welcome to us, next unto gold, than the great store of very excellent bread which we found in these *canoas;* for now our men cried, *Let us go on, we care not how far.* After that Captain *Gifford* had brought the two *canoas* to the galley, I took my barge and went to the bank's side with a dozen shot, where the *canoas* first ran themselves ashore, and landed there, sending out Captain *Gifford* and Captain *Thyn* on one hand and Captain *Caulfield* on the other, to follow those that were fled into the woods. And as I was creeping thorough the bushes, I saw an Indian basket hidden, which was the refiner's basket; for I found in it his quicksilver, saltpetre, and divers things for the trial of metals, and also the dust of such ore as he had refined; but in those *canoas* which escaped there was a good quantity of ore and gold. I then landed more men, and offered five hundred pound to what soldier soever could take one of those three Spaniards that we thought were landed. But our labours were in vain in that behalf, for they put themselves into one of the small *canoas,* and so, while the greater *canoas* were in taking, they escaped. But seeking after the Spaniards we found the *Arwacas* hidden in the woods, which were pilots for the Spaniards, and rowed their *canoas.* Of which I kept the chiefest for a pilot, and carried him with me to *Guiana;* by whom I understood where and in what countries the Spaniards had laboured for gold, though I made not the same known to all. For when the springs began to break, and the rivers to raise themselves so suddenly as by no means we could abide the digging of any mine, especially for that the richest are defended with rocks of hard stones, which we call the *white spar,* and that it required both time, men, and instruments fit for such a work, I thought it best not to hover thereabouts, lest if the same had been perceived by the company, there would have been by this time many barks and ships set out, and perchance other nations would also have gotten of ours for pilots. So as both ourselves might have been prevented, and all our care taken for good usage of the people been utterly lost, by those that only respect present profit; and such violence or insolence offered as the nations which are borderers would have changed the desire of our love and defence into hatred and violence. And for any longer stay to have brought a more quantity, which I hear hath been often objected, whosoever had seen or proved the fury of that river after it began to arise, and had been a month and odd days, as we were, from hearing aught from our ships, leaving them meanly manned 400 miles off, would perchance have turned somewhat sooner than we did, if all the mountains had been gold, or rich stones. And to say the truth, all the branches and small rivers which fell into *Orenoque* were raised with such speed, as if we waded them over the shoes in the morning outward, we were covered to the shoulders homeward the very same day; and to stay to dig our gold with our nails, had been *opus laboris* but not *ingenii.* Such a quantity as would have served our turns we could not have had, but a discovery of the mines to our infinite disadvantage we had made, and that could have been the best profit of farther search or stay; for those mines are not easily broken, nor opened in haste, and I could have returned a good quantity of gold ready cast if I had not shot at another mark than present profit.

This *Arwacan* pilot, with the rest, feared that we would have eaten them, or otherwise have put them to some cruel death: for the Spaniards, to the end that none of the people in the passage towards *Guiana,* or in *Guiana* itself, might come to speech with us, persuaded all the nations that we were men-eaters and cannibals. But when the poor men and women had seen us, and that we gave them meat, and to every one something or other which was rare and strange to them, they began to conceive the deceit and purpose of the Spaniards, who indeed, as they confessed, took from them both their wives and daughters daily . . . But I protest before the Majesty of the living God, that I neither know nor believe, that any of our company, one or other, did offer insult to any of their women, and yet we saw many hundreds, and had many in our power, and of those very young and excellently favoured, which came among us without deceit, stark naked. Nothing got us more love amongst them than this usage; for I suffered not any man to take from any of the nations so much as a *pina*[38] or a *potato* root without giving them contentment, nor any man so much as to offer to touch any of their wives or daughters; which course, so contrary to the Spaniards, who tyrannize over them in all things, drew them to admire her Majesty, whose commandment I told them it was, and also wonderfully to honour our nation. But I confess it was a very impatient work to keep the meaner sort from spoil and stealing when we came to their houses; which because in all I could not prevent, I caused my Indian interpreter at every place when we departed, to know of the loss or wrong done, and if aught were stolen or taken by violence, either the same was restored, and the party punished in their sight, or else was paid for to their uttermost demand. They also much wondered at us, after they heard that we had slain the Spaniards at *Trinidad,* for they were before resolved that no nation of Christians durst abide their presence; and they wondered more when I had made them know of the great overthrow that her Majesty's army and fleet had given them of late years in their own countries.

After we had taken in this supply of bread, with divers baskets of roots, which were excellent meat, I gave one of the *canoas* to the *Arwacas,* which belonged to the Spaniards that were escaped; and when I had dismissed all but the captain, who by the Spaniards was christened *Martin,* I sent back in the same *canoa* the old *Ciawani,* and *Ferdinando,* my first pilot, and gave them both such things as they desired, with sufficient victual to carry them back, and by them wrote a letter to the ships, which they promised to deliver, and performed it; and then I went on, with my new hired pilot, *Martin* the *Arwacan.* But the next or second day after, we came aground again with our galley, and were like to cast her away, with all our victual and provision, and so lay on the sand one whole night, and were far more in despair at this time to free her than before, because we had no tide of flood to help us, and therefore feared that all our hopes

[38] Pine-apple (see p. 365).

would have ended in mishaps. But we fastened an anchor upon the land, and with main strength drew her off; and so the fifteenth day we discovered afar off the mountains of *Guiana,* to our great joy, and towards the evening had a slent[39] of a northerly wind that blew very strong, which brought us in sight of the great river *Orenoque;* out of which this river descended wherein we were. We descried afar off three other *canoas* as far as we could discern them, after whom we hastened with our barge and wherries, but two of them passed out of sight, and the third entered up the great river, on the right hand to the westward, and there stayed out of sight, thinking that we meant to take the way eastward towards the province of *Carapana;* for that way the Spaniards keep, not daring to go upwards to *Guiana,* the people in those parts being all their enemies, and those in the *canoas* thought us to have been those Spaniards that were fled from *Trinidad,* and escaped killing. And when we came so far down as the opening of that branch into which they slipped, being near them with our barge and wherries, we made after them, and yere they could land came within call, and by our interpreter told them what we were, wherewith they came back willingly aboard us; and of such fish and *tortugas'*[40] eggs as they had gathered they gave us, and promised in the morning to bring the lord of that part with them, and to do us all other services they could. That night we came to an anchor at the parting of the three goodly rivers (the one was the river of *Amana,* by which we came from the north, and ran athwart towards the south, the other two were of *Orenoque,* which crossed from the west and ran to the sea towards the east) and landed upon a fair sand, where we found thousands of *tortugas'* eggs, which are very wholesome meat, and greatly restoring; so as our men were now well filled and highly contented both with the fare, and nearness of the land of *Guiana,* which appeared in sight.

In the morning there came down, according to promise, the lord of that border, called *Toparimaca,* with some thirty or forty followers, and brought us divers sorts of fruits, and of his wine, bread, fish, and flesh, whom we also feasted as

[39] Push. [40] Turtles.

we could; at least we drank good Spanish wine, whereof we had a small quantity in bottles, which above all things they love. I conferred with this *Toparimaca* of the next[41] way to *Guiana,* who conducted our galley and boats to his own port, and carried us from thence some mile and a-half to his town; where some of our captains garoused[42] of his wine till they were reasonable pleasant, for it is very strong with pepper, and the juice of divers herbs and fruits digested and purged. They keep it in great earthen pots of ten or twelve gallons, very clean and sweet, and are themselves at their meetings and feasts the greatest carousers and drunkards of the world. When we came to his town we found two *caciques,* whereof one was a stranger that had been up the river in trade, and his boats, people, and wife encamped at the port where we anchored; and the other was of that country, a follower of *Toparimaca.* They lay each of them in a cotton *hamaca,* which we call *Brazil* beds, and two women attending them with six cups, and a little ladle to fill them out of an earthen pitcher of wine; and so they drank each of them three of those cups at a time one to the other, and in this sort they drink drunk at their feasts and meetings.

That *cacique* that was a stranger had his wife staying at the port where we anchored, and in all my life I have seldom seen a better favoured woman. She was of good stature, with black eyes, fat of body, of an excellent countenance, her hair almost as long as herself, tied up again in pretty knots; and it seemed she stood not in that awe of her husband as the rest, for she spake and discoursed, and drank among the gentlemen and captains, and was very pleasant, knowing her own comeliness, and taking great pride therein. I have seen a lady in *England* so like to her, as but for the difference of colour, I would have sworn might have been the same.

The seat of this town of *Toparimaca* was very pleasant, standing on a little hill, in an excellent prospect, with goodly gardens a mile compass round about it, and two very fair and large ponds of excellent fish adjoining. This town is called *Arowocai;* the people are of the nation called *Nepoios,*

[41] Nearest. [42] Caroused.

and are followers of *Carapana*. In that place I saw very aged people, that we might perceive all their sinews and veins without any flesh, and but even as a case covered only with skin. The lord of this place gave me an old man for pilot, who was of great experience and travel, and knew the river most perfectly both by day and night. And it shall be requisite for any man that passeth it to have such a pilot; for it is four, five, and six miles over in many places, and twenty miles in other places, with wonderful eddies and strong currents, many great islands, and divers shoals, and many dangerous rocks; and besides upon any increase of wind so great a billow, as we were sometimes in great peril of drowning in the galley, for the small boats durst not come from the shore but when it was very fair.

The next day we hasted thence, and having an easterly wind to help us, we spared our arms from rowing; for after we entered *Orenoque,* the river lieth for the most part east and west, even from the sea unto *Quito,* in *Peru*. This river is navigable with barks little less than 1000 miles; and from the place where we entered it may be sailed up in small pinnaces to many of the best parts of *Nuevo Reyno de Granada* and of *Popayan*. And from no place may the cities of these parts of the *Indies* be so easily taken and invaded as from hence.[43] All that day we sailed up a branch of that river, having on the left hand a great island, which they call *Assapana,* which may contain some five-and-twenty miles in length, and six miles in breadth, the great body of the river running on the other side of this island. Beyond that middle branch there is also another island in the river, called *Iwana,* which is twice as big as the Isle of *Wight;* and beyond it, and between it and the main of *Guiana,* runneth a third branch of *Orenoque,* called *Arraroopana*. All three are goodly branches, and all navigable for great ships. I judge the river in this place to be at least thirty miles broad, reckoning the islands which divide the branches in it, for afterwards I sought also both the other branches.

After we reached to the head of the island called *Assapana,* a little to the westward on the right hand there opened a

[43] Raleigh regarded the occupation of 'Guiana' as a step towards the conquest of New Granada and Peru (see pp. 374-375.)

river which came from the north, called *Europa,* and fell into the great river; and beyond it on the same side we anchored for that night by another island, six miles long and two miles broad, which they call *Ocaywita.* From hence, in the morning, we landed two *Guianians,* which we found in the town of *Toparimaca,* that came with us; who went to give notice of our coming to the lord of that country, called *Putyma,* a follower of *Topiawari,* chief lord of *Aromaia,* who succeeded *Morequito,* whom (as you have heard before) *Berreo* put to death. But his town being far within the land, he came not unto us that day; so as we anchored again that night near the banks of another land, of bigness much like the other, which they call *Putapayma,* over against which island, on the main land, was a very high mountain called *Oecope.* We coveted to anchor rather by these islands in the river than by the main, because of the *tortugas'* eggs, which our people found on them in great abundance; and also because the ground served better for us to cast our nets for fish, the main banks being for the most part stony and high and the rocks of a blue, metalline colour, like unto the best steel ore, which I assuredly take it to be. Of the same blue stone are also divers great mountains which border this river in many places.

The next morning, towards nine of the clock, we weighed anchor; and the breeze increasing, we sailed always west up the river, and, after a while, opening the land on the right side, the country appeared to be champaign and the banks shewed very perfect red. I therefore sent two of the little barges with Captain *Gifford,* and with him Captain *Thyn,* Captain *Caulfield,* my cousin *Greenvile,* my nephew *John Gilbert,* Captain *Eynos,* Master *Edward Porter,* and my cousin *Butshead Gorges,* with some few soldiers, to march over the banks of that red land and to discover what manner of country it was on the other side; who at their return found it all a plain level as far as they went or could discern from the highest tree they could get upon. And my old pilot, a man of great travel, brother to the *cacique Toparimaca,* told me that those were called the plains of the *Sayma,* and that the same level reached to *Cumaná* and *Caracas,* in the *West Indies,* which are a hundred and twenty leagues to the north, and that there inhabited four principal nations. The first were the *Sayma,* the next *Assawai,* the third and greatest the *Wikiri,* by whom *Pedro Hernandez de Serpa,* before mentioned, was overthrown as he passed with 300 horse from *Cumaná* towards *Orenoque* in his enterprise of *Guiana.* The fourth are called *Aroras,* and are as black as negroes, but have smooth hair; and these are very valiant, or rather desperate, people, and have the most strong poison on their arrows, and most dangerous, of all nations, of which I will speak somewhat, being a digression not unnecessary.

There was nothing whereof I was more curious than to find out the true remedies of these poisoned arrows. For besides the mortality of the wound they make, the party shot endureth the most insufferable torment in the world, and abideth a most ugly and lamentable death, sometimes dying stark mad, sometimes their bowels breaking out of their bellies; which are presently discoloured as black as pitch, and so unsavory as no man can endure to cure or to attend them. And it is more strange to know that in all this time there was never Spaniard, either by gift or torment, that could attain to the true knowledge of the cure, although they have martyred and put to invented torture I know not how many of them. But everyone of these Indians know it not, no, not one among thousands, but their soothsayers and priests, who do conceal it, and only teach it but from the father to the son.

Those medicines which are vulgar, and serve for the ordinary poison, are made of the juice of a root called *tupara;* the same also quencheth marvellously the heat of burning fevers, and healeth inward wounds and broken veins that bleed within the body. But I was more beholding to the *Guianians* than any other; for *Antonio de Berreo* told me that he could never attain to the knowledge thereof, and yet they taught me the best way of healing as well thereof as of all other poisons. Some of the Spaniards have been cured in ordinary wounds of the common poisoned arrows with the juice of garlic. But this is a general rule for all men that shall hereafter travel the *Indies* where poisoned arrows are used, that they must abstain from drink. For if they take any liquor into their body, as they shall be marvellously provoked thereunto by drought, I say, if they drink before the wound be dressed, or soon upon it, there is no way with them but present death.

And so I will return again to our journey, which for this third day we finished, and cast anchor again near the continent on the left hand between two mountains, the one called *Aroami* and the other *Aio.* I made no stay here but till midnight; for I feared hourly lest any rain should fall, and then it had been impossible to have gone any further up, notwithstanding that there is every day a very strong breeze and easterly wind. I deferred the search of the country on *Guiana* side till my return down the river.

The next day we sailed by a great island in the middle of the river, called *Manoripano;* and, as we walked awhile on the island, while the galley got ahead of us, there came for us from the main a small *canoa* with seven or eight *Guianians,* to invite us to anchor at their port, but I deferred till my return. It was that *cacique* to whom those *Nepoios* went, which came with us from the town of *Toparimaca.* And so the fifth day we reached as high up as the province of *Aromaia,* the country of *Morequito,* whom *Berreo* executed, and anchored to the west of an island called *Murrecotima,* ten miles long and five broad. And that night the cacique *Aramiary,* to whose town we made our long and hungry voyage out of the river of *Amana,* passed by us.

The next day we arrived at the port of *Morequito,* and anchored there, sending away one of our pilots to seek the king of *Aromaia,* uncle to *Morequito,* slain by *Berreo* as aforesaid. The next day following, before noon, he came to us on foot from his house, which was fourteen English miles, himself being a hundred and ten years old, and returned on foot the same day; and with him many of the borderers, with many women and children, that came to wonder at our nation and to bring us down victual, which they did in great plenty, as venison, pork, hens, chickens, fowl, fish, with divers sorts of excellent fruits and roots, and great abundance of *pinas,* the princess of fruits that grow under the sun, especially those of *Guiana.* They brought us, also, store of bread and of their wine, and a sort of *paraquitos* no bigger than wrens, and of all other sorts both small and great. One of them gave me a beast called by the Spaniards *armadillo,* which they call *cassacam,* which seemeth to be all barred over with small plates somewhat like to a *rhinoceros,* with a white horn growing in his hinder parts as big as a great hunting-horn, which they use to wind instead of a trumpet. *Monardus*[44] writeth that a little of the powder of that horn put into the ear cureth deafness.

After this old king had rested awhile in a little tent that I caused to be set up, I began by my interpreter to discourse with him of the death of *Morequito* his predecessor, and afterward of the Spaniards; and yere I went any farther I made him know the cause of my coming thither, whose servant I was, and that the Queen's pleasure was I should undertake the voyage for their defence, and to deliver them from the tyranny of the Spaniards, dilating at large, as I had done before to those of *Trinidad,* her Majesty's greatness, her justice, her charity to all oppressed nations, with as many of the rest of her beauties and virtues as either I could express or they conceive. All which being with great admiration attentively heard and marvellously admired, I began to sound the old man as touching *Guiana* and the state thereof, what sort of commonwealth it was, how governed, of what strength and policy, how far it extended, and what nations were friends or enemies adjoining, and finally of the distance, and way to enter the same. He told me that himself and his people, with all those down the river towards the sea, as far as *Emeria,* the province of *Carapana,* were of *Guiana,* but that they called themselves *Orenoqueponi,* and that all the nations between the river and those mountains in sight, called *Wacarima,* were of the same cast and appellation; and that on the other side of those mountains of *Wacarima* there was a large plain (which after I discovered in my return) called the valley of *Amariocapana.* In all that valley the people were also of the ancient *Guianians.*

I asked what nations those were which inhabited on the further side of those mountains, beyond the valley of *Amariocapana.* He answered with a great sigh (as a man

[44] Monardes, Historia Medicinal (1574; English Version, 1577).

which had inward feeling of the loss of his country and liberty, especially for that his eldest son was slain in a battle on that side of the mountains, whom he most entirely loved) that he remembered in his father's lifetime, when he was very old and himself a young man, that there came down into that large valley of *Guiana* a nation from so far off as the sun slept (for such were his own words), with so great a multitude as they could not be numbered nor resisted, and that they wore large coats, and hats of crimson colour, which colour he expressed by shewing a piece of red wood wherewith my tent was supported, and that they were called *Orejones* and *Epuremei;* that those had slain and rooted out so many of the ancient people as there were leaves in the wood upon all the trees, and had now made themselves lords of all, even to that mountain foot called *Curaa,* saving only of two nations, the one called *Iwarawaqueri* and the other *Cassipagotos;* and that in the last battle fought between the *Epuremei* and the *Iwarawaqueri* his eldest son was chosen to carry to the aid of the *Iwarawaqueri* a great troop of the *Orenoqueponi,* and was there slain with all his people and friends, and that he had now remaining but one son; and farther told me that those *Epuremei* had built a great town called *Macureguarai* at the said mountain foot, at the beginning of the great plains of *Guiana,* which have no end; and that their houses have many rooms, one over the other, and that therein the great king of the *Orejones* and *Epuremei* kept three thousand men to defend the borders against them, and withal daily to invade and slay them; but that of late years, since the Christians offered to invade his territories and those frontiers, they were all at peace, and traded one with another, saving only the *Iwarawaqueri* and those other nations upon the head of the river of *Caroli* called *Cassipagotos,* which we afterwards discovered, each one holding the Spaniard for a common enemy.

After he had answered thus far, he desired leave to depart, saying that he had far to go, that he was old and weak, and was every day called for by death, which was also his own phrase. I desired him to rest with us that night, but I could not entreat him; but he told me that at my return from the country above he would again come to us, and in the meantime provide for us the best he could, of all that his country yielded. The same night he returned to *Orocotona,* his own town; so as he went that day eight-and-twenty miles, the weather being very hot, the country being situate between four and five degrees of the equinoctial. This *Topiawari* is held for the proudest and wisest of all the *Orenoqueponi,* and so he behaved himself towards me in all his answers, at my return, as I marvelled to find a man of that gravity and judgment and of so good discourse, that had no help of learning nor breed.

The next morning we also left the port, and sailed westward up to the river, to view the famous river called *Caroli,* as well because it was marvellous of itself, as also for that I understood it led to the strongest nations of all the frontiers, that were enemies to the *Epuremei,* which are subjects to *Inga,* emperor of *Guiana* and *Manoa.* And that night we anchored at another island called *Caiama,* of some five or six miles in length; and the next day arrived at the mouth of *Caroli.* When we were short of it as low or further down as the port of *Morequito,* we heard the great roar and fall of the river. But when we came to enter with our barge and wherries, thinking to have gone up some forty miles to the nations of the *Cassipagotos,* we were not able with a barge of eight oars to row one stone's cast in an hour; and yet the river is as broad as the Thames at Woolwich, and we tried both sides, and the middle, and every part of the river. So as we encamped upon the banks adjoining, and sent off our *Orenoquepone* which came with us from *Morequito* to give knowledge to the nations upon the river of our being there, and that we desired to see the lords of *Canuria,* which dwelt within the province upon that river, making them know that we were enemies to the Spaniards; for it was on this river side that *Morequito* slew the friar, and those nine Spaniards which came from *Manoa,* the city of *Inga,* and took from them 14,000 *pesos* of gold. So as the next day there came down a lord or *cacique,* called *Wanuretona,* with many people with him, and brought all store of provisions to entertain us, as the rest had done. And as I had before made my coming known to *Topiawari,* so did I acquaint this *cacique* therewith, and how I was sent by her Majesty for the purpose aforesaid, and gathered also what I could of him touching the estate of *Guiana*. And I found that those also of *Caroli* were not only enemies to the Spaniards, but most of all to the *Epuremei,* which abound in gold. And by this *Wanuretona* I had knowledge that on the head of this river were three mighty nations, which were seated on a great lake, from whence this river descended, and were called *Cassipagotos, Eparegotos,* and *Arawagotos;*[45] and that all those either against the Spaniards or the *Epuremei* would join with us, and that if we entered the land over the mountains of *Curaa* we should satisfy ourselves with gold and all other good things. He told us farther of a nation called *Iwarawaqueri,* before spoken of, that held daily war with the *Epuremei* that inhabited *Macureguarai,* the first civil town of *Guiana,* of the subjects of *Inga,* the emperor.

Upon this river one Captain *George,* that I took with *Berreo,* told me that there was a great silver mine, and that it was near the banks of the said river. But by this time as well *Orenoque, Caroli,* as all the rest of the rivers were risen four or five feet in height, so as it was not possible by the strength of any men, or with any boat whatsoever, to row into the river against the stream. I therefore sent Captain *Th·'n,* Captain *Greenvile,* my nephew, *John Gilbert,* my cousin *Butshead Gorges,* Captain *Clarke,* and some thirty shot more to coast the river by land, and to go to a town some twenty miles over the valley called *Amnatapoi;* and they found guides there to go farther towards the mountain foot to another great town called *Capurepana,* belonging to a *cacique* called *Haharacoa,* that was a nephew to old *Topiawari,* king of *Aromaia,* our chiefest friend, because this town and province of *Capurepana* adjoined to *Macureguarai,* which was a frontier town of the empire. And the meanwhile myself with Captain *Gifford,* Captain *Caulfield, Edward Hancock,* and some half-a-dozen shot marched overland to view the strange overfalls of the river of *Caroli,* which roared so far off; and also to see the

[45] The Purigotos and Arinagotos are still settled on the upper tributaries of the Caroni river. No such lake as that mentioned is known to exist.

plains adjoining, and the rest of the province of *Canuri*. I sent also Captain *Whiddon, William Connock,* and some eight shot with them, to see if they could find any mineral stone alongst the river's side. When we were come to the tops of the first hills of the plains adjoining to the river, we beheld that wonderful breach of waters which ran down *Caroli;* and might from that mountain see the river how it ran in three parts, above twenty miles off, and there appeared some ten or twelve overfalls in sight, every one as high over the other as a church tower, which fell with that fury, that the rebound of water made it seem as if it had been all covered over with a great shower of rain; and in some places we took it at the first for a smoke that had risen over some great town. For mine own part I was well persuaded from thence to have returned, being a very ill footman; but the rest were all so desirous to go near the said strange thunder of waters, as they drew me on by little and little, till we came into the next valley, where we might better discern the same. I never saw a more beautiful country, nor more lively prospects; hills so raised here and there over the valleys; the river winding into divers branches; the plains adjoining without bush or stubble, all fair green grass; the ground of hard sand, easy to march on, either for horse or foot; the deer crossing in every path; the birds towards the evening singing on every tree with a thousand several tunes; cranes and herons of white, crimson, and carnation, perching in the river's side; the air fresh with a gentle easterly wind; and every stone that we stooped to take up promised either gold or silver by his complexion. Your Lordship shall see of many sorts, and I hope some of them cannot be bettered under the sun; and yet we had no means but with our daggers and fingers to tear them out here and there, the rocks being most hard of that mineral spar aforesaid, which is like a flint, and is altogether as hard or harder, and besides the veins lie a fathom or two deep in the rocks. But we wanted all things requisite save only our desires and good will to have performed more if it had pleased God. To be short, when both our companies returned, each of them brought also several sorts of stones that appeared very fair, but were such as they found loose on the ground, and were for the most part but coloured, and had not any gold fixed in them. Yet such as had no judgment or experience kept all that glistered, and would not be persuaded but it was rich because of the lustre; and brought of those, and of *marcasite* withal, from *Trinidad,* and have delivered of those stones to be tried in many places, and have thereby bred an opinion that all the rest is of the same. Yet some of these stones I shewed afterward to a Spaniard of the *Caracas,* who told me that it was *El madre del oro,* that is, the mother of gold, and that the mine was farther in the ground.

But it shall be found a weak policy in me, either to betray myself or my country with imaginations; neither am I so far in love with that lodging, watching, care, peril, diseases, ill savours, bad fare, and many other mischiefs that accompany these voyages, as to woo myself again into any of them, were I not assured that the sun covereth not so much riches in any part of the earth. Captain *Whiddon,* and our chirurgeon, *Nicholas Millechamp,* brought me a kind of stones like sapphires; what they may prove I know not. I shewed them to some of the *Orenoqueponi,* and they promised to bring me to a mountain that had of them very large pieces growing diamond-wise; whether it be crystal of the mountain, *Bristol* diamond, or sapphire, I do not yet know, but I hope the best; sure I am that the place is as likely as those from whence all the rich stones are brought, and in the same height or very near.

On the left hand of this river *Caroli* are seated those nations which I called *Iwarawaqueri* before remembered, which are enemies to the *Epuremei;* and on the head of it, adjoining to the great lake *Cassipa,* are situated those other nations which also resist *Inga,* and the *Epuremei,* called *Cassipagotos, Eparegotos,* and *Arawagotos.* I farther understood that this lake of *Cassipa* is so large, as it is above one day's journey for one of their *canoas,* to cross, which may be some forty miles; and that thereinto fall divers rivers, and that great store of grains of gold are found in the summer time when the lake falleth by the banks, in those branches.

There is also another goodly river beyond *Caroli* which

is called *Arui,* which also runneth thorough the lake *Cassipa,* and falleth into *Orenoque* farther west, making all that land between *Caroli* and *Arui* an island; which is likewise a most beautiful country. Next unto *Arui* there are two rivers *Atoica* and *Caura,* and on that branch which is called *Caura* are a nation of people whose heads appear not above their shoulders; which though it may be thought a mere fable, yet for mine own part I am resolved it is true, because every child in the provinces of *Aromaia* and *Canuri* affirm the same. They are called *Ewaipanoma;* they are reported to have their eyes in their shoulders, and their mouths in the middle of their breasts, and that a long train of hair groweth backward between their shoulders. The son of *Topiawari,* which I brought with me into *England,* told me that they were the most mighty men of all the land, and use bows, arrows, and clubs thrice as big as any of *Guiana,* or of the *Orenoqueponi;* and that one of the *Iwarawaqueri* took a prisoner of them the year before our arrival there, and brought him into the borders of *Aromaia,* his father's country. And farther, when I seemed to doubt of it, he told me that it was no wonder among them; but that they were as great a nation and as common as any other in all the provinces, and had of late years slain many hundreds of his father's people, and of other nations their neighbours. But it was not my chance to hear of them till I was come away; and if I had but spoken one word of it while I was there I might have brought one of them with me to put the matter out of doubt. Such a nation was written of by *Mandeville,* whose reports were holden for fables many years; and yet since the *East Indies* were discovered, we find his relations true of such things as heretofore were held incredible.[46] Whether it be true or no, the matter is not great, neither can there be any profit in the imagination; for mine own part I saw them not, but I am resolved that so many people did not all combine or forethink to make the report.

When I came to *Cumana* in the *West Indies* afterwards by chance I spake with a Spaniard dwelling not far from

[46] Mandeville, or the author who assumed this name, placed his headless men in the East Indian Archipelago. The fable is borrowed from older writers (Herodotus, iv. 191, &c.).

thence, a man of great travel. And after he knew that I had been in *Guiana,* and so far directly west as *Caroli,* the first question he asked me was, whether I had seen any of the *Ewaipanoma,* which are those without heads. Who being esteemed a most honest man of his word, and in all things else, told me that he had seen many of them; I may not name him, because it may be for his disadvantage, but he is well known to *Monsieur Moucheron's* son of *London,* and to *Peter Moucheron,* merchant, of the Flemish ship that was there in trade; who also heard, what he avowed to be true, of those people.

The fourth river to the west of *Caroli* is *Casnero*: which falleth into the *Orenoque* on this side of *Amapaia.* And that river is greater than *Danubius,* or any of *Europe*: it riseth on the south of *Guiana* from the mountains which divide *Guiana* from *Amazons,* and I think it to be navigable many hundred miles. But we had no time, means, nor season of the year, to search those rivers, for the causes aforesaid, the winter being come upon us; although the winter and summer as touching cold and heat differ not, neither do the trees ever sensibly lose their leaves, but have always fruit either ripe or green, and most of them both blossoms, leaves, ripe fruit, and green, at one time: but their winter only consisteth of terrible rains, and overflowing of the rivers, with many great storms and gusts, thunder and lightnings, of which we had our fill ere we returned.

On the north side, the first river that falleth into the *Orenoque* is *Cari.* Beyond it, on the same side is the river of *Limo.* Between these two is a great nation of *Cannibals,* and their chief town beareth the name of the river, and is called *Acamacari.* At this town is a continual market of women for three or four hatchets apiece; they are bought by the *Arwacas,* and by them sold into the *West Indies.* To the west of *Limo* is the river *Pao,* beyond it *Caturi,* beyond that *Voari,* and *Capuri,*[47] which falleth out of the great river of *Meta,* by which *Berreo* descended from *Nuevo Reyno de Granada.* To the westward of *Capuri* is the province of *Amapaia,* where *Berreo* wintered and had so many of his people poisoned with the tawny water of the marshes of the

[47] The Apure river.

Anebas. Above *Amapaia,* toward *Nuevo Reyno,* fall in *Meto, Pato* and *Cassanar.* To the west of those, towards the provinces of the *Ashaguas* and *Catetios,* are the rivers of *Beta, Dawney,* and *Ubarro;* and toward the frontier of Peru are the provinces of *Thomebamba,* and *Caxamalca.* Adjoining to *Quito* in the north side of *Peru* are the rivers of *Guiacar* and *Goauar;* and on the other side of the said mountains the river of *Papamene* which descendeth into *Marañon* or *Amazons,* passing through the province *Motilones,* where *Don Pedro de Orsúa,* who was slain by the traitor *Aguirre* before rehearsed, built his brigandines, when he sought *Guiana* by the way of *Amazons.*

Between *Dawney* and *Beta* lieth a famous island in *Orenoque* (now called *Baraquan,* for above *Meta* it is not known by the name of *Orenoque*) which is called *Athule;*[48] beyond which ships of burden cannot pass by reason of a most forcible overfall, and current of water; but in the eddy all smaller vessels may be drawn even to *Peru* itself. But to speak of more of these rivers without the description were but tedious, and therefore I will leave the rest to the description. This river of *Orenoque* is navigable for ships little less than 1,000 miles, and for lesser vessels near 2,000. By it, as aforesaid, *Peru, Nuevo Reyno* and *Popayan* may be invaded: it also leadeth to the great empire of *Inga,* and to the provinces of *Amapaia* and *Anebas,* which abound in gold. His branches of *Casnero, Manta, Caura* descend from the middle land and valley which lieth between the easter province of *Peru* and *Guiana;* and it falls into the sea between *Marañon* and *Trinidad* in two degrees and a half. All of which your honours shall better perceive in the general description of *Guiana, Peru, Nuevo Reyno,* the kingdom of *Popayan,* and *Rodas,* with the province of *Venezuela,* to the bay of *Uraba,* behind *Cartagena,* westward, and to *Amazons* southward. While we lay at anchor on the coast of *Canuri,* and had taken knowledge of all the nations upon the head and branches of this river, and had found out so many several people, which were enemies to the *Epuremei* and the new conquerors, I thought it time lost to linger any longer in that place, especially for that the fury of *Orenoque*

[48] Cataract of Ature.

began daily to threaten us with dangers in our return. For no half day passed but the river began to rage and overflow very fearfully, and the rains came down in terrible showers, and gusts in great abundance; and withal our men began to cry out for want of shift, for no man had place to bestow any other apparel than that which he ware on his back, and that was throughly washed on his body for the most part ten times in one day; and we had now been well-near a month every day passing to the westward farther and farther from our ships. We therefore turned towards the east, and spent the rest of the time in discovering the river towards the sea, which we had not viewed, and which was most material.

The next day following we left the mouth of *Caroli,* and arrived again at the port of *Morequito* where we were before; for passing down the stream we went without labour, and against the wind, little less than a hundred miles a day. As soon as I came to anchor, I sent away one for old *Topiawari,* with whom I much desired to have further conference, and also to deal with him for some one of his country to bring with us into *England,* as well to learn the language, as to confer withal by the way, the time being now spent of any longer stay there. Within three hours after my messenger came to him, he arrived also, and with him such a rabble of all sorts of people, and every one loaden with somewhat, as if it had been a great market or fair in *England*; and our hungry companies clustered thick and threefold among their baskets, every one laying hand on what he liked. After he had rested awhile in my tent, I shut out all but ourselves and my interpreter, and told him that I knew that both the *Epuremei* and the Spaniards were enemies to him, his country and nations: that the one had conquered *Guiana* already, and the other sought to regain the same from them both; and therefore I desired him to instruct me what he could, both of the passage into the golden parts of *Guiana,* and to the civil towns and apparelled people of *Inga.* He gave me an answer to this effect: first, that he could not perceive that I meant to go onward towards the city of *Manoa,* for neither the time of the year served, neither could he perceive any sufficient numbers for such an enterprise. And if I did, I was sure with all my company to be buried there, for the emperor was of that strength, as that many times so many men more were too few. Besides, he gave me this good counsel and advised me to hold it in mind (as for himself, he knew he could not live till my return), that I should not offer by any means hereafter to invade the strong parts of *Guiana* without the help of all those nations which were also their enemies; for that it was impossible without those, either to be conducted, to be victualled, or to have aught carried with us, our people not being able to endure the march in so great heat and travail, unless the borderers gave them help, to cart with them both their meat and furniture. For he remembered that in the plains of *Macureguarai* three hundred Spaniards were overthrown, who were tired out, and had none of the borderers to their friends; but meeting their enemies as they passed the frontier, were environed on all sides, and the people setting the long dry grass on fire, smothered them, so as they had no breath to fight, nor could discern their enemies for the great smoke. He told me further that four days' journey from his town was *Macureguarai,* and that those were the next and nearest of the subjects of *Inga,* and of the *Epuremei,* and the first town of apparelled and rich people; and that all those plates of gold which were scattered among the borderers and carried to other nations far and near, came from the said *Macureguarai* and were there made, but that those of the land within were far finer, and were fashioned after the images of men, beasts, birds, and fishes. I asked him whether he thought that those companies that I had there with me were sufficient to take that town or no; he told me that he thought they were. I then asked him whether he would assist me with guides, and some companies of his people to join with us; he answered that he would go himself with all the borderers, if the rivers did remain fordable, upon this condition, that I would leave with him till my return again fifty soldiers, which he undertook to victual. I answered that I had not above fifty good men in all there; the rest were labourers and rowers, and that I had no provision to leave with them of powder, shot, apparel, or aught else, and that without those things necessary for their defence, they should be in danger of the Spaniards in my absence, who I knew would use the same measures towards mine that I offered them at *Trinidad.* And although upon the motion Captain *Caulfield,* Captain *Greenvile,* my nephew *John Gilbert* and divers others were desirous to stay, yet I was resolved that they must needs have perished. For *Berreo* expected daily a supply out of *Spain,* and looked also hourly for his son to come down from *Nuevo Reyno de Granada,* with many horse and foot, and had also in *Valencia,* in the *Caracas,* two hundred horse ready to march; and I could not have spared above forty, and had not any store at all of powder, lead, or match to have left with them, nor any other provision, either spade, pickaxe, or aught else to have fortified withal.

When I had given him reason that I could not at this time leave him such a company, he then desired me to forbear him and his country for that time; for he assured me that I should be no sooner three days from the coast but those *Epuremei* would invade him, and destroy all the remain of his people and friends, if he should any way either guide us or assist us against them. He further alleged that the Spaniards sought his death; and as they had already murdered his nephew *Morequito,* lord of that province, so they had him seventeen days in a chain before he was king of the country, and led him like a dog from place to place until he had paid an hundred plates of gold and divers chains of spleen-stones for his ransom.[49] And now, since he became owner of that province, that they had many times laid wait to take him, and that they would be now more vehement when they should understand of his conference with the English. *And because,* said he, *they would the better displant me, if they cannot lay hands on me, they have gotten a nephew of mine called* Eparacano, *whom they have christened* Don Juan, *and his son* Don Pedro, *whom they have also apparelled and armed, by whom they seek to make a party against me in mine own country. He also hath taken to wife one* Louiana, *of a strong family, which are borderers and neighbours; and myself now being old and in the hands of death am not able to travel nor to shift as when I was of*

[49] See page 344.

younger years. He therefore prayed us to defer it till the next year, when he would undertake to draw in all the borderers to serve us, and then, also, it would be more seasonable to travel; for at this time of the year we should not be able to pass any river, the waters were and would be so grown ere our return.

He farther told me that I could not desire so much to invade *Macureguarai* and the rest of *Guiana* but that the borderers would be more vehement than I. For he yielded for a chief cause that in the wars with the *Epuremei* they were spoiled of their women, and that their wives and daughters were taken from them; so as for their own parts they desired nothing of the gold or treasure for their labours, but only to recover women from the *Epuremei.* For he farther complained very sadly, as it had been a matter of great consequence, that whereas they were wont to have ten or twelve wives, they were now enforced to content themselves with three or four, and that the lords of the *Epuremei* had fifty or a hundred. And in truth they war more for women than either for gold or dominion. For the lords of countries desire many children of their own bodies to increase their races and kindreds, for in those consist their greatest trust and strength. Divers of his followers afterwards desired me to make haste again, that they might sack the *Epuremei,* and I asked them, of what? They answered, *Of their women for us, and their gold for you.* For the hope of those many of women they more desire the war than either for gold or for the recovery of their ancient territories. For what between the subjects of *Inga* and the Spaniards, those frontiers are grown thin of people; and also great numbers are fled to other nations farther off for fear of the Spaniards.

After I received this answer of the old man, we fell into consideration whether it had been of better advice to have entered *Macureguarai,* and to have begun a war upon *Inga* at this time, yea, or no, if the time of the year and all things else had sorted. For mine own part, as we were not able to march it for the rivers, neither had any such strength as was requisite, and durst not abide the coming of the winter, or to tarry any longer from our ships, I thought it were evil counsel to have attempted it at that time, although the desire for gold will answer many objections. But it would have been, in mine opinion, an utter overthrow to the enterprise, if the same should be hereafter by her Majesty attempted. For then, whereas now they have heard we were enemies to the Spaniards and were sent by her Majesty to relieve them, they would as good cheap have joined with the Spaniards at our return, as to have yielded unto us, when they had proved that we came both for one errand, and that both sought but to sack and spoil them. But as yet our desire of gold, or our purpose of invasion, is not known to them of the empire. And it is likely that if her Majesty undertake the enterprise they will rather submit themselves to her obedience than to the Spaniards, of whose cruelty both themselves and the borderers have already tasted. And therefore, till I had known her Majesty's pleasure, I would rather have lost the sack of one or two towns, although they might have been very profitable, than to have defaced or endangered the future hope of so many millions, and the great good and rich trade which *England* may be possessed of thereby. I am assured now that they will all die, even to the last man, against the Spaniards in hope of our succour and return. Whereas, otherwise, if I had either laid hands on the borderers or ransomed the lords, as *Berreo* did, or invaded the subjects of *Inga,* I know all had been lost for hereafter.

After that I had resolved *Topiawari,* lord of *Aromaia,* that I could not at this time leave with him the companies he desired, and that I was contented to forbear the enterprise against the *Epuremei* till the next year, he freely gave me his only son to take with me into *England;* and hoped that though he himself had but a short time to live, yet that by our means his son should be established after his death. And I left with him one *Francis Sparrow,* a servant of Captain *Gifford,* who was desirous to tarry, and could describe a country with his pen, and a boy of mine called *Hugh Goodwin,* to learn the language. I after asked the manner how the *Epuremei* wrought those plates of gold, and how they could melt it out of the stone. He told me that the most of the gold which they made in plates and images was not severed from the stone, but that on the lake of *Manoa,* and in a multitude of other rivers, they gathered it in grains of perfect gold and in pieces as big as small stones, and they put it to a part of copper, otherwise they could not work it; and that they used a great earthen pot with holes round about it, and when they had mingled the gold and copper together they fastened canes to the holes, and so with the breath of men they increased the fire till the metal ran, and then they cast it into moulds of stone and clay, and so make those plates and images. I have sent your honours of two sorts such as I could by chance recover, more to shew the manner of them than for the value. For I did not in any sort make my desire of gold known, because I had neither time nor power to have a great quantity. I gave among them many more pieces of gold than I received, of the new money of twenty shillings with her Majesty's picture, to wear, with promise that they would become her servants thenceforth.

I have also sent your honours of the ore, whereof I know some is as rich as the earth yieldeth any, of which I know there is sufficient, if nothing else were to be hoped for. But besides that we were not able to tarry and search the hills, so we had neither pioneers, bars, sledges, nor wedges of iron to break the ground, without which there is no working in mines. But we saw all the hills with stones of the colour of gold and silver, and we tried them to be no *marcasite,* and therefore such as the Spaniards call *El madre del oro* or 'the mother of gold,' which is an undoubted assurance of the general abundance; and myself saw the outside of many mines of the spar, which I know to be the same that all covet in this world, and of those more than I will speak of.

Having learned what I could in *Canuri* and *Aromaia,* and received a faithful promise of the principallest of those provinces to become servants to her Majesty, and to resist the Spaniards if they made any attempt in our absence, and that they would draw in the nations about the lake of *Cassipa* and those of *Iwarawaqueri,* I then parted from old *Topiawari,* and received his son for a pledge between us, and left with him two of ours as aforesaid. To *Francis Sparrow* I gave instructions to travel to *Macureguarai* with such merchandises as I left with them, thereby to learn the place, and if it were possible, to go on to the great city of *Manoa.* Which being done, we weighed anchor and coasted the river on *Guiana* side, because we came upon the north side, by the lawns of the *Saima* and *Wikiri.*

There came with us from *Aromaia* a *cacique* called *Putijma,* that commanded the province of *Warapana,* which *Putijma* slew the nine Spaniards upon *Caroli* before spoken of; who desired us to rest in the port of his country, promising to bring us unto a mountain adjoining to his town that had stones of the colour of gold, which he performed. And after we had rested there one night I went myself in the morning with most of the gentlemen of my company overland towards the said mountain, marching by a river's side called *Mana,* leaving on the right hand a town called *Tuteritona,* standing in the province of *Tarracoa,* of which *Wariaaremagoto* is principal. Beyond it lieth another town towards the south, in the valley of *Amariocapana,* which beareth the name of the said valley; whose plains stretch themselves some sixty miles in length, east and west, as fair ground and as beautiful fields as any man hath ever seen, with divers copses scattered here and there by the river's side, and all as full of deer as any forest or park in *England,* and in every lake and river the like abundance of fish and fowl; of which *Irraparragota* is lord.

From the river of *Mana* we crossed another river in the said beautiful valley called *Oiana,* and rested ourselves by a clear lake which lay in the middle of the said *Oiana;* and one of our guides kindling us fire with two sticks, we stayed awhile to dry our shirts, which with the heat hung very wet and heavy on our shoulders. Afterwards we sought the ford to pass over towards the mountain called *Iconuri,* where *Putijma* foretold us of the mine. In this lake we saw one of the great fishes, as big as a wine pipe, which they call *manati,* being most excellent and wholesome meat. But after I perceived that to pass the said river would require half-a-day's march more, I was not able myself to endure it, and therefore I sent Captain *Keymis* with six shot to go on, and gave him order not to return to the port of *Putijma,* which is called *Chiparepare,* but to take leisure, and to march down the said valley as far as a river called *Cumaca,* where I promised to meet him again, *Putijma* himself promising also to be his guide. And as they marched, they left the towns of *Emperapana* and *Capurepana* on the right hand, and marched from *Putijma's* house, down the said valley of *Amariocapana*; and we returning the same day to the river's side, saw by the way many rocks like unto gold ore, and on the left hand a round mountain which consisted of mineral stone.

From hence we rowed down the stream, coasting the province of *Parino.* As for the branches of rivers which I overpass in this discourse, those shall be better expressed in the description, with the mountains of *Aio, Ara,* and the rest, which are situate in the provinces of *Parino* and *Carricurrina.* When we were come as far down as the land called *Ariacoa,* where *Orenoque* divideth itself into three great branches, each of them being most goodly rivers, I sent away Captain *Henry Thyn,* and Captain *Greenvile* with the galley, the nearest way, and took with me Captain *Gifford,* Captain *Caulfield, Edward Porter,* and Captain *Eynos* with mine own barge and the two wherries, and went down that branch of *Orenoque* which is called *Cararoopana,* which leadeth towards *Emeria,* the province of *Carapana,* and towards the east sea, as well to find out Captain *Keymis,* whom I had sent overland, as also to acquaint myself with *Carapana,* who is one of the greatest of all the lords of the *Orenoqueponi.* And when I came to the river of *Cumaca,* to which *Putijma* promised to conduct Captain *Keymis,* I left Captain *Eynos* and Master *Porter* in the said river to expect his coming, and the rest of us rowed down the stream towards *Emeria.*

In this branch called *Cararoopana* were also many goodly islands, some of six miles long, some of ten, and some of twenty. When it grew towards sunset, we entered a branch of a river that fell into *Orenoque,* called *Winicapora;* where I was informed of the mountain of crystal, to which in truth for the length of the way, and the evil season of the year, I was not able to march, nor abide any longer upon the journey. We saw it afar off; and it appeared like a white church-tower of an exceeding height. There falleth over it a mighty river which toucheth no part of the side of the mountain, but rusheth over the top of it, and falleth to the ground with so terrible a noise and clamour, as if a thousand great bells were knocked one against another. I think there is not in the world so strange an overfall, nor so wonderful to behold. *Berreo* told me that there were diamonds and other precious stones on it, and that they shined very far off; but what it hath I know not, neither durst he or any of his men ascend to the top of the said mountain, those people adjoining being his enemies, as they were, and the way to it so impassable.

Upon this river of *Winicapora* we rested a while, and from thence marched into the country to a town called after the name of the river, whereof the captain was one *Timitwara,* who also offered to conduct me to the top of the said mountain called *Wacarima.* But when we came in first to the house of the said *Timitwara,* being upon one of their said feast days, we found them all as drunk as beggars, and the pots walking from one to another without rest. We that were weary and hot with marching were glad of the plenty, though a small quantity satisfied us, their drink being very strong and heady, and so rested ourselves awhile. After we had fed, we drew ourselves back to our boats upon the river, and there came to us all the lords of the country, with all such kind of victual as the place yielded, and with their delicate wine of *pinas,* and with abundance of hens and other provisions, and of those stones which we call spleen-stones. We understood by these chieftains of *Winicapora* that their lord, *Carapana,* was departed from *Emeria,* which was now in sight, and that he was fled to *Cairamo,* adjoining to the mountains of *Guiana,* over the valley called *Amariocapana,* being persuaded by those ten Spaniards which lay at his house that we would destroy him and his country. But after these *caciques* of *Winicapora* and *Saporatona* his followers perceived our purpose, and saw that we came as enemies to the Spaniards only, and had not so much as harmed any of those nations, no, though we found them to be of the Spaniards' own servants, they assured us that *Carapana* would be as ready to serve us as any of the lords of the provinces which we had passed; and that he durst do no other till this day but entertain the Spaniards, his country lying so directly in their way, and next of all other to any entrance that should be made in *Guiana* on that side. And they further assured us, that it was not for fear of our coming that he was removed, but to be acquitted of the Spaniards or any other that should come hereafter. For the province of *Cairoma* is situate at the mountain foot, which divideth the plains of *Guiana* from the countries of the *Orenoqueponi*; by means whereof if any should come in our absence into his towns, he would slip over the mountains into the plains of *Guiana* among the *Epuremei,* where the Spaniards durst not follow him without great force. But in mine opinion, or rather I assure myself, that *Carapana* being a notable wise and subtle fellow, a man of one hundred years of age and therefore of great experience, is removed to look on, and if he find that we return strong he will be ours; if not, he will excuse his departure to the Spaniards, and say it was for fear of our coming.

We therefore thought it bootless to row so far down the stream, or to seek any farther of this old fox; and therefore from the river of *Waricapana,* which lieth at the entrance of *Emeria,* we returned again, and left to the eastward those four rivers which fall from the mountains of *Emeria* into *Orenoque,* which are *Waracayari, Coirama, Akaniri,* and *Iparoma.* Below those four are also these branches and mouths of *Orenoque,* which fall into the east sea, whereof the first is *Araturi,* the next *Amacura,* the third *Barima,* the fourth *Wana,* the fifth *Morooca,* the sixth *Paroma,* the last *Wijmi.* Beyond them there fall out of the land between *Orenoque* and *Amazons* fourteen rivers, which I forbear to name, inhabited by the *Arwacas* and *Cannibals.*

It is now time to return towards the north, and we found it a wearisome way back from the borders of *Emeria,* to recover up again to the head of the river *Carerupana,* by which we descended, and where we parted from the galley, which I directed to take the next way to the port of *Toparimaca,* by which we entered first.

All the night it was stormy and dark, and full of thunder and great showers, so as we were driven to keep close by the banks in our small boats, being all heartily afraid both of the billow and terrible current of the river. By the next morning we recovered the mouth of the river of *Cumaca,* where we left Captain *Eynos* and *Edward Porter* to attend the coming of Captain *Keymis* overland; but when we entered the same, they had heard no news of his arrival, which bred in us a great doubt what might become of him. I rowed up a league or two farther into the river, shooting off pieces all the way, that he might know of our being there; and the next morning we heard them answer us also with a piece. We took them aboard us, and took our leave of *Putijma,* their guide, who of all others most lamented our departure, and offered to send his son with us into *England,* if we could have stayed till he had sent back to his town. But our hearts were cold to behold the great rage and increase of *Orenoque,* and therefore [we] departed, and turned toward the west, till we had recovered the parting of the three branches aforesaid, that we might put down the stream after the galley.

The next day we landed on the island of *Assapano,* which divideth the river from that branch by which we sent down to *Emeria,* and there feasted ourselves with that beast which is called *armadillo,* presented unto us before at *Winicapora.* And the day following, we recovered the galley at anchor at the port of *Toparimaca,* and the same evening departed with very foul weather, and terrible thunder and showers, for the winter was come on very far. The best was, we went no less than 100 miles a day down the river; but by the way we entered it was impossible to return, for that the river of *Amana,* being in the bottom of the bay of *Guanipa,* cannot be sailed back by any means, both the breeze and current of the sea were so forcible. And therefore we followed a branch of *Orenoque* called *Capuri,* which entered into the sea eastward of our ships, to the end we might bear with them before the wind; and it was not without need, for we had by that way as much to cross of the main sea, after we came to the river's mouth, as between *Gravelin* and *Dover,* in such boats as your honour hath heard.

To speak of what passed homeward were tedious, either to describe or name any of the rivers, islands, or villages of the *Tivitivas,* which dwell on trees; we will leave all those to the general map. And to be short, when we were arrived at the sea-side, then grew our greatest doubt, and the bitterest of all our journey forepassed; for I protest before God, that we were in a most desperate estate. For the same night which we anchored in the mouth of the river of *Capuri,* where it falleth into the sea, there arose a mighty storm, and the river's mouth was at least a league broad, so as we ran before night close under the land with our small boats, and brought the galley as near as we could. But she had as much ado to live as could be, and there wanted little of her sinking, and all those in her; for mine own part, I confess I was very doubtful which way to take, either to go over in the pestered[50] galley, there being but six foot water over the sands for two leagues together, and that also in the channel, and she drew five; or to adventure in so great a billow, and in so doubtful weather, to cross the seas in my barge. The longer we tarried the worse it was, and therefore I took Captain *Gifford,* Captain *Caulfield,* and my cousin *Greenvile* into my barge; and after it cleared up about midnight we put ourselves to God's keeping, and thrust out into the sea, leaving the galley at anchor, who durst not adventure but by daylight. And so, being all very sober and melancholy, one faintly cheering another to shew courage, it pleased God that the next day about nine o'clock, we descried the island of *Trinidad;* and steering for the nearest part of it, we kept the shore till we came to *Curiapan,* where we found our ships at anchor, than which there was never to us a more joyful sight.

Now that it hath pleased God to send us safe to our ships, it is time to leave *Guiana* to the sun, whom they worship, and steer away towards the north. I will, therefore, in a few words finish the discovery thereof. Of the several nations which we found upon this discovery I will once again make repetition, and how they are affected. At our first entrance into *Amana,* which is one of the outlets of *Orenoque,* we left on the right hand of us in the bottom of the bay, lying directly against *Trinidad,* a nation of inhuman *Cannibals,* which inhabit the rivers of *Guanipa* and *Berbeese.* In the same bay there is also a third river, which is called *Areo,*

[50] Crowded.

which riseth on *Paria* side towards *Cumaná,* and that river is inhabited with the *Wikiri,* whose chief town upon the said river is *Sayma.* In this bay there are no more rivers but these three before rehearsed and the four branches of *Amana,* all which in the winter thrust so great abundance of water into the sea, as the same is taken up fresh two or three leagues from the land. In the passages towards *Guiana,* that is, in all those lands which the eight branches of *Orenoque* fashion into islands, there are but one sort of people, called *Tivitivas,* but of two castes, as they term them, the one called *Ciawani,* the other *Waraweeti,* and those war one with another.

On the hithermost part of *Orenoque,* as at *Toparimaca* and *Winicapora,* those are of a nation called *Nepoios,* and are the followers of *Carapana,* lord of *Emeria.* Between *Winicapora* and the port of *Morequito,* which standeth in *Aromaia,* and all those in the valley of *Amariocapana* are called *Orenoqueponi,* and did obey *Morequito* and are now followers of *Topiawari.* Upon the river of *Caroli* are the *Canuri,* which are governed by a woman who is inheritrix of that province; who came far off to see our nation, and asked me divers questions of her Majesty, being much delighted with the discourse of her Majesty's greatness, and wondering at such reports as we truly made of her Highness' many virtues. And upon the head of *Caroli* and on the lake of *Cassipa* are the three strong nations of the *Cassipagotos.* Right south into the land are the *Capurepani* and *Emparepani,* and beyond those, adjoining to *Macureguarai,* the first city of *Inga,* are the *Iwarawakeri.* All these are professed enemies to the Spaniards, and to the rich *Epuremei* also. To the west of *Caroli* are divers nations of *Cannibals* and of those *Ewaipanoma* without heads. Directly west are the *Amapaias* and *Anebas,* which are also marvellous rich in gold. The rest towards *Peru* we will omit. On the north of *Orenoque,* between it and the *West Indies,* are the *Wikiri, Saymi,* and the rest before spoken of, all mortal enemies to the Spaniards. On the south side of the main mouth of *Orenoque* are the *Arwacas;* and beyond them, the *Cannibals;* and to the south of them, the *Amazons.*

To make mention of the several beasts, birds, fishes, fruits, flowers, gums, sweet woods, and of their several religions and customs, would for the first require as many volumes as those of *Gesnerus,* and for the next another bundle of *Decades.* The religion of the *Epuremei* is the same which the *Ingas,* emperors of *Peru,* used, which may be read in *Cieza* and other Spanish stories; how they believe the immortality of the soul, worship the sun, and bury with them alive their best beloved wives and treasure, as they likewise do in *Pegu* in the *East Indies,* and other places. The *Orenoqueponi* bury not their wives with them, but their jewels, hoping to enjoy them again. The *Arwacas* dry the bones of their lords, and their wives and friends drink them in powder. In the graves of the *Peruvians* the Spaniards found their greatest abundance of treasure. The like, also, is to be found among these people in every province. They have all many wives, and the lords five-fold to the common sort. Their wives never eat with their husbands, nor among the men, but serve their husbands at meals and afterwards feed by themselves. Those that are past their younger years make all their bread and drink, and work their cotton-beds, and do all else of service and labour; for the men do nothing but hunt, fish, play, and drink, when they are out of the wars.

I will enter no further into discourse of their manners, laws, and customs. And because I have not myself seen the cities of *Inga* I cannot avow on my credit what I have heard, although it be very likely that the emperor *Inga* hath built and erected as magnificent palaces in *Guiana* as his ancestors did in *Peru;* which were for their riches and rareness most marvellous, and exceeding all in *Europe,* and, I think, of the world, *China* excepted, which also the Spaniards, which I had, assured me to be true, as also the nations of the borderers, who, being but savages to those of the inland, do cause much treasure to be buried with them. For I was informed of one of the *caciques* of the valley of *Amariocapana* which had buried with him a little before our arrival a chair of gold most curiously wrought, which was made either in *Macureguarai* adjoining or in *Manoa.* But if we should have grieved them in their religion at the first, before they had been taught better, and have digged up their graves, we had lost them all. And therefore I held my first resolution, that her Majesty should either accept or refuse the enterprise ere anything should be done that might in any sort hinder the same. And if *Peru* had so many heaps of gold, whereof those *Ingas* were princes, and that they delighted so much therein, no doubt but this which now liveth and reigneth in *Manoa* hath the same humour,[51] and, I am assured, hath more abundance of gold within his territory than all *Peru* and the *West Indies*.

For the rest, which myself have seen, I will promise these things that follow, which I know to be true. Those that are desirous to discover and to see many nations may be satisfied within this river, which bringeth forth so many arms and branches leading to several countries and provinces, above 2,000 miles east and west and 800 miles south and north, and of these the most either rich in gold or in other merchandises. The common soldier shall here fight for gold, and pay himself, instead of pence, with plates of half-a-foot broad, whereas he breaketh his bones in other wars for provant[52] and penury. Those commanders and chieftains that shoot at honour and abundance shall find there more rich and beautiful cities, more temples adorned with golden images, more sepulchres filled with treasure, than either *Cortes* found in *Mexico* or *Pizarro* in *Peru*. And the shining glory of this conquest will eclipse all those so far-extended beams of the Spanish nation. There is no country which yieldeth more pleasure to the inhabitants, either for those common delights of hunting, hawking, fishing, fowling, and the rest, than *Guiana* doth; it hath so many plains, clear rivers, and abundance of pheasants, partridges, quails, rails, cranes, herons, and all other fowl; deer of all sorts, porks, hares, lions, tigers, leopards, and divers other sorts of beasts, either for chase or food. It hath a kind of beast called *cama* or *anta*,[53] as big as an English beef, and in great plenty. To speak of the several sorts of every kind I fear would be troublesome to the reader, and therefore I will omit them, and conclude that both for health, good air, pleasure, and riches, I am resolved it cannot be equalled by any region either in the east or west. Moreover the country

[51] Hakluyt reads 'honour.' [52] Provender, food. [53] The tapir.

is so healthful, as of an hundred persons and more, which lay without shift most sluttishly, and were every day almost melted with heat in rowing and marching, and suddenly wet again with great showers, and did eat of all sorts of corrupt fruits, and made meals of fresh fish without seasoning, of *tortugas*, of *lagartos* or *crocodiles*, and of all sorts good and bad, without either order or measure, and besides lodged in the open air every night, we lost not any one, nor had one ill-disposed to my knowledge; nor found any *calentura* or other of those pestilent diseases which dwell in all hot regions, and so near the equinoctial line.

Where there is store of gold it is in effect needless to remember other commodities for trade. But it hath, towards the south part of the river, great quantities of brazil-wood, and divers berries that dye a most perfect crimson and carnation; and for painting, all *France*, *Italy*, or the *East Indies* yield none such. For the more the skin is washed, the fairer the colour appeareth, and with which even those brown and tawny women spot themselves and colour their cheeks. All places yield abundance of cotton, of silk, of *balsamum*, and of those kinds most excellent and never known in *Europe*, of all sorts of gums, of Indian pepper; and what else the countries may afford within the land we know not, neither had we time to abide the trial and search. The soil besides is so excellent and so full of rivers, as it will carry sugar, ginger, and all those other commodities which the *West Indies* have.

The navigation is short, for it may be sailed with an ordinary wind in six weeks, and in the like time back again; and by the way neither lee-shore, enemies' coast, rocks, nor sands. All which in the voyages to the *West Indies* and all other places we are subject unto; as the channel of *Bahama*, coming from the *West Indies*, cannot well be passed in the winter, and when it is at the best, it is a perilous and a fearful place; the rest of the *Indies* for calms and diseases very troublesome, and the sea about the *Bermudas* a hellish sea for thunder, lightning, and storms.

This very year (1595) there were seventeen sail of Spanish ships lost in the channel of *Bahama*, and the great *Philip*, like to have sunk at the *Bermudas*, was put back to

St. Juan de Puerto Rico; and so it falleth out in that navigation every year for the most part. Which in this voyage are not to be feared; for the time of year to leave *England* is best in July, and the summer in *Guiana* is in October, November, December, January, February, and March, and then the ships may depart thence in April, and so return again into *England* in June. So as they shall never be subject to winter weather, either coming, going, or staying there: which, for my part, I take to be one of the greatest comforts and encouragements that can be thought on, having, as I have done, tasted in this voyage by the *West Indies* so many calms, so much heat, such outrageous gusts, such weather, and contrary winds.

To conclude, *Guiana* is a country that hath yet her maidenhead, never sacked, turned, nor wrought; the face of the earth hath not been torn, nor the virtue and salt of the soil spent by manurance. The graves have not been opened for gold, the mines not broken with sledges, nor their images pulled down out of their temples. It hath never been entered by any army of strength, and never conquered or possessed by any Christian prince. It is besides so defensible, that if two forts be builded in one of the provinces which I have seen, the flood setteth in so near the bank, where the channel also lieth, that no ship can pass up but within a pike's length of the artillery, first of the one, and afterwards of the other. Which two forts will be a sufficient guard both to the empire of *Inga,* and to an hundred other several kingdoms, lying within the said river, even to the city of *Quito* in *Peru.*

There is therefore great difference between the easiness of the conquest of *Guiana,* and the defence of it being conquered, and the *West* or *East Indies.* *Guiana* hath but one entrance by the sea, if it hath that, for any vessels of burden. So as whosoever shall first possess it, it shall be found unaccessible for any enemy, except he come in wherries, barges, or *canoas,* or else in flat-bottomed boats; and if he do offer to enter it in that manner, the woods are so thick 200 miles together upon the rivers of such entrance, as a mouse cannot sit in a boat unhit from the bank. By land it is more impossible to approach; for it hath the strongest situation of any region under the sun, and it is so environed with impassable mountains on every side, as it is impossible to victual any company in the passage. Which hath been well proved by the Spanish nation, who since the conquest of *Peru* have never left five years free from attempting this empire, or discovering some way into it; and yet of three-and-twenty several gentlemen, knights, and noblemen, there was never any that knew which way to lead an army by land, or to conduct ships by sea, anything near the said country. *Orellana,* of whom the river of *Amazons* taketh name, was the first, and *Don Antonio de Berreo,* whom we displanted, the last: and I doubt much whether he himself or any of his yet know the best way into the said empire. It can therefore hardly be regained, if any strength be formerly set down, but in one or two places, and but two or three crumsters[54] or galleys built and furnished upon the river within. The *West Indies* have many ports, watering places, and landings; and nearer than 300 miles to *Guiana,* no man can harbour a ship, except he know one only place, which is not learned in haste, and which I will undertake there is not any one of my companies that knoweth, whosoever hearkened most after it.

Besides, by keeping one good fort, or building one town of strength, the whole empire is guarded; and whatsoever companies shall be afterwards planted within the land, although in twenty several provinces, those shall be able all to reunite themselves upon any occasion either by the way of one river, or be able to march by land without either wood, bog, or mountain. Whereas in the *West Indies* there are few towns or provinces that can succour or relieve one the other by land or sea. By land the countries are either desert, mountainous, or strong enemies. By sea, if any man invade to the eastward, those to the west cannot in many months turn against the breeze and eastern wind. Besides, the Spaniards are therein so dispersed as they are nowhere strong, but in *Nueva España* only; the sharp mountains, the thorns, and poisoned prickles, the sandy and deep ways in the valleys, the smothering heat and air, and want of water in other places are their only and best defence; which, because those nations that invade them are not victualled or

[54] Dutch, *Kromsteven* or *Kromster,* a vessel with a bent prow.

provided to stay, neither have any place to friend adjoining, do serve them instead of good arms and great multitudes.

The *West Indies* were first offered her Majesty's grandfather by *Columbus,* a stranger, in whom there might be doubt of deceit; and besides it was then thought incredible that there were such and so many lands and regions never written of before. This Empire is made known to her Majesty by her own vassal, and by him that oweth to her more duty than an ordinary subject; so that it shall ill sort with the many graces and benefits which I have received to abuse her Highness, either with fables or imaginations. The country is already discovered, many nations won to her Majesty's love and obedience, and those Spaniards which have latest and longest laboured about the conquest, beaten out, discouraged, and disgraced, which among these nations were thought invincible. Her Majesty may in this enterprise employ all those soldiers and gentlemen that are younger brethren, and all captains and chieftains that want employment, and the charge will be only the first setting out in victualling and arming them; for after the first or second year I doubt not but to see in *London* a Contractation-House[55] of more receipt for *Guiana* than there is now in *Seville* for the *West Indies.*

And I am resolved that if there were but a small army afoot in *Guiana,* marching towards *Manoa,* the chief city of *Inga,* he would yield to her Majesty by composition so many hundred thousand pounds yearly as should both defend all enemies abroad, and defray all expenses at home; and that he would besides pay a garrison of three or four thousand soldiers very royally to defend him against other nations. For he cannot but know how his predecessors, yea, how his own great uncles, *Guascar* and *Atabalipa,* sons to *Guiana-Capac,* emperor of *Peru,* were, while they contended for the empire, beaten out by the Spaniards, and that both of late years and ever since the said conquest, the Spaniards have sought the passages and entry of his country; and of their cruelties used to the borderers he cannot be ignorant. In which respects no doubt but he will be brought to tribute with great

[55] The whole trade of Spanish America passed through the Casa de Contratacion at Seville.

gladness; if not, he hath neither shot nor iron weapon in all his empire, and therefore may easily be conquered.

And I further remember that *Berreo* confessed to me and others, which I protest before the Majesty of God to be true, that there was found among the prophecies in *Peru*, at such time as the empire was reduced to the Spanish obedience, in their chiefest temples, amongst divers others which foreshadowed the loss of the said empire, that from *Inglatierra* those *Ingas* should be again in time to come restored, and delivered from the servitude of the said conquerors. And I hope, as we with these few hands have displanted the first garrison, and driven them out of the said country, so her Majesty will give order for the rest, and either defend it, and hold it as tributary, or conquer and keep it as empress of the same. For whatsoever prince shall possess it, shall be greatest; and if the king of *Spain* enjoy it, he will become unresistible. Her Majesty hereby shall confirm and strengthen the opinions of all nations as touching her great and princely actions. And where the south border of *Guiana* reacheth to the dominion and empire of the *Amazons,* those women shall hereby hear the name of a virgin, which is not only able to defend her own territories and her neighbours, but also to invade and conquer so great empires and so far removed.

To speak more at this time I fear would be but troublesome: I trust in God, this being true, will suffice, and that he which is King of all Kings, and Lord of Lords, will put it into her heart which is Lady of Ladies to possess it. If not, I will judge those men worthy to be kings thereof, that by her grace and leave will undertake it of themselves.

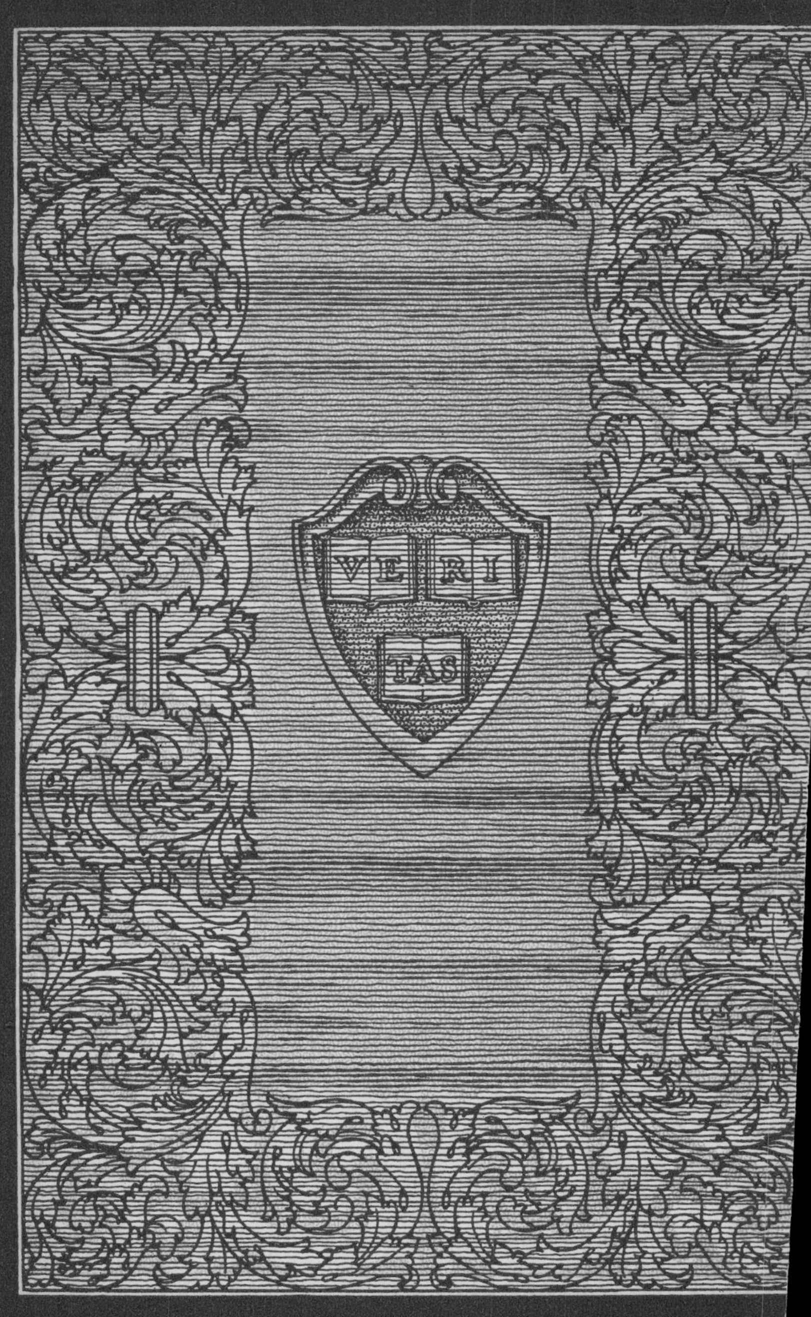
VE RI
TAS